*View*points 11

Authors

Amanda Joseph

Wendy Mathieu

Series Consultants

John Borovilos

Robert Dawe

Barbara Fullerton

Margaret Iveson

Wendy Mathieu

Dirk Verhulst

Publishing Consultant

Anthony Luengo

Assessment Consultant

Sharon Jeroski

PEARSON

Prentice Hall

Toronto

National Library of Canada Cataloguing in Publication Data

Amanda Joseph
        Viewpoints 11

ISBN 0-13-019868-4 (bound)   ISBN 0-13-019869-2 (pbk.)

1. Readers (Secondary). 2. Reading comprehension — Problems, exercises, etc. I.
Mathieu, Wendy Lee, 1959– . II. Title.

PE1121.J67 2001   428'.6   C2001-930043-3

ISBN 0-13-019868-4 (hardcover)   ISBN 0-13-019869-2 (softcover)

Publisher: Mark Cobham
Product Manager: Anita Borovilos
Managing Editor: Elynor Kagan
Project Manager: Anthony Luengo
Anthologist and Developmental Editor: Irene Cox
Copy and Production Editor: Angelie Kim
Text Researchers: Karen Alliston, Monika Croydon, Chelsea Donaldson, Todd Mercer,
Catherine Rondina, Linda Sheppard, Jennifer Sweeney, Rebecca Vogan
Proofreaders: Karen Kligman, Rebecca Vogan
Art Direction: Zena Denchik
Cover Design: Jennifer Federico
Cover Image: Horst Klemm/Masterfile
Interior Design and Layout: Jennifer Federico
Production Coordinator: Zane Kaneps, Sandra Magill
Visuals Research/Permissions: Maria DeCambra, Michaele Sinko

 3 4 5 FP 05 04 03

Printed and bound in Canada

The publisher has taken every care to meet or exceed industry specifications for the
manufacturing of textbooks. The cover of this sewn book is a premium, polymer-
reinforced material designed to provide long life and withstand rugged use. Mylar gloss
lamination has been applied for further durability.

Prentice Hall Senior English
Viewpoints/Reference Points Advisory Group

Philip Allingham
Susan Balfe
Alice Barlow-Kedves
Jamie Bell
John Borovilos
Connie Bray
Danielle Brown
Mike Budd
Jane Burningham-Ernst
Terri Carleton
Jackie Chambers
Annette Chiu
Carrie Collins
Mary Conway
Owen Davis
Robert Dawe
Dan DiGravio
Sandy Dobec
Ian Esquivel
Janis Fertuck
Barbara Fullerton
Ross Garnett
Margie Gartland
Gail Grant
Bryan Harrigan
Margaret Iveson
Sharon Jeroski
Amanda Joseph
Myra Junyk
Gabriel Kampf
Michelle Kennedy
Diana Knight

Marty Kofsky
Lorne Kulak
Gerd Laudenbach
Noël Lim
Cheryl Manny
Wendy Mathieu
Janie McTavish
Ian Mills
Yula Nouragas
Victoria Nutting
Adam Oberfrank
Keith Pearce
Robin Pearson
Larry Peters
Frank Petruzella
Louise Pivato
Sheila Powell
Peter Purcell
Judith Robinson
Tom Sbrocchi
Richard Schultz
Larry Smith
Sally Spofforth
Jim Stewart
Brian Switzer
Jean Szeles
Dirk Verhulst
Cornelia Wagner
Judy Wedeles
Darlene White
Stephen Willcock

Contents by Genre and Form

Unit 2: POETRY 210

Unit 3: NON–FICTION

Contents by Theme

■ Identity

Self

Childhood

Adolescence

Personal Challenges

Self and Culture

Stereotypes

Loss

▪ Relationships

Family

Peers

▪ Community

At Play

Rural Life

Urban Life

Civic Responsibility

Nature

South America

Africa

Europe

Asia

Australia

▪ Beyond the Everyday

Intrigue

Journeys

Moral Questions

Humour

Media Impact

Creativity

Eye on the Past

Preface

It has been said that if you take any given topic and present it to five people, you will get at least ten viewpoints in response. Each of us holds a variety of viewpoints on a wide range of topics. When exploring anything from personal relationships to the increasing role of technology and media in our lives, we all seek insights that will sharpen our viewpoints, making them more precise, more articulate, and more convincing. So, how do we achieve this goal? How does an initial impression or opinion evolve into a more powerful viewpoint?

The anthology you hold in your hands contains compelling texts from different eras, locations, and sources. You will encounter an array of selections, set in places across Canada and around the world. The genres and forms contained here range from classic poems and contemporary stories to essays, sculpture, advertisements, and Web sites.

Each selection begins with a "Context," which introduces and provides some relevant background while challenging you to make links between the selection and the environment from which it came. At the end of the selection, "Notes" are included, when appropriate, to both assist and challenge you: they enhance your comprehension and draw you into making deeper connections. Selection activities provide creative ways of further understanding the work—and, in the process, the world and also yourself. And by experimenting with new forms in your own writing or visual representations, *you* will become a more accomplished, powerful communicator. Each selection also has related themes and elements: they demonstrate how every text is made up of a wealth of interconnected features, and they help you to make links between texts.

When you interpret a short story, respond to a poem, act out a play, analyze an essay, view a painting, or study an Internet report, you enter a partnership as you engage with the rich offerings of these texts. *Viewpoints 11* challenges you to experience, consider, respond to, and evaluate many different perceptions. In this way, the book is a gateway to your own evolving viewpoints.

Acknowledgements

The authors and editors would like to thank the following educators for their contributions:

Media Consultant: Ian Esquivel
Equity Consultant: Hari Lalla
Equity and Aboriginal Consultant: Linda Laliberté

Alice Barlow-Kedves
Carrie Collins
Laura Edlund
Christine Jackson
Christel Kleitsch
Mary Ladky
Jill Lloyd-Jones
Christine McClymont
Ian Mills

We would also like to thank the following student reviewers:

Darcy Franco, Prince George Senior Secondary, Prince George, British Columbia

Sherri Henderson, West Pictou High School, Pictou, Nova Scotia

Kristin Stadnick, Radville Regional High School, Radville, Saskatchewan

Timothy Sweeney, Malvern Collegiate Institute, Toronto, Ontario

Christy Wingrove, Oak Park High School, Winnipeg, Manitoba

UNIT 1   SHORT FICTION

"When writing, I'm after the intensity of moments and layers

of meaning that come with them." ■ Alice Munro

When you read fiction, you may think, "This story did not really happen." What's important, however, is that it *could* have. It's been said that fiction offers a parallel universe: what happens in fiction is invented, but it still has to be believable to the reader. Fiction writers often start with a story idea, then begin to shape the elements of their narratives—setting, plot, character, and point of view. In honing each element, they select, arrange, discard, emphasize, and combine details to spark new ideas. Writers' distinctive voices are further shaped through their writing styles—in essence, their language choices in diction, figures of speech, and sentence rhythms. When you read a good story closely, you'll come to understand *how* writers craft their tales. As you read this unit and encounter different historical periods and cultures, confront fascinating issues, and explore universal themes, you will also gain insight into yourself. And be sure to use these stories as writing models: they offer literary patterns and techniques for you to experiment with as you fill your own stories with intensity and meaning.

The Shivering Tree

John McLeod

The Great and Mischievous Nanabush, c. 1975, Blake Debassige

LEARNING FOCUS

- Analyze the form and style of an origin myth.
- Work in a group to discover and clarify ideas.
- Write an origin myth.

CONTEXT John McLeod, an Aboriginal Canadian from Northern Ontario, is a member of the Mississauga First Nation. His story "The Shivering Tree" is a modern retelling of a trickster tale, with a structure and style that reflect the oral tradition. The story's hero is Nanabush, the Trickster, a well-known figure in Ojibwa mythology. He is half spirit and half human, both creator and spoiler, hero and clown. In this story, Nanabush becomes interlocked in a suspenseful but amusing match of wits with the evil Juggler. The story offers an explanation of the origin of two natural phenomena, and a moral lesson for human beings. What are these natural phenomena? Based on this story, how would you describe the Trickster figure in Aboriginal mythology? What lesson could be drawn from the story? ■

Nanabush was walking; he'd been walking a long time. He'd been walking a long time and he was feeling very tired and thirsty.

"My, my, my," Nanabush said to himself, "I've been walking a long time and boy oh boy am I tired and thirsty. It's a good thing I'm such a smart fellow and decided to follow this river. This way, if I get lost, I'll still know where I am even though I won't."

And he liked what he said to himself.

"Goodness me but I'm a bright fellow," Nanabush said to himself. And he had to stop in his tracks and smile and just shake his head, he was just so proud of himself for what he'd just said just before telling himself how bright he was.

"Well, Nanabush, you bright fellow, let's go down to the river and have a drink and rest our old bones for a year or two…heh, heh," Nanabush said to himself. And he agreed.

Feeling very proud of himself, Nanabush strutted down to the river. It wasn't far at all and when he got there Nanabush took a good long drink, threw some water in his face, and lay back on the sandy bank.

"It certainly is a big world," he thought. "Somewhere to the west of here are the Tall Mountains that mark the approach of the Home of the West Wind. Someday I'll go there, for I've a score to settle with that Old Fellow."

That's when his quick ears caught another sound above the voice of the river. It was another voice, a man's voice.

Nanabush sat up, fast.

"A man?" Nanabush thought. "That just can't be. No human being has come this far."

But it was a man. At least it looked like one. But that meant nothing back in those times; after all, Nanabush looked like a man—most of the time. But Nanabush was far from being human. But just who or what was this fellow anyway?

Like I said, the stranger looked human at least. He was tall and thin, clad in buckskins with long fringe that fluttered and shivered in the breeze. He wore warm leggings and moccasins as it was autumn and the weather getting colder.

The stranger was juggling something. Now that was interesting.

He was juggling with his eyes closed. And that was mighty interesting.

Nanabush stood up, slowly, never taking his eyes off the juggling stranger.

"Hello, Nanabush," The Juggler said, still juggling, his eyes still shut firmly. "It is Nanabush, isn't it?"

Nanabush felt insulted.

"Of course I'm Nanabush," Nanabush said. "Who else could I be?"

The Juggler, eyes still firmly shut, still juggling what now appeared to be a pair of small crystals, just smiled.

"Well, let me see now," The Juggler said, still juggling, his eyes still shut firmly. "You could be Me, seeing as I'm the only person in these parts, but as you are you and not me and I'm here to see it, I guess I'm me and you're you and you must be Nanabush, because I've heard you've been spotted in these parts and I'm the only person here who would have heard about you besides you."

Nanabush glared at The Juggler.

"It's a fortunate thing for you that I'm such a clever fellow," Nanabush said, "because if I wasn't I might've been confused by what you just said and I'd've become very angry."

The Juggler just kept on juggling, eyes closed and all.

Nanabush felt himself getting impatient.

"Well?" Nanabush said. "Are you going to tell me who you are?"

With a big, wide grin, The Juggler stopped what he was doing, opened his eyes, and turned to Nanabush.

"Very well," The Juggler said, "I'm a juggler and conjuror and I am known as Restless As The Wind; but most people just call me The Juggler."

"I have never heard of you," Nanabush said. He didn't like this fellow at all. No sir, Nanabush didn't like him at all.

"I was just playing around with a couple of pieces of crystal," The Juggler said. "That was nothing at all. That was just ordinary juggling that a child can do, eyes closed or not. Just watch. I'll show you some real conjuring...Look, Nanabush, look."

Quick as lightning, The Juggler plucked out his own eyes and started to juggle them, rapidly from hand to hand. He started to dance, leaping into the air, all the while juggling his eyes hand to hand, back and forth, back and forth, hand to hand.

Nanabush was stunned, couldn't move.

Now that in itself was something. It takes a great deal to shake up someone like Nanabush, and everyone knows that there just isn't anyone to compare with The Great Nanabush.

The Juggler kept it up. Juggling, hand to hand, back and forth, back and forth, hand to hand, dancing, leaping, juggling. Juggling his eyes.

"Stop," Nanabush said, shouting. "Stop, you're making me dizzy...*stop it.*"

And, just as quickly as he had started, The Juggler stopped, came to a halt just like that, arms out wide, head back, just in time for his eyes to fall right straight into their sockets.

Nanabush's own eyes almost fell out, he stared so hard.

The Juggler grinned: boy did he grin.

Nanabush still couldn't stop staring.

I don't blame The Great Nanabush one bit, my friends. A sight like that can be enough to jar anyone's preserves.

"Now that is most certainly conjuring at its best," Nanabush said, "and you may take that as the word of the very one who invented conjuring."

The Juggler grinned.

"Well, Great Nanabush, Father of Conjuring. Perhaps I can show my gratitude, indeed the gratitude of all of us Conjurors," The Juggler said, smiling. "Allow me to show you how it's done. Allow me to show you how to juggle one's own eyes in one's own hands."

Now that got to Nanabush. For great and powerful as he can be, Nanabush can make the odd blunder now and then, and when he does, it's usually a bad one. This was going to be one of the worst.

"I'm flattered," Nanabush said, smiling like a proud father. "And I'm never too old to learn."

How true that was. Nanabush was about to learn a lesson that he and we are never going to forget.

"Will you allow me, then, to show you how it is done?" The Juggler said, smiling.

"The honour will be mine," Nanabush said, stepping forward.

"Show me how it's done, Nephew."

"Removing the eyes is the really dangerous part," The Juggler said. "You have to apply some pressure just below each eye, like this."

The Juggler demonstrated how it was supposed to be done. Using his thumbs, he applied some pressure underneath his eye-sockets, and...POP...out came the eyes. Very quickly, but carefully, he caught the eyes and, quickly and just as carefully, placed them back in his sockets.

"Did you see that?" The Juggler said. "Now, very carefully, 'cause it's just the first time, try it yourself and on yourself. Not too fast. This is only the First Lesson."

Nanabush placed his thumbs under his eye-sockets, carefully applied some pressure.

"Good, good...that's good," The Juggler said, directing and urging Nanabush. "Careful now...be very careful."

Then...POP...out came Nanabush's eyes...Then...WHOOSH out shot The Juggler's right hand and grabbed Nanabush's eyes in mid-air.

"I've got them...HA HA. I've got them," The Juggler cried, leaping into the air and spinning like a top. "I've got the most powerful charms of any conjuror in The North. I have the very eyes of Nanabush...HA HA I have them."

Then, as quick as lightning, The Juggler turned and ran, ran faster than he'd ever run in his life, for Nanabush is still Nanabush, blind or not.

But Nanabush was blind. Even before The Juggler turned and ran, Nanabush had made a lunge forward, instinctively knowing that something had gone wrong.

As The Juggler ran off, laughing and whooping, Nanabush landed, face down in the river. Almost immediately, he was on his feet. Almost immediately he was the real Nanabush. He stood still, turned his fear into caution.

"I've been a fool, a vain, yes...even a blind fool. With both my eyes in my head, I was blind," he said to himself. He stood still, silent. He listened. He began to take his bearings.

The river was in front of him. He turned his back to it.

"Until I regain my sight...and I will regain my sight, I must feel my way about. I also need a weapon which I can use easily and quickly should one of my old enemies come upon me," Nanabush said to himself. "A staff, that's it. A big heavy staff, sharpened at one end; it'll act as a cane and a weapon. I must find my way to the bush."

So, stumbling over bits of driftwood and rocks, falling painfully but always getting right back up on his feet, Nanabush made his way toward the bush, feeling his way with his hands, carefully keeping his ears open for every sound.

"If a friend finds me, may he truly be a friend," Nanabush said. "If an enemy should come upon me, may he act with honour. If my enemy should save me, I will gladly be in his debt. If my enemy finds me and chooses to kill me, then fine, I will still owe him something, if only a good fight."

All around him was darkness. But he knew that to be a false darkness. The birds still sang and the warmth of the sun made itself felt on his body and he knew it to be daylight and he knew himself to be in full view of friend, foe, and stranger alike. But he stumbled on, into the bush. He knew he was in the bush, for he smelt pine needles and the odour of fallen leaves. He bent over and felt a pine cone beneath his hand.

"I must find a stout pole to carve into a pointed staff," he said, feeling about, moving more cautiously than before.

The forest was thick, for he continually bumped into trees and stumps.

"Trees, stumps, but no limbs of any good size," he thought. "At least one old enemy of mine has been at work here, Old Man Beaver and his clan."

Then his left hand touched on something, a young fallen tree. This was it. He ran his hands up and down the narrow trunk. This was exactly what he wanted. He pulled out his knife after using his great strength to break off an appropriate length of trunk. Carefully, he sat down and carefully, very carefully, he began to carve.

A staff alone won't be enough. Nanabush knew that. He'd have to find help from someone who knew the country, someone he could trust, someone who could be trusted as a guide.

But Nanabush had to concentrate on his carving. He had to be really, really careful or, in his blindness, he might cut a finger or two off.

So far, he hadn't given a thought to The Juggler.

He kept on carving, clumsily but carefully.

Then, suddenly, he stopped. Stopped everything. He had a strong feeling that he was being watched. He tightened his grip on the knife.

Though he had no eyes with which to see, he still instinctively moved his head back and forth as if scanning the area around him. He was certain that he was being watched. The feeling was even stronger.

Then he heard the voice, a deep clear voice, from somewhere above him.

"Well?" The Voice said. "Why have you stopped? You were doing well."

Knife in hand, Nanabush leaped to his feet.

"Who is there?" he snapped. "If you're an enemy, come out and fight."

"Fight?" The Voice said. "I thought you were busy working with that piece of wood."

Nanabush recognized the voice. It was indeed the voice of an enemy; a very old enemy, too.

"Owl, so it's you," Nanabush said, more on his guard than ever. "Well. What are you waiting for? Come and fight."

"I'm an old warrior, not an old fool," Owl said. "There's a thousand eyes in these woods. If I fought you and if I slew you in the condition which you are in the whole of Creation would hear of it. You'd be honoured. I'd be disgraced.

"No, Nanabush. I'm no coward. I may be your enemy, but I would like to think that I'm a worthy enemy.

"Lower your weapon. There is no danger from me, you have my word as a Warrior and as the head of my clan."

Nanabush, on hearing this solemn oath, placed his knife back into its sheath.

"I know that you're blind," said the Owl. "So will others and soon, Nanabush. Others who may not be so generous. Something must be done to restore your vision to you."

"I'll find a way myself," said Nanabush. "I'm already far too much in debt to you, Owl."

"Not if we decide to be friends," Owl said. "I am willing, for I wish there to be peace for my children. If you agree, then it's done."

"Then it's done," Nanabush said.

Their friendship sealed, the two began to talk of Nanabush's trouble.

"There is a way to restore your vision," Owl said. "I will give you a pair of eyes. I will give you my eyes."

"But Owl, my friend. That will leave you with no eyes. You will be as blind as I now am," Nanabush said.

The Owl shook his head. If he could have smiled, he would have.

"Oh no, not me," Owl said. "You see, Nanabush, I have two sets of eyes. One set for daytime and another set for night. As most of my enemies are daylight hunters like the hawk, I'll do my hunting at night from now on. During the day, I'll rest and stay safely with my family. I'll need only one set of eyes then. The other set I give to you."

Owl told Nanabush to hold out his hands. Nanabush did so, and a pair of eyes dropped into Nanabush's hands. Then...POP...Nanabush dropped the eyes into his own sockets.

"They are perfect, Owl," Nanabush said, joyously but seriously, as befits a Warrior.

"From this day, Owl, the night is yours," Nanabush declared. "From this day and for all time, you will be the Bird of The Night. You will be my eyes at night. At night your vision will be sure and your flight safe and clear. You will be to night as the Eagle and the Falcon are to the daylight. You'll rule the night skies. And out of respect for the great favour you have done for me, all who hear you call at night shall show their respect. They must not mimic your call if they hear you; that is to say, they will not answer your call. For them to do so would be to mock you. Your call will be my message in the night that I, Nanabush, never sleep but with my ears open, that even at night I watch those whom I protect, and that I keep a watch out for those who would do harm to The Creation. So call out at night, Owl, my friend and my Emissary."

Their friendship sealed for all time, Owl and Nanabush bade each other good hunting and a long life. And so they parted, Owl with his new honours, Nanabush with his new eyes.

■　■　■

Springtime.

Springtime, and Nanabush was home. New eyes and everything. "The World is very beautiful this day," Nanabush said to himself as he walked along. "All is green and fragrant with new life and the birds are back. Yes, this is truly a beautiful day."

"Can't wait till the butterflies come out," Nanabush said. "My, but it's a wonderful day. Good thing that I have my eyes to see it all."

Then came that little voice that is sometimes to be heard in the back of Nanabush's mind. "Ah, Nanabush, but they weren't always your eyes, were they?" Nanabush remembered, of course. He remembered where his new eyes had come from and he remembered also what had happened to his old eyes. For the first time in months he thought of The Juggler. That ruined his day.

"The Juggler," Nanabush thought. "If I ever again meet up with that thieving rascal, he will regret the day his parents met. He will need more than an extra pair of eyes when I get through with him."

His day was ruined, he sat down and sulked. He couldn't help but think of The Juggler, couldn't think of anything else.

In the days which followed, Nanabush was obsessed with his strange enemy. He talked of little else. He began to worry his friends and his family.

His Grandmother advised him to stop thinking about The Juggler.

"You still have a great deal of work to do in this world," Grandmother said. "You've much to do. You are the teacher, the helper of all living things. Go about your work, Grandson. Don't seek out enemies. They will find you soon enough if they are not cowards."

So Nanabush carried on as always. Sometimes sure of himself, sometimes blundering, but always leaving his mark somewhere, somehow, on the world around him, making it more and more like the world we know today.

Then, one afternoon in late summer, he felt in need of a drink of water. He was deep in the woods at this time, but he knew where there was a clear, cold pool of water not far from where he stood. Picking up his kit, he made his way through the bush. He'd just about reached the pool when he saw, through the bushes around him, that another was at the pool.

A man.

A tall, thin man.

A tall thin man who was juggling a pair of crystals hand to hand, back and forth, hand to hand, back and forth.

Nanabush's eyes narrowed; he clenched his teeth.

"I must think this out," Nanabush said to himself. "I must think quickly, though. I may not get another chance at this rascal; besides, in addition to being my enemy, he's a Sorcerer and a dangerous one. Who is to tell how much damage he has done to others besides me? This fellow is very dangerous and I must do something about him."

Quickly and quietly, as only he can do it, Nanabush changed his appearance. He took on the appearance of an old man. Then he stepped out into the open.

The Juggler gave him a quick glance but kept right on juggling.

"Good day, Old One," The Juggler said. "I'd wish you long life but it seems a good number have already done so."

"So they have, Nephew," Nanabush said. "And they did so out of respect."

"Forgive me if I sound disrespectful," The Juggler said, continuing to juggle, "but I'm a very happy fellow these days and I sometimes don't give thought to what I'm saying. It could be that you've heard of me. I'm The Juggler. My name is Restless As The Wind."

"So," Nanabush said. "You are the fellow Nanabush is looking for, the one who stole Nanabush's eyes."

"That's me all right, Old One," The Juggler said. "Tell Nanabush if you like to. Maybe I'll take his ears this time."

"He'll find you without my telling him," Nanabush said, trying to hold back a smile. "He is no longer blind, by the way. A friend gave him a new pair of eyes."

The Juggler stopped his juggling.

Nanabush, still looking like an Old Man, stepped over to the pool and took a drink of water.

"So, he's got new eyes, has he?" The Juggler said, trying not to sound as scared as he was beginning to feel. "Well, good for him. If he comes to me, I just might take his new eyes, too. I did it before and I can do it again."

Nanabush stood up.

"So you're a mighty, powerful fellow?" Nanabush said. "You think that you can beat Nanabush?"

"I am a Great Sorcerer," The Juggler said. "I can defeat anything or anyone."

"Can you beat me?" Nanabush said.

"Anyone or anything," The Juggler said, trying very hard to sound brave.

"I've heard that you can juggle with your eyes out of your head. That you don't need eyes to see," Nanabush said.

The Juggler grinned, popped out his own eyes, and juggled them, hand to hand, back and forth, hand to hand, back and forth. Then he stopped, threw his head back. Then he tossed his eyes into the air. Up went his eyes, down they came and...plunk...landed safely in their sockets.

"Is that good enough for you, Old One?" The Juggler said, grinning at Nanabush.

But it wasn't Nanabush as an old man standing there. It was Nanabush as The Juggler remembered him.

"Well. If it isn't The Great Nanabush himself," The Juggler said, grinning and trying to sound (and feel) braver than he really was.

"I've already seen that trick," Nanabush said. And he was grinning, too.

"So, Nanabush, are you tired of your new pair of eyes already?" The Juggler said. "If you want to save us both time and work, you can just hand your eyes over to me right now."

"If you really want my eyes, you're going to have to work for them, Nephew," Nanabush said.

"Fine by me. Just tell me how," The Juggler said.

"Very good, Nephew. Nothing fancy—I'll toss my eyes to you and you catch them," Nanabush said. "If you catch them, you get to keep them. If you miss you won't owe me a thing. All or nothing. Fair enough."

"Too easy," The Juggler said. "No real challenge. Tell you what, Nanabush. I'll seal my eyes shut. How does that sound?"

"Fine by me, Nephew," Nanabush said. "But I warn you. I'm going to be throwing from quite a distance, from the very rim of the world itself."

"Ha. Go to the rim of the world. Even that wouldn't be far enough. I'd know when it's coming. I'll just stand here and wait. You're the one who'll have all the work to do. If you want to walk all the way to the edge of Creation just to toss a couple of eyes, that's fine by me, I'll catch them. I never miss," The Juggler said proudly.

With a shrug of his shoulders, The Juggler obtained some sap from a nearby tree. This sap he used to seal his eyes shut. Then he stood calmly and with very great confidence.

"Well, Nanabush. I'm ready if you are. Be on your way. It's a long walk, but I'll wait. When victory is a sure thing, I can wait," The Juggler said. Then he folded his arms in front of his chest and said no more.

Nanabush walked away.

Nanabush walked away, but not to the rim of the world. He just plain walked away and didn't look back.

■   ■   ■

Nanabush went about his work of making the world what it was meant to be. He never gave The Juggler another thought. Why?

Because Nanabush knew that The Juggler, like all Sorcerers, was a vain fellow more than eager to show off his power no matter how long it took. The Juggler said he'd wait and so he did.

He's still waiting. And he will wait for all time, until The End of Time. Oh, it's not at all difficult to find him. He's very well known. He's easily recognizable.

His name, you recall, is Restless As The Wind. It's a very descriptive name. He's still to be seen standing, day in, day out, standing, rooted to the spot, his fringes and hair swaying and shivering constantly in the wind, at the slightest breeze or draught. Even when the air is perfectly still.

To pass the long hours away, you see, The Juggler, Restless As The Wind, has taken the form of a tree. A tree that never rests, whose leaves and branches still shake and shiver even when the air is still and quiet.

He's become the Shivering Tree.

The Poplar Tree.

And that's the way it is to this good day.

Nanabush also known as Nanabozho, Coyote, Hare, Old Man, Raven, and Glooscap, among other names; he is the Trickster of First Nations mythology

ANALYZE AND INTERPRET

1. a) Use a dictionary or reference guide to help you define the term "stylistic device." b) Identify as many stylistic devices in this myth as you can. c) In a chart, list the devices and an example of each. d) As a class, discuss how each device contributes to the effectiveness of the oral story.

2. Working with a small group, brainstorm a list of four or five natural phenomena that could form the basis of an origin myth, such as how thunder and lightning were created, or how the rose got its thorns. Then select one of the phenomena on your list, and create your own myth to explain its occurrence. Write out the myth, create or find appropriate illustrations for it, and read it aloud to a group. Invite the comments of group members.

3. Use the Internet and print resources to find several myths from different cultures that explain one natural or cultural phenomenon. With a group, select one myth that you like, and prepare and rehearse an oral telling of it. Present your tale to a group and listen to the group members' evaluations. For the class, identify the society that produced the myth.

MORE TO EXPLORE

Themes: Personal Challenges, Friends, Nature, Aboriginal Cultures, Canada, Intrigue, Moral Questions

Elements: characterization, dialogue, first-person point of view, myth, oral tradition, sarcasm

Learning the Language

Karen Connelly

Winter in Québec, Mark Tomalty

LEARNING FOCUS

- Explore the context and symbolism of a song.
- Identify and evaluate a literary device.
- Analyze the effect of form on style and meaning.

CONTEXT Karen Connelly was born in Calgary, Alberta, in 1969. In 1993, she was the youngest person ever to win a Governor General's Award, which she received for her memoir of travels in Thailand called *Touch the Dragon: A Thai Journal.* Her first book of poetry, *The Small Words in My Body,* won the Pat Lowther Award in 1990. Connelly has travelled extensively and lived abroad in a number of countries, including Spain, France, and Greece, in her quest for "a living knowledge of the world." Connelly has been writer-in-residence at the University of New Brunswick and Okanagan University College in Penticton, British Columbia. In the late 1990s, she settled on Vancouver Island. This story is presented as a fictional journal. Have you encountered this form before? If so, what was that story about, and why do you think the writer chose the form? Why might a writer choose to present a fictional story this way, rather than as a regular short story? ■

September 10, 1984

Monsieur Nolan is my French teacher. He's skinny, pale, and noisy as a paper bag, shaken constantly by a rough cough. His hair hangs across his forehead like charcoal splashed with silver paint. The crow Patches caught last summer reminds me of him: all-black, mournful eyes. He looks so old sometimes, when he nods his head in a certain way, when he folds his hands across his knees. But he isn't old. Mrs. Belton told us this is his first year teaching. It's not hard to tell. He can hardly speak English. His sentences come so slowly that the class turns to dissecting him.

Megan said to me today, "He wears platform shoes. And an undershirt." She suppressed a giggle. Jeff and Andrew caught the undershirt criticism and sputtered laughter out loud.

Monsieur Nolan looked confused. He's so innocent, that's the problem. "What is the…difficulty?" he said, haltingly, the words catching in his throat like snags in nylon. His pause for the right English words had taken too long.

Jeff answered, "No…dif-fi-cul-ty…at all…sir." His face reddened; his body shook with the giggles like rain puddles under wind.

Mom says it's cruel to treat anyone like that. What can I do? He's a teacher. Teachers walk all over us and we survive. Besides, they are supposed to be able to defend themselves.

November 14, 1984

I tried to get out of my French option. And I failed. After I waited to see her for half an hour, Mrs. Belton invited me into her rawhide office. (Anything that's upholstered in there is wrapped in genuine dead leather. I felt like I was in a saddle when I sat down on a chair.) When I asked about French, she said to me, slack-jawed and wide-eyed, as if it was the most shocking request she'd ever dreamed of hearing, "But why do you want to leave?"

Because I am not learning any French. Monsieur Nolan can only speak his language, he cannot teach it. I'm frustrated because I do not know how to conjugate reflexive verbs, and he can't even define them. He doesn't know the English words. *Je suis fatiguée à cause du français.* I'm exhausted because of French. School has taught me that it is better to know useless things than to know nothing at all, and I know that, in the French room, there are eighteen windowpanes, two hundred and sixteen tiles in the ceiling, and forty-eight light sections.

"Because French is boring," I said.

"Oh." Pause, a disappointed flatness slid over her face. Then out came the guilt tactic. "I don't think that's a very mature reason for refusing to be a productive member in Monsieur Nolan's class." She pronounced "mach-ure" *mat-ure*. Mom says people who do that should be fined; it's too snobbish. "Remember," Mrs. Belton continued, "French is very important in this country. Soon this entire school could be functioning bilingually…." She finished with this ominous prophecy, smiling.

Mrs. Belton is also called Madame Belton. She used to teach French.

January 7, 1985

Monsieur Nolan stood as straight as he could when we came into the classroom. He looked energetically determined, which was a change. "We are going to do something different," he said. He said it well, slowed only by his thick accent; there was no pausing for words.

"He probably practised last night in front of a mirror," Megan laughed. I refused to glance at her. He shut the door and walked to the back of the room. A slide projector was propped up on top of two scruffy books. "Over the holidays, I was in Québec," he said. "Maybe, I thought, you would be interested in these."

"That's a pretty hefty 'maybe,'" someone whispered.

With the blinds down, the room darkened. Monsieur Nolan perched on a desk at the back of the room, clicking away the slides. They weren't what I expected. There were no photographs of Louis Riel-type monuments or Wilfrid Laurier statues taken in writhing Montreal. There were no pictures of cities with their landmarks and their masses of people. A fox was caught in the camera, his legs thigh-deep in whiteness; he had a mouse in his mouth, its tail hanging between his teeth like a string of spaghetti. A herd of deer, each one in a different stage of bounce, was crossing the wind-rippled flatness of a lake. The frozen lake fringed into jagged evergreens. Spruce boughs were weighted with white, sagging to the ground. Every picture was like that, of animals or land. The wide, grey wings of an owl flying at dusk up a pale-throated cutline spread across the screen. Everything glowed white and blue-shadowed snow, like paintings lit in a dark room.

The only picture of a human being was of a girl. She stood on cross-country skis, leaning on one of her poles. Near her stood a dog, sunk in snow, panting, his pink tongue and white canines bright against the fur of his dark muzzle. The girl had loose, long, black hair; she was smiling, perhaps laughing. Monsieur Nolan did not say who she was. I looked at him. He smiled, not to me, but to the girl on the screen; it was a flighty grin, momentary. Then his expression settled into its usual lines, but a different look, as light as gauze, covered his face. It was sadness. But he didn't look like an injured crow at all. He looked human this time, grey-faced, in some quiet pain.

January 18, 1985

I understand reflexive verbs.

February 4, 1985

The last ten minutes of class, he played us music written by a man named Gilles Vigneault. I'd never heard of him until today, although everyone supposedly knows him in Quebec. It was all just a smooth blur of words that I couldn't understand because of language, my lack of it. Monsieur Nolan said that when he has the time, he will translate the words for us.

"Ha," said Megan, "he can't do it in English, the twit." That may or may not be true. I don't know. But even in French, the words had meaning. I'm just not sure what that meaning was, or of the importance of it. I only knew it was there. These are the words on the sheet he handed to us.

Mon Pays

Mon pays, ce n'est pas un pays, c'est l'hiver
Mon jardin, ce n'est pas un jardin, c'est la plaine

Mon chemin, ce n'est pas un chemin, c'est la neige
Mon pays ce n'est pas un pays, c'est l'hiver

…Où la neige au vent se marie/
Dans ce pays de poudrerie
Mon père a fait bâtir maison/
Et je m'en vais être fidèle
À sa manière à son modèle/
La chambre d'amis sera telle
Qu'on viendra des autres saisons/
Pour se bâtir à côté d'elle.…

Mon pays, ce n'est pas un pays, c'est l'hiver
Mon refrain, ce n'est pas un refrain, c'est rafale
Ma maison ce n'est pas ma maison, c'est froidure
Mon pays ce n'est pas un pays, c'est l'hiver

…Je crie…/À tous les hommes de la terre
Ma maison, c'est votre maison.

When the class finished, the halls spilled with talking people. It was like being clattered awake in the night by hailstones on the roof.

February 21, 1985

Mrs. Belton is sitting in on our classes, watching. She skulks at the back of the room sullen as a raven, periodically scratching down notes on a clipboard. We have our backs to her; we forget she's even there. But he's facing her while she looks him over, scanning him up and down like a horse at an auction. "What're his teeth like?" I can hear her say.

February 28, 1985

Worse things have happened, but not to me. Today was awful. We were supposed to have a dictation quiz, a *dictée* in French. Monsieur Nolan passed out papers and began rolling out French for us. Jeff whined.

Jeff whined again, louder. "Monsieur, you're going too fast. I can't even write this fast in English," which is probably true: he's too stupid. But his whining spread like an easily communicable disease. Andrew picked it up, gave it to his friends. Megan splayed agony and injustice all over her face.

At first, Monsieur Nolan wasn't sure of the complaints. He shook his head, then opened his mouth to talk. Instead of words, he coughed, started hacking away like a sick car engine. His back curled. With one hand, he covered his mouth; with the other he balanced himself. But his hand slid off the paper-slick wood of his desk, knocking a stack of sheets into the air. He stretched to catch them, but they fanned out fast, everywhere, feathered and graceful, sliding away across the floor top. He still gagged as the last of the pile tipped off his desk in an avalanche of white.

It happened in less than a minute. It was only a chink of time, but it was an obvious mistake. And a teacher had made it, fallen down a level, clumsily. They witnessed it: he was as clumsy as themselves. The kids were laughing. They laughed and laughed, not even trying to hold it in their mouths.

Only when Mrs. Belton stood up did they remember she had again come to the class. She walked to the front, heels cracking on the papered floor. I thought she would drag us out individually to throttle us. She didn't. "Monsieur Nolan," she said quietly, "I'll see you outside."

March 4, 1985

The sub says he has pneumonia, he's very ill, he went back. Illness isn't the only reason, though.

Mom, who never liked Mrs. Belton anyway, says she should be fired, put out of our misery.

The room was empty of his books, the slide projector, certainly all his papers. The blackboard had some writing on it. Before he left us, he wrote out the translation to "Mon Pays," that was all. And enough.

My Country

My country is not a country, it is winter
My garden is not a garden, it is the plains
My path is not a path, it is snow
My country is not a country, it is winter

…Where the snow marries the wind/
In this country of powder
My father built a house/And I will be faithful
To his method and his model/
The guestroom will be such
That other seasons will come/To build beside it.

My country is not a country, it is winter
My refrain is not a refrain, it is wind
My house is not a house, it is coldness
My country is not my country, it is winter

…I cry…/To all men of the earth
My house is your house.

NOTES

Louis Riel a Métis leader who founded Manitoba; a central figure in the North-West Rebellion, for which he was convicted of treason and executed by hanging in Saskatchewan in 1885

Wilfrid Laurier Liberal Prime Minister of Canada from 1896–1911; many viewed him as a charismatic pragmatist who promoted national unity

ANALYZE AND INTERPRET

1. With a group, find and listen to the Gilles Vigneault song "Mon Pays" and do some research into its history and significance to the people of Québec. Consider why the author included this song in the story. With your group, discuss how the song's content and mood reflect the situation in the story. How does the song contribute to the story's theme?

2. **a)** Make a list of all the similes the author uses in the story. **b)** Choose the three you find most effective, and write a sentence or two about each, explaining why you chose it. **c)** Select the three similes from your list that you

think are the weakest, and rewrite the sentences in which they appear, substituting a simile or other descriptive image of your own. **d)** Share your work with a partner. Do you think the abundance of similes contributes authenticity to the story's narrative voice? Discuss.

3. In your journal, reflect on the author's decision to write this story as a journal. What are the advantages of using a journal to tell this particular story? What are its limitations? How might the content have been different if the story were written as a letter to someone else? Next, imagine a student with different values and attitudes from those of the narrator, and retell one of the story events as this student. Ask a partner to read your work, and then discuss any changes to the tone of the story.

MORE TO EXPLORE

Themes: Adolescence, Stereotypes, Peers, At School, Canada, Moral Questions

Elements: characterization, conflict, dénouement, first-person point of view, metaphor, simile, voice

Brother Dear

Bernice Friesen

Courtesy of Edward Day Gallery

Self Portrait, 1997, William Irish

LEARNING FOCUS

- Compare your ideas, values, and perspectives with those of others.
- Rewrite from another character's viewpoint.
- Work with others to research ideas.

CONTEXT Canadian artist and author Bernice Friesen was born in Rosthern, Saskatchewan, in 1966. She studied and taught art in Saskatchewan, and her artwork has appeared in many exhibitions. As an author, she has written short stories and poetry and has won several awards. Like "Brother Dear," Friesen's stories from her anthology *The Seasons Are Horses* deal with issues of concern to young people, such as relationships, racism, and love. This story focuses on a high-school student and her older brother, and their need to define themselves as individuals. In your experience, what are some of the issues that typically bring teens and parents into conflict? At what stage do you expect to "find yourself" and feel independent of the adults in your life? What lesson does the young woman in the story learn from her brother?

Grassbank is like a lot of other small towns. We have an IGA grocery, a clinic, a drug store, among other things, and a bus depot at the pool hall. Living here, in the land of sheer boredom, can make a normally sane person want to rip off her clothes and leap to her death from the top of a grain elevator. I say "can" because several hundred people live in Grassbank—and they are not dead, though sometimes you might wonder.

I'm waiting to get out of here. It's April and next year's grade twelve, then it's escape to the University of Alberta like my brothers, like Dad wants. If I do what Dad wants. I have these dreams of running off to Europe for a couple of years, being a nanny and learning a language or two. My best friend's sister did that. If I get up the nerve to do the same, I'll tell Dad I'll do the university thing when I get back. He'll probably explode anyway.

But when I do go to university, I won't come home some weekend with a screwed up head like Greg. He's coming home today and I'm hanging out, waiting for him. I read in my psychology text that the middle kid is always the weird one. When Greg went away to school, he grew his hair long, and every time I saw it, it was a different colour. Sometimes I don't believe Greg is real. It's like, I know he exists…but not in my dimension, kind of like the Moonies, or like processed cheese food, which my mother compares to plastic and refuses to allow in the house.

And if I did happen to come home with a screwed up head, I wouldn't go shooting off my mouth in front of Dad. Mistake. Last Thanksgiving, Greg started preaching to us about how materialistic we are, about how much gas we use in the cars, about how Dad didn't really need a new motor home, and about how I buy too many shoes. I can't help it. I have a thing for shoes. After Greg left, Dad claimed to be on the verge of a coronary.

"He's a bloody Communist," Dad muttered.

"Oh, come on, Jack! It's Greenpeace he's joined," Mom laughed. She laughs at Dad a lot. Sometimes it makes him mad, but usually it calms him down and he laughs with her. They met in high school and they've been together ever since.

Mom kissed Dad on the cheek. "Besides, we *didn't* need a new motor home."

"He still has his car and everything, Dad," I said, "so don't worry. I think the free world is still pretty safe." I slapped Dad on the back. He's overweight, so sometimes I think maybe he actually is on the verge of a coronary. I imagined how his face might look if I told him I was going to Europe instead of university: boiled red, jaw hanging open: speechless, but not for long. He'd figure out a lot of things to say to me.

Dad shifted into a lower gear of panic during the Christmas holidays when Greg was home again, even though Greg had sold his car. Greg had also learned to shut up a little. They avoided each other, but the tension was still there.

"I don't like movements—environmental, social, political—I don't care," Dad said after Greg was gone. "Movements of any kind sound like they have something to do with the bowels."

Dad never uses the S-word in front of us, but we always get a lot of talk about coronaries, bowels, the pancreas, and the duod–duode-what-ever-the-heck-it-is. That's what you get when you're the daughter of a guy who inherited a John Deere dealership from his father and was always sorry he hadn't tried to be a doctor. This is why he gets so uptight about all his kids going to university. He's got a point. I aim to be the most filthy rich, the most hilariously funny CBC foreign correspondent that the world has ever seen. I know I have to go to university, but this is also a career in which you need to know a lot of languages. There are other things I want to do.

Brother dear, Greg, shows up at the front door about four o'clock, before Mom and Dad get back from work. He's carrying a green plastic garbage bag, which I assume is filled with laundry since he never brings home his garbage to wash, and his beat up army surplus backpack is hanging from his shoulder. I haven't seen him since Christmas, and I'm still not sure I'm seeing *him* because he's got a little wispy beard on the tip of his chin. He must be going for the Old Testament prophet look, but when he smiles at me, he looks more like a malnutritioned devil. I clamp my lips together, but it doesn't work. I spit all over him when I start laughing.

"What?" He frowns and looks down to check if his fly is open.

"Oh, nothing," I sputter. "Did you know that there's a small furry animal hanging from your chin?"

He looks at me in disgust. "And to think I was almost glad to see you." He drops his stuff in front of the door and heads for the kitchen. I follow him.

"You have no sense of humour," I say, as he gets himself an apple and sits down at the table. I pull a chair close to him and sit on it backwards so I can rest my chin on the back and stare at him, eyes blank and bulgy, teeth bared. He hates it when I do this.

"You've been annoying me since the day you were born," he says, trying not to look at me. Eventually he always has to look at me to see whether I'm still staring.

"Live with it. It's my mission in life." My psychology text also says that the youngest kid is always the brat of the family. I consider myself living proof. "So, you got a girlfriend yet?"

He blushes. "If I did, I wouldn't tell you. You'd broadcast it all over the neighbourhood."

"Your nostrils are flaring. You're hiding something."

He hates it when I tell him his nostrils are flaring. It just makes them flare more.

"Greg has a girlfriend! Greg has a girlfriend!"

"Shar*lene*." He swings his long hair out of his eyes and looks at the ceiling—something that always makes him look like he thinks he's better or more *mature* than me. He gets up and goes to the door, clumping his heavy hiking boots over the tile.

"So leave—snot!" I call, after he's already through the door and it's swinging behind him. His door slams upstairs and I feel awful. As if he doesn't have enough trouble getting along with Dad. I'd been looking forward to him coming home. I hadn't meant to start a fight, but he's just so bad at taking a joke. Greg and I have never been able to have fun together, not like the fun I used to have with Dennis, our older brother. Greg never wanted to play catch, to race, to play board games or cards because he's not into "the competition thing." Dad says he's got no drive, no ambition. He's not stupid, but he doesn't really care about being smart. He's in pre-law at university, but his marks are crap. I think he went into law just because Dennis did and Dad hasn't stopped cheering.

Greg doesn't come out of his room even when Dad comes in and falls over the bag of laundry in the doorway, and starts swearing and complaining about how nobody ever puts anything away in this house. Greg hides up there for over an hour, and at first, I think it's because he's mad at me, but then I'm not so sure. His marks have got to be back by now, so maybe he's avoiding Dad. He used to always hide in his room when he had bad news way back in high school.

Mom walks in the front door and falls over the laundry. I hear this big thump and some giggles even though I'm in the kitchen, where Dad and I are making supper, and then hear her feet running up the stairs. After a few minutes, Mom comes into the kitchen with Greg, her arm around his waist as if she had to drag him. "You're thinner. I know it," she says to him, prodding him in the stomach.

"I am not." He squirms and avoids looking into her eyes, but smiles. He looks over at Dad, who is already sitting, guarding his dish like a German shepherd.

"Good to have you home, Greg," Dad says happily, but his eyes aren't smiling as much as his lips. He doesn't get up. Bet you it's been a year since Dad and Greg have hugged. "Dennis doing okay?"

"I guess." Greg shrugs. "He's doing some research for one of his profs. Says it could turn into a summer job if he does it right."

Dad sits back and smiles as if when Dennis does good work, it feels as good to him as a big meal in his belly. Greg stops looking at Dad and sits on the edge of the chair next to me, like a scrawny bird about to fall off his perch. One side of his mouth curls down and his nostrils are flaring again.

"Greg has a secret," I croon, then slap my hand over my mouth, just remembering about his marks. Sometimes I have an enormous mouth.

"Leave me alone, Sharlene," he snaps, and the room becomes quiet. Dad says grace and then nobody talks, though Mom looks like she wants to. Greg eats the food around his steak. He eats the peas and the salad and starts to scrape the gravy off the potatoes, but changes his mind and smears the gravy back on.

"So. How'd exams go, Greg?" Dad chews his meat and his eyes flicker up, then down again. Greg doesn't say anything for a few seconds.

"Okay."

"Okay? That's all?" Dad leans forward and looks hard at Greg, maybe trying to figure out what he's thinking. Greg puts down his fork like he's finished and is getting ready to run.

"Aren't you going to eat your meat?" Mom says. She sometimes tries to cool things down by changing the subject. "It's your favourite."

"Um, sorry Mom. I'm sort of a vegetarian now."

"You're a—" Dad puts his coffee cup down very slowly, wearing his calm look, but I can tell the word "vegetarian" threw him because of the way his eyes dart around, like he's trying to focus on something he lost. "I'm more concerned about your economics marks than what sort of food fetish you've taken up. What about it?"

Oh, great. Last term, Greg's average in economics was 38%. On this exam, he'd have had to clear 62%, and Greg isn't much into numbers, or money for that matter. I want to put a wall of shatter-proof glass across the table to protect Greg's feelings. He shifts back in his chair.

"Didn't make it."

"What do you mean? You think you failed?" Dad's words are calm, careful.

"Well…I couldn't make it. I didn't get to the exam."

I stare at Greg in horror and admiration, hardly believing he has the nerve to tell Dad something like this. Maybe he figures it's better to get it over with sooner than later. Eventually, Dad would see the statement of grades anyway.

"You couldn't make the exam? What was it to you? Some sort of social event?" Dad's face starts to get red, and I feel like it's time for me to start sliding under the table so I won't get hit by any stray exploding brain cells. "What was so important that you 'couldn't make' the exam?"

Greg takes a deep breath and there's this rock determined look on his face which I've never seen before, which I'm sure Dad has never seen before.

"We were at a protest in Edmonton. We picketed the Legislature."

"So, I'm paying your rent and tuition at the best university in the west so you can fart away your time, huh? Ruin your future? Where's your brains? Maybe they just 'couldn't make it,' huh?"

"Some things are more important." Greg's voice is very quiet and gentle now, something he told me he learned in psychology class. It's supposed to pacify people who are screaming at you—except it doesn't seem to be working on Dad.

"And you don't have to pay my rent anymore," Greg says. "I got a job. I'm going tree planting this summer."

"You expect to make enough money for the whole year and tuition in four months? I knew your math was bad, but—"

"I'm not going back to school."

Greg puts his napkin on the table very slowly. Whenever he and Dad fight, Greg reminds me of one of those gentle, big-eyed jungle animals, like a sloth or a bush baby. He looks like he'd like to scamper up a tree and live far away above the noise and trouble of the forest floor, only this time he looks a little different, as if he'd dearly love to run, but has decided to stay put even if Dad chews him to bits.

Dad starts to blow. "What the hell are you saying? Not going back to school?" I stir my chocolate milk frantically; whenever I'm really nervous, I have to keep moving. I imagine Dad yelling at me, telling me if I don't go to university right out of high school, I probably never will. The spoon tingles against the inside of the glass, so I stop stirring.

"Jack…" Mom warns quietly, looking from Dad to Greg to the cold steak on Greg's plate.

"Well, he's ruining his life! If he'd work at it—if you weren't so damn lazy! What about when winter comes, and you can't plant trees anymore, huh? Thought of that? It's those friends of yours, those ideas they've got you into. It's no better than a cult."

"Excuse me," Greg says through his teeth, gets up and walks out the door. That's it, I think. Nobody's ever going to talk to anybody else in this family again.

Mom puts her elbows on the table and rubs her head as if she'd like to take it off and put it in a bowl of cold water in a soundproof room.

"You can't make him do what you want," she says.

Through the door crack I can see Greg's green jacket go past, and I think I hear the front door close. Mom and Dad are too busy starting a fight of their own to notice. I shove my chair back and go after him.

I see him walking down the block toward Main Street. He's got his pack and his laundry.

"Wait up!"

He stops in front of Johnsons' and stands there, not looking back, while I run up.

"You didn't even say good-bye."

"Sorry. I'm sorry. Is that all my family can ever do? Point out what's wrong with me?" He starts walking faster. I look at my watch. The bus for the city leaves at 7:00, in ten minutes. I stretch my legs to walk beside him.

"He didn't mean it—the cult stuff," I say. "You know Dad's temper." Greg keeps walking, taking long ostrich steps. "Why do you always have to run away?"

"If all you came for was to make me feel worse, you can go home. You're no different from Dad."

"He has a point, you know. You could have at least taken your finals. Now, if you ever want to go back, you've got a bad record. They might not want you back. You'll never get to be anything."

"Be something. Be something. That's all I ever get from Dad—from you now, and I know you don't want to go to university, at least not yet. Dad makes a lot of money. He did what his father wanted him to do and he's not happy. Can't you see that? Well, I'm not playing along with that anymore. Be something…Sharlene, you're not what you do. You're who you are."

We walk on and I think about this.

"So you never want to be anything?"

He stops and looks at me, his face tight, like he's two millimetres from screaming.

"Do you think I'm nothing right now? Do you think you're nothing?"

I open my mouth, then close it. I play with the zipper on my jacket and think.

"No…no, you're not nothing." If going to university is supposed to make something out of you, what are you before you go? Being in grade eleven is no big deal, but it doesn't feel like nothing. I don't feel like nothing.

"You understand what I'm saying?" He looks at me uncertainly, and looks at his watch.

"Yeah. I think I do."

He smiles. "For the first time in your life."

He starts walking and I follow. My brain feels all twisted, like I've just discovered I've been staring out of the wrong side of my head all my life. Greg suddenly seems a lot older, a lot smarter, than me.

"Don't go on the bus, Greg. Can't you just stay…until tomorrow?" We sit down on the old iron bench in front of the pool hall. I can see the bus pulling in from the highway.

"Dad isn't going to understand—ever."

"Well, he's especially not going to understand if you run away. If I were you, I'd go right back there and fight it out." I smack my fist into the palm of my hand.

"But I'm not like you. I'm like me. Maybe if I was like you, Dad would like me better."

Greg's voice is low, disappointed, and I feel terrible, terrible, because what he said is probably true. I'm the youngest, the comedian, and I do have more ambition.

"But I like you the way you are," I say, and for one long sick second, I think I'm lying. Then I think that if Greg was different, he wouldn't be Greg at all. Without Greg, who would I annoy? Who'd freak me out with all his bizarre clothes and ideas? Life wouldn't be as much fun. We smile at each other, and the sun is shining in my eyes.

"You like me the way I am?" He looks down at his hands. "So does Kristen."

"Who?"

"You were right. I do have a girlfriend. She tells me I'm just fine the way I am, and a few weeks ago, I started to believe her." He stretches his legs in front of him and grins helplessly at his boots, his cheeks pink.

I take in a huge breath of air and am about to shout "Hey, Grassbank, Greg's got a girlfriend," but I find I can't do it. I don't feel like doing something that will make him hate me. I let the air out. "That's terrific, Greg."

"I'd tell you about her, but…" He shrugs and looks up at the Greyhound.

"Well, you'll come back. Right?"

Greg watches the bus driver load his pack and his laundry into the baggage compartment.

"Right?"

"I don't suppose I'll stay away forever."

We hesitate, hug, and he gets on the bus. His shadow walks behind the smoked glass and sits alone on the other side of the bus. I look at the cracks in the sidewalk because I'm jealous. He's off on his life adventure, and I'm still stuck in grade eleven. I guess I'd like to run away, too. Someday I will—to Europe. I wave when the bus drives away. I can't see him, but maybe he can see me.

NOTES

Moonies slang name for the followers of Reverend Sun Myung Moon, Korean founder of the Unification Church, known in part for conducting mass weddings in the United States and elsewhere

Greenpeace an international environmental organization originating in Vancouver (1970) with a mandate of using nonviolent confrontation to draw public attention to ecological issues

Old Testament the Jewish Bible, or sacred scriptures containing the religious history and beliefs of the ancient Hebrews (Jewish people), or the first part of the Christian Bible

fetish an object believed to have magical powers; anything regarded with excessive reverence

ANALYZE AND INTERPRET

1. As a class, discuss how trying to accommodate parents' wishes can create conflict as young adults try to establish their own dreams.

2. Reread the story carefully, considering the perspective of a character other than the sister. As you read, jot down your views and reactions as if you were this character. Then rewrite a portion of the narrative from your chosen character's perspective, and share your rewrite with a partner.

3. **a)** With a partner, use the Internet or library to research a list of "tips" to help teenagers and parents improve their communication. **b)** Present your list to the class, identifying as a class which items appear on more than one list. Contribute any tips you feel are missing from the lists. **c)** As a class, choose the items you feel are most important, listing them in priority from most to least useful. Discuss the reasons for your choices.

MORE TO EXPLORE

Themes: Self, Adolescence, Family, Rebels, Rural Life, Canada

Elements: characterization, conflict, dialogue, empathy, first-person point of view

The Address

Marga Minco

TRANSLATED FROM THE DUTCH BY JEANNETTE K. RINGOLD

The Window Cleaner's Front Garden, Amsterdam, Maurice Sheppard

LEARNING FOCUS

- Compare ideas, values, and perspectives.
- Analyze the role of historical background in reading.
- Create an annotated diagram.

CONTEXT Marga Minco is the pseudonym of Sara Menco, who was born in the Netherlands in 1920. The Dutch writer grew up in a Jewish family of five children. During World War II, her parents, brothers, and sisters were deported. Minco, like Anne Frank, was forced to go into hiding. Today she lives and works in Amsterdam, and the effects of the Holocaust have become the subject of her writing. Minco's first book, *Bitter Herbs* (1957), which chronicles the memories of a fugitive Jewish girl in Nazi-occupied Holland, has been translated into dozens of languages. Her later works, such as the novella *The Fall* (1983), have similar themes and are characterized by her quiet, almost unemotional style. The story "The Address" relays events before and after the war. Why do you think Minco does not include what happened during the war in this story? Which moment in the story is the most moving one for you? How does the author try to help the reader understand the sense of loss the narrator feels? ■

"Do you still know me?" I asked.

The woman looked at me, inquiring; she had opened the door a crack. I came closer and stood on the front step.

"No," she said, "I don't know you."

"I'm the daughter of Mrs. S.," I said.

She kept her hand on the door as though she wanted to prevent it from opening further. Her face didn't betray any sign of recognition. She kept looking at me silently.

Maybe I'm wrong, I thought, maybe she isn't the one. I had only seen her once in passing, and that was years ago. It was quite likely that I had pushed the wrong doorbell. The woman let go of the door and stepped aside. She was wearing a green hand-knitted sweater. The wooden buttons were slightly faded from laundering. She saw that I was looking at her sweater and again hid partly behind the door. But now I knew that I was at the right address.

"You knew my mother, didn't you?" I asked.

"Did you come back?" said the woman. "I thought that no one had come back."

"Only I," I said. In the hall behind her a door opened and closed. A stale smell came out.

"I'm sorry," she said, "I can't do anything for you."

"I've come here especially on the train. I would have liked to speak with you for a moment."

"It's not convenient now," said the woman. "I can't invite you in. Another time."

She nodded and carefully closed the door, as though no one in the house should be disturbed. I remained on the front step for a moment.

The curtain of the bay window moved. "Oh, nothing," the woman would say, "it was nothing."

I looked at the nameplate once more. It said "Dorling," with black letters on white enamel. And on the doorpost, a little higher, the number. Number 46.

While slowly walking back to the station, I thought of my mother, who had once, years ago, given me the address. It was during the first half of the war. I had come home for a few days, and it had struck me right away that something had changed in the rooms. I missed all sorts of things. My mother was surprised that I'd noticed it so quickly. Then she told me about Mrs. Dorling. I had never heard of her before, but she seemed to be an old acquaintance of my mother's whom she hadn't seen in years. She had suddenly turned up and renewed the acquaintance. Since that time she had been coming regularly.

"Every time she leaves she takes something home with her," my mother said. "She took all the silver flatware at once. And then the antique plates which hung over there. She really had a tough job lugging these big vases, and I'm afraid that she hurt her back with the dishes." My mother shook her head with compassion. "I would never have dared to ask her. She suggested it herself. She even insisted. She wants to save all my beautiful things. She says that we'll lose everything when we have to leave here."

"Have you arranged with her that she'll keep everything?" I asked.

"As though that were necessary," my mother exclaimed. "It would be an insult to agree on something like that. And think of the risk she takes every time she leaves our house with a full suitcase or bag!" My mother seemed to notice that I wasn't totally convinced. She looked at me reproachfully, and after that we didn't speak of it again.

Without paying too much attention to the road I had arrived at the station. For the first time since the war I was walking again through familiar districts, but I didn't want to go further than absolutely necessary. I didn't want to torment myself with the sight of streets and houses full of memories of a cherished time. In the train back, I saw Mrs. Dorling before me again, the way I had met her the first time. It was the morning after the day my mother had told me about her. I had gotten up late, and as I went downstairs I saw that my mother was just seeing someone out. A woman with a broad back.

"There is my daughter," said my mother. She motioned to me.

The woman nodded and picked up the suitcase which stood under the coatrack. She was wearing a brown coat and a shapeless hat.

"Does she live far?" I asked after seeing how laboriously she left the house with the heavy suitcase.

"On Marconistraat," said my mother. "Number 46. Do try to remember."

I had remembered. Except that I had waited quite a long time before going there. During the first period after the liberation I felt no interest at all in all that stored stuff, and of course some fear was involved. Fear of being confronted with things that had been part of a bond which no longer existed; which had been stored in cases and boxes and were waiting in vain until they would be put back in their places; which had survived all these years because they were "things."

But gradually everything had become normal again. There was bread which was steadily becoming lighter in colour, there was a bed in which you could sleep without being threatened, a room with a view which you got more and more used to every day. And one day I noticed that I was becoming curious about all the possessions which should still be at that address. I wanted to see them, touch them, recognize them. After my first fruitless visit to Mrs. Dorling's house, I decided to try it a second time.

This time it was a girl of about fourteen who opened the door. I asked whether her mother was home. "No," she said, "my mother is just on an errand."

"That doesn't matter," I said, "I'll wait for her."

I followed the girl through the hall. Next to the mirror hung an old-fashioned menorah. We had never used it because it was much more cumbersome than candles.

"Wouldn't you like to sit down?" asked the girl. She held open the door to the room and I went in past her. Frightened, I stood still. I was in a room which I both knew and didn't know. I found myself among things I had wanted to see again but which oppressed me in the strange surroundings. Whether it was because of the tasteless manner in which everything was arranged, because of the ugly furniture or the stuffy air, I don't know, but I scarcely dared look around me anymore. The girl moved a chair. I sat down and stared at the woollen tablecloth. I touched it carefully. I rubbed it. My fingers got warm from rubbing. I followed the lines of the design. Someplace on the edge there should be a burn hole which had never been repaired.

"My mother will be back very soon," said the girl. "I had already made tea for her. Would you like a cup?"

"Please," I said. I looked up. The girl was setting out teacups on the tea table. She had a broad back. Just like her mother. She poured tea from a white pot. There was a gold edge just around the lid, I remembered. She opened a small box and took some teaspoons out of it. "That's a lovely little box." I heard my own voice. It was a strange voice. As though every sound in this room had another ring to it.

"Do you know much about that?" She had turned around and brought me my tea. She laughed. "My mother says that it is antique. We have lots more." She pointed around the room. "Just look."

I didn't need to follow her hand. I knew which things she meant. I kept looking at the still-life above the tea table. As a child I had always wanted to eat the apple that lay on the pewter plate.

"We use it for everything," she said. "We've even eaten from the plates which hang on the wall. I wanted to. But it wasn't anything special."

I had found the burn hole at the edge of the tablecloth. The girl looked at me inquiringly. "Yes," I said, "you get used to all these beautiful things at home, you hardly look at them anymore. You only notice when something is not there, because it has to be repaired, or, for example, because you've lent it to someone."

Again I heard the unnatural sound of my voice, and I continued: "I remember my mother once asking me to help her polish the silver. That was very long ago, and I must have been bored that day, or maybe I had to stay home because I was ill, for she had never asked me to do that before. I asked her which silver she meant, and she answered me, surprised, that she was of course talking about the spoons, forks, and knives. And that was of course the odd thing, I didn't know that the objects with which we ate every day were made of silver."

The girl laughed again.

"I bet you don't know that either," I said. I looked at her intently.

"What we eat with?" she asked.

"Well, do you know?"

She hesitated. She walked to the buffet and started to pull open a drawer. "I'll have to look. It's in here."

I jumped up. "I'm forgetting my time. I still have to catch my train."

She stood with her hand on the drawer. "Wouldn't you like to wait for my mother?"

"No, I have to leave." I walked to the door. The girl opened the drawer.

"I'll find my way." When I was walking through the hall I heard the clinking of spoons and forks.

At the corner of the street I looked up at the nameplate. It said Marconistraat. I had been at Number 46. The address was right. But now I no longer wanted to remember it. I would not go there again, for the objects which in your memory are linked with the familiar life of former times suddenly lose their value when you see them again, torn out of context, in strange surroundings. And what would I do with them in a small rented room in which shreds of blackout paper were still hanging along the windows and where in the narrow table drawer there was room for just a few dinner things?

I resolved to forget the address. Of all the things I should forget, that one would be the easiest.

the liberation the end of the German occupation of the Netherlands (1944) during World War II

menorah a candelabrum with seven or nine branches used in Jewish worship

ANALYZE AND INTERPRET

1. How did you respond to the decision the narrator made at the end of the story? What do you think you would have done in her place? Share your ideas with your classmates.

2. Reread the story to point out the specific paragraph at which you were able to identify its historical context. Share with your classmates anything you know about what happened to Dutch Jews during World War II. Next, do research to fill in the historical background. How does this new information add to your understanding of the story? What parallels can you draw between events described in this story and what happened to the Frank family in *The Diary of Anne Frank*?

3. The story contains many references to memories and remembering. Create a diagram that documents each of these references. Incorporate into your diagram a record of how flashbacks are used to weave memories into the story. In a group, consider the narrator and Mrs. Dorling in terms of their memories of the objects and of the events that took place during the war. Consider what they want to remember and also to forget. What broader issues about the Holocaust might the author be exploring in this story?

MORE TO EXPLORE

Themes: Self, Personal Challenges, Loss, Europe, Journeys, Moral Questions, Eye on the Past, War and Peace

Elements: dialogue, flashback, foreshadowing, mood, setting, symbol

SILVER MINE, COBALT

Yvonne McKague Housser

1930, oil on canvas, 76.2 × 88.9 cm

- Reflect on and make links to prior experience.
- Analyze a painting to discover meaning.
- Create a media text.

CONTEXT Yvonne McKague Housser was born in Toronto in 1898 and died there in 1996. She did both undergraduate and post-graduate work at the Ontario College of Art, and eventually joined the staff of that institution. She also taught at the Ryerson Polytechnic Institute (now Ryerson Polytechnic University). In 1921, she went to Paris, France, to study, later taking sketching and painting trips through Italy, England, and the United States. She first discovered the mining town of Cobalt, in Northern Ontario, on a train trip in 1917. McKague Housser was affiliated with the Group of Seven, and what are known as her "Cobalt" paintings reflect the Group's style of bold sky patterns, simplified shapes, and a sense of movement. How, specifically, does this painting reflect these characteristics? How do these characteristics help convey the message, or theme, of the painting? ◼

NOTES

Cobalt in this instance, refers to the town of Cobalt, Ontario, near the Quebec border; its silver production was ranked fourth in the world in 1910

ANALYZE AND INTERPRET

1. In a group, share descriptions of industrial buildings and sites you have visited or passed by. Describe the area around the site. What sensory details, such as sounds or smells, did you experience? Compare elements of your experience with details this artist has captured in *Silver Mine, Cobalt*.

2. As a class, consider and discuss the following question: Does this painting exalt "the machine age," represented by the mine, or does it show industry posing a threat to human beings and the natural world? In your response, make specific references to features of the painting such as content, style, composition, and colour.

3. Do some research into the life and work of Yvonne McKague Housser. Use this information to help you create a full-page newspaper advertisement for a retrospective of her paintings. Make up a name for the show that conveys the unique qualities of this artist's work. Share your work with a group, and discuss how effectively you balanced visuals and text in your advertisement.

MORE TO EXPLORE

Themes: Peers, At Work, Rural Life, Nature, Canada, Science and Technology

Elements: description, mood, setting, visual composition, visual scale

Boys and Girls

Alice Munro

Church and Horse, 1974, Alex Colville

CONTEXT Alice Munro was born in 1931 and raised on a farm in southwestern Ontario. Generally considered to be one of Canada's major contemporary writers, she has won many accolades, including three Governor General's Awards. Her short stories, which were first broadcast on CBC Radio, now appear frequently in high-profile publications such as *The New Yorker* and *The Paris Review.* Munro has commented that what interests her most in writing is observing people and the ways in which they and their circumstances change. "Boys and Girls," like most of her stories, portrays a world of small towns and outwardly quiet lives. Why do you think Munro has chosen to write this story from a first-person point of view? What stays the same and what changes for the narrator and the other main characters? How does the fact that the narrator is a girl affect what happens in the story? ■

My father was a fox farmer. That is, he raised silver foxes, in pens; and in the fall and early winter, when their fur was prime, he killed them and skinned them and sold their pelts to the Hudson's Bay Company or the Montreal Fur Traders. These companies supplied us with heroic calendars to hang, one on each side of the kitchen door. Against a background of cold blue sky and black pine forests and treacherous northern rivers, plumed adventurers planted the flags of England or of France; magnificent savages bent their backs to the portage.

For several weeks before Christmas, my father worked after supper in the cellar of our house. The cellar was white-washed, and lit by a hundred-watt bulb over the worktable. My brother Laird and I sat on the top step and watched. My father removed the pelt inside-out from the body of the fox, which looked surprisingly small, mean and rat-like, deprived of its arrogant weight of fur. The naked, slippery bodies were collected in a sack and buried at the dump. One time the hired man, Henry Bailey, had taken a swipe at me with this sack, saying, "Christmas present!" My mother thought that was not funny. In fact she disliked the whole pelting operation—that was what the killing, skinning, and preparation of the furs was called—and wished it did not have to take place in the house. There was the smell. After the pelt had been stretched inside-out on a long board my father scraped away delicately, removing the little clotted webs of blood vessels, the bubbles of fat; the smell of blood and animal fat, with the strong primitive odour of the fox itself, penetrated all parts of the house. I found it reassuringly seasonal, like the smell of oranges and pine needles.

Henry Bailey suffered from bronchial troubles. He would cough and cough until his narrow face turned scarlet, and his light blue, derisive eyes filled up with tears; then he took the lid off the stove, and, standing well back, shot out a great clot of phlegm—hsss—straight into the heart of the flames. We admired him for this performance and for his ability to make his stomach growl at will, and for his laughter, which was full of high whistlings and gurglings and involved the whole faulty machinery of his chest. It was sometimes hard to tell what he was laughing at, and always possible that it might be us.

After we had been sent to bed, we could still smell fox and still hear Henry's laugh, but these things, reminders of the warm, safe, brightly lit downstairs world, seemed lost and diminished, floating on the stale cold air upstairs. We were afraid at night in the winter. We were not afraid of *outside* though this was the time of year when snowdrifts curled around our house like sleeping whales and the wind harassed us all night, coming up from the buried fields, the frozen swamp, with its old bugbear chorus of threats and misery. We were afraid of *inside*, the room where we slept. At this time the upstairs of our house was not finished. A brick chimney went up one wall. In the middle of the floor was a square hole, with a wooden railing around it; that was where the stairs came up. On the other side of the stairwell were the things that nobody had any use for any more—a soldiery roll of linoleum, standing on end, a wicker baby carriage, a fern basket, china jugs and basins with cracks in them, a picture of the Battle of Balaclava, very sad to look at. I had told Laird, as soon as he was old enough to understand such things, that bats and skeletons lived over there; whenever a man escaped from the county jail, twenty miles away, I imagined that he had somehow let himself in the window and was hiding behind the linoleum. But we had rules to keep us safe. When the light was on, we were safe as long as we did not step off the square of worn carpet which defined our bedroom-space; when the light was off, no place was safe but the beds themselves. I had to turn out the light kneeling on the end of my bed, and stretching as far as I could to reach the cord.

In the dark we lay on our beds, our narrow life rafts, and fixed our eyes on the faint light coming up the stairwell, and sang songs. Laird sang "Jingle Bells," which he would sing any time, whether it was Christmas or not, and I sang "Danny Boy." I loved the sound of my own voice, frail and supplicating, rising in the dark. We could make out the tall frosted shapes of the windows now, gloomy and white. When I came to the part, *When I am dead, as dead I well may be*—a fit of shivering caused not by the cold sheets but by pleasurable emotion almost silenced me. *You'll kneel and say, an Ave there above me*—What was an Ave? Every day I forgot to find out.

Laird went straight from singing to sleep. I could hear his long, satisfied, bubbly breaths. Now for the time that remained to me, the most perfectly private and perhaps the best time of the whole day, I arranged myself tightly under the covers and went on with one of the stories I was telling myself from night to night. These stories were about myself, when I had grown a little older; they took place in a world that was recognizably mine, yet one that presented opportunities for courage, boldness and self-sacrifice, as mine never did. I rescued people from a bombed building (it discouraged me that the real war had gone on so far away from Jubilee). I shot two rabid wolves who were menacing the schoolyard (the teachers cowered terrified at my back). I rode a fine horse spiritedly down the main street of Jubilee, acknowledging the townspeople's gratitude for some yet-to-be-worked-out piece of heroism (nobody ever rode a horse there, except King Billy in the Orangemen's Day parade). There was always riding and shooting in these stories, though I had only been on a horse twice—bareback because we did not own a saddle—and the second time I had slid right around and dropped under the horse's feet; it had stepped placidly over me. I really was learning to shoot, but I could not hit anything yet, not even tin cans on fence posts.

Alive, the foxes inhabited a world my father made for them. It was surrounded by a high guard fence, like a medieval town, with a gate that was padlocked at night. Along the streets of this town were ranged large, sturdy pens. Each of them had a real door that a man could go through, a wooden ramp along the wire, for the foxes to run up and down on, and a kennel—something like a clothes chest with air-holes—where they slept and stayed in winter and had their young. There were feeding and watering dishes attached to the wire in such a way that they could be emptied and cleaned from the outside. The dishes were made of old tin cans, and the ramps and kennels of odds and ends of old lumber. Everything was tidy and ingenious; my father was tirelessly inventive and his favourite book in the world was *Robinson Crusoe.* He had fitted a tin drum on a wheelbarrow, for bringing water down to the pens. This was my job in summer, when the foxes had to have water twice a day. Between nine and ten o'clock in the morning, and again after supper, I filled the drum at the pump and trundled it down through the barnyard to the pens, where I parked it, and filled my watering can and went along the streets. Laird came too, with his little cream and green gardening can, filled too full and knocking against his legs and slopping water on his canvas shoes. I had the real watering can, my father's, though I could only carry it three-quarters full.

The foxes all had names, which were printed on a tin plate and hung beside their doors. They were not named when they were born, but when they survived the first year's pelting and were added to the breeding stock. Those my father had named were called names like Prince, Bob, Wally and Betty. Those I had named were called Star or Turk, or Maureen or Diana. Laird named one Maud after a hired girl we had when he was little, one Harold after a boy at school, and one Mexico, he did not say why.

Naming them did not make pets out of them, or anything like it. Nobody but my father ever went into the pens, and he had twice had blood-poisoning from bites. When I was bringing them their water they prowled up and down on the paths they had made inside their pens, barking seldom—they saved that for nighttime, when they might get up a chorus of community frenzy—but always watching me, their eyes burning, clear gold, in their pointed, malevolent faces. They were beautiful for their delicate legs and heavy, aristocratic tails and the bright fur sprinkled on dark down their backs—which gave them their name—but especially for their faces, drawn exquisitely sharp in pure hostility, and their golden eyes.

Besides carrying water I helped my father when he cut the long grass, and the lamb's quarter and flowering money-musk, that grew between the pens. He cut with the scythe and I raked into piles. Then he took a pitchfork and threw fresh-cut grass all over the top of the pens, to keep the foxes cooler and shade their coats, which were browned by too much sun. My father did not talk to me unless it was about the job we were doing. In this he was quite different from my mother, who, if she was feeling cheerful, would tell me all sorts of things—the name of a dog she had had when she was a little girl, the names of boys she had gone out with later on when she was grown up, and what certain dresses of hers had looked like—she could not imagine now what had become of them. Whatever thoughts and stories my father had were private, and I was shy of him and would never ask him questions. Nevertheless I worked willingly under his eyes, and with a feeling of pride. One time a feed salesman came down into the pens to talk to him and my father said, "Like to have you meet my new hired man." I turned away and raked furiously, red in the face with pleasure.

"Could of fooled me," said the salesman. "I thought it was only a girl."

After the grass was cut, it seemed suddenly much later in the year. I walked on stubble in the earlier evening, aware of the reddening skies, the entering silences, of fall. When I wheeled the tank out of the gate and put the padlock on, it was almost dark. One night at this time I saw my mother and father standing talking on the little rise of ground we called the gangway, in front of the barn. My father had just come from the meathouse; he had his stiff bloody apron on, and a pail of cut-up meat in his hand.

It was an odd thing to see my mother down at the barn. She did not often come out of the house unless it was to do something—hang out the wash or dig potatoes in the garden. She looked out of place, with her bare lumpy legs, not touched by the sun, her apron still on and damp across the stomach from the supper dishes. Her hair was tied up in a kerchief, wisps of it falling out. She would tie her hair up like this in the morning, saying she did not have time to do it properly, and it would stay tied up all day. It was true, too; she really did not have time. These days our back porch was piled with baskets of peaches and grapes and pears, bought in town, and onions and tomatoes and cucumbers grown at home, all waiting to be made into jelly and jam and preserves, pickles and chili sauce. In the kitchen there was a fire in the stove all day, jars clinked in boiling water, sometimes a cheesecloth bag was strung on a pole between two chairs, straining blue-black grape pulp for jelly. I was given jobs to do and I would sit at the table peeling peaches that had been soaked in hot water, or cutting up onions, my eyes smarting and streaming. As soon as I was done, I ran out of the house, trying to get out of earshot before my mother thought of what she wanted me to do next. I hated the hot dark kitchen in summer, the green blinds and the flypapers, the same old oilcloth table and wavy mirror and bumpy linoleum. My mother was too tired and preoccupied to talk to me, she had no heart to tell about the Normal School Graduation Dance; sweat trickled over her face and she was always counting under her breath, pointing at jars, dumping cups of sugar. It seemed to me that work in the house was endless, dreary and peculiarly depressing; work done out of doors, and in my father's service, was ritualistically important.

I wheeled the tank up to the barn, where it was kept, and I heard my mother saying, "Wait till Laird gets a little bigger, then you'll have a real help."

What my father said I did not hear. I was pleased by the way he stood listening, politely as he would to a salesman or a stranger, but with an air of wanting to get on with his real work. I felt my mother had no business down here and I wanted him to feel the same way. What did she mean about Laird? He was no help to anybody. Where was he now? Swinging himself sick on the swing, going around in circles, or trying to catch caterpillars. He never once stayed with me till I was finished.

"And then I can use her more in the house," I heard my mother say. She had a dead-quiet, regretful way of talking about me that always made me uneasy. "I just get my back turned and she runs off. It's not like I had a girl in the family at all."

I went and sat on a feed bag in the corner of the barn, not wanting to appear when this conversation was going on. My mother, I felt, was not to be trusted. She was kinder than my father and more easily fooled, but you could not depend on her, and the real reasons for the things she said and did were not to be known. She loved me, and she sat up late at night making a dress of the difficult style I wanted, for me to wear when school started, but she was also my enemy. She was always plotting. She was plotting now to get me to stay in the house more, although she knew I hated it (*because* she knew I hated it) and keep me from working for my father. It seemed to me she would do this simply out of perversity, and to try her power. It did not occur to me that she could be lonely, or jealous. No grown-up could be; they were too fortunate. I sat and kicked my heels monotonously against a feed bag, raising dust, and did not come out till she was gone.

At any rate, I did not expect my father to pay any attention to what she said. Who could imagine Laird doing my work—Laird remembering the padlock and cleaning out the watering-dishes with a leaf on the end of a stick, or even wheeling the tank without it tumbling over? It showed how little my mother knew about the way things really were.

I have forgotten to say what the foxes were fed. My father's bloody apron reminded me. They were fed horsemeat. At this time most farmers still kept horses, and when a horse got too old to work, or broke a leg or got down and would not get up, as they sometimes did, the owner would call my father, and he and Henry went out to the farm in the truck. Usually they shot and butchered the horse there, paying the farmer from five to twelve dollars. If they had already too much meat on hand, they would bring the horse back alive, and keep it for a few days or weeks in our stable, until the meat was needed. After the war the farmers were buying tractors and gradually getting rid of horses altogether, so it sometimes happened that we got a good healthy horse, that there was just no use for any more. If this happened in the winter we might keep the horse in our stable till spring, for we had plenty of hay and if there was a lot of snow—and the plow did not always get our road cleared—it was convenient to be able to go to town with a horse and cutter.

The winter I was eleven years old we had two horses in the stable. We did not know what names they had had before, so we called them Mack and Flora. Mack was an old black workhorse, sooty and indifferent. Flora was a sorrel mare, a driver. We took them both out in the cutter. Mack was slow and easy to handle. Flora was given to fits of violent alarm, veering at cars and even at other horses, but we loved her speed and high-stepping, her general air of gallantry and abandon. On Saturdays we went down to the stable and as soon as we opened the door on its cosy, animal-smelling darkness Flora threw up her head, rolled her eyes, whinnied despairingly and pulled herself through a crisis of nerves on the spot. It was not safe to go into her stall; she would kick.

This winter also I began to hear a great deal more on the theme my mother had sounded when she had been talking in front of the barn. I no longer felt safe. It seemed that in the minds of the people around me there was a steady undercurrent of thought, not to be deflected, on this one subject. The word *girl* had formerly seemed to me innocent and unburdened, like the word *child*; now it appeared that it was no such thing. A girl was not, as I had supposed, simply what I was; it was what I had to become. It was a definition, always touched with emphasis, with reproach and disappointment. Also it was a joke on me. Once Laird and I were fighting, and for the first time ever, I had to use all my strength against him; even so, he caught and pinned my arm for a moment, really hurting me. Henry saw this, and laughed, saying, "Oh, that there Laird's gonna show you, one of these days!" Laird was getting a lot bigger. But I was getting bigger too.

My grandmother came to stay with us for a few weeks and I heard other things. "Girls don't slam doors like that." "Girls keep their knees together when they sit down." And worse still, when I asked some questions, "That's none of girls' business." I continued to slam the doors and sit as awkwardly as possible, thinking that by such measures I kept myself free.

When spring came, the horses were let out in the barnyard. Mack stood against the barn wall trying to scratch his neck and haunches, but Flora trotted up and down and reared at the fences, clattering her hooves against the rails. Snowdrifts dwindled quickly, revealing the hard grey and brown earth, the familiar rise and fall of the ground, plain and bare after the fantastic landscape of winter. There was a great feeling of opening-out, of release. We just wore rubbers now, over our shoes; our feet felt ridiculously light. One Saturday we went out to the stable and found all the doors open, letting in the unaccustomed sunlight and fresh air. Henry was there, just idling around looking at his collection of calendars which were tacked up behind the stalls in a part of the stable my mother had probably never seen.

"Come to say goodbye to your old friend Mack?" Henry said. "Here, you give him a taste of oats." He poured some oats into Laird's cupped hands and Laird went to feed Mack. Mack's teeth were in bad shape. He ate very slowly, patiently shifting the oats around in his mouth, trying to find a stump of a molar to grind it on. "Poor old Mack," said Henry mournfully. "When a horse's teeth's gone, he's gone. That's about the way."

"Are you going to shoot him today?" I said. Mack and Flora had been in the stable so long I had almost forgotten they were going to be shot.

Henry didn't answer me. Instead he started to sing in a high, trembly, mocking-sorrowful voice, *Oh, there's no more work, for poor Uncle Ned, he's gone where the good darkies go.* Mack's thick, blackish tongue worked diligently at Laird's hand. I went out before the song was ended and sat down on the gangway.

I had never seen them shoot a horse, but I knew where it was done. Last summer Laird and I had come upon a horse's entrails before they were buried. We had thought it was a big black snake, coiled up in the sun. That was around in the field that ran up beside the barn. I thought that if we went inside the barn, and found a wide crack or a knothole to look through, we would be able to see them do it. It was not something I wanted to see; just the same, if a thing really happened, it was better to see it, and know.

My father came down from the house, carrying the gun.

"What are you doing here?" he said.

"Nothing."

"Go on up and play around the house."

He sent Laird out of the stable. I said to Laird, "Do you want to see them shoot Mack?" and without waiting for an answer led him around to the front door of the barn, opened it carefully, and went in. "Be quiet or they'll hear us," I said. We could hear Henry and my father talking in the stable, then the heavy, shuffling steps of Mack being backed out of his stall.

In the loft it was cold and dark. Thin, crisscrossed beams of sunlight fell through the cracks. The hay was low. It was a rolling country, hills and hollows, slipping under our feet. About four feet up was a beam going around the walls. We piled hay up in one corner and I boosted Laird up and hoisted myself. The beam was not very wide; we crept along it with our hands flat on the barn walls. There were plenty of knotholes, and I found one that gave me the view I wanted—a corner of the barnyard, the gate, part of the field. Laird did not have a knothole and began to complain.

I showed him a widened crack between two boards. "Be quiet and wait. If they hear you you'll get us in trouble."

My father came in sight carrying the gun. Henry was leading Mack by the halter. He dropped it and took out his cigarette papers and tobacco; he rolled cigarettes for my father and himself. While this was going on Mack nosed around in the old, dead grass along the fence. Then my father opened the gate and they took Mack through. Henry led Mack away from the path to a patch of ground and they talked together, not loud enough for us to hear. Mack again began searching for a mouthful of fresh grass, which was not to be found. My father walked away in a straight line, and stopped short at a distance which seemed to suit him. Henry was walking away from Mack too, but sideways, still negligently holding on to the halter. My father raised the gun and Mack looked up as if he had noticed something and my father shot him.

Mack did not collapse at once, but swayed, lurched sideways and fell, first on his side; then he rolled over on his back and, amazingly, kicked his legs for a few seconds in the air. At this Henry laughed, as if Mack had done a trick for him. Laird, who had drawn a long, groaning breath of surprise when the shot was fired, said out loud, "He's not dead." And it seemed to me it might be true. But his legs stopped, he rolled on his side again, his muscles quivered and sank. The two men walked over and looked at him in a businesslike way; they bent down and examined his forehead where the bullet had gone in, and now I saw his blood on the brown grass.

"Now they just skin him and cut him up," I said. "Let's go." My legs were a little shaky and I jumped gratefully down into the hay. "Now you've seen how they shoot a horse," I said in a congratulatory way, as if I had seen it many times before. "Let's see if any barn cat's had kittens in the hay." Laird jumped. He seemed young and obedient again. Suddenly I remembered how, when he was little, I had brought him into the barn and told him to climb the ladder to the top beam. That was in the spring, too, when the hay was low. I had done it out of a need for excitement, a desire for something to happen so that I could tell about it. He was wearing a little bulky brown and white checked coat, made down from one of mine. He went all the way up, just as I told him, and sat down on the top beam with the hay far below him on one side, and the barn floor and some old machinery on the other. Then I ran screaming to my father, "Laird's up on the top beam!" My father came, my mother came, my father went up the ladder talking very quietly and brought Laird down under his arm, at which my mother leaned against the ladder and began to cry. They said to me, "Why weren't you watching him?" but nobody ever knew the truth. Laird did not know enough to tell. But whenever I saw the brown and white checked coat hanging in the closet, or at the bottom of the rag bag, which was where it ended up, I felt a weight in my stomach, the sadness of unexorcised guilt.

I looked at Laird who did not even remember this, and I did not like the look on his thin, winter-pale face. His expression was not frightened or upset, but remote, concentrating. "Listen," I said, in an unusually bright and friendly voice, "you aren't going to tell, are you?"

"No," he said absently.

"Promise."

"Promise," he said. I grabbed the hand behind his back to make sure he was not crossing his fingers. Even so, he might have a nightmare; it might come out that way. I decided I had better work hard to get all thoughts of what he had seen out of his mind—which, it seemed to me, could not hold very many things at a time. I got some money I had saved and that afternoon we went into Jubilee and saw a show, with Judy Canova, at which we both laughed a great deal. After that I thought it would be all right.

Two weeks later I knew they were going to shoot Flora. I knew from the night before, when I heard my mother ask if the hay was holding out all right, and my father said, "Well, after tomorrow there'll just be the cow, and we should be able to put her out to grass in another week." So I knew it was Flora's turn in the morning.

This time I didn't think of watching it. That was something to see just one time. I had not thought about it very often since, but sometimes when I was busy, working at school, or standing in front of the mirror combing my hair and wondering if I would be pretty when I grew up, the whole scene would flash into my mind: I would see the easy, practised way my father raised the gun, and hear Henry laughing when Mack kicked his legs in the air. I did not have any great feeling of horror and opposition, such as a city child might have had; I was too used to seeing the death of animals as a necessity by which we lived. Yet I felt a little ashamed, and there was a new wariness, a sense of holding-off, in my attitude to my father and his work.

It was a fine day, and we were going around the yard picking up tree branches that had been torn off in winter storms. This was something we had been told to do, and also we wanted to use them to make a teepee. We heard Flora whinny, and then my father's voice and Henry's shouting, and we ran down to the barnyard to see what was going on.

The stable door was open. Henry had just brought Flora out, and she had broken away from him. She was running free in the barnyard, from one end to the other. We climbed up on the fence. It was exciting to see her running, whinnying, going up on her hind legs, prancing and threatening like a horse in a Western movie, an unbroken ranch horse, though she was just an old driver, an old sorrel mare. My father and Henry ran after her and tried to grab the dangling halter. They tried to work her into a corner, and they had almost succeeded when she made a run between them, wild-eyed, and disappeared around the corner of the barn. We heard the rails clatter down as she got over the fence, and Henry yelled, "She's into the field now!"

That meant she was in the long L-shaped field that ran up by the house. If she got around the centre, heading toward the lane, the gate was open; the truck had been driven into the field this morning. My father shouted to me, because I was on the other side of the fence, nearest the lane, "Go shut the gate!"

I could run very fast. I ran across the garden, past the tree where our swing was hung, and jumped across a ditch into the lane. There was the open gate. She had not got out, I could not see her up on the road; she must have run to the other end of the field. The gate was heavy. I lifted it out of the gravel and carried it across the roadway. I had it half-way across when she came in sight, galloping straight toward me. There was just time to get the chain on. Laird came scrambling through the ditch to help me.

Instead of shutting the gate, I opened it as wide as I could. I did not make any decision to do this, it was just what I did. Flora never slowed down; she galloped straight past me, and Laird jumped up and down, yelling, "Shut it, shut it!" even after it was too late. My father and Henry appeared in the field a moment too late to see what I had done. They only saw Flora heading for the township road. They would think I had not got there in time.

They did not waste any time asking about it. They went back to the barn and got the gun and the knives they used, and put these in the truck; then they turned the truck around and came bouncing up the field toward us. Laird called to them, "Let me go too, let me go too!" and Henry stopped the truck and they took him in. I shut the gate after they were all gone.

I supposed Laird would tell. I wondered what would happen to me. I had never disobeyed my father before, and I could not understand why I had done it. Flora would not really get away. They would catch up with her in the truck. Or if they did not catch her this morning, somebody would see her and telephone us this afternoon or tomorrow. There was no wild country here for her to run to, only farms. What was more, my father had paid for her, we needed the meat to feed the foxes, we needed the foxes to make our living. All I had done was make more work for my father who worked hard enough already. And when my father found out about it he was not going to trust me any more; he would know that I was not entirely on his side. I was on Flora's side, and that made me no use to anybody, not even to her. Just the same, I did not regret it; when she came running at me and I held the gate open, that was the only thing I could do.

I went back to the house, and my mother said, "What's all the commotion?" I told her that Flora had kicked down the fence and got away. "Your poor father," she said, "now he'll have to go chasing over the countryside. Well, there isn't any use planning dinner before one." She put up the ironing board. I wanted to tell her, but thought better of it and went upstairs and sat on my bed.

Lately I had been trying to make my part of the room fancy, spreading the bed with old lace curtains, and fixing myself a dressing-table with some leftovers of cretonne for a skirt. I planned to put up some kind of barricade between my bed and Laird's, to keep my section separate from his. In the sunlight, the lace curtains were just dusty rags. We did not sing at night any more. One night when I was singing, Laird said, "You sound silly," and I went right on, but the next night, I did not start. There was not so much need to anyway, we were no longer afraid. We knew it was just old furniture over there, old jumble and confusion. We did not keep to the rules. I still stayed awake after Laird was asleep and told myself stories, but even in these stories something different was happening, mysterious alterations took place. A story might start off in the old way, with a spectacular danger, a fire or wild animals, and for a while I might rescue people; then things would change around, and instead, somebody would be rescuing me. It might be a boy from our class at school, or even Mr. Campbell, our teacher, who tickled girls under the arms. And at this point the story concerned itself at great length with what I looked like—how long my hair was, and what kind of dress I had on; by the time I had these details worked out the real excitement of the story was lost.

It was later than one o'clock when the truck came back. The tarpaulin was over the back, which meant there was meat in it. My mother had to heat dinner up all over again. Henry and my father had changed from their bloody overalls into ordinary working overalls in the barn, and they washed their arms and necks and faces at the sink, and splashed water on their hair and combed it. Laird lifted his arm to show off a streak of blood. "We shot old Flora," he said, "and cut her up in fifty pieces."

"Well I don't want to hear about it," my mother said. "And don't come to my table like that."

My father made him go and wash the blood off.

We sat down and my father said grace and Henry pasted his chewing-gum on the end of his fork, the way he always did; when he took it off he would have us admire the pattern. We began to pass the bowls of steaming, overcooked vegetables. Laird looked across the table at me and said proudly, distinctly, "Anyway it was her fault Flora got away."

"What?" my father said.

"She could of shut the gate and she didn't. She just open' it up and Flora run out."

"Is that right?" my father said.

Everybody at the table was looking at me. I nodded, swallowing food with great difficulty. To my shame, tears flooded my eyes.

My father made a curt sound of disgust. "What did you do that for?"

I did not answer. I put down my fork and waited to be sent from the table, still not looking up.

But this did not happen. For some time nobody said anything, then Laird said matter-of-factly, "She's crying."

"Never mind," my father said. He spoke with resignation, even good humour, the words which absolved and dismissed me for good. "She's only a girl," he said.

I didn't protest that, even in my heart. Maybe it was true.

Notes

Hudson's Bay Company established in 1760 by royal decree, the Hudson's Bay Trading Company monopolized nearly all trade through the Hudson Strait for over a century

derisive mocking

Battle of Balaclava one of the major battles of the Crimean War (1854–1856); immortalized in Tennyson's poem, "The Charge of the Light Brigade." Balaclava is located in Russia, on the Crimean peninsula.

Ave short for Ave Maria, a Roman Catholic prayer; from the Latin word *avēre*, meaning "fare well"

unexorcised not released; pent up

Analyze and Interpret

1. Choose the character in the story with whom you identify either the most or the least, and with a partner discuss the reasons why.

2. How do the narrator's carefully described "adventure stories" relate to the theme of "Boys and Girls"? With the class, discuss what these stories suggest about the world she lives in and the world she would like to live in.

3. With your partner, assume the role of the narrator and write a short story that serves as a sequel to "Boys and Girls." Share your writing with your peers, and have them evaluate how well your sequel propels the plot forward and provides a satisfying read.

More to Explore

Themes: Self, Childhood, Stereotypes, Family, Rebels, Rural Life, Canada

Elements: characterization, conflict, description, first-person point of view, plot

FIRE DOWN ON THE LABRADOR

David Blackwood

1980, etching, 32" × 20"

- Present and compare responses to a visual text.
- Explain how the choices made by an author influence meaning.
- Research information to plan and deliver an oral presentation.

CONTEXT *Fire Down on the Labrador* is a large etching produced in 1980 by artist David Blackwood, who was born in 1941 in Wesleyville, Newfoundland. Though much of Blackwood's work recreates the Newfoundland landscape, he now lives and works in Ontario. Blackwood's artwork is popular internationally, but he intentionally keeps his prices far below market value so that they are affordable to a greater number of people. By his own account, Blackwood is a visual storyteller, engaged with the world of his Newfoundland ancestors who earned their living as sailors and fishermen. What narrative is occurring here? What do you think are the main themes Blackwood explores in this etching? ■

ANALYZE AND INTERPRET

1. a) List each aspect of this image that catches your eye. b) Place your list in order according to what aspect you noticed first to what you noticed last. c) Now reorder the list from what holds your attention the longest to what is least interesting to you. d) Share and discuss your list with a partner and attempt to explain any differences or similarities in your reactions.

2. Numerous threats to human beings are illustrated in this etching. With a partner, list each threatening element in the image and describe how the artist has depicted the potential danger. Evaluate each threat both in terms of its artistic presentation and what the reality of the situation would be. In a short essay explain why, in your opinion, the artist has made the choices that he has.

3. Using the Internet or print resources, research what happened historically when fire broke out on the *Labrador*, or investigate another maritime incident that occurred on a ship such as the *Marie Celeste*, *Prince of Wales*, *Repulse*, *Lusitania*, or *Kon-Tiki*. Prepare an oral telling of the event and present it to a small group. Use details to lend impact and authenticity to your presentation.

MORE TO EXPLORE

Themes: At Work, Nature, Canada, Intrigue, Eye on the Past, Crisis

Elements: mood, setting, tone, tragedy, visual composition, visual scale

The Lamp at Noon

Sinclair Ross

LEARNING FOCUS

- Analyze the factors that influence personal responses.
- Analyze the use of literary devices such as personification and mood.
- Plan, draft, revise, and edit a research essay.

CONTEXT Sinclair Ross grew up on the prairies of Saskatchewan during the Depression. Born in 1908, Ross was compelled to leave school early to support his fatherless family. He took a job at the Royal Bank of Canada, and worked for the bank until his retirement in 1968. To this point, except for a brief time in the army, he had not been outside of Canada. Upon retiring, he travelled and lived abroad, mainly in Spain and Greece. He eventually returned to live in Vancouver, where he died in 1996. Ross' short stories and novels are celebrated for their vividly realized settings and their exploration of the effects of place on the human spirit. In "The Lamp at Noon," how do the weather and climate play a role in the characters' shifting moods? If you found yourself in a perpetual dust storm, how might you be affected? ■

A little before noon she lit the lamp. Demented wind fled keening past the house: a wail through the eaves that died every minute or two. Three days now without respite it had held. The dust was thickening to an impenetrable fog.

She lit the lamp, then for a long time stood at the window motionless. In dim, fitful outline the stable and oat granary still were visible; beyond, obscuring fields and landmarks, the lower of dust clouds made the farmyard seem an isolated acre, poised aloft above a sombre void. At each blast of wind it shook, as if to topple and spin hurtling with the dust-reel into space.

From the window she went to the door, opening it a little, and peering toward the stable again. He was not coming yet. As she watched there was a sudden rift overhead, and for a moment through the tattered clouds the sun raced like a wizened orange. It shed a soft, diffused light, dim and yellow as if it were the light from the lamp reaching out through the open door.

She closed the door, and going to the stove tried the potatoes with a fork. Her eyes all the while were fixed and wide with a curious immobility. It was the window. Standing at it, she had let her forehead press against the pane until the eyes were strained apart and rigid. Wide like that they had looked out to the deepening ruin of the storm. Now she could not close them.

The baby started to cry. He was lying in a homemade crib over which she had arranged a tent of muslin. Careful not to disturb the folds of it, she knelt and tried to still him, whispering huskily in a singsong voice that he must hush and go to sleep again. She would have liked to rock him, to feel the comfort of his little body in her arms, but a fear had obsessed her that in the dust-filled air he might contract pneumonia. There was dust sifting everywhere. Her own throat was parched with it. The table had been set less than ten minutes, and already a film was gathering on the dishes. The little cry continued, and with wincing, frightened lips she glanced around as if to find a corner where the air was less oppressive. But while the lips winced the eyes maintained their wide, immobile stare. "Sleep," she whispered again. "It's too soon for you to be hungry. Daddy's coming for his dinner."

He seemed a long time. Even the clock, still a few minutes off noon, could not dispel a foreboding sense that he was longer than he should be. She went to the door again—and then recoiled slowly to stand white and breathless in the middle of the room. She mustn't. He would only despise her if she ran to the stable looking for him. There was too much grim endurance in his nature ever to let him understand the fear and weakness of a woman. She must stay quiet and wait. Nothing was wrong. At noon he would come—and perhaps after dinner stay with her awhile.

Yesterday, and again at breakfast this morning, they had quarrelled bitterly. She wanted him now, the assurance of his strength and nearness, but he would stand aloof, wary, remembering the words she had flung at him in her anger, unable to understand it was only the dust and wind that had driven her.

Tense, she fixed her eyes upon the clock, listening. There were two winds: the wind in flight, and the wind that pursued. The one sought refuge in the eaves, whimpering, in fear; the other assailed it there, and shook the eaves apart to make it flee again. Once as she listened this first wind sprang inside the room, distraught like a bird that has felt the graze of talons on its wing; while furious the other wind shook the walls, and thudded tumbleweeds against the window till its quarry glanced away again in fright. But only to return—to return and quake among the feeble eaves, as if in all this dust-mad wilderness it knew no other sanctuary.

Then Paul came. At his step she hurried to the stove, intent upon the pots and frying-pan. "The worst wind yet," he ventured, hanging up his cap and smock. "I had to light the lantern in the tool shed, too."

They looked at each other, then away. She wanted to go to him, to feel his arms supporting her, to cry a little just that he might soothe her, but because his presence made the menace of the wind seem less, she gripped herself and thought, "I'm in the right. I won't give in. For his sake, too, I won't."

He washed, hurriedly, so that a few dark welts of dust remained to indent upon his face a haggard strength. It was all she could see as she wiped the dishes and set the food before him: the strength, the grimness, the young Paul growing old and hard, buckled against a desert even grimmer than his will. "Hungry?" she asked, touched to a twinge of pity she had not intended. "There's dust in everything. It keeps coming faster than I can clean it up."

He nodded. "Tonight, though, you'll see it go down. This is the third day."

She looked at him in silence a moment, and then as if to herself muttered broodingly, "Until the next time. Until it starts again."

There was a dark resentment in her voice now that boded another quarrel. He waited, his eyes on her dubiously as she mashed a potato with her fork. The lamp between them threw strong lights and shadows on their faces. Dust and drought, earth that betrayed alike his labour and his faith, to him the struggle had given sternness, an impassive courage. Beneath the whip of sand his youth had been effaced. Youth, zest, exuberance—there remained only a harsh and clenched virility that yet became him, that seemed at the cost of more engaging qualities to be fulfillment of his inmost and essential nature. Whereas to her the same debts and poverty had brought a plaintive indignation, a nervous dread of what was still to come. The eyes were hollowed, the lips pinched dry and colourless. It was the face of a woman that had aged without maturing, that had loved the little vanities of life, and lost them wistfully.

"I'm afraid, Paul," she said suddenly. "I can't stand it any longer. He cries all the time. You will go, Paul—say you will. We aren't living here—not really living—"

The pleading in her voice now, after its shrill bitterness yesterday, made him think that this was only another way to persuade him. He answered evenly, "I told you this morning, Ellen; we keep on right where we are. At least I do. It's yourself you're thinking about, not the baby."

This morning such an accusation would have stung her to rage; now, her voice swift and panting, she pressed on, "Listen, Paul—I'm thinking of all of us—you, too. Look at the sky—what's happening. Are you blind? Thistles and tumbleweeds—it's a desert. You won't have a straw this fall. You won't be able to feed a cow or a chicken. Please, Paul, say we'll go away—"

"Go where?" His voice as he answered was still remote and even, inflexibly in unison with the narrowed eyes and the great hunch of muscle-knotted shoulder. "Even as a desert it's better than sweeping out your father's store and running his errands. That's all I've got ahead of me if I do what you want."

"And here—" she faltered. "What's ahead of you here? At least we'll get enough to eat and wear when you're sweeping out his store. Look at it—look at it, you fool. Desert—the lamp lit at noon—"

"You'll see it come back. There's good wheat in it yet."

"But in the meantime—year after year—can't you understand, Paul? We'll never get them back—"

He put down his knife and fork and leaned toward her across the table. "I can't go, Ellen. Living off your people—charity—stop and think of it. This is where I belong. I can't do anything else."

"Charity!" she repeated him, letting her voice rise in derision. "And this—you call this independence! Borrowed money you can't even pay the interest on, seed from the government—grocery bills—doctor bills—"

"We'll have crops again," he persisted. "Good crops—the land will come back. It's worth waiting for."

"And while we're waiting, Paul!" It was not anger now, but a kind of sob. "Think of me—and him. It's not fair. We have our lives, too, to live."

"And you think that going home to your family—taking your husband with you—"

"I don't care—anything would be better than this. Look at the air he's breathing. He cries all the time. For his sake, Paul. What's ahead of him here, even if you do get crops?"

He clenched his lips a minute, then, with his eyes hard and contemptuous, struck back, "As much as in town, growing up a pauper. You're the one who wants to go, it's not for his sake. You think that in town you'd have a better time—not so much work—more clothes—"

"Maybe—" she dropped her head defencelessly. "I'm young still. I like pretty things."

There was silence now—a deep fastness of it enclosed by rushing wind and creaking walls. It seemed the yellow lamplight cast a hush upon them. Through the haze of dusty air the walls receded, dimmed, and came again. At last she raised her head and said listlessly, "Go on—your dinner's getting cold. Don't sit and stare at me. I've said it all."

The spent quietness in her voice was even harder to endure than her anger. It reproached him, against his will insisted that he see and understand her lot. To justify himself he tried, "I was a poor man when you married me. You said you didn't mind. Farming's never been easy, and never will be."

"I wouldn't mind the work or the skimping if there was something to look forward to. It's the hopelessness—going on—watching the land blow away."

"The land's all right," he repeated. "The dry years won't last forever."

"But it's not just dry years, Paul!" The little sob in her voice gave way suddenly to a ring of exasperation. "Will you never see? It's the land itself—the soil. You've plowed and harrowed it until there's not a root or fibre left to hold it down. That's why the soil drifts—that's why in a year or two there'll be nothing left but the bare clay. If in the first place you farmers had taken care of your land—if you hadn't been so greedy for wheat every year—"

She had taught school before she married him, and of late in her anger there had been a kind of disdain, an attitude almost of condescension, as if she no longer looked upon the farmers as her equals. He sat still, his eyes fixed on the yellow lamp flame, and seeming to know how her words had hurt him, she went on softly, "I want to help you, Paul. That's why I won't sit quiet while you go on wasting your life. You're only thirty—you owe it to yourself as well as me."

He sat staring at the lamp without answering, his mouth sullen. It seemed indifference now, as if he were ignoring her, and stung to anger again she cried, "Do you ever think what my life is? Two rooms to live in—once a month to town, and nothing to spend when I get there. I'm still young—I wasn't brought up this way."

"You're a farmer's wife now. It doesn't matter what you used to be, or how you were brought up. You get enough to eat and wear. Just now that's all I can do. I'm not to blame that we've been dried out five years."

"Enough to eat!" she laughed back shrilly. "Enough salt pork—enough potatoes and eggs. And look—" Springing to the middle of the room she thrust out a foot for him to see the scuffed old slipper. "When they're completely gone I suppose you'll tell me I can go barefoot—that I'm a farmer's wife—that it's not your fault we're dried-out—"

"And what about these?" He pushed his chair away from the table now to let her see what he was wearing. "Cowhide—hard as boards—but my feet are so calloused I don't feel them any more."

Then he stood up, ashamed of having tried to match her hardships with his own. But frightened now as he reached for his smock she pressed close to him. "Don't go yet. I brood and worry when I'm left alone. Please, Paul—you can't work on the land anyway."

"And keep on like this? You start before I'm through the door. Week in and week out—I've troubles enough of my own."

"Paul—please stay—" The eyes were glazed now, distended a little as if with the intensity of her dread and pleading. "We won't quarrel any more. Hear it! I can't work—I just stand still and listen—"

The eyes frightened him, but responding to a kind of instinct that he must withstand her, that it was his self-respect and manhood against the fretful weakness of a woman, he answered unfeelingly, "In here safe and quiet—you don't know how well off you are. If you were out in it—fighting it—swallowing it—"

"Sometimes, Paul, I wish I was. I'm so caged—if I could only break away and run. See—I stand like this all day. I can't relax. My throat's so tight it aches—"

With a jerk he freed his smock from her clutch. "If I stay we'll only keep on all afternoon. Wait till tomorrow—we'll talk things over when the wind goes down."

Then without meeting her eyes again he swung outside, and, doubled low against the buffets of the wind, fought his way slowly toward the stable. There was a deep hollow calm within, a vast darkness engulfed beneath the tides of moaning wind. He stood breathless a moment, hushed almost to a stupor by the sudden extinction of the storm and the stillness that enfolded him. It was a long, far-reaching stillness. The first dim stalls and rafters led the way into cavern-like obscurity, into vaults and recesses that extended far beyond the stable walls. Nor in these first quiet moments did he forbid the illusion, the sense of release from a harsh, familiar world into one of peace and darkness. The contentious mood that his stand against Ellen had roused him to, his tenacity and clenched despair before the ravages of wind, it was ebbing now, losing itself in the cover of darkness. Ellen and the wheat seemed remote, unimportant. At a whinny from the bay mare, Bess, he went forward and into her stall. She seemed grateful for his presence, and thrust her nose deep between his arm and body. They stood a long time motionless, comforting and assuring each other.

For soon again the first deep sense of quiet and peace was shrunken to the battered shelter of the stable. Instead of release or escape from the assaulting wind, the walls were but a feeble stand against it. They creaked and sawed as if the fingers of a giant hand were tightening to collapse them; the empty loft sustained a pipelike cry that rose and fell but never ended. He saw the dust-black sky again, and his fields blown smooth with drifted soil.

But always, even while listening to the storm outside, he could feel the tense and apprehensive stillness of the stable. There was not a hoof that clumped or shifted, not a rub of halter against manger. And yet, though it had been a strange stable, he would have known, despite the darkness, that every stall was filled. They, too, were all listening.

From Bess he went to the big grey gelding, Prince. Prince was twenty years old, with rib-grooved sides, and high, protruding hip-bones. Paul ran his hand over the ribs, and felt a sudden shame, a sting of fear that Ellen might be right in what she said. For wasn't it true—nine years a farmer now on his own land, and still he couldn't even feed his horses? What, then, could he hope to do for his wife and son?

There was much he planned. And so vivid was the future of his planning, so real and constant, that often the actual present was but half felt, but half endured. Its difficulties were lessened by a confidence in what lay beyond them. A new house—land for the boy—land and still more land—or education, whatever he might want.

But all the time was he only a blind and stubborn fool? Was Ellen right? Was he trampling on her life, and throwing away his own? The five years since he married her, were they to go on repeating themselves, five, ten, twenty, until all the brave future he looked forward to was but a stark and futile past?

She looked forward to no future. She had no faith or dream with which to make the dust and poverty less real. He understood suddenly. He saw her face again as only a few minutes ago it had begged him not to leave her. The darkness round him now was as a slate on which her lonely terror limned itself. He went from Prince to the other horses, combing their manes and forelocks with his fingers, but always it was her face before him, its staring eyes and twisted suffering. "See, Paul,—I stand like this all day. I just stand still—My throat's so tight it aches—"

And always the wind, the creak of walls, the wild lipless wailing through the loft. Until at last as he stood there, staring into the livid face before him, it seemed that this scream of wind was a cry from her parched and frantic lips. He knew it couldn't be, he knew that she was safe within the house, but still the wind persisted as a woman's cry. The cry of a woman with eyes like those that watched him through the dark. Eyes that were mad now—lips that even as they cried still pleaded, "See, Paul—I stand like this all day. I just stand still—so caged! If I could only run!"

He saw her running, pulled and driven headlong by the wind, but when at last he returned to the house, compelled by his anxiety, she was walking quietly back and forth with the baby in her arms. Careful, despite his concern, not to reveal a fear or weakness that she might think capitulation to her wishes, he watched a moment through the window, and then went off to the tool shed to mend harness. All afternoon he stitched and riveted. It was easier with the lantern lit and his hands occupied. There was a wind whining high past the tool shed too, but it was only wind. He remembered the arguments with which Ellen had tried to persuade him away from the farm, and one by one he defeated them. There would be rain again—next year or the next. Maybe in his ignorance he had farmed his land the wrong way, seeding wheat every year, working the soil till it was lifeless dust—but he would do better now. He would plant clover and alfalfa, breed cattle, acre by acre and year by year restore to his land its fibre and fertility. That was something to work for, a way to prove himself. It was ruthless wind, blackening the sky with his earth, but it was not his master. Out of his land it had made a wilderness. He now, out of the wilderness, would make a farm and home again.

Tonight he must talk with Ellen. Patiently, when the wind was down, and they were both quiet again. It was she who had told him to grow fibrous crops, who had called him an ignorant fool because he kept on with summer fallow and wheat. Now she might be gratified to find him acknowledging her wisdom. Perhaps she would begin to feel the power and steadfastness of the land, to take a pride in it, to understand that he was not a fool, but working for her future and their son's.

And already the wind was slackening. At four o'clock he could sense a lull. At five, straining his eyes from the tool shed doorway, he could make out a neighbour's buildings half a mile away. It was over— three days of blight and havoc like a scourge—three days so bitter and so long that for a moment he stood still, unseeing, his senses idle with a numbness of relief.

But only for a moment. Suddenly he emerged from the numbness; suddenly the fields before him struck his eyes to comprehension. They lay black, naked. Beaten and mounded smooth with dust as if a sea in gentle swell had turned to stone. And though he had tried to prepare himself for such a scene, though he had known since yesterday that not a blade would last the storm, still now, before the utter waste confronting him, he sickened and stood cold. Suddenly like the fields he was naked. Everything that had sheathed him a little from the realities of existence: vision and purpose, faith in the land, in the future, in himself—it was all rent now, stripped away. "Desert," he heard her voice begin to sob. "Desert, you fool—the lamp lit at noon!"

In the stable again, measuring out their feed to the horses, he wondered what he would say to her tonight. For so deep were his instincts of loyalty to the land that still, even with the images of his betrayal stark upon his mind, his concern was how to withstand her, how to go on again and justify himself. It had not occurred to him yet that he might or should abandon the land. He had lived with it too long. Rather was his impulse still to defend it—as a man defends against the scorn of strangers even his most worthless kin.

He fed his horses, then waited. She too would be waiting, ready to cry at him, "Look now—that crop that was to feed and clothe us! And you'll still keep on! You'll still say 'Next year—there'll be rain next year'!"

But she was gone when he reached the house. The door was open, the lamp blown out, the crib empty. The dishes from their meal at noon were still on the table. She had perhaps begun to sweep, for the broom was lying in the middle of the floor. He tried to call, but a terror clamped upon his throat. In the wan, returning light it seemed that even the deserted kitchen was straining to whisper what it had seen. The tatters of the storm still whimpered through the eaves, and in their moaning told the desolation of the miles they had traversed. On tiptoe at last he crossed to the adjoining room; then at the threshold, without even a glance inside to satisfy himself that she was really gone, he wheeled again and plunged outside.

He ran a long time—distraught and headlong as a few hours ago he had seemed to watch her run—around the farmyard, a little distance into the pasture, back again blindly to the house to see whether she had returned—and then at a stumble down the road for help.

They joined him in the search, rode away for others, spread calling across the fields in the direction she might have been carried by the wind—but nearly two hours later it was himself who came upon her. Crouched down against a drift of sand as if for shelter, her hair in matted strands around her neck and face, the child clasped tightly in her arms.

The child was quite cold. It had been her arms, perhaps, too frantic to protect him, or the smother of dust upon his throat and lungs. "Hold him," she said as he knelt beside her. "So—with his face away from the wind. Hold him until I tidy my hair."

Her eyes were still wide in an immobile stare, but with her lips she smiled at him. For a long time he knelt transfixed, trying to speak to her, touching fearfully with his fingertips the dust-grimed cheeks and eyelids of the child. At last she said, "I'll take him again. Such clumsy hands—you don't know how to hold a baby yet. See how his head falls forward on your arm."

Yet it all seemed familiar—a confirmation of what he had known since noon. He gave her the child, then, gathering them up in his arms, struggled to his feet, and turned toward home.

It was evening now. Across the fields a few spent clouds of dust still shook and fled. Beyond, as if through smoke, the sunset smouldered like a distant fire.

He walked with a long dull stride, his eyes before him, heedless of her weight. Once he glanced down and with her eyes she still was smiling. "Such strong arms, Paul—and I was so tired just carrying him...."

He tried to answer, but it seemed that now the dusk was drawn apart in breathless waiting, a finger on its lips until they passed. "You were right, Paul...." Her voice came whispering, as if she too could feel the hush. "You said tonight we'd see the storm go down. So still now, and a red sky—it means tomorrow will be fine."

Notes

reproached shamed or disgraced

condescension patronizing behaviour characterized by an air of superiority

distended stretched out or blown up from internal pressure

stupor mental confusion; daze

tenacity courage or perseverance

capitulation surrender

Analyze and Interpret

1. With a partner, discuss your reactions to the characters. Then, in a small group, describe how these reactions might be affected by factors such as your gender, family, life experiences, culture, and values.

2. The author has almost made the wind into a character in this story through his extensive use of personification. With a partner, skim the story, read aloud the descriptive sections about the wind, and discuss the effectiveness of the personification. What atmosphere might it create?

3. What do you think Ross is saying about how the Depression affected human relationships? Plan to write an essay in which you discuss how the events in the story relate to its historical context. First, use the library or on-line resources to research Depression-era farm life on the Canadian Prairies. Next, write down your ideas in an outline. Ask a partner to read your outline to suggest ways to strengthen your content and organization. Write a first draft, then have your partner edit it for clarity and style.

More to Explore

Themes: Personal Challenges, Family, At Work, Rural Life, Nature, Canada, Eye on the Past, Crisis

Elements: characterization, description, foreshadowing, narration, personification, setting, third-person point of view, tragedy

Ramu and Rani

Iqbal Ahmad

New Beginnings, 1998, Shanti Panchal

CONTEXT Iqbal Ahmad was born in Agra, India, in 1921, where he was edu-cated in English mission schools, and later studied at the University of Allahabad. Ahmad taught English at that university and at Karachi University in Pakistan before immigrating to Canada in 1964. He received a Ph.D. from York University, Toronto, in 1974, writing his thesis on the well-known literary critic Northrop Frye. He continued teaching English literature at the University of Waterloo and what is now Ryerson Polytechnic University. With his wife and two children, Ahmad lived mainly in Toronto until his death in 1993. "Ramu and Rani" comes from Ahmad's first book, *The Opium Eater and Other Stories* (1992). One reviewer noted his gentle, humorous style of storytelling. What makes this story, and the story-within-the-story, so romantic? What fea-tures of the story resemble traditional myths or folk tales? ■

"The boatman is here," announced one of the servants.

We were sitting, my sister Adiba and I, on the terrace at the back of the house. A hundred feet away and twenty feet below flowed the river, the Ganga, brimming and blue in the clear November after-noon. "What a view!" I had exclaimed, when we sat down to a light lunch, soon after my arrival in Kherabad.

I had come to Kherabad primarily to discuss my wedding plans with my sister. I was getting married in December during the Christmas holidays, and my sister was to go in advance to our ances-tral home in Agra to get things ready for the guests, mostly relatives, some of whom were coming from as far as Hydrabad Deccan, and to make the necessary arrangements for the *nikah* ceremony, the wed-ding feast and the music party.

Adiba's husband was the District Magistrate of Kherabad, hence the princely house with the choice location. From Kherabad I was going to Bhimsa, a village by the Ganga, in connection with some taxation problems that the Provincial Government was having with that *tehsil*. I was going there to see the *Tehsildar* of the region.

Hameed, Adiba's husband, had suggested that I should take the river route, which would be much nicer than a bus ride on a dusty road. The scenery, he said, was fantastic. We would pass the thickly wooded Jinga Hills and, finally, I could get some duck-hunting done along the way. I had jumped at the offer. He had arranged for the boat to come to the very doorsteps.

Hanif, the young servant boy, carried my bedding-roll—I was spending the night at the village—and a small hamper of food that my sister insisted I should take with me. We descended the river bank and I met Nathu, the boatman. He was a strong gentle man in his mid-thirties. Soon we were underway. We floated down the river, with Nathu plying the oars rhythmically at a leisurely pace. He was not very talkative, which suited me fine. I was enjoying the wind, the water, the blue sky, and above all my reverie of life with Razia, the girl I was about to marry.

I had met her at a party and had fallen head over heels in love with her. She grew to like me too after we had met a few times. Yes, she would marry me, she had said in answer to my inevitable query. But her parents put up a stiff resistance. I did not have a glamorous job and they were sure that their beautiful daughter would attract much better suitors. But when Razia firmly, though indirectly—that is through her mother—communicated to her father that she wanted to marry me, they gave in. And here I was looking at the world through the filter of her beauty.

"Those are not ducks?" I asked Nathu, pointing to some dark spots in the far distance on the white sand along the river.

"No, they are geese," he said.

"Oh, I absolutely must have a crack at them," I exclaimed, with the enthusiasm of the amateur sportsman.

"Okay. What you do is get behind that mound," he said, pointing to a sand dune not far from where the geese were lying in the sun.

"Get off there," he said, inclining his head toward a break in the river bank.

He took me there and I jumped out. Then ducking, crawling, dragging myself on my belly and carrying my gun in front of me, I made my way to the vantage point, behind which the geese were snoozing. As my head topped the curve of the sandy rise, the sentinel bird gave the alarm, and, as if released by a spring, the whole honking flock rose into the air. I too jumped to my feet and let go with both the barrels, dropping one bird. Excited and happy, I carried it back to the boat.

"Not bad! That's a fat bird," said Nathu, and again we were on our way, gliding down the river.

After a couple of hours, Nathu said, more to himself than to me, "I don't like it."

"You don't like what?" I queried him.

"That black cloud over there," he said. To my eyes it was no more than a little grey stain on the horizon.

"It's a storm cloud," he said. "I don't think we have more than half an hour to find a shelter." And he increased the pace of his rowing.

"I know a place not far from here, an arm of the river that goes into those hills. I'll be able to make it there," he said. The hills were at quite some distance, but then, he was rowing quickly.

Soon enough little rags of wind blew past us. The little speck we had seen on the horizon was now moving over us like a giant grey sliding roof. The wind turned to squalls and the first big drops of rain fell on our heads as Nathu left the river and entered a narrow creek.

We had an umbrella of trees arching over us now and the rain was only lightly filtering through the green canopy. As the clouds raced overhead, it quickly grew much darker. We rowed about half a mile inland up the narrow tributary, penetrating the thick vegetation.

We stopped near what was a crudely constructed cottage, abandoned now, a part of which had fallen in. There were no doors in the doorways and the shutterless windows were open squares in the bare walls. We hauled our things in. Inside, the shack was not as bad as it appeared from the outside. It would protect us from the weather well enough.

"I'm afraid we'll have to spend the night here," said Nathu. "It's not going to clear up in a hurry."

"That's all right," I said. I was not at all put about by the inconvenience.

We made a fire, had our supper, and, as it was quite dark now, we lay down to sleep. It hadn't really rained a great deal, but the wind and the lightning were truly terrible.

"You found a great spot for a night like this," I said to Nathu.

"Oh, I have spent many nights here," he replied, and then added, "I had better build a fire to last us through the night. It will keep the wild animals away. We are inside the Jinga Hills, miles away from the nearest village." He got up and added to the fire and lay down again. Soon we were fast asleep.

It must have been about three o'clock in the morning when my sleep was broken by the sound of someone laughing outside. It was a woman's laugh, musical like silver bells. I got up and went to the shutterless window to see who it was.

There was mottled moonlight outside—the trees near the cottage were not close set—and the ground looked like a carpet of light and grey patches. I looked up. The sky, all that I could see, was crystal clear. The storm had blown over and the moon was shining in its splendour, full and bright, almost like the day. In the lighted patches things were perfectly visible, and even in the shade under the trees visibility was not bad. But I saw no one. Who could have been laughing?

Then I saw her, a young woman, her form silvery like the moon even in the shade. She was dressed from the shoulders to the knees in an almost transparent length of muslin that was floating rather than fitted around her body. She was playfully running about and giving out little musical peals of laughter while she was being pursued by a young man, who was strong and brown like the earth, and who was wearing a *dhoti* that covered him from his waist to his calves. He was trying to catch her, but she eluded his grasp by dodging behind trees or escaping to the other side of the puddles that the rain water had formed, and emitting those silvery peals.

They played this game for a while and he eventually caught her. He held her in his embrace and she playfully went on resisting him, throwing her head back and laughing, laughing all the time, till they tumbled to the ground and rolled on the grass, where he victoriously kissed her. She lay in his arms for some time. Then they sat up and, holding hands, leaned their backs against a tree. What they said to each other I could not hear.

After a while they got up, strolled toward a swing that was suspended from a tall tree and got up on it. They sat side by side on its wooden seat, each with an arm behind the other as they grasped the ropes. Then they pushed off and started pumping the swing with their feet. Going back and forth the swing rose higher and higher till it was almost parallel to the ground at its highest points. As they shot up and swept down in that wide arc and the wind whistled through her hair, the woman again let out her musical shrieks of pleasure.

After some time they slowed down, stopped and got off. They were quiet now, and arm in arm walked in their bare feet through the puddles of rain water and, finally, disappeared under the trees.

I remained watching at my station for a long time, waiting for them to come back, but they did not. I rubbed my eyes. Was it a vision? Did I really see them or was I dreaming? I looked down at my rolled-out bedding. Yes, it was there. I looked at Nathu. He lay sound asleep. The fire had gone out, but the thought of the wild animals did not even cross my mind. I lay down happy and went back to sleep.

"*Babu,* wake up!" Nathu was saying. I opened my eyes; it was broad daylight. I got up, rolled up my bedding and got dressed. Nathu made a fire and boiled some water. We made tea and had our breakfast.

"The fire went out in the night," he said.

"Yes, I saw it when I got up sometime after midnight. I was awakened by some sounds that I heard," I said.

A worried look came over his face and he asked, "It wasn't a tiger or a bear?"

"No, no, it wasn't a tiger or a bear. In fact, I am not even sure if I got up at all. Maybe it was all a dream." I told him what I had seen, or what I believed I had seen. He listened intently to my story, not interrupting even once, and all the time a quiet smile played upon his simple face.

"Are you in love?" he asked when I had finished.

"Why, was it a lover's dream?"

"No, it was not a dream," he said. "What you saw was there all right; but only those who are in love can see it. I know some other people who have seen them. But I myself never have, although I have spent many nights here. But perhaps I didn't love the woman I married in the playful and moonlight kind of way that you saw." And he told me about his wife, saying, "Jasho was a fisherman's daughter. I am a fisherman. She was strong and as good as myself at casting the net and hauling in the catch. We are partners in water. Perhaps that's not love for Ramu and Rani."

"Who are Ramu and Rani?" I asked.

"The man and woman you saw last night," he replied.

"Do they live here?" I asked. "No, they died long ago," he said.

"What!" I exclaimed.

"I'll tell you about them when we get back on the river."

We packed up, put out the fire, loaded our things onto the boat and worked our way through the tunnel of lush greenery. When we emerged on the vast expanse of the river, the water was glimmering in the gorgeous morning light. We resumed our journey and Nathu told me about the moon-coloured woman and the earth-coloured man.

"About fifty miles down the river, well beyond the cluster of the wild Jinga Hills, in which we have spent the night, is a village called Premabad. It was there that Rani's father lived long ago. He was almost like a king to the villagers; he was the top *zamindar,* owner of almost all the land in and around the village. He lived in a *haveli,* a big house, surrounded by his wealth and his beautiful family, of whom the most beautiful was his youngest child, a girl who went by the name of Rani or 'the queen.'

"Apart from his wealth and rank that earned him honour and respect, there was his high caste too. He was a Brahmin. But he was not a fanatic. With the exception of his cook, who was always a Brahmin, most of his servants were from the lower castes. And the man who looked after his cows was indeed of the *shudra* caste, from the so-called 'untouchables.' But everybody touched Ghasita, the cowherd, and he was in and out of the *haveli* all the time.

"Ramu was Ghasita's son and from his childhood he was Rani's playmate. The two of them romped together in the fields, chased the cows and played together all the time. No one minded it, that is, as long as they were children. But when Rani was fifteen, restrictions were imposed.

"Soon she would be married, she was told, and go to her husband's home and assume responsibility of a whole household as a grown woman. It was not good for her to be seen in the company of a boy, and a *shudra* boy at that. People talk and say all kinds of malicious things. Now that she was of a marriageable age she should exercise more prudence.

"Ramu was flatly ordered not to seek Rani's company. In fact, he was not to come into the *haveli* at all. However, he was often in the nearby cowsheds, assisting his father. And it was there that they secretly would meet, Rani and he. She would quietly steal into one of the little barns where he would be waiting for her.

"The family, secure in their aristocratic superiority, could not even imagine that the two lovers were still meeting. It was only when Rani's mother went by chance into one of the sheds that she saw them sitting in a corner holding hands.

"The *zamindar* was furious. He called the girl up to his room and shouted at her. Where was her shame? She was playing with filth. She was not thinking of the family's honour, not even of her own future. He told her that he had ordered Ramu to be sent to another village where he would live with his uncle. If he ever came back, and if the two of them were seen together again, he would simply have him beaten to death.

"The next day Ramu was gone. Ghasita was treated with greater care than before, but he could not look anyone in the eye. The guilt of his son made him feel guilty too, and he moved like one who was trying to be invisible. And if the *zamindar* spoke a kind word to him, which he sometimes did, he would immediately stoop down and touch his feet.

"'You are mother and father to us, lord,' he would say, with tears of gratitude showing in his eyes and the demon of fear gripping his heart.

"The *zamindar* also earnestly embarked on finding a match for his daughter, who herself was now very quiet and withdrawn. She did not protest; she did nothing either to oppose or support what he was doing. Her father liked to think that she had dutifully submitted to his will, but in his heart of hearts he was not really convinced.

"He didn't have to try very hard to find a mate for Rani. There were so many young men wanting to marry this beautiful and wealthy girl; proposals poured in.

"Finally, a match was decided upon. Rani would go to Pritamgarh as the daughter-in-law, not of a *zamindar* like her father, but of the Rajah of Pritamgarh. The father and mother were elated at the prospect. They did not name her Rani for nothing, her mother said; she was destined to be a queen.

"As the wedding date approached, Rani sank deeper into silence and dejection. Her usually lively and cheerful face was now habitually melancholy and pensive. Her mother and father and brothers tried to cheer her up. Girls get married, they said; they have to leave the homes of their childhood. Certainly, she would be separated from those she had lived with and loved all her life, and who on their part had doted on her. But she would have an equally good home now and lots and lots of love from her husband and the people she was going to.

"They never talked of Ramu. They, in fact, would have been surprised if somebody had told them what the cause of her grief was, so deeply into the dark depths of their minds had they thrust the idea of a liking existing between a Brahmin girl and a *shudra* boy.

"The wedding day arrived. Rani had not eaten, or had eaten next to nothing, for a whole week, and when one of her maids went to her bedroom to awaken her and begin preparing the bride for the evening ceremony—the bridegroom's party was arriving in the afternoon—she came out howling and sobbing. Rani was dead.

"The whole household was thrown into a commotion. The mother beat her breast and tore her hair. The father moaned and cried and said why did he live to see this day?

"The news of the *zamindar's* daughter's death on her wedding day spread like wildfire in the village and beyond. A man was rushed to Pritamgarh to inform the bridegroom's party of the tragedy that had struck before they started. By noon people from far and near were pouring in to comfort the *zamindar* in his bereavement.

"In another part of the house preparations were under way to take the body to the cremation ghat for burning.

"Evening had fallen by the time the pundits had finished the religious rituals, chanted the prayers, and got the bier ready. Rani's body was wrapped in a white shroud and was placed on a long narrow frame made of two bamboos joined firmly together by a number of cross-sticks. It was heaped high with flowers. Two men, one in front, the other behind, lifted the light bier on to their shoulders, and the sad procession started out. Crying 'Ram nam sat hai' they slowly wound their way toward the river.

"It was completely dark when they reached the cremation ghat. The sky was overcast and a few drops of rain began to fall. The priests proceeded with the last ceremony. They arranged the fire logs many layers deep, into a funeral pyre, lavishly poured ghee over it, and placed the body on top of the pile. The mother and father uttered heart-rending shrieks, and then the mother collapsed, falling to the ground, where she kept banging her head. Loving hands helped her up.

"Finally, the funeral pyre was torched. It was at that precise moment that the rain came pouring down. The flames fed with fat were rising and trying to establish themselves, and the rain, now falling in sheets, was dousing them. Then the whole world lit up as a huge ball of light-ning hit the ground yards away from the mourners, followed by a deaf-ening crash of thunder that sent waves of terror through them. And when the roaring thunder hurled another immense fire-ball, and this time in their very midst, the crowd stampeded. Everybody ran. The older, fatter ladies of the *haveli,* who could not run, had to be lifted up and carried by the servants, as everybody headed for home. They ran, and as they ran they looked back and saw more balls of fire bouncing on the burning ghat. The thunder pursued them and they ran harder.

"The storm was as short as it was violent. When it was over, there was not a soul near the dead body except a young man who was stand-ing near the now cold funeral pyre. The rain drenched him to the skin, but he was oblivious to it; he was drowning in grief. The fire on the *chita* had gone out, but he was burning inside.

"The rain had stopped, the lightning and thunder were gone, and the wind had died down. Everything was quiet and the young man stood like a statue, when he heard a groan and saw a movement inside the winding sheet.

"Like a wild animal he jumped onto the pyre and began to tear off the partly singed and completely soaked shroud. Rani sat up and opened her eyes.

"'Where are we?' she said.

"'It's all right; it's all right,' he kept repeating as he extricated her from the winding sheet, lifted her off the log pile, and set her down on the ground. She stood there, naked, by his side. He flung away the torn cloth of the dead, took off his *kurta* and put it on her.

"Then they started walking, away from the ghat, away from the village, along the river bank, toward the distant Jinga Hills. And they talked. Ramu told her what had happened. Probably, he said, she had the disease that he once heard old Vedji talk about in which heartbeat and breathing are almost gone as is the heat of the body. They thought she was dead and brought her to the cremation ground. And then about the fearsome thunder and lightning and how everybody ran.

"She asked him where he had come from. He told her he had heard of her death and had come to the village. He was there around noon, but he did not go in; he hung around at the outskirts. Later on, when the funeral procession started, he had followed it at a distance, keeping out of sight. And then at the burning ghat he watched from a distance, standing behind a tree. And when everyone had gone, he had come out and had been standing there ever since.

"They kept walking, hand in hand. They walked all night.

"The next morning the *zamindar* returned to the site with his priests to complete the unfinished rites, and they were all very surprised to find the body gone. They found the shroud. It had been torn, and there were some blood stains on it. They concluded that wild animals had taken away the body. They grieved some more and went home.

"It was years later that reports began to circulate that a young couple lived in the dangerous forest of the Jinga Hills. They were also sighted a few times on the bank of the river. But they never stayed for more than a fleeting glimpse. And then the story was slowly pieced together as to who they were."

"Some believe," Nathu concluded, "that they are still alive. But that cannot be. They came here more than a hundred years ago."

When he had finished his story, I emerged from a sort of trance, and all I could think of saying was, "So you never saw them?"

"No," he said. "I told you my wife and I are partners in water, not players in the moonlight."

I smiled at his simple answer, but in the dim and dreaming part of my mind I saw a moonlike face that was Razia's.

NOTES

Ganga another name for the Ganges River, located in northern India and Bangladesh

Agra a city in northern India containing the Taj Mahal, a romantic memorial to the emperor Shah Jahan's favourite wife, Mahal

Babu in Hindi, a word used to address an educated man or a gentleman

zamindar a landowner; an Urdu word, originally from the Persian *zamīn,* meaning "land," and *dār,* meaning "owner"

Brahmin in traditional Hindu society, a member of the highest caste (originally scholars and priests); from the Sanskrit *brahman,* meaning "priest"

shudra the lowest caste, or "untouchables," in traditional Hindu society

Rajah a prince or ruler; from the Hindi *rājān,* originally from the Sanskrit *rājan,* meaning "king"

ghat a wide flight of steps at a riverbank

pundit a learned man; an expert in Hindu religion and law or the Sanskrit language

ghee a Hindi word meaning clarified butter, used in cookery across India

kurta loose-fitting, collarless tunic

ANALYZE AND INTERPRET

1. As a class, discuss why you think the author chose "Ramu and Rani" as the title for this story, and whether or not you think it is effective. Note that sometimes writers will select a phrase from a piece of writing as its title. Find a phrase within the story that you think could be a suitable title, and defend your choice to your classmates.

2. Consider the three romantic couples in this story: Ramu and Rani, the narrator and his fiancée, and Nathu and his wife. In a group, discuss each of these relationships in terms of the following aspects of love: love at first sight, overcoming obstacles to love, death due to love, eternal love, and love as a lifelong partnership. Write an essay about the portrayal of love in this story, in which you compare the three couples. You might wish to make reference to other literary romantic couples such as Romeo and Juliet or Beauty and the Beast.

3. With a partner, improvise a conversation between the narrator and his fiancée, Razia, in which he describes his experiences in the forest. In your conversation, does Razia accept the story of Ramu and Rani as easily as the narrator does? How does Razia's reaction to his story affect the way the narrator feels about her? Present your dialogue to your classmates and ask them to evaluate it in terms of their understanding of the characters.

MORE TO EXPLORE

Themes: Self and Culture, Stereotypes, Family, Romance, Rebels, Canada, Asia, Crisis

Elements: archetype, description, empathy, first-person point of view, myth, pathos, setting

A Walk to the Jetty

Jamaica Kincaid

Caribbean Coconut Harvest

- Use feedback from a partner to revise your work.
- Make a visual display of places in a story.
- Compare a character's experience with your own.

CONTEXT Jamaica Kincaid was born on the Caribbean island of Antigua in 1949, but left her birthplace at the age of seventeen. Born Elaine Potter Richardson, she changed her name and created a new life for herself in the United States. She worked first in New York City as a nanny, then went to college to study photography. She began writing for *The New Yorker* magazine, for which she was a regular contributor for twenty years. Kincaid, who now lives in Vermont, admits that much of her writing is haunted by the tortured relationship she had with her mother. In discussing her work, Kincaid claims that she doesn't like happy endings, saying "Life is difficult, and that's that." How does "A Walk to the Jetty" confirm her viewpoint? What evidence in this short story suggests that it is autobiographically based? ■

"My name is Annie John." These were the first words that came into my mind as I woke up on the morning of the last day I spent in Antigua, and they stayed there, lined up one behind the other, marching up and down, for I don't know how long. At noon on that day, a ship on which I was to be a passenger would sail to Barbados, and there I would board another ship, which would sail to England, where I would study to become a nurse. My name was the last thing I saw the night before, just as I was falling asleep; it was written in big, black letters all over my trunk, sometimes followed by my address in Antigua, sometimes followed by my address as it would be in England. I did not want to go to England, I did not want to be a nurse, but I would have chosen going off to live in a cavern and keeping house for seven unruly men rather than go on with my life as it stood. I never wanted to lie in this bed again, my legs hanging out way past the foot of it, tossing and turning on my mattress, with its cotton stuffing all lumped just where it wasn't a good place to be lumped. I never wanted to lie in my bed again and hear Mr. Ephraim driving his sheep to pasture—a signal to my mother that she should get up to prepare my father's and my bath and breakfast. I never wanted to lie in bed and hear her get dressed, washing her face, brushing her teeth, and gargling. I especially never wanted to lie in my bed and hear my mother gargling again.

Lying there in the half-dark of my room, I could see my shelf, with my books—some of them prizes I had won in school, some of them gifts from my mother—and with photographs of people I was supposed to love forever no matter what, and with my old thermos, which was given to me for my eighth birthday, and some shells I had gathered at different times I spent at the sea. In one corner stood my washstand and its beautiful basin of white enamel with blooming red hibiscus painted at the bottom and an urn that matched. In another corner were my old school shoes and my Sunday shoes. In still another corner, a bureau held my old clothes. I knew everything in this room, inside out and outside in. I had lived in this room for thirteen of my seventeen years. I could see in my mind's eye even the day my father was adding it onto the rest of the house. Everywhere I looked stood something that had meant a lot to me, that had given me pleasure at some point, or could remind me of a time that was a happy time. But as I was lying there my heart could have burst open with joy at the thought of never having to see any of it again.

If someone had asked me for a little summing up of my life at that moment as I lay in bed, I would have said, "My name is Annie John. I was born on the fifteenth of September, seventeen years ago, at Holberton Hospital, at five o'clock in the morning. At the time I was born, the moon was going down at one end of the sky and the sun was coming up at the other. My mother's name is Annie also. My father's name is Alexander, and he is thirty-five years older than my mother. Two of his children are four and six years older than she is. Looking at how sickly he has become and looking at the way my mother now has to run up and down for him, gathering the herbs and barks that he boils in water, which he drinks instead of the medicine the doctor has ordered for him, I plan not only never to marry an old man but certainly never to marry at all. The house we live in my father built with his own hands. The bed I am lying in my father built with his own hands. If I get up and sit on a chair, it is a chair my father built with his own hands. When my mother uses a large wooden spoon to stir the porridge we sometimes eat as part of our breakfast, it will be a spoon that my father has carved with his own hands. The sheets on my bed my mother made with her own hands. The curtains hanging at my window my mother made with her own hands. The nightie I am wearing, with scalloped neck and hem and sleeves, my mother made with her own hands. When I look at things in a certain way, I suppose I should say that the two of them made me with their own hands. For most of my life, when the three of us went anywhere together I stood between the two of them or sat between the two of them. But then I got too big, and there I was, shoulder to shoulder with them more or less, and it became not very comfortable to walk down the street together. And so now there they are together and here I am apart. I don't see them now the way I used to, and I don't love them now the way I used to. The bitter thing about it is that they are just the same and it is I who have changed, so all the things I used to be and all the things I used to feel are as false as the teeth in my father's head. Why, I wonder, didn't I see the hypocrite in my mother when, over the years, she said that she loved me and could hardly live without me, while at the same time proposing and arranging separation after separation, including this one, which, unbeknownst to her, *I* have arranged to be permanent? So now I, too, have hypocrisy, and sharp eyes, and I have made a vow never to be fooled again."

Lying in my bed for the last time, I thought, This is what I add up to. At that, I felt as if someone had placed me in a hole and was forcing me first down and then up against the pressure of gravity. I shook myself and prepared to get up. I said to myself, "I am getting up out of this bed for the last time." Everything I would do that morning until I got on the ship that would take me to England I would be doing for the last time, for I had made up my mind that, come what may, the road for me now went only in one direction: away from my home, away from my mother, away from my father, away from the everlasting blue sky, away from the everlasting hot sun, away from people who said to me, "This happened during the time your mother was carrying you." If I had been asked to put into words why I felt this way, if I had been given years to reflect and come up with the words of why I felt this way, I would not have been able to come up with so much as the letter "A." I only knew that I felt the way I did, and that this feeling was the strongest thing in my life.

The Anglican church bell struck seven. My father had already bathed and dressed and was in his workshop puttering around. As if the day of my leaving were something to celebrate, they were treating it as a holiday, and nothing in the usual way would take place. My father would not go to work at all. When I got up, my mother greeted me with a big, bright "Good morning"—so big and bright that I shrank before it. I bathed quickly in some warm bark water that my mother had prepared for me. I put on my underclothes—all of them white and all of them smelling funny. Along with my earrings, my neck chain, and my bracelets, all made of gold from British Guiana, my underclothes had been sent to my mother's obeah woman, and whatever she had done to my jewellery and underclothes would help protect me from evil spirits and every kind of misfortune. The things I never wanted to see or hear or do again now made up at least three weeks' worth of grocery lists. I placed a mark against obeah women, jewellery, and white underclothes. Over my underclothes, I put on an around-the-yard dress of my mother's. The clothes I would wear for my voyage were a dark-blue pleated skirt and a blue-and-white checked blouse (the blue in the blouse matched exactly the blue of my skirt) with a large sailor collar and with a tie made from the same material as the skirt—a blouse that came down a long way past my waist, over my skirt. They were lying on a chair, freshly ironed by my mother. Putting on my clothes was the last thing I would do just before leaving the house. Miss Cornelia came and pressed my hair and then shaped it into what felt like a hundred corkscrews, all lying flat against my head so that my hat would fit properly.

At breakfast, I was seated in my usual spot, with my mother at one end of the table, my father at the other, and me in the middle, so that as they talked to me or to each other I would shift my head to the left or to the right and get a good look at them. We were having a Sunday breakfast, a breakfast as if we had just come back from Sunday-morning services: salt fish and antroba and souse and hard-boiled eggs, and even special Sunday bread from Mr. Daniel, our baker. On Sundays, we ate this big breakfast at eleven o'clock and then we didn't eat again until four o'clock, when we had our big Sunday dinner. It was the best breakfast we ate, and the only breakfast better than that was the one we ate on Christmas morning. My parents were in a festive mood, saying what a wonderful time I would have in my new life, what a wonderful opportunity this was for me, and what a lucky person I was. They were eating away as they talked, my father's false teeth making that clop-clop sound like a horse on a walk as he talked, my mother's mouth going up and down like a donkey's as she chewed each mouthful thirty-two times. (I had long ago counted, because it was something she made me do also, and I was trying to see if this was just one of her rules that applied only to me.) I was looking at them with a smile on my face but disgust in my heart when my mother said, "Of course, you are a young lady now, and we won't be surprised if in due time you write to say that one day soon you are to be married."

Without thinking, I said, with bad feeling that I didn't hide very well, "How absurd!"

My parents immediately stopped eating and looked at me as if they had not seen me before. My father was the first to go back to his food. My mother continued to look. I don't know what went through her mind, but I could see her using her tongue to dislodge food stuck in the far corners of her mouth.

Many of my mother's friends now came to say goodbye to me, and to wish me God's blessings. I thanked them and showed the proper amount of joy at the glorious things they pointed out to me that my future held and showed the proper amount of sorrow at how much my parents and everyone else who loved me would miss me. My body ached a little at all this false going back and forth, at all this taking in of people gazing at me with heads tilted, love and pity on their smiling faces. I could have left without saying any goodbyes to them and I wouldn't have missed it. There was only one person I felt I should say goodbye to, and that was my former friend Gwen. We had long ago drifted apart, and when I saw her now my heart nearly split in two with embarrassment at the feelings I used to have for her and things I had shared with her. She had now degenerated into complete silliness, hardly able to complete a sentence without putting in a few giggles. Along with the giggles, she had developed some other schoolgirl traits that she did not have when she was actually a schoolgirl, so beneath her were such things then. When we were saying our goodbyes, it was all I could do not to say cruelly, "Why are you behaving like such a monkey?" Instead, I put everything on a friendly plain, wishing her well and the best in the future. It was then that she told me that she was more or less engaged to a boy she had known while growing up early on in Nevis, and that soon, in a year or so, they would be married. My reply to her was "Good luck," and she thought I meant her well, so she grabbed me and said, "Thank you. I knew you would be happy about it." But to me it was as if she had shown me a high point from which she was going to jump and hoped to land in one piece on her feet. We parted, and when I turned away I didn't look back.

My mother had arranged with a stevedore to take my trunk to the jetty ahead of me. At ten o'clock on the dot, I was dressed, and we set off for the jetty. An hour after that, I would board a launch that would take me out to sea, where I then would board the ship. Starting out, as if for old time's sake and without giving it a thought, we lined up in the old way: I walking between my mother and my father. I loomed way above my father and could see the top of his head. We must have made a strange sight: a grown girl all dressed up in the middle of a morning, in the middle of the week, walking in step in the middle between her two parents, for people we didn't know stared at us. It was all of half an hour's walk from our house to the jetty, but I was passing through most of the years of my life. We passed by the house where Miss Dulcie, the seamstress that I had been apprenticed to for a time, lived, and just as I was passing by, a wave of bad feeling for her came over me, because I suddenly remembered that in the months I spent with her all she had me do was sweep the floor, which was always full of threads and pins and needles, and I never seemed to sweep it clean enough to please her. Then she would send me to the store to buy buttons or thread, though I was only allowed to do this if I was given a sample of the button or thread, and then she would find fault even though they were an exact match of the samples she had given me. And all the while she said to me, "A girl like you will never learn to sew properly, you know." At the time, I don't suppose I minded it, because it was customary to treat the first-year apprentice with such scorn, but now I placed on the dustheap of my life Miss Dulcie and everything that I had had to do with her.

We were soon on the road that I had taken to school, to church, to Sunday school, to choir practice, to Brownie meetings, to Girl

Guide meetings, to meet a friend. I was five years old when I first walked on this road unaccompanied by someone to hold my hand. My mother had placed three pennies in my little basket, which was a duplicate of her bigger basket, and sent me to the chemist's shop to buy a pennyworth of senna leaves, a pennyworth of eucalyptus leaves, and a pennyworth of camphor. She then instructed me on what side of the road to walk, where to make a turn, where to cross, how to look carefully before I crossed, and if I met anyone that I knew to politely pass greetings and keep on my way. I was wearing a freshly ironed yellow dress that had printed on it scenes of acrobats flying through the air and swinging on a trapeze. I had just had a bath, and after it, instead of powdering me with my baby-smelling talcum powder, my mother had, as a special favour, let me use her own talcum powder, which smelled quite perfumy and came in a can that had painted on it people going out to dinner in nineteenth-century London and was called Mazie. How it pleased me to walk out the door and bend my head down to sniff at myself and see that I smelled just like my mother. I went to the chemist's shop, and he had to come from behind the counter and bend down to hear what it was that I wanted to buy, my voice was so little and timid then. I went back just the way I had come, and when I walked into the yard and presented my basket with its three packages to my mother, her eyes filled with tears and she swooped me up and held me high in the air and said that I was wonderful and good and that there would never be anybody better. If I had just conquered Persia, she couldn't have been more proud of me.

We passed our church—the church in which I had been christened and received and had sung in the junior choir. We passed by a house in which a girl I used to like and was sure I couldn't live without had lived. Once, when she had mumps, I went to visit her against my mother's wishes, and we sat on her bed and ate the cure of roasted, buttered sweet potatoes that had been placed on her swollen jaws, held there by a piece of white cloth. I don't know how, but my mother found out about it, and I don't know how, but she put an end to our friendship. Shortly after, the girl moved with her family across the sea to somewhere else. We passed the doll store, where I would go with my mother when I was little and point out the doll I wanted that year for Christmas. We passed the store where I bought the much-fought-over shoes I wore to church to be received in. We passed the bank. On my sixth birthday, I was given, among other things, the present of a sixpence. My mother and I then went to this bank, and with the sixpence I opened my own savings account. I was given a little grey book with my name in big letters on it, and in the balance column it said "6d." Every Saturday morning after that, I was given a sixpence—later a shilling, and later a two-and-sixpence piece—and I would take it to the bank for deposit. I had never been allowed to withdraw even a farthing from my bank account until just a few weeks before I was to leave; then the whole account was closed out, and I received from the bank the sum of six pounds ten shillings and two and half pence.

We passed the office of the doctor who told my mother three times that I did not need glasses, that if my eyes were feeling weak a glass of carrot juice a day would make them strong again. This happened when I was eight. And so every day at recess I would run to my school gate and meet my mother, who was waiting for me with a glass of juice from carrots she had just grated and then squeezed, and I would drink it and then run back to meet my chums. I knew there was nothing at all wrong with my eyes, but I had recently read a story in *The Schoolgirl's Own Annual* in which the heroine, a girl a few years older than I was then, cut such a figure to my mind with the way she was always adjusting her small, round, horn-rimmed glasses that I felt I must have a pair exactly like them. When it became clear that I didn't need glasses, I began to complain about the glare of the sun being too much for my eyes, and I walked around with my hands shielding them—especially in my mother's presence. My mother then bought for me a pair of sunglasses with the exact horn-rimmed frames I wanted, and how I enjoyed the gestures of blowing on the lenses, wiping them with the hem of my uniform, adjusting the glasses when they slipped down my nose, and just removing them from their case and putting them on. In three weeks, I grew tired of them and they found a nice resting place in a drawer, along with some other things that at one time or another I couldn't live without.

We passed the store that sold only grooming aids, all imported from England. This store had in it a large porcelain dog—white, with black spots all over and a red ribbon of satin tied around its neck. The dog sat in front of a white porcelain bowl that was always filled with fresh water, and it sat in such a way that it looked as if it had just taken a long drink. When I was a small child, I would ask my mother, if ever we were near this store, to please take me to see the dog, and I would stand in front of it, bent over slightly, my hands resting on my knees, and stare at it and stare at it. I thought this dog more beautiful and more real than any actual dog I had ever seen or any actual dog I would ever see. I must have outgrown my interest in the dog, for when it disappeared I never asked what became of it. We passed the library, and if there was anything on this walk that I might have wept over leaving, this most surely would have been the thing. My mother had been a member of the library long before I was born. And since she took me everywhere with her when I was quite little, when she went to the library she took me along there, too. I would sit in her lap very quietly as she read books that she did not want to take home with her. I could not read the words yet, but just the way they looked on the page was interesting to me. Once, a book she was reading had a large picture of a man in it, and when I asked her who he was she told me that he was Louis Pasteur and that the book was about his life. It stuck in my mind, because she said it was because of him that she boiled my milk to purify it before I was allowed to drink it, that it was his idea, and that that was why the process was called pasteurization. One of the things I had put away in my mother's old trunk in which she kept all my childhood things was my library card. At that moment, I owed seven-pence in overdue fees.

As I passed by all these places, it was as if I were in a dream, for I didn't notice the people coming and going in and out of them, I didn't feel my feet touch ground, I didn't even feel my own body—I just saw these places as if they were hanging in the air, not having top or bottom, and as if I had gone in and out of them all in the same moment. The sun was bright; the sky was blue and just above my head. We then arrived at the jetty.

My heart now beat fast, and no matter how hard I tried, I couldn't keep my mouth from falling open and my nostrils from spreading to the ends of my face. My old fear of slipping between the boards of the jetty and falling into the dark-green water where the dark-green eels lived came over me. When my father's stomach started to go bad, the doctor had recommended a walk every evening right after he ate his dinner. Sometimes he would take me with him. When he took me with him, we usually went to the jetty, and there he would sit and talk to the night watchman about cricket or some other thing that didn't interest me, because it was not personal; they didn't talk about their wives, or their children, or their parents, or about any of their likes and dislikes. They talked about things in such a strange way, and I didn't see what they found funny, but sometimes they made each other laugh so much that their guffaws would bound out to sea and send back an echo. I was always sorry when we got to the jetty and saw that the night watchman on duty was the one he enjoyed speaking to; it was like being locked up in a book filled with numbers and diagrams and what-ifs. For the thing about not being able to understand and enjoy what they were saying was I had nothing to take my mind off my fear of slipping in between the boards of the jetty.

Now, too, I had nothing to take my mind off what was happening to me. My mother and father—I was leaving them forever. My home on an island—I was leaving it forever. What to make of everything? I felt a familiar hollow space inside. I felt I was being held down against my will. I felt I was burning up from head to toe. I felt that someone was tearing me up into little pieces and soon I would be able to see all the little pieces as they floated out into nothing in the deep blue sea. I didn't know whether to laugh or cry. I could see that it would be better not to think too clearly about any one thing. The launch was being made ready to take me, along with some other passengers, out to the ship that was anchored in the sea. My father paid our fares, and we joined a line of people waiting to board. My mother checked my bag to make sure that I had my passport, the money she had given me, and a sheet of paper placed between some pages in my Bible on which were written the names of the relatives—people I had not known existed—with whom I would live in England. Across from the jetty was a wharf, and some stevedores were loading and unloading barges. I don't know why seeing that struck me so, but suddenly a wave of strong feeling came over me, and my heart swelled with a great gladness as the words "I shall never see this again" spilled out inside me. But then, just as quickly, my heart shrivelled up and the words "I shall never see this again" stabbed at me. I don't know what stopped me from falling in a heap at my parents' feet.

When we were all on board, the launch headed out to sea. Away from the jetty, the water became the customary blue, and the launch left a wide path in it that looked like a road. I passed by sounds and smells that were so familiar that I had long ago stopped paying any attention to them. But now here they were, and the ever-present "I shall never see this again" bobbed up and down inside me. There was the sound of the seagull diving down into the water and coming up with something silverish in its mouth. There was the smell of the sea and the sight of small pieces of rubbish floating around in it. There were boats filled with fishermen coming in early. There was the sound of their voices as they shouted greetings to each other. There was the hot sun, there was the blue sea, there was the blue sky. Not very far away, there was the white sand of the shore, with the run-down houses all crowded in next to each other, for in some places only poor people lived near the shore. I was seated in the launch between my parents, and when I realized that I was gripping their hands tightly I glanced quickly to see if they were looking at me with scorn, for I felt sure that they must have known of my never-see-this-again feelings. But instead my father kissed me on the forehead and my mother kissed me on the mouth, and they both gave over their hands to me, so that I could grip them as much as I wanted. I was on the verge of feeling that it had all been a mistake, but I remembered that I wasn't a child anymore, and that now when I made up my mind about something I had to see it through. At that moment, we came to the ship, and that was that.

The goodbyes had to be quick, the captain said. My mother introduced herself to him and then introduced me. She told him to keep an eye on me, for I had never gone this far away from home on my own. She gave him a letter to pass on to the captain of the next ship that I would board in Barbados. They walked me to my cabin, a small space that I would share with someone else—a woman I did not know. I had never before slept in a room with someone I did not know. My father kissed me goodbye and told me to be good and to write home often. After he said this, he looked at me, then looked at the floor and swung his left foot, then looked at me again. I could see that he wanted to say something else, something that he had never said to me before, but then he just turned and walked away. My mother said, "Well," and then she threw her arms around me. Big tears streamed down her face, and it must have been that—for I could not bear to see my mother cry—which started me crying, too. She then tightened her arms around me and held me to her close, so that I felt that I couldn't breathe. With that, my tears dried up and I was suddenly on my guard. "What does she want now?" I said to myself. Still holding me close to her, she said, in a voice that raked across my skin, "It doesn't matter what you do or where you go, I'll always be your mother and this will always be your home."

I dragged myself away from her and backed off a little, and then I shook myself, as if to wake myself out of a stupor. We looked at each other for a long time with smiles on our faces, but I know the opposite of that was in my heart. As if responding to some invisible cue, we both said, at the very same moment, "Well." Then my mother turned around and walked out the cabin door. I stood there for I don't know how long, and then I remembered that it was customary to stand on deck and wave to your relatives who were returning to shore. From the deck, I could not see my father, but I could see my mother facing the ship, her eyes searching to pick me out. I removed from my bag a red cotton handkerchief that she had earlier given me for this purpose, and I waved it wildly in the air. Recognizing me immediately, she waved just as wildly, and we continued to do this until she became just a dot in the matchbox-size launch swallowed up in the big blue sea.

I went back to my cabin and lay down on my berth. Everything trembled as if it had a spring at its very centre. I could hear the small waves lap-lapping around the ship. They made an unexpected sound, as if a vessel filled with liquid had been placed on its side and now was slowly emptying out.

Notes

jetty a pier or dock

obeah a person who uses supernatural forces to gain success, protection, or cures for clients; practice of magic originating in Africa; from a West African language, probably Twi or Efik

antroba a Northern Caribbean word for eggplant

souse in this instance, pickled pork trimmings served cold with onions, cucumber, and red pepper; from the Old French *souser,* meaning "to pickle," originally from the Old Saxon *sultia* or Old High German *sulza,* meaning "salt" or "brine"

senna plant with yellow flowers, often used as medicine

Louis Pasteur French chemist (1822–1895) who discovered the process of heating liquids to kill bacteria; hence the verb "to pasteurize"

Analyze and Interpret

1. With a partner, locate within the story the sentence "I shall never see this again," and discuss in what ways it conveys the conflicting emotions of Annie John as she prepares to leave Antigua. Work with your partner to find specific examples that reinforce your ideas. Each of you can then use your shared ideas as the basis for the first draft of a short essay on this topic. Edit and proofread each other's drafts before writing a final copy.

2. As Annie walks to the jetty, various places along the way evoke memories for her. Working in a small group, make a map or a diorama of the walk to the jetty. Indicate and label all the places referred to in the story. Explain, in a paragraph under your map, the effect the setting has had on the story and its main character. Display the finished visuals in the classroom.

3. Imagine that you are about to leave your home. Draw up a personal list of things "I shall never see again." Separate your list into those things that you will be happy to leave and those that you will miss. Share and discuss your list with a partner. Then reflect in your journal about how easy or difficult it was to create your list, and whether any of the items on your list surprised you.

More to Explore

Themes: Self, Childhood, Adolescence, Family, Caribbean, Journeys

Elements: anecdote, description, first-person point of view, setting, simile, voice

The Charmer

Budge Wilson

A Young Man, 1959, Gerald Scott

CONTEXT Budge Wilson came to the craft of writing in 1984 after a successful career as an art teacher and illustrator. Since then, her work as a writer has won her numerous awards in Canada. Wilson was born in Halifax in 1927. A great deal of her fiction is set in the Nova Scotian landscape of her birth, the province where she has spent much of her life. The focus of this story is not setting, however, but the voice of the narrator as she comes to learn the truth about her brother. To what extent can people be naïve about the faults of those they love? Do you think that making sense of the past genuinely helps us solve the problems of the present? ■

I am thirty-three years old now, and I no longer wake up each morning with a hard lump of anger pressing against my chest.

It seems I've come full circle. Way back when I was a little girl, I was not angry at all, not ever. Like everyone else, I was too charmed to be irritated. But perhaps *charmed* is too mild a term. At that age, I felt something more intense. I was bewitched. My heart lay open and eager. He could take it and me, and do with us what he would. When he beckoned, I followed, at top speed. If he said, "How be you wash my bike for me, Posie, love?" I would be halfway to the kitchen for bucket and rags before he stopped speaking. When he said, "Go get my baseball, kid," I ran and got it. "Thanks, Posie," he'd say, grabbing the ball and disappearing to the park.

My name is not Posie. It's Winnifred. Winnifred means *friend of peace*. Later I would have a grim laugh or two about that. He always called me Posie when he wanted me to do something for him, or when he wished to make it clear to me that I had measured up. It was payment for good behaviour, and an insurance policy for future services. Collect my baseball and you will get your reward—my flashing Colgate smile and your pet name. He was my brother.

His name was Zachary, and he was eleven years older than I was. Wouldn't you know they'd call him Zachary and me Winnifred? Zachary has such an exotic ring to it, and when all his friends took to calling him Zack, it was like he was a movie star or a TV hero or something. It has always seemed to me that the most compellingly male, the most electric, movie and rock stars have short names. I watch a lot of late-night movies on the tube, and I should know. Clark Gable, John Wayne, Kirk Douglas, Steve McQueen. And nearer to the present day, Mick Jagger, John Lennon, Burt Reynolds. Take Tyrone Power, now. A lot of women have admired Tyrone Power. But to my way of thinking, he was as flimsy, as pretty, as his name.

But Winnifred. Winnifred is on a par with Edna, Maud, Ernestine— terrible names, all of them. It's true that, for a while, I thought Winnifred might be special. In Sunday School, we sang a hymn that went,

"Winnie cometh, Winnie cometh,
To make up His jewels…"

The hymns were thrown onto a screen, in huge block letters, and at first I was too young to read the words. What delicious prestige to be that Winnie whom everyone was singing about! Placed in a hymn and written on the wall for all to see. Chosen to inherit His jewels—rubies, diamonds, opals. Then, of course, I learned to read, and found out the truth.

"When He cometh, when He cometh,
To make up His jewels…"

And I realized I'd be precious lucky to be even one of those jewels. Besides, I wasn't really Winnie, anyway. I was Winnifred. Don't ask me why, but I just wasn't the kind of kid who ended up with a nickname. So you can imagine the effect that *Posie* had upon my spirit. As early as three years old, I knew that a posie was a bouquet of flowers.

I was Zachary's willing slave. Slavery, in fact, was in vogue in our house. Mom would make a chocolate layer cake for the church bazaar and leave it on the kitchen table with a sign beside it: FOR CHURCH BAZAAR. DEATH TO ANYONE WHO TOUCHES IT. Chances are she'd come home from town, two hours before the bazaar, to find a large wedge cut out of the side, crumbs all over the floor, and the sign turned upside down. Then Zack would arrive just as she was tying on her apron to make another cake. Brown from the sun, black curls glistening from the Municipal Pool, he would enter the kitchen, dancing a little jig on the doormat. Then his mouth would go all mock-sad and quivering at the corners. "My mother, my queen!" he might say. "How could someone with any taste buds at all ignore the creation of so great a cook? The master cook of the whole of this city!" Then he would give her one of his special bear hugs. Or he might get down on one or even both of his knees. "Forgive me, duchess," he would say, and then unbutton his shirt, laying bare his marvellous brown chest. "For the knife," he would continue. "For death."

Then my mother would laugh, we'd *all* laugh, and Mom would mix up the batter for the new cake, a smile playing upon her lips. "Go ahead!" she'd say, with a fake sigh. "Have another piece. You certainly are the limit!"

My two little sisters and I would stand there grinning, while Zack sat down and ate half the cake. Then the three of us would wash up the old baking dishes and the new baking dishes and his plate and fork and glass. And sweep up his crumbs. Before he left, he would probably bow once more to Mom, and say, "Thank you, my angel." She'd put her head on one side, with that adoring look of hers, and say, "Be off with you! You're a real devil!"

Which, of course, he was. But anyone who knows anything about devils knows that they're fallen angels, and can often fool you for a very long time. We studied a chunk of *Paradise Lost* in grade thirteen. Milton's Satan certainly had a lot more going for him than the angels who hovered over the garden, exuding piety.

Even Dad took a long time to wake up. You wouldn't think a fourteen- or sixteen-year-old boy could hoodwink a father, but he could, he could. Zack lied over trifles, and periodically stole money out of wallets that were left lying around. He started smoking at thirteen, and was into the liquor cabinet by fourteen. At sixteen, he smashed up our car one night after a poker party. Once he dumped Dad's red tool box, tools and all, in the river, during one of his rages. The tool box seemed to bother Dad even more than the car. But afterwards, Zack delivered apologies that would have brought tears to a preacher's eyes. That kind of dramatic repentance has a lot more clout than simple, everyday good behaviour, and he really knew how to bring it off. Zack'd been in Sunday School himself long enough to be able to quote from the parable of the prodigal son on appropriate occasions, and the first twenty-two or so times he did it, he really convinced us when he said he was "no longer worthy to be called thy son." The part about making him "one of thy hired servants" always left Mom in tatters. Later on, Dad would just leave the room and go out to his work shed and sit and rock and rock in that old chair of his.

People probably thought we were deficient in brain power to be taken in by such cheap tricks. But just try putting yourself in our shoes. He was the only son, the only brother, the oldest child. He was intelligent and fun, and knew how to bring laughter out of a stone. He was surrounded by a bevy of admirers; everywhere he went, he trailed friends. He was athletic, won races, amassed trophies. He got lead parts in school plays. He won class elections. And he was beautiful. His face was rugged and laughing; his body was muscular and golden, even in January. He moved with the grace of a tiger. He dazzled. He shone.

By the time I was thirteen, Zachary's halo was dimming, but I still adored him. He was twenty-four years old, still living at home, still gorging chocolate cakes, still borrowing the car. He needed money for his girlfriends and his liquor and his poker, and home was a cheap place to live. Cranky and delightful, moody and captivating, he still played the hero's role in our house.

Then Lizzie got sick. She wasn't just sick. She had leukemia, and every one of us knew she was going to die. She was the youngest, the quiet one, the gentle one. She idolized Zack even more than the rest of us, because she was only seven, too young to see any of his flaws. He was her knight in shining armour, and she was forever looking for him to ride by her hospital room. "Why doesn't Zack come?" she kept asking.

Once, just once, he arrived with a comic book for her, and her white little face lit up so brightly that you could almost convince yourself she might get better. He even made her laugh, and all our hearts went out to him in gratitude. But apart from that, he never once visited her during those last awful six weeks in the hospital. He was on a bender, day after day, or else he'd sober up enough to spend a week trying to win liquor money at the poker table.

One day Mom had the courage to plead, "Please, Zachary. Go see Lizzie. She keeps asking for you. *Please.*"

He sat down and put his head in his hands, saying, "I'm in terrible pain, Mom. I'm so frustrated. I can't help her." To which she replied, stiffly, "You can. You can visit her."

Then he rose from his chair and threw a book on the floor. "Quit nagging!" he snapped at her. "I'm too old for that. I can handle my own life. I sure don't need you telling me what to do."

Zack lost a job and got another, and then lost that one, too. He was forever taking off in the family car, just as we were needing it to go to the hospital. But Mom forgave him everything. "He's sensitive," she'd say. "He's taking it hard, and he can't face what's ahead for us. This is his way of coping. He's probably suffering more than the rest of us." Suffering my foot, I thought.

That last day, the day that Lizzie died, we were all at the hospital, watching it happen—all, of course, except Zachary. Then the doctor came in and said that no, Lizzie was not asleep, she was gone.

There she was, our Lizzie, tubes coming out of her all over, machines ticking away, and nothing left of her at all. I tasted the words *Gone, Dead,* and they had no meaning at all for me. The closest I could come to a definition was *not there anymore*, but this was too large a concept for me to absorb. I could only understand the rage and the grief.

When we all walked out into the corridor, there he was. Zachary. Sobered up, dressed in the outfit Lizzie loved best—the tight jeans and the Mickey Mouse shirt. He stood there, grinning, his arms overflowing with gifts—a hot-pink teddy bear, a bundle of comics, a Barbie Doll in a bride's dress, a bouquet of five orchids. "*Hail the conquering hero comes.*" Orchids, I thought. *Orchids.* I fled to the hospital washroom and was sick into the basin.

Four days later, he came home. He'd been heaven knows where in the meantime. He had on a clean white shirt, open at the neck, and his jeans. It was summer, and his skin was shining, gleaming tanned, so that you knew he'd been at the beach a lot—at Fox Point, maybe. He'd never looked more handsome. Scudding across my mind came the thought: if you can't find a job, Zack, try Simpson's catalogue, Men's Clothing division. You're a photographer's dream.

He sat down, head in his hands, of course. Don't move, I silently begged my mother. *Don't move.* But she went over and sat down beside him, placing her hand on his back. Then the words came, but no tears, "I'm sorry, I'm sorry," and variations on the theme. Start the prodigal son bit, I thought, and I'll kill you. But he did. "…no longer worthy to be called thy son," he finished, his voice suitably uneven. "Make me as one of thy hired servants." My mother was kissing his hand and crying. I had a terrible desire to spit. Truly, it was all I could do to keep from standing up and spitting on the carpet beside his feet. My father did stand up.

"I agree one hundred per cent," he said, his voice soft and even, although the tears continued to roll down his cheeks. I marvelled that he could do this. If I were to try to speak while crying, I know that my speech would be peppered with hiccups and sobs, that my mouth and face would be all distorted and screwed up. "About being unworthy, I mean," he went on. "Over the years, I been wondering what to do about forgiveness. The Bible is all the time saying we should forgive one another. Your mother seems to be able to do it real easy, but I find I'm no good at it at all anymore. Seems to me that even the good Lord Himself wouldn't have wanted us all to just lie down and be walked over."

Zachary was looking at the floor now, his hands clasped tight, eyes dry and moving to and fro, as if he were memorizing the pattern on the carpet.

"You got two choices, my boy," said Dad, his words still firm and quiet. "You can stick around and be just what you suggest. You can be one of our hired servants. I should've taken you up on that offer fourteen years back. You can bake cakes and scrub floors and wash dishes and mow lawns, and clean all your junk out of the garage. You can paint the house. You can iron your own shirts. You can spread your charm around on a daily basis, instead of saving it all up for special occasions."

There was a long silence. I think my dad was breathing hard, or doing whatever it took to get himself under control. Then he started to speak again.

"I hate to bring more misery into this house than we already got, Zachary, but I'm giving you another choice." He looked hard at Zack, and then he shouted, so that we all jumped, "*Look at me, Zachary!*"

Zachary looked. He looked up from under his lids, and I thought, He looks shifty. He doesn't even seem handsome to me anymore. Cheap, I thought. Cheap and shifty.

"If you don't like the first choice," said my dad, his voice quiet again, "there's always the second. You can clear out."

Nothing happened for maybe as long as five minutes. Zack was staring at the carpet again, eyes darting. Nobody spoke. You could hear Mom sniffling, and from time to time a chainsaw somewhere down the street whined, but mostly the silence was pressing in on our ears. I sat there counting the roses on the wallpaper so that I wouldn't be tempted to look at him.

Then Zachary rose and went upstairs to his room. We could hear him moving around up there, shuffling about, opening drawers, thunking things down. In about half an hour, he came down the stairs carrying two suitcases. He stopped at the bottom, and then went over and touched Mom on the shoulder. That's all. Then he just walked out the door without a word.

I grieved a lot after Zack left. I grieved for Lizzie, of course, and I grieved for Mom and Dad, and I grieved for my own broken dream. Zack rode the rails out west, and we heard from Alberta friends that he drifted around the small towns out there, trying this job and that, playing poker, drinking cheap wine, always moving on.

I think Mom saw the justice of what Dad did, but I don't think she ever forgave him for it. She'd lost two children in one week, and that's too many for someone who only had four to begin with. She became senile early—in her late sixties—and she used to sit all day in a chair in the nursing home common room, with her head drooped over on one side. Her hair was straight and ragged, her eyes open but empty. Her hands would often be clasped in front of her, knuckles white, and she'd be forever and ever muttering, "All my fault. All my fault." Occasionally she'd yell, in a loud, tormented voice, "Too late! Too late!" Then the nurses would come running and give her a sedative.

I'm married now, with three children, and I hardly ever think about Zachary anymore. I'm too busy with my own life and my own family. My children are all girls, two of them quiet and sweet, but the third like quicksilver, pretty and mischievous, quick-tempered and full of laughter. Our home revolves around the magic of her personality. She sheds light upon all of us. Her name is Stephanie, and she's thirteen years old. The other day she became angry at something one of her friends had done. Racing into our kitchen, she pushed her two sisters aside, and, seizing a jug of milk from the table, hurled it at the opposite wall. There was a loud crash as crockery and milk flew in all directions. Then Stephanie sat down on a chair with her head in her hands. Finally she lifted up her beautiful little face, framed by her long golden hair, and looked at me from under a fringe of curling lashes.

"Mom, darling," she began, voice faltering, "I'm so sorry. I'm *so, so, so* sorry. I've gone and done it again." She rose from the chair with a familiar grace, and passed her hand across her forehead, sighing. "I can't imagine what came over me. Mom, sweetie. Can you forgive me? I could die with being sorry. Tell me what I can do to make me feel good again. I feel so terrible, I can hardly bear it."

I looked at her, listened to her, and longed to hold her in my arms and whisper consolation. But somewhere in the back of my head, I could hear a voice shouting, "Too late! Too late!"

I looked at Stephanie again. Despite her agonized expression, her eyes were dry. I recalled that these temper tantrums had been pretty frequent of late, as had the moving speeches of regret and apology. I had put it all down to the shifting hormones of a thirteen-year-old, and assumed that the violence would eventually pass. I looked now at the wall. The pitcher had cracked the paint where it hit, and there was milk from one side of the room to the other. The floor was a lake, and drops of sticky milk were clinging to windows, curtains, kitchen utensils, dishes.

Something else. My two other daughters were watching this drama from the doorway. They were looking at Stephanie and they were studying me. I did not like the look on their faces.

"Stephanie," I began, keeping my voice friendly, "if you want to do something to feel better, I'll help you." She smiled a grateful smile. "I'm going over to Mrs. Vincent's," I continued, "to help her hang her new living room curtains. While I'm gone, I want you to clean up the milk and the broken china. There are rags and a pail at the bottom of the basement stairs. The curtains will have to be washed by hand, because the red dye runs. They're cotton, so you'll have to iron them. You'll also find milk on all those utensils in their container, as well as on most surfaces. Those china jugs are on sale at Zellers, and I'd like you to take that allowance money you've been saving and go out to the Mall for a new one. We have some green paint left over from when we painted the kitchen, so fortunately you won't have to buy that. You can repaint that wall on Saturday morning. I'll see that no one gets in your way."

Then, lest I weaken at the sight of her stricken face, I tiptoed through the milk and walked out of the kitchen.

"Thank you, Zachary," I said.

"*What?*" she said.

"Nothing important," I lied, and shut the door behind me.

NOTES

Tyrone Power a star of the early Hollywood studios, Power (1914–1958) was less an actor than a dashing movie idol

Paradise Lost an epic poem written by the English writer John Milton in 1667, in which he depicts the fall of humanity from God's grace

piety devotion or reverence, usually in a religious sense

prodigal extravagant or wasteful. The "prodigal son" refers to the biblical story about a son who takes his inheritance and leaves his family; when he returns, he is embraced by his father

bevy a group or flock

ANALYZE AND INTERPRET

1. Work with a partner. One of you will list words from the story that the narrator as an adult uses to describe Zack. The other will list words the narrator uses when she is a child to describe him. Use jot notes in your list to provide specific examples from the story that justify her descriptions. Present your lists to each other one word at a time, speaking alternately and explaining your interpretation of each word. Then make and display an illustrative diagram of Zack that reveals the two perceptions of him.

2. Work in a group of three to produce three monologues at the time of Lizzie's death, in the voices of the mother, the father, and Zack. Read the monologues aloud in your group, and comment on the differing perspectives and how they aid in the comprehension of the situation as a whole.

3. Using the library or on-line resources, find and read the parable of the prodigal son. In point form, note the similarities and differences between this selection and the parable. With specific references to both texts, write a short formal essay examining how an understanding of the parable enriches the story. With a partner, edit and proofread each other's essays and produce a final, polished copy.

MORE TO EXPLORE

Themes: Childhood, Adolescence, Personal Challenges, Loss, Family, Canada, Moral Questions, Crisis

Elements: allegory, allusion, characterization, climax, conflict, first-person point of view, flashback, parable

To Da-duh,
in Memoriam

Paule Marshall

CONTEXT Paule Marshall, originally named Valenza Pauline Burke, was born in Brooklyn, New York, in 1929, soon after her parents had emigrated from Barbados. As a child, she listened intently to her mother's Caribbean-born friends, who would gather daily in the kitchen to talk and tell stories. Marshall began writing fiction when illness forced her to take a break from college. Much of her writing, such as her first novel, *Brown Girl, Brownstones* (1959), is autobiographical, focusing on the theme of a young black woman's search for identity. Another theme she explores in her fiction is the need for African-Americans to reclaim their African heritage. Her third novel, *Praisesong for the Widow* (1983), established her reputation as a major writer, and she has won many awards, including the MacArthur Prize Fellowship. How might Marshall's childhood experiences have inspired this story? In what ways do the grandmother and granddaughter bridge the enormous gap between them? What makes the ending of the story so appropriate and yet so moving? ∎

"…Oh Nana! All of you is not involved in this evil business Death,
Nor all of us in life."

—From "At My Grandmother's Grave," by Lebert Bethune

I did not see her at first I remember. For not only was it dark inside the crowded disembarkation shed in spite of the daylight flooding in from outside, but standing there waiting for her with my mother and sister I was still somewhat blinded by the sheen of tropical sunlight on the water of the bay which we had just crossed in the landing boat, leaving behind us the ship that had brought us from New York lying in the offing. Besides, being only nine years of age at the time and knowing nothing of islands I was busy attending to the alien sights and sounds of Barbados, the unfamiliar smells.

I did not see her, but I was alerted to her approach by my mother's hand which suddenly tightened around mine, and looking up I traced her gaze through the gloom in the shed until I finally made out the small, purposeful, painfully erect figure of the old woman headed our way.

Her face was drowned in the shadow of an ugly rolled-brim brown felt hat, but the details of her slight body and of the struggle taking place within it were clear enough—an intense, unrelenting struggle between her back which was beginning to bend ever so slightly under the weight of her eighty-odd years and the rest of her which sought to deny those years and hold that back straight, keep it in line. Moving swiftly toward us (so swiftly it seemed she did not intend stopping when she reached us, but would sweep past us out the doorway which opened onto the sea and like Christ walk upon the water!), she was caught between the sunlight at her end of the building and the darkness inside—and for a moment she appeared to contain them both: the light in the long severe old-fashioned white dress she wore which brought the sense of a past that was still alive into our bustling present and in the snatch of white at her eye; the darkness in her black high-top shoes and in her face which was visible now that she was closer.

It was as stark and fleshless as a death mask, that face. The maggots might have already done their work, leaving only the framework of bone beneath the ruined skin and deep wells at the temple and jaw. But her eyes were alive, unnervingly so for one so old, with a sharp light that flicked out of the dim clouded depths like a lizard's tongue to snap up all in her view. Those eyes betrayed a child's curiosity about the world, and I wondered vaguely seeing them, and seeing the way the bodice of her ancient dress had collapsed in on her flat chest (what had happened to her breasts?), whether she might not be some kind of child at the same time that she was a woman, with fourteen children, my mother included, to prove it. Perhaps she was both, both child and woman, darkness and light, past and present, life and death—all the opposites contained and reconciled in her.

"My Da-duh," my mother said formally and stepped forward. The name sounded like thunder fading softly in the distance.

"Child," Da-duh said, and her tone, her quick scrutiny of my mother, the brief embrace in which they appeared to shy from each other rather than touch, wiped out the fifteen years my mother had been away and restored the old relationship. My mother, who was such a formidable figure in my eyes, had suddenly with a word been reduced to my status.

"Yes, God is good," Da-duh said with a nod that was like a tic. "He has spared me to see my child again."

We were led forward then, apologetically because not only did Da-duh prefer boys but she also liked her grandchildren to be "white," that is, fair-skinned; and we had, I was to discover, a number of cousins, the outside children of white estate managers and the like, who qualified. We, though, were as black as she.

My sister being the oldest was presented first. "This one takes after the father," my mother said and waited to be reproved.

Frowning, Da-duh tilted my sister's face toward the light. But her frown soon gave way to a grudging smile, for my sister with her large mild eyes and little broad winged nose, with our father's high-cheeked Barbadian cast to her face, was pretty.

"She's goin' be lucky," Da-duh said and patted her once on the cheek. "Any girl child that takes after the father does be lucky."

She turned then to me. But oddly enough she did not touch me. Instead leaning close, she peered hard at me, and then quickly drew back. I thought I saw her hand start up as though to shield her eyes. It was almost as if she saw not only me, a thin truculent child who it was said took after no one but myself, but something in me which for some reason she found disturbing, even threatening. We looked silently at each other for a long time there in the noisy shed, our gaze locked. She was the first to look away.

"But Adry," she said to my mother and her laugh was cracked, thin, apprehensive. "Where did you get this one here with this fierce look?"

"We don't know where she came out of, my Da-duh," my mother said, laughing also. Even I smiled to myself. After all I had won the encounter. Da-duh had recognized my small strength—and this was all I ever asked of the adults in my life then.

"Come, soul," Da-duh said and took my hand. "You must be one of those New York terrors you hear so much about."

She led us, me at her side and my sister and mother behind, out of the shed into the sunlight that was like a bright driving summer rain and over to a group of people clustered beside a decrepit lorry. They were our relatives, most of them from St. Andrews although Da-duh herself lived in St. Thomas, the women wearing bright print dresses, the colours vivid against their darkness, the men rusty black suits that encased them like straitjackets. Da-duh, holding fast to my hand, became my anchor as they circled round us like a nervous sea, exclaiming, touching us with their calloused hands, embracing us shyly. They laughed in awed bursts: "But look Adry got big-big children!" / "And see the nice things they wearing, wrist watch and all!" / "I tell you, Adry has done all right for sheself in New York...."

Da-duh, ashamed at their wonder, embarrassed for them, admonished them the while. "But oh Christ," she said, "why you all got to get on like you never saw people from 'Away' before? You would think New York is the only place in the world to hear wunna. That's why I don't like to go anyplace with you St. Andrews people, you know. You all ain't been colonized."

We were in the back of the lorry finally, packed in among the barrels of ham, flour, cornmeal and rice and the trunks of clothes that my mother had brought as gifts. We made our way slowly through Bridgetown's clogged streets, part of a funereal procession of cars and open-sided buses, bicycles, and donkey carts. The dim little limestone shops and offices along the way marched with us, at the same mournful pace, toward the same grave ceremony—as did the people, the women balancing huge baskets on top their heads as if they were no more than hats they wore to shade them from the sun. Looking over the edge of the lorry I watched as their feet slurred the dust. I listened, and their voices, raw and loud and dissonant in the heat, seemed to be grappling with each other high overhead.

Da-duh sat on a trunk in our midst, a monarch amid her court. She still held my hand, but it was different now. I had suddenly become her anchor, for I felt her fear of the lorry with its asthmatic motor (a fear and distrust, I later learned, she held of all machines) beating like a pulse in her rough palm.

As soon as we left Bridgetown behind though, she relaxed, and while the others around us talked she gazed at the canes standing tall on either side of the winding marl road. "C'dear," she said softly to herself after a time. "The canes this side are pretty enough."

They were too much for me. I thought of them as giant weeds

that had overrun the island, leaving scarcely any room for the small tottering houses of sunbleached pine we passed or the people, dark streaks as our lorry hurtled by. I suddenly feared that we were journeying, unaware that we were, toward some dangerous place where the canes, grown as high and thick as a forest, would close in on us and run us through with their stiletto blades. I longed then for the familiar: for the street in Brooklyn where I lived, for my father who had refused to accompany us ("Blowing out good money on foolishness," he had said of the trip), for a game of tag with my friends under the chestnut tree outside our aging brownstone house.

"Yes, but wait till you see St. Thomas canes," Da-duh was saying to me. "They's canes father, bo," she gave a proud arrogant nod. "Tomorrow, God willing, I goin' take you out in the ground and show them to you."

True to her word Da-duh took me with her the following day out into the ground. It was a fairly large plot adjoining her weathered board and shingle house and consisting of a small orchard, a good-sized canepiece and behind the canes, where the land sloped abruptly down, a gully. She had purchased it with Panama money sent her by her eldest son, my uncle Joseph, who had died working on the canal. We entered the ground along a trail no wider than her body and as devious and complex as her reasons for showing me her land. Da-duh strode briskly ahead, her slight form filled out this morning by the layers of sacking petticoats she wore under her working dress to protect her against the damp. A fresh white cloth, elaborately arranged around her head, added to her height, and lent her a vain, almost roguish air.

Her pace slowed once we reached the orchard, and glancing back at me occasionally over her shoulder, she pointed out the various trees.

"This here is a breadfruit," she said. "That one yonder is a papaw. Here's a guava. This is a mango. I know you don't have anything like these in New York. Here's a sugar apple." (The fruit looked more like artichokes than apples to me.) "This one bears limes...." She went on for some time, intoning the names of the trees as though they were those of her gods. Finally, turning to me, she said, "I know you don't have anything this nice where you come from." Then, as I hesitated:

"I said I know you don't have anything this nice where you come from...."

"No," I said and my world did seem suddenly lacking.

Da-duh nodded and passed on. The orchard ended and we were on the narrow cart road that led through the canepiece, the canes clashing like swords above my cowering head. Again she turned and her thin muscular arms spread wide, her dim gaze embracing the small field of canes, she said—and her voice almost broke under the weight of her pride, "Tell me, have you got anything like these in that place where you were born?"

"No."

"I din' think so. I bet you don't even know that these canes here and the sugar you eat is one and the same thing. That they does throw the canes into some damn machine at the factory and squeeze out all the little life in them to make sugar for you all so in New York to eat. I bet you don't know that."

"I've got two cavities and I'm not allowed to eat a lot of sugar."

But Da-duh didn't hear me. She had turned with an inexplicably angry motion and was making her way rapidly out of the canes and down the slope at the edge of the field which led to the gully below. Following her apprehensively down the incline amid a stand of banana plants whose leaves flapped like elephants' ears in the wind, I found myself in the middle of a small tropical wood—a place dense and damp and gloomy and tremulous with the fitful play of light and shadow as the leaves high above moved against the sun that was almost hidden from view. It was a violent place, the tangled foliage fighting each other for a chance at the sunlight, the branches of the trees locked in what seemed an immemorial struggle, one both necessary and inevitable. But despite the violence, it was pleasant, almost peaceful in the gully, and beneath the thick undergrowth the earth smelled like spring.

This time Da-duh didn't even bother to ask her usual question, but simply turned and waited for me to speak.

"No," I said, my head bowed. "We don't have anything like this in New York."

"Ah," she cried, her triumph complete. "I din' think so. Why, I've heard that's a place where you can walk till you drop and never see a tree."

"We've got a chestnut tree in front of our house," I said.

"Does it bear?" She waited. "I ask you, does it bear?"

"Not anymore," I muttered. "It used to, but not anymore."

She gave the nod that was like a nervous twitch. "You see," she said. "Nothing can bear there." Then, secure behind her scorn, she added, "But tell me, what's this snow like that you hear so much about?"

Looking up, I studied her closely, sensing my chance, and then I told her, describing at length and with as much drama as I could summon not only what snow in the city was like, but what it would be like here, in her perennial summer kingdom.

"…And you see all these trees you got here," I said. "Well, they'd be bare. No leaves, no fruit, nothing. They'd be covered in snow. You see your canes. They'd be buried under tons of snow. The snow would be higher than your head, higher than your house, and you wouldn't be able to come down into this here gully because it would be snowed under…."

She searched my face for the lie, still scornful, but intrigued. "What a thing, huh?" she said finally, whispering it softly to herself.

"And when it snows, you couldn't dress like you are now," I said. "Oh no, you'd freeze to death. You'd have to wear a hat and gloves and galoshes and ear muffs so your ears wouldn't freeze and drop off, and a heavy coat. I've got a Shirley Temple coat with fur on the collar. I can dance. You wanna see?"

Before she could answer I began, with a dance called the Truck which was popular back then in the 1930s. My right forefinger waving, I trucked around the nearby trees and around Da-duh's awed and rigid form. After the Truck, I did the Suzy-Q, my lean hips swishing, my sneakers sidling zigzag over the ground. "I can sing," I said and did so, starting with "I'm Gonna Sit Right Down and Write Myself a Letter," then without pausing, "Tea for Two," and ending with "I Found a Million Dollar Baby in a Five and Ten Cent Store."

For long moments afterwards Da-duh stared at me as if I were a creature from Mars, an emissary from some world she did not know but which intrigued her and whose power she both felt and feared. Yet something about my performance must have pleased her, because bending down she slowly lifted her long skirt and then, one by one, the layers of petticoats until she came to a drawstring purse dangling at the end of a long strip of cloth tied round her waist. Opening the purse, she handed me a penny. "Here," she said half-smiling against her will. "Take this to buy yourself a sweet at the shop up the road. There's nothing to be done with you, soul."

From then on, whenever I wasn't taken to visit relatives, I accompanied Da-duh out into the ground, and alone with her amid the canes or down in the gully I told her about New York. It always began with some slighting remark on her part: "I know they don't have anything this nice where you come from," or "Tell me, I hear those foolish people in New York does do such and such...." But as I answered, re-creating my towering world of steel and concrete and machines for her, building the city out of words, I would feel her give way. I came to know the signs of her surrender: the total stillness that would come over her little hard dry form, the probing gaze that like a surgeon's knife sought to cut through my skull to get at the images there, to see if I were lying; above all, her fear, a fear nameless and profound, the same one I had felt beating in the palm of her hand that day in the lorry.

Over the weeks I told her about refrigerators, radios, gas stoves, elevators, trolley cars, wringer washing machines, movies, airplanes, the cyclone at Coney Island, subways, toasters, electric lights: "At night, see, all you have to do is flip this little switch on the wall and all the lights in the house go on. Just like that. Like magic. It's like turning on the sun at night."

"But tell me," she said to me once with a faint mocking smile, "do the white people have all these things too or it's only the people looking like us?"

I laughed. "What d'ya mean," I said. "The white people have even better." Then: "I beat up a white girl in my class last term."

"Beating up white people!" Her tone was incredulous.

"How you mean!" I said, using an expression of hers. "She called me a name."

For some reason Da-duh could not quite get over this and repeated in the same hushed, shocked voice, "Beating up white people now! Oh, the lord, the world's changing up so I can scarce recognize it anymore."

One morning toward the end of our stay, Da-duh led me into a part of the gully that we had never visited before, an area darker and more thickly overgrown than the rest, almost impenetrable. There in a small clearing amid the dense bush, she stopped before an incredibly tall royal palm which rose cleanly out of the ground, and drawing the eye up with it, soared high above the trees around it into the sky. It appeared to be touching the blue dome of sky, to be flaunting its dark crown of fronds right in the blinding white face of the late morning sun.

Da-duh watched me a long time before she spoke, and then she said very quietly, "All right, now, tell me if you've got anything this tall in that place you're from."

I almost wished, seeing her face, that I could have said no. "Yes," I said. "We've got buildings hundreds of times this tall in New York. There's one called the Empire State Building that's the tallest in the world. My class visited it last year and I went all the way to the top. It's got over a hundred floors. I can't describe how tall it is. Wait a minute. What's the name of that hill I went to visit the other day, where they have the police station?"

"You mean Bissex?"

"Yes, Bissex. Well, the Empire State Building is way taller than that."

"You're lying now!" she shouted, trembling with rage. Her hand lifted to strike me.

"No, I'm not," I said. "It really is, if you don't believe me I'll send you a picture postcard of it soon as I get back home so you can see for yourself. But it's way taller than Bissex."

All the fight went out of her at that. The hand poised to strike me fell limp to her side, and as she stared at me, seeing not me, but the building that was taller than the highest hill she knew, the small stubborn light in her eyes (it was the same amber as the flame in the kerosene lamp she lit at dusk) began to fail. Finally, with a vague gesture that even in the midst of her defeat still tried to dismiss me and my world, she turned and started back through the gully, walking slowly, her steps groping and uncertain, as if she were suddenly no longer sure of the way, while I followed triumphant yet strangely saddened behind.

The next morning I found her dressed for our morning walk but stretched out on the Berbice chair in the tiny drawing room where she sometimes napped during the afternoon heat, her face turned to the window beside her. She appeared thinner and suddenly indescribably old.

"My Da-duh," I said.

"Yes, nuh," she said. Her voice was listless and the face she slowly turned my way was, now that I think back on it, like a Benin mask, the features drawn and almost distorted by an ancient abstract sorrow.

"Don't you feel well?" I asked.

"Girl, I don't know."

"My Da-duh, I goin' boil you some bush tea," my aunt, Da-duh's youngest child, who lived with her, called from the shed roof kitchen.

"Who tell you I need bush tea?" she cried, her voice assuming for a moment its old authority. "You can't even rest nowadays without some malicious person looking for you to be dead. Come girl," she motioned me to a place beside her on the old-fashioned lounge chair, "give us a tune."

I sang for her until breakfast at eleven, all my brash irreverent Tin Pan Alley songs, and then just before noon we went out into the ground. But it was a short, dispirited walk. Da-duh didn't even notice that the mangoes were beginning to ripen and would have to be picked before the village boys got to them. And when she paused occasionally and looked out across the canes or up at her trees it wasn't as if she were seeing them but something else. Some huge, monolithic shape had imposed itself, it seemed, between her and the land, obstructing her vision. Returning to the house she slept the entire afternoon on the Berbice chair.

She remained like this until we left, languishing away the mornings on the chair at the window gazing out at the land as if it were already doomed; then, at noon, taking the brief stroll with me through the ground during which she seldom spoke, and afterwards returning home to sleep till almost dusk sometimes.

On the day of our departure she put on the austere, ankle length white dress, the black shoes and brown felt hat (her town clothes she called them), but she did not go with us to town. She saw us off on the road outside her house and in the midst of my mother's tearful protracted farewell, she leaned down and whispered in my ear, "Girl, you're not to forget now to send me the picture of that building, you hear."

By the time I mailed her the large coloured picture postcard of the Empire State Building she was dead. She died during the famous '37 strike which began shortly after we left. On the day of her death, England sent planes flying low over the island in a show of force—so low, according to my aunt's letter, that the downdraft from them shook the ripened mangoes from the trees in Da-duh's orchard. Frightened, everyone in the village fled into the canes. Except Da-duh. She remained in the house at the window so my aunt said, watching as the planes came swooping and screaming like monstrous birds down over the village, over her house, rattling her trees and flattening the young canes in her field. It must have seemed to her lying there that they did not intend pulling out of their dive, but like the hard-back beetles which hurled themselves with suicidal force against the walls of the house at night, those menacing silver shapes would hurl themselves in an ecstasy of self-immolation onto the land, destroying it utterly.

NOTES

wunna all of you, "you-all"

marl a mixture of clays, carbons, and shells used as a fertilizer

"They's canes father, bo" "Those canes are tremendous, boy!"

Shirley Temple child star (born 1928) and top box office draw in American movies from 1936–1938, famous for her golden ringlets

the cyclone at Coney Island a ride at a Long Island, N.Y., amusement park

Berbice chair a reclining armchair designed for the verandahs of grand plantation houses; after the Berbice River, which flows through eastern Guyana and was named after the Dutch colony of Berbice

Benin masks elaborately carved, ceremonial masks from the kingdom of Benin in West Africa (now part of Nigeria), which flourished from the fifteenth to seventeenth centuries

Tin Pan Alley legendary district of New York; the original centre of the pop music industry, due to the supposed resemblance of pop music to the clanging of pots and pans

ANALYZE AND INTERPRET

1. In fiction, authors often reveal characterization through the following methods: appearance, dialogue, actions, and interactions. Reread the story, making jot notes as you learn about Da-duh through each of these methods.

2. One description of Da-duh in the story is the following: "Perhaps she was…both child and woman, darkness and light, past and present, life and death—all the opposites contained and reconciled in her." Explain how each of these pairs of opposites, or paradoxes, applies to her. Work with a partner to list any other opposites you can think of that exemplify either Da-duh or other aspects of the story. Share your list with the class, explaining your ideas. Decide which pair of opposites best expresses the theme of the story.

3. Imagine the scene on the last day of Da-duh's life, as she watches the British planes. Write a monologue expressing what she might be thinking. What connection might she make between the planes and the conversations she had with her granddaughter? Why didn't she leave the village with the others? How does she feel about her fate? Present your monologue to your classmates, and invite them to ask questions regarding your interpretation of Da-duh's character. Then incorporate ideas raised in the discussion into a revision of your monologue.

MORE TO EXPLORE

Themes: Childhood, Self and Culture, Loss, Family, Urban Life, Caribbean, Journeys, Eye on the Past

Elements: description, dialect, hyperbole, metaphor, paradox, plot, simile, symbol

A Handful of Dates

Tayeb Salih

TRANSLATED BY DENYS JOHNSON-DAVIES

CONTEXT Tayeb Salih was born in 1929 in the northeast African nation of Sudan. Salih descended from farmers and Islamic teachers, who influenced his early plan to work in agriculture and education. He studied at Khartoum University in the United Arab Emirates, and in England, where he later became the head of the BBC's drama programming in Arabic. His first book, *The Wedding of Zein and Other Stories*, was published when he was thirty-nine years old, and has been translated into many languages. Today Salih is considered a leading Arabic writer. This story has a powerful dénouement, in which the narrator's feelings change suddenly and dramatically. Why does he react so strongly to his grandfather's actions? What feelings does the end of the story evoke in you? ■

I must have been very young at the time. While I don't remember exactly how old I was, I do remember that when people saw me with my grandfather, they would pat me on the head and give my cheek a pinch—things they didn't do to my grandfather. The strange thing was that I never used to go out with my father, rather it was my grandfather who would take me with him wherever he went, except for the mornings when I would go to the mosque to learn the Koran. The mosque, the river and the fields—these were the landmarks in our life. While most of the children of my age grumbled at having to go to the mosque to learn the Koran, I used to love it. The reason was, no doubt, that I was quick at learning by heart and the Sheikh always asked me to stand up and recite the Chapter of the Merciful whenever we had visitors, who would pat me on my head and cheek just as people did when they saw me with my grandfather.

Yes, I used to love the mosque, and I loved the river too. Directly after we finished our Koran reading in the morning I would throw down my wooden slate and dart off, quick as a genie, to my mother, hurriedly swallow down my breakfast, and run off for a plunge in the river. When tired of swimming about, I would sit on the bank and gaze at the strip of water that wound away eastwards and hid behind a thick wood of acacia trees. I loved to give rein to my imagination and picture to myself a tribe of giants living behind that wood, a people tall and thin with white beards and sharp noses, like my grandfather. Before my grandfather ever replied to my many questions he would rub the tip of his nose with his forefinger. As for his beard, it was soft and luxuriant and as white as cotton-wood—never in my life have I seen anything of purer whiteness or greater beauty. My grandfather must also have been extremely tall, for I never saw anyone in the whole area address him without having to look up at him, nor did I see him enter a house without having to bend so low that I was put in mind of the way the river wound round behind the wood of acacia trees. I loved him and would imagine myself, when I grew to be a man, tall and slender like him, walking along with great strides.

I believe I was his favourite grandchild: no wonder, for my cousins were a stupid bunch and I—so they say—was an intelligent child. I used to know when my grandfather wanted me to laugh, when to be silent; also I would remember the times for his prayers and would bring him his prayer-rug and fill the ewer for his ablutions without his having to ask me. When he had nothing else to do, he enjoyed listening to me reciting to him from the Koran in a lilting voice, and I could tell from his face that he was moved.

One day I asked him about our neighbour Masood. I said to my grandfather: "I fancy you don't like our neighbour Masood?"

To which he answered, having rubbed the tip of his nose: "He's an indolent man and I don't like such people."

I said to him: "What's an indolent man?"

My grandfather lowered his head for a moment, then looking across at the wide expanse of field, he said: "Do you see it stretching out from the edge of the desert up to the Nile bank? A hundred feddans. Do you see all those date palms? And those trees—sant, acacia, and sayal? All this fell into Masood's lap, was inherited by him from his father."

Taking advantage of the silence that had descended upon my grandfather, I turned my gaze from him to the vast area defined by his words. "I don't care," I told myself, "who owns those date palms, those trees or this black, cracked earth—all I know is that it's the arena for my dreams and my playground."

My grandfather then continued: "Yes, my boy, forty years ago all this belonged to Masood—two-thirds of it is now mine."

This was news to me for I had imagined that the land had belonged to my grandfather ever since God's Creation.

"I didn't own a single feddan when I first set foot in this village. Masood was then the owner of all these riches. The position has changed now, though, and I think that before Allah calls to him, I shall have bought the remaining third as well."

I do not know why it was I felt fear at my grandfather's words— and pity for our neighbour Masood. How I wished my grandfather wouldn't do what he'd said! I remembered Masood's singing, his beautiful voice and powerful laugh that resembled the gurgling of water. My grandfather never used to laugh.

I asked my grandfather why Masood had sold his land.

"Women," and from the way my grandfather pronounced the word, I felt that "women" was something terrible. "Masood, my boy, was a much-married man. Each time he married, he sold me a feddan or two." I made the quick calculation that Masood must have married some ninety women. Then I remembered his three wives, his shabby appearance, his lame donkey and its dilapidated saddle, his djellaba with the torn sleeves. I had all but rid my mind of the thoughts that jostled in it when I saw the man approaching us, and my grandfather and I exchanged glances.

"We'll be harvesting the dates today," said Masood. "Don't you want to be there?"

I felt, though, that he did not really want my grandfather to attend. My grandfather, however, jumped to his feet and I saw that his eyes sparkled momentarily with an intense brightness. He pulled me by the hand and we went off to the harvesting of Masood's dates.

Someone brought my grandfather a stool covered with an ox-hide, while I remained standing. There was a vast number of people there, but though I knew them all, I found myself, for some reason, watching Masood: aloof from the great gathering of people he stood as though it were no concern of his, despite the fact that the date palms to be harvested were his own. Sometimes his attention would be caught by the sound of a huge clump of dates crashing down from on high. Once he shouted up at the boy perched on the very summit of the date palm who had begun hacking at a clump with his long, sharp sickle: "Be careful you don't cut the heart of the palm."

No one paid any attention to what he said and the boy seated at the very summit of the date palm continued, quickly and energetically, to work away at the branch with his sickle till the clump of dates began to drop like something descending from the heavens.

I, however, had begun to think about Masood's phrase "the heart of the palm." I pictured the palm tree as something with feeling, something possessed of a heart that throbbed. I remembered Masood's remark to me when he had once seen me playing about with the branch of a young palm tree: "Palm trees, my boy, like humans, experience joy and suffering." And I had felt an inward and unreasoned embarrassment.

When I again looked at the expanse of ground stretching before me, I saw my young companions swarming like ants around the trunks of the palm trees, gathering up dates and eating most of them. The dates were collected into high mounds. I saw people coming along and weighing them into measuring bins and pouring them into sacks, of which I counted thirty. The crowd of people broke up, except for Hussein the merchant, Mousa the owner of the field next to ours on the east, and two men I'd never seen before.

I heard a low whistling sound and saw that my grandfather had fallen asleep. Then I noticed that Masood had not changed his stance, except that he had placed a stalk in his mouth and was munching at it like someone surfeited with food who doesn't know what to do with the mouthful he still has.

Suddenly my grandfather woke up, jumped to his feet and walked toward the sacks of dates. He was followed by Hussein the merchant, Mousa the owner of the field next to ours, and the two strangers. I glanced at Masood and saw that he was making his way toward us with extreme slowness, like a man who wants to retreat, but whose feet insist on going forward. They formed a circle round the sacks of dates and began examining them, some taking a date or two to eat. My grandfather gave me a fistful, which I began munching. I saw Masood filling the palms of both hands with dates and bringing them up close to his nose, then returning them.

Then I saw them dividing up the sacks between them. Hussein the merchant took ten; each of the strangers took five. Mousa the owner of the field next to ours on the eastern side took five, and my grandfather took five. Understanding nothing, I looked at Masood and saw that his eyes were darting about to left and right like two mice that have lost their way home.

"You're still fifty pounds in debt to me," said my grandfather to Masood. "We'll talk about it later."

Hussein called his assistants and they brought along donkeys, the two strangers produced camels, and the sacks of dates were loaded on to them. One of the donkeys let out a braying which set the camels frothing at the mouth and complaining noisily. I felt myself drawing close to Masood, felt my hand stretch out toward him as though I wanted to touch the hem of his garment. I heard him make a noise in his throat like the rasping of a lamb being slaughtered. For some unknown reason, I experienced a sharp sensation of pain in my chest.

I ran off into the distance. Hearing my grandfather call after me, I hesitated a little, then continued on my way. I felt at that moment that I hated him. Quickening my pace, it was as though I carried within me a secret I wanted to rid myself of. I reached the river bank near the bend it made behind the wood of acacia trees. Then, without knowing why, I put my finger into my throat and spewed up the dates I'd eaten.

NOTES

Koran the sacred text of Islam understood to contain the revelations made by Allah to Mohammed

acacia a family of tropical trees, many of which produce gums that have a variety of uses

ewer a large, wide-mouthed pitcher or jug

ablutions a washing or cleansing of the body, especially connected with religious practice

indolent lazy; wishing to avoid activity or exertion

surfeited fed to fullness or to excess

ANALYZE AND INTERPRET

1. In a group of three, you will produce three diary entries. Placing yourselves in the story just after the date-picking, one of you will write as the narrator, the second as the grandfather, and the third as Masood. Share the diary entries within your group, and comment on ways they help you to understand the story.

2. Write a short story from the first-person point of view that includes the following elements: **a)** a young person, **b)** his or her elder, **c)** a seemingly trivial but significant event, **d)** a changed perspective, **e)** a symbolic action. Read your stories aloud in a group of four or five, and provide each other with positive critical feedback.

3. The author, Tayeb Salih, has developed the physical and social setting of this story in great detail. Isolate 10 specific features of the setting and indicate in writing how each adds to your comprehension of the selection and the effectiveness of the story. Share your analysis with a partner, and together brainstorm the changes needed to move the story into a different geographic location, such as Canada.

MORE TO EXPLORE

Themes: Self, Childhood, Family, Rural Life, Africa, Moral Questions

Elements: characterization, conflict, dénouement, narration, parable, personification, setting, simile

Companions Past
and Present

Daphne Odjig

1983, acrylic on canvas, 61.0 × 50.8 cm

- Describe feelings and make predictions in writing.
- Analyze the visual elements of a painting.
- Work with others to research and explain an artist's style.

CONTEXT Born in 1919 on the Wikwemikong Indian Reserve on Manitoulin Island, Ontario, artist Daphne Odjig is the daughter of an Odawa father and an English mother. Her mother died when she was very young, and she was raised by her English grandmother. As a result, she lost sight of her First Nations identity for many years. Living in Toronto and British Columbia, Odjig studied the European masters. In the 1960s, a move to Manitoba stimulated her rediscovery of her Ojibwa and Potawatomi roots. Odjig's exploration of Aboriginal mythology led to powerful paintings in bold acrylic colours, and by the 1970s her work had received international exposure. In 1976, she returned to British Columbia, where her art entered a more personal phase. Odjig's style, which includes rhythmic lines and circular motifs, is based on an abstracted human form. Her monumental mural for the Museum of Civilization in Ottawa (1978) concentrates on her past experiences and dreams, while her more recent paintings, done in softer oil pastels, reflect the gentle browns and greens of the forests in British Columbia. In *Companions Past and Present*, what do you think is happening in the picture? Which elements represent the past, and which the present? ■

ANALYZE AND INTERPRET

1. In a journal entry, describe ways in which you feel connected to past and present generations of your family. Include how important these family ties are to you now and how you think they will change as you grow older.

2. In a group, discuss how Odjig has created a particular mood in this painting by a careful combination of visual elements, such as "colour value" (lightness and darkness). How is repetition used to highlight the atmosphere and theme of the work?

3. Working in a small group, use the Internet and print resources to compile a collection of images by another Aboriginal artist. Make a display of the images that focuses on one aspect of the artist's work, such as the subject matter, medium, use of colour, or style. Annotate the images you have found with paragraphs that explain features of the aspect you have chosen.

MORE TO EXPLORE

Themes: Self and Culture, Family, Friends, Role Models, Nature, Aboriginal Cultures, Canada

Elements: comparison, mood, setting, symbol, tone, visual composition, visual scale

Love Must Not Be Forgotten

Zhang Jie
TRANSLATED BY GLADYS YANG

LEARNING FOCUS

- Use a graphic organizer to prepare information for writing.
- Analyze and use a voice and style appropriate to the diary form.
- Research and explain the effect of cultural and historical values on the meaning of texts.

CONTEXT Zhang Jie is one of China's most popular—and controversial—writers. Born in Beijing in 1937, she trained as an economist and worked for the Chinese government for many years. Much of her writing reflects her first-hand experience of China's "Cultural Revolution." Proclaimed by Mao Zedong in 1966, it was a decade-long array of sanctions imposed by the government on the political, social, economic, and cultural lives of Chinese citizens as a means of creating a perfect Socialist society. Many people were persecuted during this often violent upheaval that split families and destroyed institutions. Zhang Jie published her first story at the age of forty, and went on to write scripts for the Beijing Film Studio. In 1981 her first novel, *Leaden Wings*, brought her international attention with its satire of government bureaucracy and traditional Chinese attitudes toward marriage. Zhang Jie's short-story collection, *Love Must Not Be Forgotten*, was published in English in 1986. Some of the stories were hailed as China's first contribution to feminist fiction. What part does the Cultural Revolution play in this story? What is the narrator's vision of the ideal marriage of the future? ■

I am thirty, the same age as our People's Republic. For a republic thirty is still young. But a girl of thirty is virtually on the shelf.

Actually, I have a bona fide suitor. Have you seen the Greek sculptor Myron's Discobolus? Qiao Lin is the image of that discus thrower. Even the padded clothes he wears in winter fail to hide his fine physique. Bronzed, with clear-cut features, a broad forehead, and large eyes, his appearance alone attracts most girls to him.

But I can't make up my mind to marry him. I'm not clear what attracts me to him, or him to me.

I know people are gossiping behind my back: "Who does she think she is, to be so choosy?"

To them, I'm a nobody playing hard to get. They take offence at such preposterous behaviour.

Of course, I shouldn't be captious. In a society where commercial production still exists, marriage like most other transactions is still a form of barter.

I have known Qiao Lin for nearly two years, yet still cannot fathom whether he keeps so quiet from aversion to talking or from having nothing to say. When, by way of a small intelligence test, I demand his opinion of this or that, he says "good" or "bad" like a child in kindergarten.

Once I asked, "Qiao Lin, why do you love me?" He thought the question over seriously for what seemed an age. I could see from his normally smooth but now wrinkled forehead that the little grey cells in his handsome head were hard at work cogitating. I felt ashamed to have put him on the spot.

Finally he raised his clear childlike eyes to tell me, "Because you're good!"

Loneliness flooded my heart. "Thank you, Qiao Lin!" I couldn't help wondering, if we were to marry, whether we could discharge our duties to each other as husband and wife. Maybe, because law and morality would have bound us together. But how tragic simply to comply with law and morality! Was there no stronger bond to link us?

When such thoughts cross my mind I have the strange sensation that instead of being a girl contemplating marriage I am an elderly social scientist.

Perhaps I worry too much. We can live like most married couples, bringing up children together, strictly true to each other according to the law…. Although living in the seventies of the twentieth century, people still consider marriage the way they did millennia ago, as a means of continuing the race, a form of barter, or a business transaction in which love and marriage can be separated. As this is the common practice, why shouldn't we follow suit?

But I still can't make up my mind. As a child, I remember, I often cried all night for no rhyme or reason, unable to sleep and disturbing the whole household. My old nurse, a shrewd though uneducated woman, said an ill wind had blown through my ear. I think this judgment showed prescience, because I still have that old weakness. I upset myself over things which really present no problem, upsetting other people at the same time. One's nature is hard to change.

I think of my mother too. If she were alive, what would she say about my attitude to Qiao Lin and my uncertainty about marrying him?

My thoughts constantly turn to her, not because she was such a strict mother that her ghost is still watching over me since her death. No, she was not just my mother but my closest friend. I loved her so much that the thought of her leaving me makes my heart ache.

She never lectured me, just told me quietly in her deep, unwomanly voice about her successes and failures, so that I could learn from her experience. She had evidently not had many successes—her life was full of failures.

During her last days she followed me with her fine, expressive eyes, as if wondering how I would manage on my own and as if she had some important advice for me but hesitated to give it. She must have been worried by my naïveté and sloppy ways. She suddenly blurted out, "Shanshan, if you aren't sure what you want, don't rush into marriage—better live on your own!"

Other people might think this strange advice from a mother to her daughter, but to me it embodied her bitter experience. I don't think she underestimated me or my knowledge of life. She loved me and didn't want me to be unhappy.

"I don't want to marry, Mum!" I said, not out of bashfulness or a show of coyness. I can't think why a girl should pretend to be coy. She had long since taught me about things not generally mentioned to girls.

"If you meet the right man, then marry him. Only if he's right for you!"

"I'm afraid no such man exists!"

"That's not true. But it's hard. The world is so vast, I'm afraid you may never meet him." Whether I married or not was not what concerned her, but the quality of the marriage.

"Haven't you managed fine without a husband?"

"Who says so?"

"I think you've done fine."

"I had no choice…." She broke off, lost in thought, her face wistful. Her wistful lined face reminded me of a withered flower I had pressed in a book.

"Why did you have no choice?"

"You ask too many questions," she parried, not ashamed to confide in me but afraid that I might reach the wrong conclusion. Besides, everyone treasures a secret to carry to the grave. Feeling a bit put out, I demanded bluntly, "Didn't you love my dad?"

"No, I never loved him."

"Did he love you?"

"No, he didn't."

"Then why get married?"

She paused, searching for the right words to explain this mystery, then answered bitterly, "When you're young you don't always know what you're looking for, what you need, and people may talk you into getting married. As you grow older and more experienced you find out your true needs. By then, though, you've done many foolish things for which you could kick yourself. You'd give anything to be able to make a fresh start and live more wisely. Those content with their lot will always be happy, they say, but I shall never enjoy that happiness." She added self-mockingly, "A wretched idealist, that's all I am."

Did I take after her? Did we both have genes which attracted ill winds?

"Why don't you marry again?"

"I'm afraid I'm still not sure what I really want." She was obviously unwilling to tell me the truth.

I cannot remember my father. He and Mother split up when I was very small. I just recall her telling me sheepishly that he was a fine handsome fellow. I could see she was ashamed of having judged by appearances and made a futile choice. She told me, "When I can't sleep at night, I force myself to sober up by recalling all those stupid blunders I made. Of course it's so distasteful that I often hide my face in the sheet for shame, as if there were eyes watching me in the dark. But distasteful as it is, I take some pleasure in this form of atonement."

I was really sorry that she hadn't remarried. She was such a fascinating character, if she'd married a man she loved, what a happy household ours would surely have been. Though not beautiful, she had the simple charm of an ink landscape. She was a fine writer too. Another author who knew her well used to say teasingly, "Just reading your works is enough to make anyone love you!"

She would retort, "If he knew that the object of his affection was a white-haired old crone, that would frighten him away."

At her age, she must have known what she really wanted, so this was obviously an evasion. I say this because she had quirks which puzzled me.

For instance, whenever she left Beijing on a trip, she always took with her one of the twenty-seven volumes of Chekhov's stories published between 1950 and 1955. She also warned me, "Don't touch these books. If you want to read Chekhov, read that set I bought you." There was no need to caution me. Having a set of my own why should I touch hers? Besides, she'd told me this over and over again. Still she was on her guard. She seemed bewitched by those books.

So we had two sets of Chekhov's stories at home. Not just because we loved Chekhov, but to parry other people like me who loved Chekhov. Whenever anyone asked to borrow a volume, she would lend one of mine. Once, in her absence, a close friend took a volume from her set. When she found out she was frantic, and at once took a volume of mine to exchange for it.

Ever since I can remember, those books were on her bookcase. Although I admire Chekhov as a great writer, I was puzzled by the way she never tired of reading him. Why, for over twenty years, had she had to read him every single day?

Sometimes, when tired of writing, she poured herself a cup of strong tea and sat down in front of the bookcase, staring raptly at that set of books. If I went into her room then it flustered her, and she either spilt her tea or blushed like a girl discovered with her lover.

I wondered: Has she fallen in love with Chekhov? She might have if he'd still been alive.

When her mind was wandering just before her death, her last words to me were: "That set...." She hadn't the strength to give it its complete title. But I knew what she meant. "And my diary…'Love Must Not Be Forgotten'…. Cremate them with me."

I carried out her last instruction regarding the works of Chekhov, but couldn't bring myself to destroy her diary. I thought, if it could be published, it would surely prove the most moving thing she had written. But naturally publication was out of the question.

At first I imagined the entries were raw material she had jotted down. They read neither like stories, essays, a diary, or letters. But after reading the whole I formed a hazy impression, helped out by my imperfect memory. Thinking it over, I finally realized that this was no lifeless manuscript I was holding, but an anguished, loving heart. For over twenty years one man had occupied her heart, but he was not for her. She used these diaries as a substitute for him, a means of pouring out her feelings to him, day after day, year after year.

No wonder she had never considered any eligible proposals, had turned a deaf ear to idle talk whether well-meant or malicious. Her heart was already full, to the exclusion of anybody else. "No lake can compare with the ocean, no cloud with those on Mount Wu." Remembering those lines I often reflected sadly that few people in real life could love like this. No one would love me like this.

I learned that toward the end of the thirties, when this man was doing underground work for the Party in Shanghai, an old worker had given his life to cover him, leaving behind a helpless wife and daughter. Out of a sense of duty, of gratitude to the dead and deep class feeling, he had unhesitatingly married the girl. When he saw the endless troubles caused by "love" of couples who had married for "love," he may have thought, "Thank Heaven, though I didn't marry for love, we get on well, able to help each other." For years, as man and wife they lived through hard times.

He must have been my mother's colleague. Had I ever met him? He couldn't have visited our home. Who was he?

In the spring of 1962, Mother took me to a concert. We went on foot, the theatre being quite near.

A black limousine pulled up silently by the pavement. Out stepped an elderly man with white hair in a black serge tunic-suit. What a striking shock of white hair! Strict, scrupulous, distinguished, transparently honest—that was my impression of him. The cold glint of his flashing eyes reminded me of lightning or swordplay. Only ardent love for a woman really deserving his love could fill cold eyes like those with tenderness.

He walked up to Mother and said, "How are you, Comrade Zhong Yu? It's been a long time."

"How are you!" Mother's hand holding mine suddenly turned icy cold and trembled a little.

They stood face to face without looking at each other, each appearing upset, even stern. Mother fixed her eyes on the trees by the roadside, not yet in leaf. He looked at me. "Such a big girl already. Good, fine—you take after your mother."

Instead of shaking hands with Mother he shook hands with me. His hand was as icy as hers and trembling a little. As if transmitting an electric current, I felt a sudden shock. Snatching my hand away I cried, "There's nothing good about that!"

"Why not?" he asked with a surprised expression grown-ups always have when children speak out frankly.

I glanced at Mother's face. I did take after her, to my disappointment. "Because she's not beautiful!"

He laughed, then said teasingly, "Too bad that there should be a child who doesn't find her own mother beautiful. Do you remember in '53, when your mum was transferred to Beijing, she came to our ministry to report for duty? She left you outside on the verandah, but like a monkey you climbed all the stairs, peeped through the cracks in doors, and caught your finger in the door of my office. You sobbed so bitterly that I carried you off to find her."

"I don't remember that." I was annoyed at his harking back to a time when I was still in open-seat pants.

"Ah, we old people have better memories." He turned abruptly and remarked to Mother, "I've read that last story of yours. Frankly speaking, there's something not quite right about it. You shouldn't have condemned the heroine…. There's nothing wrong with falling in love, as long as you don't spoil someone else's life…. In fact, the hero might have loved her too. Only for the sake of a third person's happiness, they had to renounce their love…."

A policeman came over to where the car was parked and ordered the driver to move on. When the driver made some excuse, the old man looked round. After a hasty "Goodbye" he strode to the car and told the policeman, "Sorry. It's not his fault, it's mine...."

I found it amusing watching this old cadre listening respectfully to the policeman's strictures. When I turned to Mother with a mischievous smile, she looked as upset as a first-form primary schoolchild standing forlornly in front of the stern headmistress. Anyone would have thought she was the one being lectured by the policeman.

The car drove off, leaving a puff of smoke. Very soon even this smoke vanished with the wind, as if nothing at all had happened. But the incident stuck in my mind.

Analyzing it now, he must have been the man whose strength of character won Mother's heart. That strength came from his firm political convictions, his narrow escapes from death in the Revolution, his active brain, his drive at work, his well-cultivated mind. Besides, strange to say, he and Mother both liked the oboe. Yes, she must have worshipped him. She once told me that unless she worshipped a man, she couldn't love him even for one day.

But I could not tell whether he loved her or not. If not, why was there this entry in her diary?

> "This is far too fine a present. But how did you know
> that Chekhov's my favourite writer?"
> "You said so."
> "I don't remember that."
> "I remember. I heard you mention it when you were
> chatting with someone."

So he was the one who had given her the *Selected Stories of Chekhov.* For her that was tantamount to a love letter.

Maybe this man, who didn't believe in love, realized by the time his hair was white that in his heart was something which could be called love. By the time he no longer had the right to love, he made the tragic discovery of this love for which he would have given his life. Or did it go deeper than that?

This is all I remember about him.

How wretched Mother must have been, deprived of the man to whom she was devoted! To catch a glimpse of his car or the back of his head through its rear window, she carefully figured out which roads he would take to work and back. Whenever he made a speech, she sat at the back of the hall watching his face rendered hazy by cigarette smoke and poor lighting. Her eyes would brim with tears, but she swallowed them back. If a fit of coughing made him break off, she wondered anxiously why no one persuaded him to give up smoking. She was afraid he would get bronchitis again. Why was he so near yet so far?

He, to catch a glimpse of her, looked out of the car window every day, straining his eyes to watch the streams of cyclists, afraid that she might have an accident. On the rare evenings on which he had no meetings, he would walk by a roundabout way to our neighbourhood, to pass our compound gate. However busy, he would always make time to look in papers and journals for her work.

His duty had always been clear to him, even in the most difficult times. But now confronted by this love he became a weakling, quite helpless. At his age it was laughable. Why should life play this trick on him?

Yet when they happened to meet at work, each tried to avoid the other, hurrying off with a nod. Even so, this would make Mother blind and deaf to everything around her. If she met a colleague named Wang she would call him Guo and mutter something unintelligible.

It was a cruel ordeal for her. She wrote:

> We agreed to forget each other. But I deceived you, I have never forgotten. I don't think you've forgotten either. We're just deceiving each other, hiding our misery. I haven't deceived you deliberately, though; I did my best to carry out our agreement. I often stay far away from Beijing, hoping time and distance will help me to forget you. But on my return, as the train pulls into the station, my head reels. I stand on the platform looking round intently, as if someone were waiting for me. Of course there is no one. I realize then that I have forgotten nothing. Everything is unchanged. My love is like a tree the roots of which strike deeper year after year—I have no way to uproot it.
>
> At the end of every day, I feel as if I've forgotten something important. I may wake with a start from my dreams wondering what has happened. But nothing has

happened. Nothing. Then it comes home to me that you are missing! So everything seems lacking, incomplete, and there is nothing to fill up the blank. We are nearing the ends of our lives, why should we be carried away by emotion like children? Why should life submit people to such ordeals, then unfold before you your lifelong dream? Because I started off blindly I took the wrong turning, and now there are insuperable obstacles between me and my dream.

Yes, Mother never let me go to the station to meet her when she came back from a trip, preferring to stand alone on the platform and imagine that he had met her. Poor Mother with her greying hair was as infatuated as a girl.

Not much space in the diary was devoted to their romance. Most entries dealt with trivia: Why one of her articles had not come off; her fear that she had no real talent; the excellent play she missed by mistaking the time on the ticket; the drenching she got by going out for a stroll without her umbrella. In spirit they were together day and night, like a devoted married couple. In fact, they spent no more than twenty-four hours together in all. Yet in that time they experienced deeper happiness than some people in a whole lifetime. Shakespeare makes Juliet say, "I cannot sum up half my sum of wealth." And probably that is how Mother felt.

He must have been killed in the Cultural Revolution. Perhaps because of the conditions then, that section of the diary is ambiguous and obscure. Mother had been so fiercely attacked for her writing, it amazed me that she went on keeping a diary. From some veiled allusions I gathered that he had queried the theories advanced by that "theoretician" then at the height of favour, and had told someone, "This is sheer Rightist talk." It was clear from the tear-stained pages of Mother's diary that he had been harshly denounced; but the steadfast old man never knuckled under to the authorities. His last words were, "When I go to meet Marx, I shall go on fighting my case!"

That must have been in the winter of 1969, because that was when Mother's hair turned white overnight, though she was not yet fifty. And she put on a black arm-band. Her position then was extremely difficult.

She was criticized for wearing this old-style mourning, and ordered to say for whom she was in mourning.

"For whom are you wearing that, Mum?" I asked anxiously.

"For my lover." Not to frighten me she explained, "Someone you never knew."

"Shall I put one on too?" She patted my cheeks, as she had when I was a child. It was years since she had shown me such affection. I often felt that as she aged, especially during these last years of persecution, all tenderness had left her, or was concealed in her heart, so that she seemed like a man.

She smiled sadly and said, "No, you needn't wear one."

Her eyes were as dry as if she had no more tears to shed. I longed to comfort her or do something to please her. But she said, "Off you go."

I felt an inexplicable dread, as if dear Mother had already half left me. I blurted out, "Mum!"

Quick to sense my desolation, she said gently, "Don't be afraid. Off you go. Leave me alone for a little." I was right. She wrote:

> You have gone. Half my soul seems to have taken flight with you.
>
> I had no means of knowing what had become of you, much less of seeing you for the last time. I had no right to ask either, not being your wife or friend.... So we are torn apart. If only I could have borne that inhuman treatment for you, so that you could have lived on! You should have lived to see your name cleared and take up your work again, for the sake of those who loved you. I knew you could not be a counter-revolutionary. You were one of the finest men killed. That's why I love you—I am not afraid now to avow it.
>
> Snow is whirling down. Could God be using this whiteness to cover up your blood and the scandal of your murder?
>
> I have never set store by my life. But now I keep wondering whether anything I say or do would make you contract your shaggy eyebrows in a frown. I must live a worthwhile life like you, and do some honest work for our country. Things can't go on like this—those criminals will get what's coming to them.
>
> I used to walk alone along that small asphalt road, the only place where we once walked together, hearing my footsteps in the silent night.... I always paced to and fro and lingered

there, but never as wretchedly as now. Then, though you were not beside me, I knew you were still in this world and felt that you were keeping me company. Now I can hardly believe that you have gone.

At the end of the road I would retrace my steps, then walk along it again.

Rounding the fence I always looked back, as if you were still standing there waving goodbye. We smiled faintly, like casual acquaintances, to conceal our undying love. That ordinary evening in early spring, a chilly wind was blowing as we walked silently away from each other. You were wheezing a little because of your chronic bronchitis. That upset me. I wanted to beg you to slow down, but somehow I couldn't. We both walked very fast, as if some important business were waiting for us. How we prized that single stroll we had together, but we were afraid we might lose control of ourselves and burst out with "I love you"—those three words which had tormented us for years. Probably no one else could believe that we never once even clasped hands!

No, Mother, I believe it. I am the only one able to see into your locked heart.

Ah, that little asphalt road, so haunted by bitter memories. We shouldn't overlook the most insignificant spots on earth. For who knows how much secret grief and joy they may hide.

No wonder that when tired of writing, she would pace slowly along that little road behind our window. Sometimes at dawn after a sleepless night, sometimes on a moonless, windy evening. Even in winter during howling gales which hurled sand and pebbles against the window pane.... I thought this was one of her eccentricities, not knowing that she had gone to meet him in spirit.

She liked to stand by the window too, staring at the small asphalt road. Once I thought from her expression that one of our closest friends must be coming to call. I hurried to the window. It was a late autumn evening. The cold wind was stripping dead leaves from the trees and blowing them down the small empty road.

She went on pouring out her heart to him in her diary as she had when he was alive. Right up to the day when the pen slipped from her fingers. Her last message was:

I am a materialist, yet I wish there were a Heaven. For then, I know, I would find you there waiting for me. I am going there to join you, to be together for eternity. We need never be parted again or keep at a distance for fear of spoiling someone else's life. Wait for me, dearest, I am coming—

I do not know how Mother, on her deathbed, could still love so ardently with all her heart. To me it seemed not love but a form of madness, a passion stronger than death. If undying love really exists, she reached its extreme. She obviously died happy, because she had known true love. She had no regrets.

Now these old people's ashes have mingled with the elements. But I know that, no matter what form they may take, they still love each other. Though not bound together by earthly laws or morality, though they never once clasped hands, each possessed the other completely. Nothing could part them. Centuries to come, if one white cloud trails another, two grasses grow side by side, one wave splashes another, a breeze follows another...believe me, that will be them.

Each time I read that diary "Love Must Not Be Forgotten" I cannot hold back my tears. I often weep bitterly, as if I myself experienced their ill-fated love. If not a tragedy it was too laughable. No matter how beautiful or moving I find it, I have no wish to follow suit!

Thomas Hardy wrote that "the call seldom produces the comer, the man to love rarely coincides with the hour for loving." I cannot censure them from conventional moral standards. What I deplore is that they did not wait for a "missing counterpart" to call them.

If everyone could wait, instead of rushing into marriage, how many tragedies could be averted!

When we reach communism, will there still be cases of marriage without love? Maybe, because since the world is so vast, two kindred spirits may be unable to answer each other's call. But how tragic! However, by that time, there may be ways to escape such tragedies.

Why should I split hairs?

Perhaps after all we are responsible for these tragedies. Who knows? Maybe we should take the responsibility for the old ideas handed down from the past. Because if someone never marries, that is a challenge to these ideas. You will be called neurotic, accused of having guilty secrets or having made political mistakes. You may be regarded as an eccentric who looks down on ordinary people, not respecting age-old customs—a heretic. In short they will trump up endless vulgar and futile charges to ruin your reputation. Then you have to knuckle under to those ideas and marry willy-nilly. But once you put the chains of a loveless marriage around your neck, you will suffer for it for the rest of your life.

I long to shout: "Mind your own business! Let us wait patiently for our counterparts. Even waiting in vain is better than willy-nilly marriage. To live single is not such a fearful disaster. I believe it may be a sign of a step forward in culture, education, and the quality of life."

NOTES

Myron's Discobolus Greek sculpture from the fifth century BCE of an Olympic athlete in action

captious hard to please

prescience foresight; knowledge of the future

parried responded, countered; the terms "thrust" and "parry" are used in the sport of fencing

Chekhov Anton Chekhov (1860–1904), a Russian author famous for his short stories and plays such as *The Cherry Orchard*

cadre civil servant

the Revolution the triumph of communism with the founding of the People's Republic of China under Mao Zedong in 1949

Thomas Hardy English poet and novelist (1840–1928) who created the rich fictional world of "Wessex," and whose writing reveals a pessimistic view of life

ANALYZE AND INTERPRET

1. Reread the story, creating as you go a chart of pros and cons as to whether the narrator should marry Qiao Lin. Using your chart to provide details, write a letter to the narrator in which you present your advice on whether she should proceed with marrying him.

2. Much of what the narrator believes about her mother's relationship is determined by reading her mother's diary. Consider in what ways the narrator's assumptions could be problematic. Discuss with the class to what extent diaries are truthful and realistic. Then work with a partner to write a diary entry by the Comrade. Be sure to write in a style that reflects his character as it is depicted in the story.

3. Historically, the phrase "Love Must Not Be Forgotten" was the rallying cry for Chinese writers involved in the "Literature Wounded Movement," which became stronger after the death of Mao Zedong. Writers in this movement were reacting against the government's attempts to suppress personal feelings in literature. Do research into the "Literature Wounded Movement" in China in order to discover how such suppression affected the literature of the country. Write a short research report on your findings.

MORE TO EXPLORE

Themes: Childhood, Self and Culture, Loss, Family, Romance, Rebels, Asia, Eye on the Past

Elements: allusion, characterization, conflict, empathy, first-person point of view, flashback, setting, tragedy

A Television Drama

Jane Rule

LEARNING FOCUS

- Communicate orally in a small group to debate an issue.
- Select and use references to defend an interpretation.
- Create and present a storyboard for a news report based on a story you have read.

CONTEXT Born in New Jersey in 1931, Jane Rule came to Canada in 1956. She worked at various jobs, mostly to gather background material for her writing. A lecturer in English at the University of British Columbia for many years, Rule has lived on Galiano Island, British Columbia, since the mid-1970s. She began to write full-time in 1974, and her published work includes the novel *The Desert of the Heart*, which was made into a feature film in 1984. Rule's fiction often explores relationships and portrays multiple perspectives within one narrative. As the title suggests, this story deals with the medium of television. One impact of television is that people may be increasingly aware of world events while at times feeling curiously detached from events in their own lives. Can you remember the last time you "experienced" a tragedy through television? Did you feel like merely an onlooker or were you emotionally affected? ■

At one-thirty in the afternoon, Carolee Mitchell was running the vacuum cleaner, or she would have heard the first sirens and looked out. After the first, there weren't any others. The calling voices, even the number of dogs barking, could have been students on their way back to school, high-spirited in the bright, cold earliness of the year. Thinking back on the sounds, Carolee remembered a number of car doors being slammed, that swallow of air and report which made her smooth her hair automatically even if she wasn't expecting anyone. But what caught her eye finally was what always caught her eye: the flight of a bird from a treetop in the ravine out over the fringe of trees at the bottom of her steeply sloping front lawn, nearly private in the summer, exposed now to the startling activity of the street.

Three police cars were parked in front of the house, a motorcycle like a slanted stress in the middle of the intersection, half a dozen more police cars scattered up and down the two blocks. There were men in uniform up on her neighbour's terrace with rifles and field glasses. Police with dogs were crossing the empty field at the bottom of the ravine. More cars were arriving, police and reporters with cameras and sound equipment. Mingling among the uniforms and equipment were the neighbours: Mrs. Rolston from the house across the street who had obviously not taken time to put on a coat and was rubbing her arms absent-mindedly as she stood and talked, Jane Carey from next door with a scarf tied round her head and what looked like one of her son's jackets thrown over her shoulders, old Mr. Monkson, a few small children. Cars and people kept arriving. Suddenly there was a voice magnified to reach even Carolee, surprised and unbelieving behind her picture window.

"Clear the street. All householders return to or stay in your houses. Clear the street."

Mrs. Rolston considered the idea for a moment but did not go in. The others paid no attention at all. Carolee wondered if she should go out just to find out what on earth was going on. Perhaps she should telephone someone, but everyone she might phone was already in the street. Was it a gas main? Not with all those dogs. A murder? It seemed unlikely that anyone would kill anyone else on this street, where every child had his own bedroom and most men either studies or basement workshops to retreat into. In any case, it was the middle of the afternoon. Mrs. Cole had come out on her balcony with field glasses focused on the place where the dogs and police had entered the ravine. Field glasses. Where were Pete's field glasses? Carolee thought she knew, but she did not move to get them. She would not know what she was looking for in the undergrowth or the gardens.

"Clear the street. All householders return to or stay in your houses."

Police radios were now competing with each other. "Suspect last apprehended in the alley between..." "House to house search..." "Ambulance..."

If one of those policemen standing about on the street would come to search the house, Carolee could at least find out what was going on. Was that a TV crew? Dogs were barking in the ravine. Did police dogs bark? Nobody on the street seemed to be doing anything, except for the motorcycle policeman who was turning away some cars. Maybe Carolee should go empty the dishwasher and then come back. It was pointless to stand here by the window. Nothing was happening, or, if something was happening, Carolee couldn't see the point of it. She went to the window in Pete's study to see if she could discover activity on the side street. There were more policemen, and far up the block an ambulance was pulling away without a siren, its red light slowly circling. Carolee watched it until it turned the corner at the top of the hill. Then she turned back toward the sound of barking dogs and radios, but paused as she turned.

There, sitting against the curve of the laurel hedge by the lily pond, was a man, quite a young man, his head down, his left hand against his right shoulder. He was sick or hurt or dead. Or not really there at all, something Carolee's imagination had put there to explain the activity in the street, part of a collage, like an unlikely photograph in the middle of a painting. But he raised his head slightly then, and Carolee saw the blood on his jacket and trousers.

"I must call the police," she said aloud, but how could she call the police when they were already there, three of them standing not seventy feet away, just below the trees on the parking strip? She must call someone, but all the neighbours were still out of doors. And what if the police did discover him? He might be shot instead of helped. Carolee wanted to help him, whoever he was. It was such an odd way he was sitting, his legs stretched out in front of him so that he couldn't possibly have moved quickly. He might not be able to move at all. But she couldn't get to him, not without being seen. Suddenly he got to his feet, his left hand still against his right shoulder and also holding the lower part of his ducked face. He walked to the end of the curve of hedge as if it was very difficult for him to move, and then he began a stumbling run across the front lawn, through the trees, and out onto the parking strip. There he turned, hesitated, and fell on his back. Carolee had heard no shot. Now her view was blocked by a gathering of police and reporters drawn to that new centre like leaves to a central drain.

"Suspect apprehended on…"

What had he done? What had that hurt and stumbling boy done? Carolee was standing with her hand on the transistor radio before it occurred to her to turn it on.

"We interrupt this program with a news bulletin. A suspect has been apprehended on…"

He had robbed a bank, run a car into a tree, shot a policeman, been shot at.

"And now, here is our reporter on the scene."

Carolee could see the reporter quite clearly, standing in the street in front of the house, but she could hear only the radio voice, explaining what had happened.

"And now the ambulance is arriving…" as indeed it was. "The suspect, suffering from at least three wounds, who seems near death, is being lifted onto a stretcher…" This she couldn't see. It seemed to take a very long time before police cleared a path for the ambulance, again silent, its red light circling, to move slowly down the block and out of sight.

A newspaper reporter was walking up the front path, but Carolee didn't answer the door. She stood quietly away from the window and waited until he was gone. Then she went to the kitchen and began to empty the dishwasher. It was two o'clock. She turned on the radio again to listen to the regular news report. The details were the same. At three o'clock the hospital had reported that the policeman was in the operating room having a bullet removed from his right lung. At four o'clock the suspect was reported in only fair condition from wounds in the shoulder, jaw, leg and hand.

At five o'clock Pete came home, the evening paper in his hand. "Well, you've had quite a day," he said. "Are you all right?"

"Yes," Carolee said, her hands against his cold jacket, her cheek against his cold face. "Yes, I'm all right. What did the paper say?"

"It's all diagrams," he said, holding out the front page to her.

There was a map of the whole neighbourhood, a sketched aerial map, a view of the roof of their house Carolee had never had. She followed the dots and arrows to the hood of a car crumpled under a flower of foliage, on again across the ravine, up their side hill, and there was the laurel hedge and the jelly bean lily pond, but the dots didn't stop there, arced round rather and immediately down through the trees to a fallen doll, all alone, not a policeman or reporter in sight, lying there exposed to nothing but a God's-eye view.

"You must have seen him," Pete said.

"Yes," Carolee agreed, still looking down on the rooftops of all her neighbours' houses.

"Did it frighten you?" Pete asked.

"Not exactly. It was hard to believe, and everything seemed to happen so very slowly."

"Did you get a good look at him?"

"I guess not really," Carolee said. Had he sat there by the laurel hedge at all, his long, stiff legs stretched out in front of him? The map didn't show it.

"Something has got to be done about all this violence," Pete said.

His tone and the look on his face made Carolee realize that Pete had been frightened, much more frightened than she was. Those dotted lines across his front lawn, that figure alone in the landscape—Carolee felt herself shaken by a new fear, looking at what Pete had seen.

"I'll get us a drink," Pete said.

Once they sat down, Carolee tried to tell her husband what it had been like, all those women just standing out in the street. She told him about the guns and field glasses and dogs and cameras. She did not tell him about the man, hurt, by the laurel hedge.

Pete turned on the television, and they watched three minutes of fast-moving images, first the policeman lifted into an ambulance, then officers and dogs running through the field, finally glimpses of the suspect on the ground and then shifted onto a stretcher; and, while they watched, a voice told them of the robbery, the chase, the capture. Finally several people were quickly interviewed, saying such things as, "I saw him go over the fence" or "He fell practically at my feet." That was Mrs. Rolston, still rubbing her cold arms in the winter day.

"I'm glad you had the good sense to stay inside," Pete said. He was holding her hand, beginning to relax into indignation and relief.

Carolee wasn't there, nor was the man there. If she had spoken to that reporter, if she had said then, "I saw him. He was sitting by the laurel hedge," would the dots in the paper have changed? Would the cameras have climbed into their nearly exposed winter garden? Would she believe now what she couldn't quite believe even then, that she stood at that window and saw a man dying in her garden?

Now a labour union boss was talking, explaining the unfair practices of the compensation board. Nearly at once, young marines were running, firing, falling. Planes were dropping bombs. Carolee wasn't there, but it seemed real to her, terribly real, so that for a moment she forgot Pete's hand in hers, her safe house on a safe street, and was afraid.

NOTES

report in this instance, an explosive sound

ANALYZE AND INTERPRET

1. With a group, discuss the impact of witnessing violence. What are the differences between seeing an actual violent incident first-hand and watching a violent news clip on television? How does seeing a news clip of real violence differ from watching fictitious violence in a movie or television show? What views are expressed on these topics in "A Television Drama"?

2. In the role of Carolee, write the diary entry she might make on the day of the story. Share your writing with a group, and be prepared to defend your depiction of Carolee with specific references to the story.

3. With a partner, create a storyboard for a news report of the incident in the story. a) Consider what impact you want your story to have on the viewer. b) Create your storyboard by including sketches of the visual elements of your report, such as maps or diagrams, photographs, and film footage. c) Annotate your images with the words to be spoken by a newscaster or on-the-scene reporter. d) Present your storyboard to a group and invite members' comments.

MORE TO EXPLORE

Themes: Self, Urban Life, Civic Responsibility, Canada, Intrigue, Media Impact, Crisis

Elements: empathy, irony, narration, paradox, third-person point of view

The Pedestrian

Ray Bradbury

LEARNING FOCUS

- Explore how the element of setting functions in a story.
- Create a text with a specific point of view.
- Adapt a story into a screenplay.

CONTEXT Science-fiction author Ray Bradbury was born in Illinois in 1920. He and his family lived there and in Arizona before they moved to Los Angeles when he was fourteen years old. Bradbury's formal education ended with graduation from Los Angeles High School, but he continued to spend his days writing stories and his nights studying at the library. After his first story was published in 1938, he supported himself for four years by selling newspapers on Los Angeles street corners. Bradbury is the author of over thirty books, and has written for the theatre, cinema, and television. He has won an Emmy award and many literary prizes, and was nominated for an Academy Award. In 1982, Bradbury created what are known as the "interior metaphors" for Spaceship Earth in the Epcot Center at Disney World in Florida. What elements or details of this story suggest that Bradbury wrote it some time ago? Do you think it's possible for authors of science fiction to write stories that remain relevant despite changes in technology? Why or why not? ■

To enter out into that silence that was the city at eight o'clock of a misty evening in November, to put your feet upon that buckling concrete walk, to step over grassy seams and make your way, hands in pockets, through the silences, that was what Mr. Leonard Mead most dearly loved to do. He would stand upon the corner of an intersection and peer down long moonlit avenues of sidewalk in four directions, deciding which way to go, but it really made no difference; he was alone in this world of A.D. 2053, or as good as alone, and with a final decision made, a path selected, he would stride off, sending patterns of frosty air before him like the smoke of a cigar.

Sometimes he would walk for hours and miles and return only at midnight to his house. And on his way he would see the cottages and homes with their dark windows, and it was not unequal to walking through a graveyard where only the faintest glimmers of firefly light appeared in flickers behind the windows. Sudden grey phantoms seemed to manifest upon inner room walls where a curtain was still undrawn against the night, or there were whisperings and murmurs where a window in a tomb-like building was still open.

Mr. Leonard Mead would pause, cock his head, listen, look, and march on, his feet making no noise on the lumpy walk. For long ago he had wisely changed to sneakers when strolling at night, because the dogs in intermittent squads would parallel his journey with barkings if he wore hard heels, and lights might click on and faces appear and an entire street be startled by the passing of a lone figure, himself, in the early November evening.

On this particular evening he began his journey in a westerly direction, toward the hidden sea. There was a good crystal frost in the air; it cut the nose and made the lungs blaze like a Christmas tree inside; you could feel the cold light going on and off, all the branches filled with invisible snow. He listened to the faint push of his soft shoes through autumn leaves with satisfaction, and whistled a cold quiet whistle between his teeth, occasionally picking up a leaf as he passed, examining its skeletal pattern in the infrequent lamplights as he went on, smelling its rusty smell.

"Hello, in there," he whispered to every house on every side as he moved. "What's up tonight on Channel 4, Channel 7, Channel 9? Where are the cowboys rushing, and do I see the United States Cavalry over the next hill to the rescue?"

The street was silent and long and empty, with only his shadow moving like the shadow of a hawk in midcountry. If he closed his eyes and stood very still, frozen, he could imagine himself upon the centre of a plain, a wintry, windless American desert with no house in a thousand miles, and only dry river beds, the streets, for company.

"What is it now?" he asked the houses, noticing his wristwatch. "Eight-thirty p.m.? Time for a dozen assorted murders? A quiz? A revue? A comedian falling off the stage?"

Was that a murmur of laughter from within a moonwhite house? He hesitated, but went on when nothing more happened. He stumbled over a particularly uneven section of sidewalk. The cement was vanishing under flowers and grass. In ten years of walking by night or day, for thousands of miles, he had never met another person walking, not once in all that time.

He came to a cloverleaf intersection which stood silent where two main highways crossed the town. During the day it was a thunderous surge of cars, the gas stations open, a great insect rustling and a ceaseless jockeying for position as the scarab-beetles, a faint incense puttering from their exhausts, skimmed homeward to the far directions. But now these highways, too, were like streams in a dry season, all stone and bed and moon radiance.

He turned back on a side street, circling around toward his home. He was within a block of his destination when the lone car turned a corner quite suddenly and flashed a fierce white cone of light upon him. He stood entranced, not unlike a night moth, stunned by the illumination, and then drawn toward it.

A metallic voice called to him:

"Stand still. Stay where you are! Don't move!"

He halted.

"Put up your hands!"

"But—" he said.

"Your hands up! Or we'll shoot!"

The police, of course, but what a rare, incredible thing; in a city of three million, there was only *one* police car left, wasn't that correct? Ever since a year ago, 2052, the election year, the force had been cut down from three cars to one. Crime was ebbing; there was no need now for the police, save for this one lone car wandering and wandering the empty streets.

"Your name?" said the police car in a metallic whisper. He couldn't see the men in it for the bright light in his eyes.

"Leonard Mead," he said.

"Speak up!"

"Leonard Mead!"

"Business or profession?"

"I guess you'd call me a writer."

"No profession," said the police car, as if talking to itself. The light held him fixed, like a museum specimen, needle thrust through chest.

"You might say that," said Mr. Mead. He hadn't written in years.

Magazines and books didn't sell any more. Everything went on in the tomblike houses at night now, he thought, continuing his fancy. The tombs, ill-lit by television light, where the people sat like the dead, the grey or multicoloured lights touching their faces, but never really touching them.

"No profession," said the phonograph voice, hissing. "What are you doing out?"

"Walking," said Leonard Mead.

"Walking!"

"Just walking," he said simply, but his face felt cold.

"Walking, just walking, walking?"

"Yes, sir."

"Walking where? For what?"

"Walking for air. Walking to see."

"Your address!"

"Eleven South Saint James Street."

"And there is air *in* your house, you have an *air conditioner,* Mr. Mead?"

"Yes."

"And you have a viewing screen in your house to see with?"

"No."

"No?" There was a crackling quiet that in itself was an accusation.

"Are you married, Mr. Mead?"

"No."

"Not married," said the police voice behind the fiery beam. The moon was high and clear among the stars and the houses were grey and silent.

"Nobody wanted me," said Leonard Mead with a smile.

"Don't speak unless you're spoken to!"

Leonard Mead waited in the cold night.

"Just *walking,* Mr. Mead?"

"Yes."

"But you haven't explained for what purpose."

"I explained; for air, and to see, and just to walk."

"Have you done this often?"

"Every night for years."

The police car sat in the centre of the street with its radio throat faintly humming.

"Well, Mr. Mead," it said.

"Is that all?" he asked politely.

"Yes," said the voice. "Here." There was a sigh, a pop. The back door of the police car sprang wide. "Get in."

"Wait a minute. I haven't done anything!"

"Get in."

"I protest!"

"Mr. Mead."

He walked like a man suddenly drunk. As he passed the front window of the car he looked in. As he had expected there was no one in the front seat, no one in the car at all.

"Get in."

He put his hand to the door and peered into the back seat, which was a little cell, a little black jail with bars. It smelled of riveted steel. It smelled of harsh antiseptic; it smelled too clean and hard and metallic. There was nothing soft there.

"Now if you had a wife to give you an alibi," said the iron voice, "But—"

"Where are you taking me?"

The car hesitated, or rather gave a faint whirring click, as if information, somewhere, was dropping card by punch-slotted card under electric eyes. "To the Psychiatric Centre for Research on Regressive Tendencies."

He got in. The door shut with a soft thud. The police car rolled through the night avenues, flashing its dim lights ahead.

They passed one house on one street a moment later, one house in an entire city of houses that were dark, but this one particular house had all of its electric lights brightly lit, every window a loud yellow illumination, square and warm in the cool darkness.

"That's *my* house," said Leonard Mead.

No one answered him.

The car moved down the empty riverbed streets and off away, leaving the empty streets with the empty sidewalks, and no sound and no motion all the rest of the chill November night.

ANALYZE AND INTERPRET

1. Write a short essay explaining how the setting functions in the story "The Pedestrian." **a)** Use the following questions to prompt jot notes for an outline: What important background information is conveyed by the description of the setting? What aspects of the story conflict are introduced in the setting? What does the setting tell about the main character? What mood or atmosphere does the setting create? **b)** Write a first draft of your essay in which you incorporate quotations from the story to illustrate the points you make. **c)** Exchange essays with a partner to edit each other's work.

2. Write an editorial that might appear in a local newspaper, in which you comment on the arrest of Mr. Leonard Mead. What course of action will your editorial propose? Use your writing to reinforce the attitudes and values of the society in which Mead lives.

3. Work with a partner to rewrite "The Pedestrian" as a script for a short film. Use the format of the screenplay excerpt from "Sense and Sensibility" in this anthology as your model. Ask another group of students to read your script and comment on how successfully it conveys the mood of the original story.

MORE TO EXPLORE

Themes: Self and Culture, Rebels, Urban Life, Civic Responsibility, Intrigue, Moral Questions, Media Impact, Eye on the Future, Science and Technology

Elements: analogy, conflict, description, mood, motif, setting, simile, third-person point of view

The Storyteller

Saki (H.H. Munro)

Gloucester Old Spot, 1989, James Lynch

CONTEXT Saki, whose real name was Hector Hugh Munro, was born in 1870 in Burma, now known as Myanmar, and was educated in England. When Munro joined the staff of a London newspaper, he chose his pseudonym from a book called *The Rubáiyát* by Omar Khayyám, a Persian poet and astronomer. Saki wrote a series of highly popular, lightly satirical articles for the *Westminster Gazette*, and also became well known for his short stories and two novels. After enlisting in the British army at the outbreak of World War I, Saki was killed in action in France in 1916. The fiction of Saki was influenced by his childhood experiences as well as by the lives of Britain's middle and upper classes, whom he viewed with wit and sometimes biting irony. Which character in "The Storyteller" is being skewered by Saki's wit? How have manners and mores—especially those that relate to raising children—changed since Saki's time? ■

It was a hot afternoon, and the railway carriage was correspondingly sultry, and the next stop was at Templecombe, nearly an hour ahead. The occupants of the carriage were a small girl, and a smaller girl, and a small boy. An aunt belonging to the children occupied one corner seat, and the further corner seat on the opposite side was occupied by a bachelor who was a stranger to their party, but the small girls and the small boy emphatically occupied the compartment. Both the aunt and the children were conversational in a limited, persistent way, reminding one of the attentions of a housefly that refused to be discouraged. Most of the aunt's remarks seemed to begin with "Don't," and nearly all of the children's remarks began with "Why?" The bachelor said nothing out loud.

"Don't, Cyril, don't," exclaimed the aunt, as the small boy began smacking the cushions of the seat, producing a cloud of dust at each blow.

"Come and look out of the window," she added.

The child moved reluctantly to the window. "Why are those sheep being driven out of that field?" he asked.

"I expect they are being driven to another field where there is more grass," said the aunt weakly.

"But there is lots of grass in that field," protested the boy; "there's nothing else but grass there. Aunt, there's lots of grass in that field."

"Perhaps the grass in the other field is better," suggested the aunt fatuously.

"Why is it better?" came the swift, inevitable question.

"Oh, look at those cows!" exclaimed the aunt. Nearly every field along the line had contained cows or bullocks, but she spoke as though she were drawing attention to a rarity.

"Why is the grass in the other field better?" persisted Cyril.

The frown on the bachelor's face was deepening to a scowl. He was a hard, unsympathetic man, the aunt decided in her mind. She was utterly unable to come to any satisfactory decision about the grass in the other field.

The smaller girl created a diversion by beginning to recite "On the

Road to Mandalay." She only knew the first line, but she put her limited knowledge to the fullest possible use. She repeated the line over and over again in a dreamy but resolute and very audible voice; it seemed to the bachelor as though someone had had a bet with her that she could not repeat the line aloud two thousand times without stopping. Whoever it was who had made the wager was likely to lose his bet.

"Come over here and listen to a story," said the aunt, when the bachelor had looked twice at her and once at the communication cord.

The children moved listlessly toward the aunt's end of the carriage. Evidently her reputation as a storyteller did not rank high in their estimation.

In a low, confidential voice, interrupted at frequent intervals by loud, petulant questions from her listeners, she began an unenterprising and deplorably uninteresting story about a little girl who was good, and made friends with everyone on account of her goodness, and was finally saved from a mad bull by a number of rescuers who admired her moral character.

"Wouldn't they have saved her if she hadn't been good?" demanded the bigger of the small girls. It was exactly the question that the bachelor had wanted to ask.

"Well, yes," admitted the aunt lamely, "but I don't think they would have run quite so fast to her help if they had not liked her so much."

"It's the stupidest story I've ever heard," said the bigger of the small girls, with immense conviction.

"I didn't listen after the first bit, it was so stupid," said Cyril.

The smaller girl made no actual comment on the story, but she had long ago recommenced a murmured repetition of her favourite line.

"You don't seem to be a success as a storyteller," said the bachelor suddenly from his corner.

The aunt bristled in instant defence at this unexpected attack.

"It's a very difficult thing to tell stories that children can both understand and appreciate," she said stiffly.

"I don't agree with you," said the bachelor.

"Perhaps *you* would like to tell them a story," was the aunt's retort.

"Tell us a story," demanded the bigger of the small girls.

"Once upon a time," began the bachelor, "there was a little girl called Bertha, who was extraordinarily good."

The children's momentarily-aroused interest began at once to flicker; all stories seemed dreadfully alike, no matter who told them.

"She did all that she was told, she was always truthful, she kept her clothes clean, ate milk puddings as though they were jam tarts, learned her lessons perfectly, and was polite in her manners."

"Was she pretty?" asked the bigger of the small girls.

"Not as pretty as any of you," said the bachelor, "but she was horribly good."

There was a wave of reaction in favour of the story; the word horrible in connection with goodness was a novelty that commended itself. It seemed to introduce a ring of truth that was absent from the aunt's tales of infant life.

"She was so good," continued the bachelor, "that she won several medals for goodness, which she always wore, pinned on to her dress. There was a medal for obedience, another medal for punctuality, and a third for good behaviour. They were large metal medals and they clinked against one another as she walked. No other child in the town where she lived had as many as three medals, so everybody knew that she must be an extra good child."

"Horribly good," quoted Cyril.

"Everybody talked about her goodness, and the Prince of the country got to hear about it, and he said that as she was so very good she might be allowed once a week to walk in his park, which was just outside the town. It was a beautiful park, and no children were ever allowed in it, so it was a great honour for Bertha to be allowed to go there."

"Were there any sheep in the park?" demanded Cyril.

"No," said the bachelor, "there were no sheep."

"Why weren't there any sheep?" came the inevitable question arising out of that answer.

The aunt permitted herself to smile, which might almost have been described as a grin.

"There were no sheep in the park," said the bachelor, "because the Prince's mother had once had a dream that her son would either be killed by a sheep or else by a clock falling on him. For that reason the Prince never kept a sheep in his park or a clock in his palace."

The aunt suppressed a gasp of admiration.

"Was the Prince killed by a sheep or by a clock?" asked Cyril.

"He is still alive, so we can't tell whether the dream will come true," said the bachelor unconcernedly; "anyway, there were no sheep in the park, but there were lots of little pigs running all over the place."

"What colour were they?"

"Black with white faces, white with black spots, black all over, grey with white patches, and some were white all over."

The storyteller paused to let a full idea of the park's treasures sink into the children's imaginations; then he resumed:

"Bertha was rather sorry to find that there were no flowers in the park. She had promised her aunts, with tears in her eyes, that she would not pick any of the kind Prince's flowers, and she had meant to keep her promise, so of course it made her feel silly to find that there were no flowers to pick."

"Why weren't there any flowers?"

"Because the pigs had eaten them all," said the bachelor promptly. "The gardeners had told the Prince that you couldn't have pigs and flowers, so he decided to have pigs and no flowers."

There was a murmur of approval at the excellence of the Prince's decision; so many people would have decided the other way.

"There were lots of other delightful things in the park. There were ponds with gold and blue and green fish in them, and trees with beautiful parrots that said clever things at a moment's notice, and hummingbirds that hummed all the popular tunes of the day. Bertha walked up and down and enjoyed herself immensely, and thought to herself: 'If I were not so extraordinarily good I should not have been allowed to come into this beautiful park and enjoy all that there is to be seen in it,' and her three medals clinked against one another as she walked and helped to remind her how very good she really was. Just then an enormous wolf came prowling into the park to see if it could catch a fat little pig for its supper."

"What colour was it?" asked the children, amid an immediate quickening of interest.

"Mud-colour all over, with a black tongue, and pale grey eyes that gleamed with unspeakable ferocity. The first thing that it saw in the park was Bertha; her pinafore was so spotlessly white and clean that it could be seen from a great distance. Bertha saw the wolf and saw that it was stealing toward her, and she began to wish that she had never been allowed to come into the park. She ran as hard as she could, and the wolf came after her with huge leaps and bounds. She managed to reach a shrubbery of myrtle bushes and she hid herself in one of the thickest of the bushes. The wolf came sniffing among the branches, its black tongue lolling out of its mouth and its pale grey eyes glaring with rage. Bertha was terribly frightened, and thought to herself: 'If I had not been so extraordinarily good I should have been safe in the town at this moment.' However, the scent of the myrtle was so strong that the wolf could not sniff out where Bertha was hiding, and the bushes were so thick that he might have hunted about in them for a long time without catching sight of her, so he thought he might as well go off and catch a little pig instead. Bertha was trembling very much at having the wolf prowling and sniffing so near her and as she trembled the medal for obedience clinked against the medals for good conduct and punctuality. The wolf was just moving away when he heard the sound of the medals clinking and stopped to listen; they clinked again in a bush quite near him. He dashed into the bush, his pale grey eyes gleaming with ferocity and triumph, and dragged Bertha out and devoured her to the last morsel. All that was left of her were her shoes, bits of clothing, and the three medals for goodness."

"Were any of the little pigs killed?"

"No, they all escaped."

"The story began badly," said the smaller of the small girls, "but it had a beautiful ending."

"It is the most beautiful story that I ever heard," said the bigger of the small girls, with immense decision.

"It is the *only* beautiful story I have ever heard," said Cyril.

A dissentient opinion came from the aunt.

"A most improper story to tell to young children! You have undermined the effects of years of careful teaching."

"At any rate," said the bachelor, collecting his belongings preparatory to leaving the carriage, "I kept them quiet for ten minutes, which was more than you were able to do."

"Unhappy woman!" he observed to himself as he walked down the platform of Templecombe station; "for the next six months or so those children will assail her in public with demands for an improper story!"

NOTES

"On the Road to Mandalay" a poem by English poet Rudyard Kipling (1865–1936); Mandalay is a city in Burma (now Myanmar)

dissentient dissenting; not in agreement

ANALYZE AND INTERPRET

1. With your classmates, discuss the art of storytelling. Consider what characterics make a good story and a good storyteller. How do the attitudes of the aunt and the bachelor toward storytelling affect their methods? Saki's stories are often described as "witty," "whimsical," and "cynical." Which of these words do you think applies to this story? Discuss whether or not you consider Saki a good storyteller, and why. Support your response.

2. Saki wrote during the late nineteenth and early twentieth centuries. How does the author's style affect your enjoyment of the story? List examples from the story of either old-fashioned or formal diction and sentence structure. Then rephrase your examples in contemporary or informal language.

3. Work with a group of classmates to adapt "The Storyteller" as a stage play or screenplay. **a)** Study a play or screenplay to determine the conventions of the form you have chosen. **b)** As you write your first draft, keep in mind that you can invent new characters, dialogue, or short scenes in order to flesh out the narrative. **c)** Note that the setting of the story is very static. Consider different ways of dealing with this problem. **d)** You will also need to work out how your adaptation will present the stories told by the aunt and the bachelor in a visually interesting way. **e)** Read your completed script to your classmates. Invite them to comment on how your adaptation has developed the possibilities of the medium you chose.

MORE TO EXPLORE

Themes: Childhood, Stereotypes, Family, Rebels, At Play, Europe, Humour, Creativity

Elements: allusion, characterization, hyperbole, satire, third-person point of view

A Cap for Steve

Morley Callaghan

LEARNING FOCUS

- Analyze how a writer uses characterization.
- Evaluate the use of plot devices.
- Write a comparative essay.

CONTEXT Morley Callaghan, one of the best-known Canadian writers of the twentieth century, was born in Toronto in 1903 and died there in 1990. Educated at the University of Toronto and Osgoode Hall Law School, Callaghan published his first stories in 1926, and his first novel, *Strange Fugitive*, two years later. He worked as a broadcaster in the 1950s, and won the Governor General's Award in 1951 for his novel *The Loved and the Lost*. His memoir of his life in 1929, called *That Summer in Paris* (1963), is considered a classic of Canadian non-fiction. Callaghan's fiction often explores the conflict between the practical demands of everyday living and the need to believe and trust. In what ways have you experienced this conflict? To what extent is it reflected in the story "A Cap for Steve"? ■

Dave Diamond, a poor man, a carpenter's assistant, was a small, wiry, quick-tempered individual who had learned how to make every dollar count in his home. His wife, Anna, had been sick a lot, and his twelve-year-old son, Steve, had to be kept in school. Steve, a big-eyed, shy kid, ought to have known the value of money as well as Dave did. It had been ground into him.

But the boy was crazy about baseball, and after school, when he could have been working as a delivery boy or selling papers, he played ball with the kids. His failure to appreciate that the family needed a few extra dollars disgusted Dave. Around the house he wouldn't let Steve talk about baseball, and he scowled when he saw him hurrying off with his glove after dinner.

When the Phillies came to town to play an exhibition game with the home team and Steve pleaded to be taken to the ball park, Dave, of course, was outraged. Steve knew they couldn't afford it. But he had got his mother on his side. Finally Dave made a bargain with them.

He said that if Steve came home after school and worked hard helping to make some kitchen shelves he would take him that night to the ball park.

Steve worked hard, but Dave was still resentful. They had to coax him to put on his good suit. When they started out Steve held aloof, feeling guilty, and they walked down the street like strangers; then Dave glanced at Steve's face and, half-ashamed, took his arm more cheerfully.

As the game went on, Dave had to listen to Steve's recitation of the batting average of every Philly that stepped up to the plate; the time the boy must have wasted learning these averages began to appall him. He showed it so plainly that Steve felt guilty again and was silent.

After the game Dave let Steve drag him onto the field to keep him company while he tried to get some autographs from the Philly players, who were being hemmed in by gangs of kids blocking the way to the clubhouse. But Steve, who was shy, let the other kids block him off from the players. Steve would push his way in, get blocked out, and come back to stand mournfully beside Dave. And Dave grew impatient. He was wasting valuable time. He wanted to get home; Steve knew it and was worried.

Then the big, blond Philly outfielder, Eddie Condon, who had been held up by a gang of kids tugging at his arm and thrusting their score cards at him, broke loose and made a run for the clubhouse. He was jostled, and his blue cap with the red peak, tilted far back on his head, fell off. It fell at Steve's feet, and Steve stooped quickly and grabbed it. "Okay, son," the outfielder called, turning back. But Steve, holding the hat in both hands, only stared at him.

"Give him his cap, Steve," Dave said, smiling apologetically at the big outfielder who towered over them. But Steve drew the hat closer to his chest. In an awed trance he looked up at big Eddie Condon. It was an embarrassing moment. All the other kids were watching. Some shouted, "Give him his cap."

"My cap, son," Eddie Condon said, his hand out.

"Hey, Steve," Dave said, and he gave him a shake. But he had to jerk the cap out of Steve's hands.

"Here you are," he said.

The outfielder, noticing Steve's white, worshipping face and pleading eyes, grinned and then shrugged. "Aw, let him keep it," he said.

"No, Mr. Condon, you don't need to do that," Dave protested.

"It's happened before. Forget it," Eddie Condon said, and he trotted away to the clubhouse.

Dave handed the cap to Steve; envious kids circled around them and Steve said, "He said I could keep it, Dad. You heard him, didn't you?"

"Yeah, I heard him," Dave admitted. The wonder in Steve's face made him smile. He took the boy by the arm and they hurried off the field.

On the way home Dave couldn't get him to talk about the game; he couldn't get him to take his eyes off the cap. Steve could hardly believe in his own happiness. "See," he said suddenly, and he showed Dave that Eddie Condon's name was printed on the sweatband. Then he went on dreaming. Finally he put the cap on his head and turned to Dave with a slow, proud smile. The cap was away too big for him; it fell down over his ears. "Never mind," Dave said. "You can get your mother to take a tuck in the back."

When they got home Dave was tired and his wife didn't understand the cap's importance, and they couldn't get Steve to go to bed. He swaggered around wearing the cap and looking in the mirror every ten minutes. He took the cap to bed with him.

Dave and his wife had a cup of coffee in the kitchen, and Dave told her again how they had got the cap. They agreed that their boy must have an attractive quality that showed in his face, and that Eddie Condon must have been drawn to him—why else would he have singled Steve out from all the kids?

But Dave got tired of the fuss Steve made over that cap and of the way he wore it from the time he got up in the morning until the time he went to bed. Some kid was always coming in, wanting to try on the cap. It was childish, Dave said, for Steve to go around assuming that the cap made him important in the neighbourhood, and to keep telling them how he had become a leader in the park a few blocks away where he played ball in the evenings. And Dave wouldn't stand for Steve's keeping the cap on while he was eating. He was always scolding his wife for accepting Steve's explanation that he'd forgotten he had it on.

Just the same, it was remarkable what a little thing like a ball cap could do for a kid, Dave admitted to his wife as he smiled to himself.

One night Steve was late coming home from the park. Dave didn't realize how late it was until he put down his newspaper and watched his wife at the window. Her restlessness got on his nerves. "See what comes from encouraging the boy to hang around with those park loafers," he said. "I don't encourage him," she protested. "You do," he insisted irritably, for he was really worried now. A gang hung around the park until midnight. It was a bad park. It was true that on one side there was a good district with fine, expensive apartment houses, but the kids from that neighbourhood left the park to the kids from the poorer homes. When his wife went out and walked down to the corner it was his turn to wait and worry and watch at the open window. Each waiting moment tortured him. At last he heard his wife's voice and Steve's voice, and he relaxed and sighed; then he remembered his duty and rushed angrily to meet them.

"I'll fix you, Steve, once and for all," he said. "I'll show you you can't start coming into the house at midnight."

"Hold your horses, Dave," his wife said. "Can't you see the state he's in?" Steve looked utterly exhausted and beaten.

"What's the matter?" Dave asked quickly.

"I lost my cap," Steve whispered; he walked past his father and threw himself on the couch in the living room and lay with his face hidden.

"Now, don't scold him, Dave," his wife said.

"Scold him. Who's scolding him?" Dave asked, indignantly. "It's his cap, not mine. If it's not worth his while to hang on to it, why should I scold him?" But he was implying resentfully that he alone recognized the cap's value.

"So you are scolding him," his wife said. "It's his cap. Not yours. What happened, Steve?"

Steve told them he had been playing ball and he found that when he ran the bases the cap fell off; it was still too big despite the tuck his mother had taken in the band. So the next time he came to bat he tucked the cap in his hip pocket. Someone had lifted it, he was sure.

"And he didn't even know whether it was still in his pocket," Dave said sarcastically.

"I wasn't careless, Dad," Steve said. For the last three hours he had been wandering around to the homes of the kids who had been in the park at the time; he wanted to go on, but he was too tired. Dave knew the boy was apologizing to him, but he didn't know why it made him angry.

"If he didn't hang on to it, it's not worth worrying about now," he said, and he sounded offended.

After that night they knew that Steve didn't go to the park to play ball; he went to look for the cap. It irritated Dave to see him sit around listlessly, or walk in circles, trying to force his memory to find a particular incident which would suddenly recall to him the moment when the cap had been taken. It was no attitude for a growing, healthy boy to take, Dave complained. He told Steve firmly once and for all he didn't want to hear any more about the cap.

One night, two weeks later, Dave was walking home with Steve from the shoemaker's. It was a hot night. When they passed an ice-cream parlour Steve slowed down. "I guess I couldn't have a soda, could I?" Steve said. "Nothing doing," Dave said firmly. "Come on now," he added as Steve hung back, looking in the window.

"Dad, look!" Steve cried suddenly, pointing at the window. "My cap! There's my cap! He's coming out!"

A well-dressed boy was leaving the ice-cream parlour; he had on a blue ball cap with a red peak, just like Steve's cap. "Hey, you!" Steve cried, and he rushed at the boy, his small face fierce and his eyes wild. Before the boy could back away Steve had snatched the cap from his head. "That's my cap!" he shouted.

"What's this?" the bigger boy said. "Hey, give me my cap or I'll give you a poke on the nose."

Dave was surprised that his own shy boy did not back away. He watched him clutch the cap in his left hand, half crying with excitement as he put his head down and drew back his right fist; he was willing to fight. And Dave was proud of him.

"Wait, now," Dave said. "Take it easy, son," he said to the other boy, who refused to back away.

"My boy says it's his cap," Dave said.

"Well, he's crazy. It's my cap."

"I was with him when he got this cap. When the Phillies played here. It's a Philly cap."

"Eddie Condon gave it to me," Steve said. "And you stole it from me, you jerk."

"Don't call me a jerk, you little squirt. I never saw you before in my life."

"Look," Steve said, pointing to the printing on the cap's sweatband. "It's Eddie Condon's cap. See? See, Dad?"

"Yeah. You're right, son. Ever see this boy before, Steve?"

"No," Steve said reluctantly.

The other boy realized he might lose the cap. "I bought it from a guy," he said. "I paid him. My father knows I paid him." He said he got the cap at the ballpark. He groped for some magically impressive words and suddenly found them. "You'll have to speak to my father," he said.

"Sure, I'll speak to your father," Dave said. "What's your name? Where do you live?"

"My name's Hudson. I live about ten minutes away on the other side of the park." The boy appraised Dave, who wasn't any bigger than he was and who wore a faded blue windbreaker and no tie. "My father is a lawyer," he said boldly. "He wouldn't let me keep the cap if he didn't think I should."

"Is that a fact?" Dave asked belligerently. "Well, we'll see. Come on. Let's go." And he got between the two boys and they walked along the street. They didn't talk to each other. Dave knew the Hudson boy was waiting to get to the protection of his home, and Steve knew it, too, and he looked up apprehensively at Dave. And Dave, reaching for his hand, squeezed it encouragingly and strode along, cocky and belligerent, knowing that Steve relied on him.

The Hudson boy lived in that row of fine apartment houses on the other side of the park. At the entrance to one of these houses Dave tried not to hang back and show he was impressed, because he could feel Steve hanging back. When they got into the small elevator Dave didn't know why he took off his hat. In the carpeted hall on the fourth floor the Hudson boy said, "Just a minute," and entered his own apartment. Dave and Steve were left alone in the corridor, knowing that the other boy was preparing his father for the encounter. Steve looked anxiously at his father, and Dave said, "Don't worry, son," and he added resolutely, "No one's putting anything over on us."

A tall, balding man in a brown velvet smoking jacket suddenly opened the door. Dave had never seen a man wearing one of these jackets, although he had seen them in department-store windows. "Good evening," he said, making a deprecatory gesture at the cap Steve still clutched tightly in his left hand. "My boy didn't get your name. My name is Hudson."

"Mine's Diamond."

"Come on in," Mr. Hudson said, putting out his hand and laughing good-naturedly. He led Dave and Steve into his living room. "What's this about that cap?" he asked. "The way kids can get excited about a cap. Well, it's understandable, isn't it?"

"So it is," Dave said, moving closer to Steve, who was awed by the broadloom rug and the fine furniture. He wanted to show Steve he was at ease himself, and he wished Mr. Hudson wouldn't be so polite. That meant Dave had to be polite and affable, too, and it was hard to manage when he was standing in the middle of the floor in his old windbreaker.

"Sit down, Mr. Diamond," Mr. Hudson said. Dave took Steve's arm and sat him down beside him on the chesterfield. The Hudson boy watched his father. And Dave looked at Steve and saw that he wouldn't face Mr. Hudson or the other boy; he kept looking up at Dave, putting all his faith in him.

"Well, Mr. Diamond, from what I gathered from my boy, you're able to prove this cap belonged to your boy."

"That's a fact," Dave said.

"Mr. Diamond, you'll have to believe my boy bought that cap from some kid in good faith."

"I don't doubt it," Dave said. "But no kid can sell something that doesn't belong to him. You know that's a fact, Mr. Hudson."

"Yes, that's a fact," Mr. Hudson agreed. "But that cap means a lot to my boy, Mr. Diamond."

"It means a lot to my boy, too, Mr. Hudson."

"Sure it does. But supposing we called in a policeman. You know what he'd say? He'd ask you if you were willing to pay my boy what he paid for the cap. That's usually the way it works out," Mr. Hudson said, friendly and smiling, as he eyed Dave shrewdly.

"But that's not right. It's not justice," Dave protested. "Not when it's my boy's cap."

"I know it isn't right. But that's what they do."

"All right. What did you say your boy paid for the cap?" Dave said reluctantly.

"Two dollars."

"Two dollars!" Dave repeated. Mr. Hudson's smile was still kindly, but his eyes were shrewd, and Dave knew that the lawyer was counting on his not having the two dollars. Mr. Hudson thought he had Dave sized up; he looked at him and decided he was broke. Dave's pride was hurt, and he turned to Steve. What he saw in Steve's face was more powerful than the hurt to his pride; it was the memory of how difficult it had been to get an extra nickel, the talk he heard about the cost of food, the worry in his mother's face as she tried to make ends meet, and the bewildered embarrassment that he was here in a rich man's home, forcing his father to confess that he couldn't afford to spend two dollars. Then Dave grew angry and reckless. "I'll give you the two dollars," he said.

Steve looked at the Hudson boy and grinned brightly. The Hudson boy watched his father.

"I suppose that's fair enough," Mr. Hudson said. "A cap like this can be worth a lot to a kid. You know how it is. Your boy might want to sell—I mean be satisfied. Would he take five dollars for it?"

"Five dollars?" Dave repeated. "Is it worth five dollars, Steve?" he asked uncertainly.

Steve shook his head and looked frightened.

"No thanks, Mr. Hudson," Dave said firmly.

"I'll tell you what I'll do," Mr. Hudson said. "I'll give you ten dollars. The cap has sentimental value for my boy, a Philly cap, a big-leaguer's cap. It's only worth about a buck and a half really," he added. But Dave shook his head again. Mr. Hudson frowned. He looked at his own boy with indulgent concern, but now he was embarrassed. "I'll tell you what I'll do," he said. "This cap—well, it's worth as much as a day at the circus to my boy. Your boy should be recompensed. I want to be fair. Here's twenty dollars," and he held out two ten-dollar bills to Dave.

That much money for a cap, Dave thought, and his eyes brightened. But he knew what the cap had meant to Steve; to deprive him of it now that it was within his reach would be unbearable. All the things he needed in his life gathered around him; his wife was there, saying he couldn't afford to reject the offer, he had no right to do it; and he turned to Steve to see if Steve thought it wonderful that the cap could bring them twenty dollars.

"What do you say, Steve?" he asked uneasily.

"I don't know," Steve said. He was in a trance. When Dave smiled, Steve smiled too, and Dave believed that Steve was as impressed as he was, only more bewildered, and maybe even more aware that they could not possibly turn away that much money for a ball cap.

"Well, here you are," Mr. Hudson said, and he put the two bills in Steve's hand. "It's a lot of money. But I guess you had a right to expect as much."

With a dazed, fixed smile Steve handed the money slowly to his father, and his face was white.

Laughing jovially, Mr. Hudson led them to the door. His own boy followed a few paces behind.

In the elevator Dave took the bills out of his pocket. "See, Stevie," he whispered eagerly. "That windbreaker you wanted! And ten dollars for your bank! Won't Mother be surprised?"

"Yeah," Steve whispered, the little smile still on his face. But Dave had to turn away quickly so their eyes wouldn't meet, for he saw that it was a scared smile.

Outside, Dave said, "Here, you carry the money home, Steve. You show it to your mother."

"No, you keep it," Steve said, and then there was nothing to say. They walked in silence.

"It's a lot of money," Dave said finally. When Steve didn't answer him, he added angrily, "I turned to you, Steve. I asked you, didn't I?"

"That man knew how much his boy wanted that cap," Steve said.

"Sure. But he recognized how much it was worth to us."

"No, you let him take it away from us," Steve blurted.

"That's unfair," Dave said. "Don't dare say that to me."

"I don't want to be like you," Steve muttered, and he darted across the road and walked along on the other side of the street.

"It's unfair," Dave said angrily, only now he didn't mean that Steve was unfair, he meant that what had happened in the prosperous Hudson home was unfair, and he didn't know quite why. He had been trapped, not just by Mr. Hudson, but by his own life. Across the road Steve was hurrying along with his head down, wanting to be alone. They walked most of the way home on opposite sides of the street, until Dave could stand it no longer. "Steve," he called, crossing the street. "It was very unfair. I mean, for you to say..." but Steve started to run. Dave walked as fast as he could and Steve was getting beyond him, and he felt enraged and suddenly he yelled, "Steve!" and he started to chase his son. He wanted to get hold of Steve and pound him, and he didn't know why. He gained on him, he gasped for breath and he almost got him by the shoulder. Turning, Steve saw his father's face in the street light and was terrified; he circled away, got to the house, and rushed in, yelling, "Mother!"

"Son, son!" she cried, rushing from the kitchen. As soon as she threw her arms around Steve, shielding him, Dave's anger left him and he felt stupid. He walked past them into the kitchen.

"What happened?" she asked anxiously. "Have you both gone crazy? What did you do, Steve?"

"Nothing," he said sullenly.

"What did your father do?"

"We found the boy with my ball cap, and he let the boy's father take it from us."

"No, no," Dave protested. "Nobody pushed us around. The man didn't put anything over us." He felt tired and his face was burning. He told what had happened; then he slowly took the two ten-dollar bills out of his wallet and tossed them on the table and looked up guiltily at his wife.

It hurt him that she didn't pick up the money, and that she didn't rebuke him. "It is a lot of money, son," she said slowly. "Your father was only trying to do what he knew was right, and it'll work out, and you'll understand." She was soothing Steve, but Dave knew she felt that she needed to be gentle with him, too, and he was ashamed.

When she went with Steve to his bedroom, Dave sat by himself. His son had contempt for him, he thought. His son, for the first time, had seen how easy it was for another man to handle him, and he had judged him and had wanted to walk alone on the other side of the street. He looked at the money and he hated the sight of it.

His wife returned to the kitchen, made a cup of tea, talked soothingly, and said it was incredible that he had forced the Hudson man to pay him twenty dollars for the cap, but all Dave could think of was Steve was scared of me.

Finally, he got up and went into Steve's room. The room was in darkness, but he could see the outline of Steve's body on the bed, and he sat down beside him and whispered, "Look, son, it was a mistake. I know why. People like us—in circumstances where money can scare us. No, no," he said, feeling ashamed and shaking his head apologetically; he was taking the wrong way of showing the boy they were together; he was covering up his own failure. For the failure had been his, and it had come out of being so separated from his son that he had been blind to what was beyond the price in a boy's life. He longed now to show Steve he could be with him from day to day. His hand went out hesitantly to Steve's shoulder. "Steve, look," he said eagerly. "The trouble was I didn't realize how much I enjoyed it that night at the ball park. If I had watched you playing for your own team—the kids around here say you could be a great pitcher. We could take that money and buy a new pitcher's glove for you, and a catcher's mitt. Steve, Steve, are you listening? I could catch you, work with you in the lane. Maybe I could be your coach...watch you become a great pitcher." In the half-darkness he could see the boy's pale face turn to him.

Steve, who had never heard his father talk like this, was shy and wondering. All he knew was that his father, for the first time, wanted to be with him in his hopes and adventures. He said, "I guess you do know how important that cap was." His hand went out to his father's arm. "With that man the cap was—well it was just something he could buy, eh Dad?" Dave gripped his son's hand hard. The wonderful generosity of childhood—the price a boy was willing to pay to be able to count on his father's admiration and approval made him feel humble, then strangely exalted.

NOTES

Phillies the Philadelphia Phillies, the major-league baseball team founded in that city in 1883

deprecatory belittling; expressing disapproval or criticism

chesterfield an old-fashioned, chiefly Canadian term referring to a sofa

ANALYZE AND INTERPRET

1. In a group, discuss your response to the characters in this story. Consider the following questions in your discussion: Which character do you identify with most? Do any of the characters either remind you of people you know, or have qualities which you would like to develop in yourself? Did you change your opinion of any of the characters as you read? Do you think the author provided adequate motivation for the actions of the characters? Do you think any of the characters are stereotypes?

2. In a skilfully written story, the author achieves a delicate balance between fore-shadowing and suspense. In a small group, identify what you think the climax and the resolution of this story might be. With the class, discuss whether the story contains adequate foreshadowing to prepare you for this climax and the resolution. At what points in the story did you experience the greatest suspense? Did you find the story too predictable?

3. Obtain and read the story by Morley Callaghan entitled "Luke Baldwin's Vow." Write a comparative essay in which you explore the similarities and differences between these two stories by Callaghan. In preparation for writing, create a chart with these headings: Events, Characters, and Themes. Reread each story, filling in your chart with jot notes as the basis for your first draft. Ask several classmates to read your draft and comment on how well you used transition words to clarify similarities and differences. Use their comments to help you revise your essay.

MORE TO EXPLORE

Themes: Childhood, Personal Challenges, Stereotypes, Family, Peers, Role Models, Canada, Moral Questions

Elements: characterization, climax, conflict, dénouement, foreshadowing, pathos, symbol, third-person point of view

Sunday in the Park

Bel Kaufman

Sandpit, France, Andrew Macara

Bel Kaufman was born in Berlin, Germany, in 1913, into a family with a strong writing tradition. Her grandfather was the famous Yiddish humorist Sholom Aleichem. She spent her childhood in Russia, and did not learn English until she immigrated with her family to the United States at the age of twelve. Kaufman's most famous work is the darkly funny novel *Up the Down Staircase*, the story of a young English teacher's experiences in an inner-city New York high school. This novel, which has been translated into sixteen languages, was adapted for the stage and screen. Kaufman's other writing includes the novel *Love, Etc.*, as well as short stories and magazine articles. By the age of eighty-seven, Kaufman was still busy travelling, giving talks about her grandfather, and ballroom dancing twice a week. In "Sunday in the Park," how does an incident between two children lead to a clash between their parents? What would you have done as a parent in this situation? Why might this incident continue to cast a shadow long after the crisis is over? ■

It was still warm in the late-afternoon sun, and the city noises came muffled through the trees in the park. She put her book down on the bench, removed her sunglasses, and sighed contentedly. Morton was reading the *Times Magazine* section, one arm flung around her shoulder; their three-year-old son, Larry, was playing in the sandbox: a faint breeze fanned her hair softly against her cheek. It was five-thirty of a Sunday afternoon, and the small playground, tucked away in a corner of the park, was all but deserted. The swings and seesaws stood motionless and abandoned, the slides were empty, and only in the sandbox two little boys squatted diligently side by side. *How good this is,* she thought, and almost smiled at her sense of well-being. They must go out in the sun more often: Morton was so city-pale, cooped up all week inside the grey factorylike university. She squeezed his arm affectionately and glanced at Larry, delighting in the pointed little face frowning in concentration over the tunnel he was digging. The other boy suddenly stood up and with a quick, deliberate swing of his chubby arm threw a spadeful of sand at Larry. It just missed his head. Larry continued digging; the boy remained standing, shovel raised, stolid and impassive.

"No, no, little boy." She shook her finger at him, her eyes searching for the child's mother or nurse. "We mustn't throw sand. It may get in someone's eyes and hurt. We must play nicely in the nice sandbox."

The boy looked at her in unblinking expectancy. He was about Larry's age but perhaps ten pounds heavier, a husky little boy with none of Larry's quickness and sensitivity in his face. Where was his mother? The only other people left in the playground were two women and a little girl on roller skates leaving now through the gate, and a man on a bench a few feet away. He was a big man, and he seemed to be taking up the whole bench as he held the Sunday comics close to his face. She supposed he was the child's father. He did not look up from his comics, but spat once deftly out of the corner of his mouth. She turned her eyes away.

At that moment, as swiftly as before, the fat little boy threw another spadeful of sand at Larry. This time some of it landed on his hair and forehead. Larry looked up at his mother, his mouth tentative; her expression would tell him whether to cry or not.

Her first instinct was to rush to her son, brush the sand out of his hair, and punish the other child, but she controlled it. She always said that she wanted Larry to learn to fight his own battles.

"Don't *do* that, little boy," she said sharply, leaning forward on the bench. "You mustn't throw sand!"

The man on the bench moved his mouth as if to spit again, but instead he spoke. He did not look at her, but at the boy only.

"You go right ahead, Joe," he said loudly. "Throw all you want. This here is a *public* sandbox."

She felt a sudden weakness in her knees as she glanced at Morton. He had become aware of what was happening. He put his *Times* down carefully on his lap and turned his fine, lean face toward the man, smiling the shy, apologetic smile he might have offered a student in pointing out an error in his thinking. When he spoke to the man, it was with his usual reasonableness.

"You're quite right," he said pleasantly, "but just because this is a public place…"

The man lowered his funnies and looked at Morton. He looked at him from head to foot, slowly and deliberately. "Yeah?" His insolent voice was edged with menace. "My kid's got just as good a right here as yours, and if he feels like throwing sand, he'll throw it, and if you don't like it, you can take your kid the hell out of here."

The children were listening, their eyes and mouths wide open, their spades forgotten in small fists. She noticed the muscle in Morton's jaw tighten. He was rarely angry; he seldom lost his temper. She was suffused with a tenderness for her husband and an impotent rage against the man for involving him in a situation so alien and so distasteful to him.

"Now, just a minute," Morton said courteously, "you must realize…"

"Aw, shut up," said the man.

Her heart began to pound. Morton half rose; the *Times* slid to the ground. Slowly the other man stood up. He took a couple of steps toward Morton, then stopped. He flexed his great arms, waiting. She pressed her trembling knees together. Would there be violence, fighting? How dreadful, how incredible…. She must do something, stop them, call for help. She wanted to put her hand on her husband's sleeve, to pull him down, but for some reason she didn't.

Morton adjusted his glasses. He was very pale. "This is ridiculous," he said unevenly. "I must ask you…"

"Oh, yeah?" said the man. He stood with his legs spread apart, rocking a little, looking at Morton with utter scorn. "You and who else?"

For a moment the two men looked at each other nakedly. Then Morton turned his back on the man and said quietly. "Come on, let's get out of here." He walked awkwardly, almost limping with self-consciousness, to the sandbox. He stooped and lifted Larry and his shovel out.

At once Larry came to life; his face lost its rapt expression and he began to kick and cry. "I don't *want* to go home, I want to play better, I don't *want* any supper, I don't *like* supper…." It became a chant as they walked, pulling their child between them, his feet dragging on the ground. In order to get to the exit gate they had to pass the bench where the man sat sprawling again. She was careful not to look at him. With all the dignity she could summon, she pulled Larry's sandy, perspiring little hand, while Morton pulled the other. Slowly and with head high she walked with her husband and child out of the playground.

Her first feeling was one of relief that a fight had been avoided, that no one was hurt. Yet beneath it there was a layer of something else, something heavy and inescapable. She sensed that it was more than just an unpleasant incident, more than defeat of reason by force. She felt dimly it had something to do with her and Morton, something acutely personal, familiar, and important.

Suddenly Morton spoke. "It wouldn't have proved anything."

"What?" she asked.

"A fight. It wouldn't have proved anything beyond the fact that he's bigger than I am."

"Of course," she said.

"The only possible outcome," he continued reasonably, "would have been—what? My glasses broken, perhaps a tooth or two replaced, a couple of days' work missed—and for what? For justice? For truth?"

"Of course," she repeated. She quickened her step. She wanted only to get home and to busy herself with her familiar tasks; perhaps then the feeling, glued like heavy plaster on her heart, would be gone. *Of all the stupid, despicable bullies,* she thought, pulling harder on Larry's hand. The child was still crying. Always before she had felt a tender pity for his defenceless little body, the frail arms, the narrow shoulders with sharp, winglike shoulder blades, the thin and unsure legs, but now her mouth tightened in resentment.

"Stop crying," she said sharply. "I'm ashamed of you!" She felt as if all three of them were tracking mud along the street. The child cried louder.

If there had been an issue involved, she thought, *if there had been something to fight for.... But what else could he possibly have done? Allow himself to be beaten? Attempt to educate the man? Call a policeman? "Officer, there's a man in the park who won't stop his child from throwing sand on mine...."* The whole thing was as silly as that, and not worth thinking about.

"Can't you keep him quiet, for Pete's sake?" Morton asked irritably.

"What do you suppose I've been trying to do?" she said.

Larry pulled back, dragging his feet.

"If you can't discipline this child, I will," Morton snapped, making a move toward the boy.

But her voice stopped him. She was shocked to hear it, thin and cold and penetrating with contempt. "Indeed?" she heard herself say. "You and who else?

NOTES

funnies the comics section of the newspaper

ANALYZE AND INTERPRET

1. Think about how you feel when you get angry. Consider how you respond physically and emotionally. Under what circumstances do you speak your mind, and when do you keep your anger to yourself? With whom do you feel most comfortable expressing your anger? Discuss your responses with a small group and then share your findings with the class.

2. As you read the story, take notes on the main points of action. Work with a partner to create a story graph which shows the rising action, climax, and dénouement. As a class, locate the climax on your graphs. What does the climax tell you about the author's purpose in writing this story? In what way does the placement of the climax affect the interpretation of this story?

3. This story demonstrates two contrasting approaches to conflict resolution. Work with a partner to research the topic of conflict resolution. Use your research to design a Web page or pamphlet for families to help them deal with conflict. As a class, brainstorm criteria for an effective publication, considering such elements as layout and the accuracy of information. Have a few students view your work while you create it to offer suggestions for improvement.

MORE TO EXPLORE

Themes: Stereotypes, Family, Peers, At Play, Urban Life, Moral Questions

Elements: climax, conflict, dénouement, dialogue, foreshadowing, plot, third-person point of view

The Gentlemen of the Jungle

Jomo Kenyatta

Porcupine, Elephant, Panther and Gazelle, Kivuthi Mbuno

LEARNING FOCUS

- Explore a form's purpose and audience.
- Debate an important social issue.
- Write and revise a fable with help from others.

CONTEXT Jomo Kenyatta was the president of the African nation of Kenya from 1964 to 1978. The son of a poor farmer, he went on to study in London, England, where he earned a Ph.D. in anthropology. On his return to Kenya, he was imprisoned for his political activities but eventually helped lead Kenya to independence from Britain in 1963. Although much of his writing is non-fiction, "The Gentlemen of the Jungle" is a fictional beast fable in the same vein as George Orwell's *Animal Farm*. Fables, by definition, not only include a moral lesson but serve as allegories that comment on contemporary politics or social events, often through the use of irony. Is using a plot with animals far-fetched, or do readers see the parallels to humanity? Why? What might be a possible social or political interpretation of this story? How does the story's final line, "Peace is costly, but it's worth the expense," relate to its narrative? ■

Once upon a time an elephant made a friendship with a man. One day a heavy thunderstorm broke out, the elephant went to his friend, who had a little hut at the edge of the forest, and said to him: "My dear good man, will you please let me put my trunk inside your hut to keep it out of this torrential rain?" The man, seeing what situation his friend was in, replied: "My dear good elephant, my hut is very small, but there is room for your trunk and myself. Please put your trunk in gently." The elephant thanked his friend, saying: "You have done me a good deed and one day I shall return your kindness." But what followed? As soon as the elephant put his trunk inside the hut, slowly he pushed his head inside, and finally flung the man out in the rain, and then lay down comfortably inside his friend's hut, saying: "My dear good friend, your skin is harder than mine, and as there is not enough room for both of us, you can afford to remain in the rain while I am protecting my delicate skin from the hailstorm."

The man, seeing what his friend had done to him, started to grumble; the animals in the nearby forest heard the noise and came to see what was the matter. All stood around listening to the heated argument between the man and his friend the elephant. In this turmoil the lion came along roaring, and said in a loud voice: "Don't you all know that I am the King of the Jungle! How dare any one disturb the peace of my kingdom?" On hearing this the elephant, who was one of the high ministers in the jungle kingdom, replied in a soothing voice, and said: "My lord, there is no disturbance of the peace in your kingdom. I have only been having a little discussion with my friend here as to the possession of this little hut which your lordship sees me occupying." The lion, who wanted to have "peace and tranquillity" in his kingdom, replied in a noble voice, saying: "I command my ministers to appoint a Commission of Enquiry to go thoroughly into this matter and report accordingly." He then turned to the man and said: "You have done well by establishing friendship with my people, especially with the elephant, who is one of my honourable ministers of state. Do not grumble any more, your hut is not lost to you. Wait until the sitting of my Imperial Commission, and there you will be given plenty of opportunity to state your case. I am sure that you will be pleased with the findings of the Commission." The man was very pleased by these sweet words from the King of the Jungle, and innocently waited for his opportunity, in the belief that naturally the hut would be returned to him.

The elephant, obeying the command of his master, got busy with other ministers to appoint the Commission of Enquiry. The following elders of the jungle were appointed to sit in the Commission: (1) Mr. Rhinoceros; (2) Mr. Buffalo; (3) Mr. Alligator; (4) The Rt. Hon. Mr. Fox to act as chairman; and (5) Mr. Leopard to act as Secretary to the Commission. On seeing the personnel, the man protested and asked if it was not necessary to include in this Commission a member from his side. But he was told that it was impossible, since no one from his side was well enough educated to understand the intricacy of jungle law. Further, that there was nothing to fear, for the members of the Commission were all men of repute for their impartiality in justice, and as they were gentlemen chosen by God to look after the interests of races less adequately endowed with teeth and claws, he might rest assured that they would investigate the matter with the greatest care and report impartially.

The Commission sat to take the evidence. The Rt. Hon. Mr. Elephant was first called. He came along with a superior air, brushing his tusks with a sapling which Mrs. Elephant had provided, and in an authoritative voice said: "Gentlemen of the Jungle, there is no need for me to waste your valuable time in relating a story which I am sure you all know. I have always regarded it as my duty to protect the interests of my friends, and this appears to have caused the misunderstanding between myself and my friend here. He invited me to save his hut from being blown away by a hurricane. As the hurricane had gained access owing to the unoccupied space in the hut, I considered it necessary, in my friend's own interests, to turn the undeveloped space to a more economic use by sitting in it myself; a duty which any of you would undoubtedly have performed with equal readiness in similar circumstances."

After hearing the Rt. Hon. Mr. Elephant's conclusive evidence, the Commission called Mr. Hyena and other elders of the jungle, who all supported what Mr. Elephant had said. They then called the man, who began to give his own account of the dispute. But the Commission cut him short, saying: "My good man, please confine yourself to relevant issues. We have already heard the circumstances from various unbiased sources; all we wish you to tell us is whether the undeveloped space in your hut was occupied by any one else before Mr. Elephant assumed his position?" The man began to say: "No, but—" But at this point, the Commission declared that they had heard sufficient evidence from both sides and retired to consider their decision. After enjoying a delicious meal at the expense of the Rt. Hon. Mr. Elephant, they reached their verdict, called the man, and declared as follows: "In our opinion this dispute has arisen through a regrettable misunderstanding due to the backwardness of your ideas. We consider that Mr. Elephant has fulfilled his sacred duty of protecting your interests. As it is clearly for your good that the space should be put to its most economic use, and as you yourself have not reached the stage of expansion which would enable you to fill it, we consider it necessary to arrange a compromise to suit both parties. Mr. Elephant shall continue his occupation of your hut, but we give you permission to look for a site where you can build another hut more suited to your needs, and we will see that you are well protected."

The man, having no alternative, and fearing that his refusal might expose him to the teeth and claws of members of the Commission, did as they suggested. But no sooner had he built another hut than Mr. Rhinoceros charged in with his horn lowered and ordered the man to quit. A Royal Commission was again appointed to look into the matter, and the same finding was given. This procedure was repeated until Mr. Buffalo, Mr. Leopard, Mr. Hyena and the rest were all accommodated with new huts. Then the man decided that he must adopt an effective method of protection, since Commissions of Enquiry did not seem to be of any use to him. He sat down and said: "*Ng'enda thi ndagaga motegi*," which literally means "there is nothing that treads on the earth that cannot be trapped," or in other words, you can fool people for a time, but not for ever.

Early one morning, when the huts already occupied by the jungle lords were all beginning to decay and fall to pieces, he went out and built a bigger and better hut a little distance away. No sooner had Mr. Rhinoceros seen it than he came rushing in, only to find that Mr.

Elephant was already inside, sound asleep. Mr. Leopard next came to the window, Mr. Lion, Mr. Fox and Mr. Buffalo entered the doors, while Mr. Hyena howled for a place in the shade and Mr. Alligator basked on the roof. Presently they all began disputing about their rights of penetration, and from disputing they came to fighting, and while they were all embroiled together the man set the hut on fire and burnt it to the ground, jungle lords and all. Then he went home, saying: "Peace is costly, but it's worth the expense," and lived happily ever after.

ANALYZE AND INTERPRET

1. In a group, consider the features and the purpose of a fable. Briefly outline the plots of some fables you know. As a class, discuss the following: How is your reading of this story affected by the fact that it is a fable? Why do you think the author chose to convey his theme in this form? Who might his audience be?

2. The man in the story resorts to violent action to rid himself of his oppressors. Discuss whether the man has alternatives to his actions, given the circumstances outlined in the story. Do you think the author believes that violence is necessary in some circumstances? If so, has he convinced you? What other courses of action might be available to oppressed people? Work with a group to prepare a debate on the use of violence versus non-violence to bring about social or political change.

3. a) Choose an issue that concerns you and write a fable expressing your ideas about it. b) Review the features of a fable and incorporate them into your work. c) Read your fable to your classmates to test whether you were able to effectively relay your message. d) As a class, make a chart of all of the issues dealt with in the fables. What are the similarities and/or differences in the issues that were chosen? e) In a class discussion, analyze which of these issues are the result of modern conditions and which are timeless. Then consider what factors contributed to your conclusions.

MORE TO EXPLORE

Themes: Self and Culture, Rebels, Africa, Moral Questions, War and Peace

Elements: allegory, conflict, dénouement, hyperbole, irony, oral tradition, parable, plot, third-person point of view

Do Seek Their Meat from God

Charles G.D. Roberts

Last Refuge, Yvonne Delvo

- Explain how stylistic techniques influence your reading.
- Support your interpretations with evidence.
- Respond in the voice of a character.

CONTEXT Sir Charles G.D. Roberts was a Canadian poet and historian with an international reputation. He is probably best known today for his animal stories. He was born in 1860 in Douglas, New Brunswick, near wilderness areas that inspired him to observe wild animals closely. Roberts published his first collection of animal stories in 1896 and the popular novel *Red Fox* a few years later. After a decade of teaching in Nova Scotia, he left Canada to live in New York, Paris, Munich, and finally London, England, where he worked during World War I. Roberts returned to Canada in 1925 to live his final years in Toronto. He died in 1943. "Do Seek Their Meat from God" was his first published animal story. What does it reveal about the place of animals and human beings in nature? Where do you think Roberts' sympathies lie? ■

One side of the ravine was in darkness. The darkness was soft and rich, suggesting thick foliage. Along the crest of the slope treetops came into view—great pines and hemlocks of the ancient unviolated forest—revealed against the orange disk of a full moon just rising. The low rays slanting through the moveless tops lit strangely the upper portion of the opposite steep—the western wall of the ravine, barren, unlike its fellow, bossed with great rocky projections and harsh with stunted junipers. Out of the sluggish dark that lay along the ravine as in a trough rose the brawl of a swollen, obstructed stream.

Out of a shadowy hollow behind a long white rock, on the lower edge of that part of the steep which lay in the moonlight, came softly a great panther. In common daylight his coat would have shown a warm fulvous hue, but in the elvish decolourizing rays of that half-hidden moon he seemed to wear a sort of spectral grey. He lifted his smooth round head to gaze on the increasing flame, which presently he greeted with a shrill cry. That terrible cry, at once plaintive and menacing, with an undertone like the fierce protestations of a saw beneath the file, was a summons to his mate, telling her that the hour had come when they should seek their prey. From the lair behind the rock, where the cubs were being suckled by their dam, came no immediate answer. Only a pair of crows, that had their nest in a giant fir tree across the gulf, woke up and croaked harshly their indignation. These three summers past they had built in the same spot, and had been nightly awakened to vent the same rasping complaints.

The panther walked restlessly up and down, half a score of paces each way, along the edge of the shadow, keeping his wide-open green eyes upon the rising light. His short, muscular tail twitched impatiently, but he made no sound. Soon the breadth of confused brightness had spread itself farther down the steep, disclosing the foot of the white rock, and the bones and antlers of a deer which had been dragged thither and devoured.

By this time the cubs had made their meal, and their dam was ready for such enterprise as must be accomplished ere her own hunger, now grown savage, could hope to be assuaged. She glided supplely forth into the glimmer, raised her head, and screamed at the moon in a voice as terrible as her mate's. Again the crows stirred, croaking harshly; and the two beasts, noiselessly mounting the steep, stole into the shadows of the forest that clothed the high plateau.

The panthers were fierce with hunger. These two days past their hunting had been well-nigh fruitless. What scant prey they had slain had for the most part been devoured by the female; for had she not those small blind cubs at home to nourish, who soon must suffer at any lack of hers? The settlements of late had been making great inroads on the world of ancient forest, driving before them the deer and smaller game. Hence the sharp hunger of the panther parents, and hence it came that on this night they hunted together. They purposed to steal upon the settlements in their sleep, and take tribute of the enemies' flocks. Through the dark of the thick woods, here and there pierced by the moonlight, they moved swiftly and silently. Now and again a dry twig would snap beneath the discreet and padded footfalls. Now and again, as they rustled some low tree, a pewee or a nuthatch would give a startled chirp. For an hour the noiseless journeying continued, and ever and anon the two grey, sinuous shapes would come for a moment into the view of the now well-risen moon. Suddenly there fell upon their ears, far off and faint, but clearly defined against the vast stillness of the Northern forest, a sound which made those stealthy hunters pause and lift their heads. It was the voice of a child crying—crying long and loud, hopelessly, as if there were no one by to comfort it. The panthers turned aside from their former course and glided toward the sound. They were not yet come to the outskirts of the settlement, but they knew of a solitary cabin lying in the thick of the woods a mile and more from the nearest neighbour. Thither they bent their way, fired with fierce hope. Soon they would break their bitter fast.

Up to noon of the previous day the lonely cabin had been occupied. Then its owner, a shiftless fellow, who spent his days for the most part at the corner tavern three miles distant, had suddenly grown disgusted with a land wherein one must work to live, and had betaken himself with his seven-year-old boy to seek some more indolent clime. During the long lonely days when his father was away at the tavern, the little boy had been wont to visit the house of the next neighbour, to play with a child of some five summers, who had no other playmate. The next neighbour was a prosperous pioneer, being master of a substantial frame-house in the midst of a large and well-tilled clearing. At times, though rarely, because it was forbidden, the younger child would make his way by a rough wood road to visit his poor little disreputable playmate. At length it had appeared that the five-year-old was learning unsavoury language from the elder boy, who rarely had an opportunity of hearing speech more desirable. To the bitter grief of both children, the companionship had at length been stopped by unalterable decree of the master of the frame-house.

Hence it had come to pass that the little boy was unaware of his comrade's departure. Yielding at last to an eager longing for that comrade, he had stolen away late in the afternoon, traversed with endless misgivings the lonely stretch of wood road, and reached the cabin, only to find it empty. The door, on its leathern hinges, swung idly open. The one room had been stripped of its few poor furnishings. After looking in the rickety shed, whence darted two wild and hawk-like chickens, the child had seated himself on the hacked threshold, and sobbed passionately with a grief that he did not fully comprehend. Then seeing the shadows lengthen across the tiny clearing, he had grown afraid to start for home. As the dusk gathered, he had crept trembling into the cabin, whose door would not stay shut. When it grew quite dark, he crouched in the inmost corner of the room, desperate with fear and loneliness, and lifted up his voice piteously. From time to time his lamentations would be choked by sobs or he would grow breathless, and in the terrifying silence would listen hard to hear if anyone or anything were coming. Then again would the shrill childish wailings arise, startling the unexpectant night and piercing the forest depths, even to the ears of those great beasts which had set forth to seek their meat from God.

The lonely cabin stood some distance, perhaps a quarter of a mile, back from the highway connecting the settlements. Along this main road a man was plodding wearily. All day he had been walking, and now as he neared home his steps began to quicken with anticipation of rest. Over his shoulder projected a double-barrelled fowling-piece, from which was slung a bundle of such necessities as he had purchased in town that morning. It was the prosperous settler, the master of the frame-house. His mare being with foal, he had chosen to make the tedious journey on foot.

The settler passed the mouth of the wood road leading to the cabin. He had gone perhaps a furlong beyond, when his ears were startled by the sound of a child crying in the woods. He stopped, lowered his burden to the road, and stood straining ears and eyes in the direction of the sound. It was just at this time that the two panthers also stopped and lifted their heads to listen. Their ears were keener than those of the man, and the sound had reached them at a greater distance.

Presently the settler realized whence the cries were coming. He called to mind the cabin, but he did not know the cabin's owner had departed. He cherished a hearty contempt for the drunken squatter; and on the drunken squatter's child he looked with small favour, especially as a playmate for his own boy. Nevertheless, he hesitated before resuming his journey.

"Poor little devil!" he muttered, half in wrath. "I reckon his precious father's drunk down at 'the Corners,' and him crying for loneliness!" Then he reshouldered his burden and strode on doggedly.

But louder, shriller, more hopeless and more appealing, arose the childish voice, and the settler paused again, irresolute and with deepening indignation. In his fancy he saw the steaming supper his wife would have awaiting him. He loathed the thought of retracing his steps, and then stumbling a quarter of a mile through the stumps and bog of the wood road. He was foot-sore as well as hungry, and he cursed the vagabond squatter with serious emphasis; but in that waiting was a terror which would not let him go on. He thought of his own little one left in such a position, and straightway his heart melted. He turned, dropped his bundle behind some bushes, grasped his gun, and made speed back for the cabin.

"Who knows," he said to himself, "but that drunken idiot has left his youngster without a bite to eat in the whole miserable shanty? Or maybe he's locked out, and the poor little beggar's half scared to death. Sounds as if he was scared"; and at this thought the settler quickened his pace.

As the hungry panthers drew near the cabin and the cries of the lonely child grew clearer, they hastened their steps, and their eyes opened to a wider circle, flaming with a greener fire. It would be thoughtless superstition to say the beasts were cruel. They were simply keen with hunger and alive with the eager passion of the chase. They were not ferocious with any anticipation of battle, for they knew the voice was the voice of a child, and something in the voice told them the child was solitary. Theirs was no hideous or unnatural rage, as it is the custom to describe it. They were but seeking with the strength, the cunning, the deadly swiftness given them to that end, the food convenient for them. On their success in accomplishing that for which nature had so exquisitely designed them depended not only their own, but the lives of their blind and helpless young, now whimpering in the cave on the slope of the moonlit ravine. They crept through a wet alder thicket, bounded lightly over the ragged brush fence, and paused to reconnoitre on the edge of the clearing in the full glare of the moon. At the same moment the settler emerged from the darkness of the wood-road on the opposite side of the clearing. He saw the two great beasts, heads down and snouts thrust forward, gliding toward the open cabin door.

For a few moments the child had been silent. Now his voice rose again in pitiful appeal, a very ecstasy of loneliness and terror. There was a note in the cry that shook the settler's soul. He had a vision of his own boy, at home with his mother, safeguarded from even the thought of peril. And here was this little one left to the wild beasts! "Thank God! Thank God I came!" murmured the settler, as he dropped on one knee to take a sure aim. There was a loud report (not like the sharp crack of a rifle), and the female panther, shot through the loins, fell in a heap, snarling furiously and striking with her forepaws.

The male walked around her in fierce and anxious amazement. As the smoke lifted, he discerned the settler kneeling for a second shot. With a high screech of fury, the lithe brute sprang upon his enemy, taking a bullet full in his chest without seeming to know he was hit. Ere the man could slip in another cartridge, the beast was upon him, bearing him to the ground and fixing keen fangs in his shoulder. Without a word, the man set his strong fingers desperately into the brute's throat, wrenched himself partly free, and was struggling to rise when the panther's body collapsed upon him all at once, a dead weight which he easily flung aside. The bullet had done its work just in time.

Quivering from the swift and dreadful contest, bleeding profusely from his mangled shoulder, the settler stepped up to the cabin door and peered in. He heard sobs in the darkness.

"Don't be scared, sonny," he said in a reassuring voice. "I'm going to take you home along with me. Poor little lad, *I'll* look after you if folks that ought to don't."

Out of the dark corner came a shout of delight, in a voice which made the settler's heart stand still. "Daddy, daddy," it said, "I knew you'd come. I was so frightened when it got dark!" And a little figure launched itself into the settler's arms and clung to him trembling. The man sat down on the threshold and strained the child to his breast. He remembered how near he had been to disregarding the far-off cries, and great beads of sweat broke out upon his forehead.

Not many weeks afterwards, the settler was following the fresh trail of a bear which had killed his sheep. The trail led him at last along the slope of a deep ravine, from whose bottom came the brawl of a swollen and obstructed stream. In the ravine he found a shallow cave, behind a great white rock. The cave was plainly a wild beast's lair, and he entered circumspectly. There were bones scattered about, and on some dry herbage in the deepest corner of the den he found the dead bodies, now rapidly decaying, of two small panther cubs.

NOTES

fulvous of a red-yellow or brown-yellow colour

dam female parent of a four-legged animal

fowling-piece light gun for shooting wild birds

furlong Imperial measurement equal to an eighth of a mile (0.2 km); from the Old English *fuhrlang,* from *fuhr,* meaning "furrow," and *lang,* meaning "long"

ANALYZE AND INTERPRET

1. With a partner, consider how the author balances our sympathies for the animals and the human beings in this story. Find specific passages in the text to support your views. As a class, discuss how you would have felt if the story had ended differently—with the settler finding the remains of his son in the abandoned cabin.

2. How does the author create suspense in this story? At what point did you experience the greatest suspense? How does the element of suspense contribute to your enjoyment of the story? Discuss your response with your classmates.

3. In the role of the settler, write a diary entry for the day that you find the bodies of the panther cubs. How does this discovery affect your response to the story events? Make an audio recording of your diary entry and then listen to it. Consider how effectively your writing reflects the voice of someone living more than a hundred years ago, and make any revisions to the language to create a more historical feel.

MORE TO EXPLORE

Themes: Family, Rural Life, Nature, Canada, Intrigue, Moral Questions, Crisis

Elements: description, irony, narrator, pathos, plot, setting, simile, third-person point of view

Initiation

Sylvia Plath

LEARNING FOCUS

- Organize and interpret two sides of an issue.
- Analyze an author's use of climax.
- Use dialogue to interpret character.

CONTEXT Sylvia Plath was born in 1933. The backdrop to her life and work was her comfortable upbringing in the American city of Boston. It was not long, however, before she rebelled against class, status, and the confining roles assigned to women. Plath attended Smith College, and went on to marry the poet Ted Hughes. The rest of her brief life was lived with Hughes in England. A poet from a young age, Plath is famous today as much for *The Bell Jar*, a stark and moving autobiographical novel published shortly before her death in 1963, as for her numerous poetry collections. "Initiation" focuses on themes found in her poetry, including the exploration of social hierarchies and personal freedom. In the story, the free-spirited and imaginative Millicent finds what she needs to survive through the image of the heather birds. What might the heather birds symbolize? What aspects of this story, written about half a century ago, are similar to or different from life in your school today? ■

The basement room was dark and warm, like the inside of a sealed jar, Millicent thought, her eyes getting used to the strange dimness. The silence was soft with cobwebs, and from the small, rectangular window set high in the stone wall there sifted a faint bluish light that must be coming from the full October moon. She could see now that what she was sitting on was a woodpile next to the furnace.

Millicent brushed back a strand of hair. It was stiff and sticky from the egg that they had broken on her head as she knelt blindfolded at the sorority altar a short while before. There had been a silence, a slight crunching sound, and then she had felt the cold, slimy egg-white flattening and spreading on her head and sliding down her neck. She had heard someone smothering a laugh. It was all part of the ceremony.

Then the girls had led her here, blindfolded still, through the corridors off Betsy Johnson's house and shut her in the cellar. It would be an hour before they came to get her, but then Rat Court would be all over and she would say what she had to say and go home.

For tonight was the grand finale, the trial by fire. There really was no doubt now that she would get in. She could not think of anyone who had ever been invited into the high school sorority and failed to get through initiation time. But even so, her case would be quite different. She would see to that. She could not exactly say what had decided her revolt, but it definitely had something to do with Tracy and something to do with the heather birds.

What girl at Lansing High would not want to be in her place now? Millicent thought, amused. What girl would not want to be one of the elect, no matter if it did mean five days of initiation before and after school, ending in the climax of Rat Court on Friday night when they made the new girls members? Even Tracy had been wistful when she heard that Millicent had been one of the five girls to receive an invitation.

"It won't be any different with us, Tracy," Millicent had told her. "We'll still go around together like we always have, and next year you'll surely get in."

"I know, but even so," Tracy had said quietly, "you'll change, whether you think you will or not. Nothing ever stays the same."

And nothing does, Millicent had thought. How horrible it would be if one never changed...if she were condemned to be the plain, shy Millicent of a few years back for the rest of her life. Fortunately there was always the changing, the growing, the going on.

It would come to Tracy, too. She would tell Tracy the silly things the girls had said, and Tracy would change also, entering eventually into the magic circle. She would grow to know the special ritual as Millicent had started to last week.

"First of all," Betsy Johnson, the vivacious blonde secretary of the sorority, had told the five new candidates over sandwiches in the school cafeteria last Monday, "first of all, each of you has a big sister. She's the one who bosses you around, and you just do what she tells you."

"Remember the part about talking back and smiling," Louise Fullerton had put in, laughing. She was another celebrity in high school, pretty and dark and vice-president of the student council. "You can't say anything unless your big sister asks you something or tells you to talk to someone. And you can't smile, no matter how you're dying to." The girls had laughed a little nervously, and then the bell had rung for the beginning of afternoon classes.

It would be rather fun for a change, Millicent mused, getting her books out of her locker in the hall, rather exciting to be part of a closely knit group, the exclusive set at Lansing High. Of course, it wasn't a school organization. In fact, the principal, Mr. Cranton, wanted to do away with initiation week altogether, because he thought it was undemocratic and disturbed the routine of school work. But there wasn't really anything he could do about it. Sure, the girls had to come to school for five days without any lipstick on and without curling their hair, and of course everybody noticed them, but what could the teachers do?

Millicent sat down at her desk in the big study hall. Tomorrow she would come to school, proudly, laughingly, without lipstick, with her brown hair straight and shoulder length, and then everybody would know, even the boys would know, that she was one of the elect. Teachers would smile helplessly, thinking perhaps: So now they've picked Millicent Arnold. I never would have guessed it.

A year or two ago, not many people would have guessed it. Millicent had waited a long time for acceptance, longer than most. It was as if she had been sitting for years in a pavilion outside a dance floor, looking in through the windows at the golden interior, with the lights clear and the air like honey, wistfully watching the couples waltzing to the never-ending music, laughing in pairs and groups together, no one alone.

But now at last, amid a week of fanfare and merriment, she would answer her invitation to enter the ballroom through the main entrance marked "Initiation." She would gather up her velvet skirt, her silken train, or whatever the disinherited princesses wore in the story books, and come into her rightful kingdom.... The bell rang to end study hall.

"Millicent, wait up!" It was Louise Fullerton behind her, Louise who had always before been very nice, very polite, friendlier than the rest, even long ago, before the invitation had come.

"Listen," Louise walked down the hall with her to Latin, their next class, "are you busy right after school today? Because I'd like to talk to you about tomorrow."

"Sure. I've got lots of time."

"Well, meet me in the hall after homeroom then, and we'll go down to the drugstore or something."

Walking beside Louise on the way to the drugstore, Millicent felt a surge of pride. For all anyone could see, she and Louise were the best of friends.

"You know, I was so glad when they voted you in," Louise said.

Millicent smiled. "I was really thrilled to get the invitation," she said frankly, "but kind of sorry that Tracy didn't get in, too."

Tracy, she thought. If there is such a thing as a best friend, Tracy has been just that this last year.

"Yes, Tracy," Louise was saying, "she's a nice girl, and they put her up on the slate, but...well, she had three blackballs against her."

"Blackballs? What are they?"

"Well, we're not supposed to tell anybody outside the club, but seeing as you'll be in at the end of the week I don't suppose it hurts." They were at the drugstore now.

"You see," Louise began explaining in a low voice after they were seated in the privacy of the booth, "once a year the sorority puts up all the likely girls that are suggested for membership...."

Millicent sipped her cold, sweet drink slowly, saving the ice cream to spoon up last. She listened carefully to Louise who was going on, "...and then there's a big meeting, and all the girls' names are read off and each girl is discussed."

"Oh?" Millicent asked mechanically, her voice sounding strange.

"Oh, I know what you're thinking," Louise laughed. "But it's really not as bad as all that. They keep it down to a minimum of catting. They just talk over each girl and why or why not they think she'd be good for the club. And then they vote. Three blackballs eliminate a girl."

"Do you mind if I ask you what happened to Tracy?" Millicent said.

Louise laughed a little uneasily. "Well, you know how girls are.

They notice little things. I mean, some of them thought Tracy was just a bit *too* different. Maybe you could suggest a few things to her."

"Like what?"

"Oh, like maybe not wearing knee socks to school, or carrying that old bookbag. I know it doesn't sound like much, but well, it's things like that which set someone apart. I mean, you know that no girl at Lansing would be seen dead wearing knee socks, no matter how cold it gets, and it's kiddish and kind of green to carry a bookbag."

"I guess so," Millicent said.

"About tomorrow," Louise went on. "You've drawn Beverly Mitchell for a big sister. I wanted to warn you that she's the toughest, but if you get through all right it'll be all the more credit to you."

"Thanks, Lou," Millicent said gratefully, thinking, this is beginning to sound serious. Worse than a loyalty test, this grilling over the coals. What's it supposed to prove anyway? That I can take orders without flinching? Or does it just make them feel good to see us run around at their beck and call?

"All you have to do really," Louise said, spooning up the last of her sundae, "is be very meek and obedient when you're with Bev and do just what she tells you. Don't laugh or talk back or try to be funny, or she'll just make it harder for you, and believe me, she's a great one for doing that. Be at her house at seven-thirty."

And she was. She rang the bell and sat down on the steps to wait for Bev. After a few minutes the front door opened and Bev was standing there, her face serious.

"Get up, gopher," Bev ordered.

There was something about her tone that annoyed Millicent. It was almost malicious. And there was an unpleasant anonymity about the label "gopher," even if that was what they always called the girls being initiated. It was degrading, like being given a number. It was a denial of individuality.

Rebellion flooded through her.

"I said get up. Are you deaf?"

Millicent got up, standing there.

"Into the house, gopher. There's a bed to be made and a room to be cleaned at the top of the stairs."

Millicent went up the stairs mutely. She found Bev's room and started making the bed. Smiling to herself, she was thinking: How absurdly funny, me taking orders from this girl like a servant.

Bev was suddenly there in the doorway. "Wipe that smile off your face," she commanded.

There seemed something about this relationship that was not all fun. In Bev's eyes, Millicent was sure of it, there was a hard, bright spark of exultation.

On the way to school, Millicent had to walk behind Bev at a distance of ten paces, carrying her books. They came up to the drugstore where there already was a crowd of boys and girls from Lansing High waiting for the show.

The other girls being initiated were there, so Millicent felt relieved. It would not be so bad now, being part of the group.

"What'll we have them do?" Betsy Johnson asked Bev. That morning Betsy had made her "gopher" carry an old coloured parasol through the square and sing "I'm Always Chasing Rainbows."

"I know," Herb Dalton, the good-looking basketball captain, said.

A remarkable change came over Bev. She was all at once very soft and coquettish.

"You can't tell them what to do," Bev said sweetly. "Men have nothing to say about this little deal."

"All right, all right," Herb laughed, stepping back and pretending to fend off a blow.

"It's getting late," Louise had come up. "Almost eight-thirty. We'd better get them marching on to school."

The "gophers" had to do a Charleston step all the way to school, and each one had her own song to sing, trying to drown out the other four. During school, of course, you couldn't fool around, but even then, there was a rule that you mustn't talk to boys outside of class or at lunchtime…or any time at all after school. So the sorority girls would get the most popular boys to go up to the "gophers" and ask them out, or try to start them talking, and sometimes a "gopher" was taken by surprise and began to say something before she could catch herself. And then the boy reported her and she got a black mark.

Herb Dalton approached Millicent as she was getting an ice cream at the lunch counter that noon. She saw him coming before he spoke to her, and looked down quickly, thinking: He is too princely, too dark and smiling. And I am much too vulnerable. Why must he be the one I have to be careful of?

I won't say anything, she thought, I'll just smile very sweetly. She smiled up at Herb very sweetly and mutely. His return grin was rather miraculous. It was surely more than was called for in the line of duty.

"I know you can't talk to me," he said, very low. "But you're doing fine, the girls say. I even like your hair straight and all."

Bev was coming toward them, then, her red mouth set in a bright, calculating smile. She ignored Millicent and sailed up to Herb.

"Why waste your time with gophers?" she carolled gaily. "Their tongues are tied, but completely."

Herb managed a parting shot. "But that one keeps *such* an attractive silence."

Millicent smiled as she ate her sundae at the counter with Tracy. Generally, the girls who were outsiders now, as Millicent had been, scoffed at the initiation antics as childish and absurd to hide their secret envy. But Tracy was understanding, as ever.

"Tonight's the worst, I guess, Tracy," Millicent told her. "I hear that the girls are taking us on a bus over to Lewiston and going to have us performing in the square."

"Just keep a poker face outside," Tracy advised. "But keep laughing like mad inside."

Millicent and Bev took a bus ahead of the rest of the girls; they had to stand up on the way to Lewiston Square. Bev seemed very cross about something. Finally she said, "You were talking with Herb Dalton at lunch today."

"No," said Millicent honestly.

"Well, I *saw* you smile at him. That's practically as bad as talking. Remember not to do it again."

Millicent kept silent.

"It's fifteen minutes before the bus gets into town," Bev was saying then. "I want you to go up and down the bus asking people what they eat for breakfast. Remember, you can't tell them you're being initiated."

Millicent looked down the aisle of the crowded bus and felt suddenly quite sick. She thought: How will I ever do it, going up to all those stony-faced people who are staring coldly out of the window.

"You heard me, gopher."

"Excuse me, madam," Millicent said politely to the lady in the first seat of the bus, "but I'm taking a survey. Could you please tell me what you eat for breakfast?"

"Why…er…just orange juice, toast, and coffee," she said.

"Thank you very much." Millicent went on to the next person, a young business man. He ate eggs sunny side up, toast and coffee.

By the time Millicent got to the back of the bus, most of the people were smiling at her. They obviously know, she thought, that I'm being initiated into something.

Finally, there was only one man left in the corner of the back seat. He was small and jolly, with a ruddy, wrinkled face that spread into a beaming smile as Millicent approached. In his brown suit with the forest-green tie he looked something like a gnome or a cheerful leprechaun.

"Excuse me, sir," Millicent smiled, "but I'm taking a survey. What do you eat for breakfast?"

"Heather birds' eyebrows on toast," the little man rattled off.

"What?" Millicent exclaimed.

"Heather birds' eyebrows," the little man explained. "Heather birds live on the mythological moors and fly about all day long, singing wild and sweet in the sun. They're bright purple and have *very* tasty eyebrows."

Millicent broke out into spontaneous laughter. Why, this was wonderful, the way she felt a sudden comradeship with a stranger.

"Are you mythological, too?"

"Not exactly," he replied, "but I certainly hope to be someday. Being mythological does wonders for one's ego."

The bus was swinging into the station now; Millicent hated to leave the little man. She wanted to ask him more about the birds.

And from that time on, initiations didn't bother Millicent at all. She went gaily about Lewiston Square from store to store asking for broken crackers and mangoes, and she just laughed inside when people stared and then brightened, answering her crazy questions as if she were quite serious and really a person of consequence. So many people were shut up tight inside themselves like boxes, yet they would open up, unfolding quite wonderfully, if only you were interested in them. And really, you didn't have to belong to a club to feel related to other human beings.

One afternoon Millicent had started talking with Liane Morris, another of the girls being initiated, about what it would be like when they were finally in the sorority.

"Oh, I know pretty much what it'll be like," Liane had said. "My sister belonged before she graduated from high school two years ago."

"Well, just what *do* they do as a club?" Millicent wanted to know.

"Why, they have a meeting once a week…each girl takes turns entertaining at her house…."

"You mean it's just a sort of exclusive social group…."

"I guess so…though that's a funny way of putting it. But it sure gives a girl prestige value. My sister started going steady with the captain of the football team after she got in. Not bad, I say."

No, it wasn't bad, Millicent had thought, lying in bed on the morning of Rat Court and listening to the sparrows chirping in the gutters. She thought of Herb. Would he ever have been so friendly if she were without the sorority label? Would he ask her out (if he ever did) just for herself, no strings attached?

Then there was another thing that bothered her. Leaving Tracy on the outskirts. Because that is the way it would be; Millicent had seen it happen before.

Outside, the sparrows were still chirping, and as she lay in bed Millicent visualized them, pale grey-brown birds in a flock, one like the other, all exactly alike.

And then, for some reason, Millicent thought of the heather birds. Swooping carefree over the moors, they would go singing and cooing out across the great spaces of air, dipping and darting, strong and proud in their freedom and their sometime loneliness. It was then that she made her decision.

Seated now on the woodpile in Betsy Johnson's cellar, Millicent knew that she had come triumphant through the trial of fire, the sear-ing period of the ego which could end in two kinds of victory for her. The easiest of which would be her coronation as a princess labelling her conclusively as one of the select flock.

The other victory would be much harder, but she knew that it was what she wanted. It was not that she was being noble or anything. It was just that she had learned there were other ways of getting into the great hall, blazing with lights, of people and of life.

It would be hard to explain to the girls tonight, of course, but she could tell Louise later just how it was. How she had proved something to herself by going through everything, even Rat Court, and then deciding not to join the sorority after all. And how she could still be friends with everybody. Sisters with everybody. Tracy, too.

The door behind her opened and a ray of light sliced across the soft gloom of the basement room.

"Hey Millicent, come on out now. This is it." There were some of the girls outside.

"I'm coming," she said, getting up and moving out of the soft darkness into the glare of light, thinking: This is it, all right. The worst part, the hardest part, the part of initiation that I figured out myself.

But just then, from somewhere far off, Millicent was sure of it, there came a melodic fluting, quite wild and sweet, and she knew that it must be the song of the heather birds as they went wheeling and gliding against wide blue horizons through vast spaces of air, their wings flashing quick and purple in the bright sun.

Within Millicent another melody soared, strong and exuberant, a triumphant answer to the music of the darting heather birds that sang so clear and lilting over the far lands. And she knew that her own private initiation had just begun.

1. When people are faced with difficult decisions, they sometimes list the "pros and cons" of their dilemma on a chart. **a)** Create the chart Millicent might have made about joining the sorority. **b)** In a small group, discuss which items on your list you think were most important in helping her make up her mind. **c)** Consider what you think you would have done in Millicent's place, and why.

2. With a partner, use this anthology's glossary and your dictionary to research the literary term "climax." Discuss with your partner which scene in "Initiation" forms the climax. Then join with another pair to discuss what happens in the climax, and its impact on Millicent.

3. At the end of the story, Millicent feels that, even though she isn't going to join the sorority, she can still be "sisters with everybody." With a partner, create a dialogue between Millicent and Tracy in which they discuss the aftermath of Millicent's decision. Consider such questions as the following: How have the sorority girls reacted? Is Herb Dalton still interested in Millicent? Does Millicent regret what she did? Work with another pair of classmates. Listen to one another's dialogue and then compare your interpretations of the characters' responses.

MORE TO EXPLORE

Themes: Self, Adolescence, Personal Challenges, Peers, Friends, Rebels, At School, Moral Questions

Elements: characterization, climax, conflict, description, irony, symbol, third-person point of view

Wrap-Up

1. Use the Internet and other sources to do research for a formal essay that traces the history and development of the short story. Be sure to include in your essay answers to the following questions: What purposes have short stories served over time? In what ways has the form changed, and in what ways has it remained consistent? What trends and attitudes have influenced the genre? Why has the short story as a literary form endured?

2. Some of the stories you encountered in this unit were easy to understand; others may have been more difficult. Write a journal entry in which you reflect on and describe the reading strategies you used to help you understand the more complex stories. Comment on the effectiveness of each strategy, and how you might modify it for future reading. Next, identify additional strategies you could use to assist in comprehension. Consider also whether you would use the same or different strategies in reading other genres.

3. With a small group, research the time period and geographical setting of a story in this unit. Then create several pages of a newspaper from this era and locale. Include news, pictures, editorials, cartoons, and advertisements that would be typical of the time and place. Use a page layout or desktop publishing program to design and print a professional-looking publication.

4. Work with a partner to create a story based on a visual in this unit. Consider the characters, narrative, and mood. After developing a story outline, get feedback on its effectiveness from another pair. Write the first draft, then have a third pair analyze your draft's ability to do the following: develop a strong sense of place; include realistic dialogue; "show" readers rather than tell them the story; and include only details relevant to the main conflict. Edit and proofread your story before reading it to the class.

5. With a partner, choose a selection from this unit that includes non-English words or phrases. First, discuss why you think the author has included them. Is their meaning clear from the context in which they appear, or did you have to check them in a dictionary or elsewhere? Can you identify any English words that are derived from these non-English words? If so, investigate how they made their way into the English language. When might you appropriately use these words in your own writing or when speaking? Share your findings with the class, using visuals, as needed, to support your presentation.

6. Which of the stories in this unit do you think could best be turned into a novel? Why? In several paragraphs, describe how you would adapt this story. Would you modify the story's theme, and, if so, how? What would you do with elements such as the setting and mood? How would you develop the characters and the plot?

"If I stopped writing poetry, I would feel a very personal,

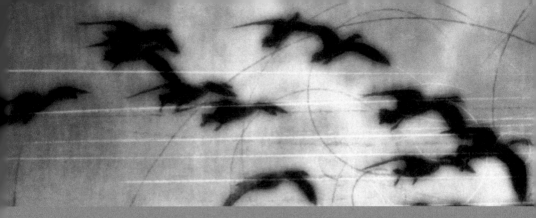

private, intimate whisper was lost." ■ Michael Ondaatje

As ancient as the earliest civilizations, as modern as today, poetry remains a powerful genre for us to tell stories, comment on ideas, and express our most intense emotions. Poetry is incredibly versatile. In this unit, you will encounter poets who communicate plot through narrative poems, present strong feelings through lyric poems, and work their wonder within highly structured forms, such as the sonnet and tanka. The free verse selections here reveal that poetry can be stunningly evocative—and provocative—when free of regular rhythm, rhyme, and stanza form. Virtually all poetry appeals to our hearts and minds through the senses. As you read and listen to each poem, think about how it affects your ears through rhyme and rhythm. Think, too, about how it appeals to your mind's eye through imagery created by metaphors, similes, and symbols. In poetry, each word must be carefully chosen and arranged. To appreciate the contribution each word makes to an entire poem's purpose and effect, you will need to be rigorous in your reading and rereading. The results can be rewarding: insight and beauty can be experienced in a matter of minutes, and re-experienced for a lifetime.

SOS

LEARNING FOCUS

- Analyze and interpret an oral reading.
- Extend an existing literary text to enhance understanding.

CONTEXT Dorothy Livesay's life spanned nearly the entire twentieth century; her immense output of poetry reflects many of the historical shifts of this era. Born in Winnipeg, Manitoba, in 1909, Livesay was greatly influenced by the emerging philosophy of socialism and by early feminism. She published her first book of poems at the age of eighteen and, soon after, obtained her B.A. in modern languages at the University of Toronto. Livesay travelled to France during the 1930s, returning to Canada with even stronger political concerns. Her later poetry, written after 1960, reflects a move toward more personal subjects, including the exploration of womanhood and the effects of aging. Among the numerous accolades Livesay received for her poetry were the Officer of the Order of Canada and two Governor General's Awards. She died in 1996. "SOS" is typical of Livesay's middle-period work. What poetic devices contribute to the rhythmic effect in this poem? How has she captured sounds, and what effect do these sounds have? ■

SOS

Dorothy Livesay

Deet deet deet remorseless as rain
He hammers out the code, channelled in deep-sea pit,
The waters now assembling in a cloud
Formation, meeting in thunder grip—
A knife-slash on her deck, then slow ooze back
Followed by sprouting spray, a wreathe of hair
Shaped to a masthead, fastened to the prow.

Deet deet deet da da. The shriek
Of raw metallic language. Comrades here
Call help. Send greetings to green worlds.
Deet deet deet. The pumps. The captain says
If not next moment's puff, then looming NOW
Time nosing forward like an iceberg snout
Upon us! Only the women in the boats—
The operator's left above, the girl untorn
From grim assertion on the forward deck.
Now not to break or beat, up hand and heart
Da da deet deet quick quicker unity
Unless you court defeat and lick old sores
Reverse your engines! Set your compass here…

Too late. The splutter-spitting da-de-da
Is tattered rag and shattered SOS.
"Hold on" voice cried, "together here"—
Then waters licked her nostril's lip
With salt, and sprayed the foaming brain.
This sea invasion, barricading hordes
Flooded her passages: the signalling
Spluttered da da, alighted, stopped.

After, a scouting plane might spy
(Searching with gulls the empty sea)
A bloated face, dead messages
Curled carelessly in the wave's arm
Their meaning blotted out; might hear
The sea heave endlessly above the sound
Of rotting timbers, ship's bell clanging under sand.

AN ELEGY ON THE DEATH OF A MAD DOG

CONTEXT Oliver Goldsmith was born in Ireland around 1730. After graduating from Trinity College, Dublin, he went on an extended walking tour of France, Germany, Switzerland, and Italy. Apparently, in one of these countries he acquired a medical degree, but when he returned to London, England, he took up the pen instead. Goldsmith wrote whimsical essays and nostalgic poetry, but his reputation rests primarily on the comedic drama *She Stoops to Conquer* (1773) and his novel *The Vicar of Wakefield* (1766). His comedies injected realism into the dull, sentimental theatre of the day and, like his novel, are imbued with warm humanity. A member of Samuel Johnson's circle, Goldsmith was praised for being kind, spontaneous, and funny. He died in 1774. Consider the definition of the term "parody" and how it relates to this poem. Is a parody intended as a good-natured way of poking fun at someone or something, or is it intended as a serious critique? Does this poem qualify as a parody? Why or why not? ■

An Elegy on the Death of a Mad Dog

Oliver Goldsmith

Good people all, of every sort,
Give ear unto my song;
And if you find it wondrous short,
It cannot hold you long.

In Islington there was a man
Of whom the world might say,
That still a godly race he ran—
Whene'er he went to pray.

A kind and gentle heart he had,
To comfort friends and foes;
The naked every day he clad—
When he put on his clothes.

And in that town a dog was found,
As many dogs there be,
Both mongrel, puppy, whelp, and hound,
And curs of low degree.

This dog and man at first were friends;
But when a pique began,
The dog, to gain some private ends,
Went mad, and bit the man.

Around from all the neighbouring streets
The wond'ring neighbours ran,
And swore the dog had lost its wits
To bite so good a man.

The wound it seemed both sore and sad
To every Christian eye;
And while they swore the dog was mad,
They swore the man would die.

But soon a wonder came to light
That showed the rogues they lied,—
The man recovered of the bite,
The dog it was that died!

SOMETIMES MY BODY LEAVES ME

CONTEXT Lorna Crozier was born in 1941 in Swift Current, Saskatchewan. Just as she was establishing her reputation as a Prairie poet, she travelled abroad, and eventually moved permanently to Victoria, British Columbia, taking up a position in the Creative Writing Department at the University of Victoria. Today, Crozier is considered a leader in Canadian poetry, her work offering, in the words of the poet Dennis Lee, "the literate vernacular" of everyday speech. Her collection *Inventing the Hawk* was awarded the Governor General's Award in 1992. What have you read or seen recently that focuses attention on contradictory signals sent by our minds and our bodies? Are you convinced that this contradiction can happen? Why or why not? ■

Sometimes My Body Leaves Me

Lorna Crozier

Sometimes my body leaves me,
goes into another room
and locks the door. There

it bangs about
like an angry thief.
What is it looking for?

Then there are its silences
stretched thin and taut
between us, invisible

as a fishing line
falling through layers
and layers of green.

I don't know what it feels,
if it feels anything;
or what it remembers,
if each cell holds a memory.

I don't know what sounds to make
to call it back.

What does it do when it sits alone
without a book or anything
resembling love?

ANALYZE AND INTERPRET

1. With a partner, read the poem aloud several times. When it is your turn to listen, close your eyes so that you can concentrate on the sound of the poem.
   Discuss what you noticed during the oral reading by answering the following: **a)** Which parts of the poem do you read more slowly? Where do you naturally speed up? How does the poet achieve this effect? **b)** What alliterations
   and vowel sounds stood out as you listened? Why do you think the poet
   chose to emphasize these particular sounds? **c)** What lines and phrases are
   repeated in the poem? What is the effect of these repetitions? **d)** Which
   parts of the poem made the biggest impact on you when you were listening? Why? Keep notes during your discussion, and share your observations
   with the rest of the class.

2. "SOS" tells a story. Use your imagination to add to the story by writing
   either a poem or short story about what happened before or after the events
   in this poem. Before you start, plan the events of your narrative in a brief plot
   summary. Be sure to incorporate figurative and descriptive language in your
   narrative to create a sense of atmosphere.

MORE TO EXPLORE

Themes: Loss, At Work, Nature, Canada, Science and Technology, Crisis

Elements: alliteration, assonance, motif, rhythm

An Elegy on the Death of a Mad Dog   Oliver Goldsmith

ANALYZE AND INTERPRET

1. With a partner, use the glossary in this anthology and your dictionary to
   help you write a definition of the term "elegy." Next, discuss and then summarize what the main message or meaning of this poem might be. Then
   analyze and discuss the tone of the poem. With a small group, discuss your
   findings and consider these questions: What is the relationship between
   the message and the tone? Why is this poem an elegy, and what bearing
   does this form have on the message and tone of the poem?

2. You will work with a group of classmates to present an oral interpretation of
   this poem in the form of a choral reading. **a)** First, experiment with individual voices, pairs of speakers, and reading in unison. **b)** As you experiment,
   consider how you can enhance your reading by varying your pitch, tempo, volume, and stress. **c)** How might you use sound effects, gestures, and move-

ment for dramatic effect? **d)** Mark up a copy of the poem to indicate how it is to be read. **e)** Videotape your performance and play it for the class. **f)** Discuss how your understanding and appreciation of the poem have deepened as a result of preparing it as a choral reading.

MORE TO EXPLORE

Themes: Personal Challenges, Peers, Europe, Humour

Elements: metre, paradox, parody, rhyme, satire

Sometimes My Body Leaves Me   Lorna Crozier

ANALYZE AND INTERPRET

1. In a few paragraphs, write a character sketch of the narrator of this poem. In your sketch, speculate on features of this narrator such as temperament, experiences, and background. Then exchange sketches with a partner, and discuss their similarities and differences. Use evidence from the poem to explain your character analysis.

2. Using the library and the Internet, find a list of books of literary criticism on Lorna Crozier's work. Use the information you find to create a bibliography of secondary sources for Crozier. Be sure to use a correct, consistent format for listing these citations in your bibliography.

MORE TO EXPLORE

Themes: Self, Canada, Intrigue

Elements: personification, rhetorical question, tone

IN PROGRESS

Head of Andromeda, 1868, Dante Gabriel Rossetti

LEARNING FOCUS

- Participate in analyzing and presenting an interpretation.
- Consider how the context of an author's life affects writing.

CONTEXT Christina Rossetti lived from 1830 to 1894. Throughout her life, she remained close to home and family, partly as a result of ill health. Rossetti was publishing poetry by the time she was twenty, but used a pseudonym. Later, under her own name, she wrote in a variety of forms, including devotional texts influenced by her intense Anglican upbringing. She was also strongly influenced by the milieu of the Pre-Raphaelites, a group of artists whose founders included her brother Dante Gabriel Rossetti. This art movement championed such ideals as nature's beauty, moral seriousness, and the literary imagination. The title of this poem refers to a person. In what ways are individuals a "work in progress"? How do people develop? In your opinion, are we capable of really changing as we age? ■

In Progress

Christina Rossetti

Ten years ago it seemed impossible
      That she should ever grow so calm as this,
      With self-remembrance in her warmest kiss
And dim dried eyes like an exhausted well.
Slow-speaking when she had some fact to tell,
      Silent with long-unbroken silences,
      Centred in self yet not unpleased to please,
Gravely monotonous like a passing bell.
Mindful of drudging daily common things,
      Patient at pastime, patient at her work,
         Wearied perhaps but strenuous certainly.
         Sometimes I fancy we may one day see
      Her head shoot forth seven stars from where they lurk
And her eyes lightnings and her shoulders wings.

HOLY SONNET 10

LEARNING FOCUS

- Speculate on a meaning, citing evidence.
- Research literary forms and devices, and relate them to a text.

CONTEXT John Donne was born in London, England, in 1572. He began university at the age of eleven, studying for three years at Oxford University, and another three at Cambridge University. He was considered too young, however, to receive a degree from either institution. Donne's life took many turns, including studying law, joining naval expeditions to Spain and the Azores Islands, attaining a post in Queen Elizabeth I's Parliament, and becoming an Anglican minister. He wrote numerous books of poetry and prose, as well as 160 published sermons. All of his writing was noted for its elaborate metaphors, flair for drama, wide knowledge, and quick wit. At the age of forty-five, Donne's wife died, a heartbreaking event that led him to write his Holy Sonnets. Why is it sometimes helpful to write down feelings and views about a painful experience? How might metaphors help a writer to express and deal with such an experience? ■

Holy Sonnet 10
John Donne

Death, be not proud, though some have called thee
Mighty and dreadful, for thou art not so;
For those whom thou think'st thou dost overthrow
Die not, poor Death, nor yet canst thou kill me.
From rest and sleep, which but thy pictures be,
Much pleasure; then from thee much more must flow,
And soonest our best men with thee do go,
Rest of their bones, and soul's delivery.
Thou art slave to fate, chance, kings, and desperate men,
And dost with poison, war, and sickness dwell.
And poppy or charms can make us sleep as well
And better than thy stroke; why swell'st thou then?
One short sleep past, we wake eternally
And death shall be no more; Death, thou shalt die.

MY LAST DUCHESS

LEARNING FOCUS

- Work with a group to write a dramatic monologue.
- Record an oral reading to express an interpretation.

CONTEXT The Victorian poet Robert Browning was born in London, England, in 1812. Browning received little formal education but made good use of his father's extensive library. In his twenties, Browning befriended the British writers Shelley, Carlyle, Dickens, and Tennyson, and he travelled to Russia and Italy. He attempted to write stage plays, but these early works received mixed reviews. At the age of thirty-four, Browning married the poet Elizabeth Barrett. In 1869 he wrote what many consider his finest work, *The Ring and the Book*. He died in 1889. "My Last Duchess" is a dramatic monologue spoken by a duke, a character probably based on the actual sixteenth-century Duke of Ferrara, Alphonso II. The duke is betrothed to the daughter of a count. In this poem, the duke addresses the count's representative, who is negotiating a dowry. The duke proudly shows off a painting of his former wife, egotistically describing her as he would a possession. He notes that earlier in her life, she was more enamoured of simple things than of his great reputation, and that later in life she lost her joyful demeanour. Why do you think the poet chose the dramatic monologue form to present this situation? Have you ever encountered a similar interaction in a film, on television, or in a piece of fiction? How does that situation compare with the one in the poem? ■

My Last Duchess

Robert Browning

Ferrara

That's my last Duchess painted on the wall,
Looking as if she were alive. I call
That piece a wonder, now: Frà Pandolf's hands
Worked busily a day, and there she stands.
Will't please you sit and look at her? I said
"Frà Pandolf" by design, for never read
Strangers like you that pictured countenance,
The depth and passion of its earnest glance,
But to myself they turned (since none puts by
The curtain I have drawn for you, but I)
And seemed as they would ask me, if they durst,
How such a glance came there; so, not the first
Are you to turn and ask thus Sir, 'twas not
Her husband's presence only, called that spot
Of joy into the Duchess' cheek: perhaps
Frà Pandolf chanced to say "Her mantle laps
Over my lady's wrist too much," or "Paint
Must never hope to reproduce the faint
Half-flush that dies along her throat": such stuff
Was courtesy, she thought, and cause enough
For calling up that spot of joy. She had
A Heart—how shall I say?—too soon made glad,
Too easily impressed; she liked whate'er
She looked on, and her looks went everywhere.
Sir, 'twas all one! My favour at her breast,

The dropping of the daylight in the West,
The bough of cherries some officious fool
Broke in the orchard for her, the white mule
She rode with round the terrace—all and each
Would draw from her alike the approving speech,
Or blush, at least. She thanked men—good! But thanked
Somehow—I know not how—as if she ranked
My gift of a nine-hundred-years-old name
With anybody's gift. Who'd stoop to blame
This sort of trifling? Even had you skill
In speech—(which I have not)—to make your will
Quite clear to such an one, and say, "Just this
Or that in you disgusts me; here you miss,
Or there exceed the mark"—and if she let
Herself be lessoned so, nor plainly set
Her wits to yours, forsooth, and made excuse
—E'en then would be some stooping; and I choose
Never to stoop. Oh sir, she smiled, no doubt,
Whene'er I passed her; but who passed without
Much the same smile? This grew; I gave commands;
Then all smiles stopped together. There she stands
As if alive. Will't please you rise? We'll meet
The company below, then. I repeat,
The Count your master's known munificence
Is ample warrant that no just pretence
Of mine for dowry will be disallowed;
Though his fair daughter's self, as I avowed
At starting, is my object. Nay, we'll go
Together down, sir. Notice Neptune, though,
Taming a sea horse, thought a rarity,
Which Claus of Innsbruck cast in bronze for me!

ANALYZE AND INTERPRET

1. In a group of three, discuss the relationship among this poem's title, content, and theme. Present the results of your discussion to the entire class, and respond to questions and comments.

2. This poem is written from the third-person point of view; however, it may be based on Rossetti's own life. **a)** In a group, research biographical information about Rossetti. **b)** Discuss any information you found that might be relevant to this poem. **c)** Present your findings. **d)** As a class, discuss the value of researching an author's biography to assist in interpreting her or his works.

MORE TO EXPLORE

Themes: Personal Challenges, Self and Culture, Europe

Elements: alliteration, assonance, couplet, iambic pentameter, irony, page layout, rhyme, sonnet

---

Holy Sonnet 10   John Donne

NOTES

dost old-fashioned term meaning "do" or "does"

poppy refers to the flower of the plant from which the narcotic opium is extracted; in Donne's era, the drug was not known to be dangerously addictive and was used to assist in sleep and for medicinal purposes

swell'st old-fashioned contraction for "swellest," meaning "swell up"; in this instance, indicates "swelling with pride"

ANALYZE AND INTERPRET

1. What might the last two lines of the poem mean? What is the speaker's attitude toward the subject of the sonnet? Identify words and phrases that communicate this attitude.

2. With a partner, research the characteristics of the English and the Italian sonnet forms. How is this sonnet a combination of the two? How has Donne used the form of the sonnet to organize his ideas? Summarize your discussion and share your notes with another group.

MORE TO EXPLORE

Themes: Personal Challenges, Nature, Europe, Journeys

Elements: archetype, formal language, metre, rhyme, sonnet, thesis

NOTES

Ferrara the speaker of this dramatic monologue, the Duke of Ferrara

Frà Pandolf refers to the artist who created the painting of the Duchess

countenance refers to her face as an indication of character or mood

durst old-fashioned term meaning "if they would dare"

mantle a cloak

officious marked by excessive eagerness in offering unwanted services

nine-hundred-years-old name here, the Duke is indicating that he comes from a well-established aristocratic lineage

trifling in this instance, frivolous

forsooth an old fashioned term for "in truth"; often used sarcastically

e'en the old-fashioned contraction for "even"

munificence lavish generosity

dowry the money, goods, or estate a woman is expected to bring to a marriage in some cultures

Neptune the Roman god of the sea

Claus of Innsbruck refers to another artist

ANALYZE AND INTERPRET

1. This poem takes the form of a dramatic monologue. Work in a group to read the poem aloud several times, and then discuss the story it is telling. With your group, rewrite the poem as a dramatic monologue spoken by the count's representative. Retain as much of the original content as you can.

2. Read lines 21 through 35 with a partner, and discuss what they tell about the duchess. What does the duke reveal about himself in these lines? Practise reading the lines as you think the duke would say them, and then record yourself. Ask a partner to listen to your tape and comment on how effectively you were able to recreate the personality of the duke.

MORE TO EXPLORE

Themes: Self and Culture, Stereotypes, Romance, Europe, Intrigue, Moral Questions, Eye on the Past

Elements: couplet, dramatic monologue, formal language, irony, metaphor, metre

THE
TABLES
TURNED

CONTEXT William Wordsworth was born in 1770 in northern England's Lake District, where he lived much of his life. With Samuel Taylor Coleridge, Wordsworth started the English Romantic movement in 1798 on publication of their collection of poetry called *Lyrical Ballads*. While many poets still used a grandiose style to write about ancient heroes, Wordsworth focused on nature, common people, and children, using ordinary diction of the time to express his feelings. He defined poetry as "the spontaneous overflow of powerful feelings" arising from "emotion recollected in tranquility." This revolution in how poetry was written went on to influence several generations of poets in many countries. Wordsworth studied at Cambridge University and travelled to numerous European countries. His early work was considered to be his best, although he wrote up until his death at the age of eighty in 1850. Why do you think people are inspired by nature? What are we able to learn from nature that we cannot learn from academic pursuits? ■

The Tables Turned

William Wordsworth

Up! up! my Friend, and quit your books;
Or surely you'll grow double:
Up! up! my Friend, and clear your looks;
Why all this toil and trouble?

The sun, above the mountain's head,
A freshening lustre mellow
Through all the long green fields has spread,
His first sweet evening yellow.

Books! 'tis a dull and endless strife:
Come, hear the woodland linnet,
How sweet his music! on my life,
There's more of wisdom in it.

And hark! how blithe the throstle sings!
He, too, is no mean preacher:
Come forth into the light of things,
Let Nature be your Teacher.

She has a world of ready wealth,
Our minds and hearts to bless—
Spontaneous wisdom breathed by health,
Truth breathed by cheerfulness.

One impulse from a vernal wood
May teach you more of man,
Of moral evil and of good,
Than all the sages can.

Sweet is the lore which Nature brings;
Our meddling intellect
Mis-shapes the beauteous forms of things:—
We murder to dissect.

Enough of Science and of Art;
Close up those barren leaves;
Come forth, and bring with you your heart
That watches and receives.

ODE TO AUTUMN

Autumn, 1940, Franklin Carmichael

CONTEXT John Keats is considered to be one of England's major Romantic poets. He was born in 1795 and lost both his parents before he reached the age of fourteen. While still a teenager, he began training as an apothecary, or pharmacist, but demonstrated a keen yearning to write. After passing his examination as an apothecary, he worked as a medical practitioner for less than a year before embracing the financially precarious life of a full-time poet in 1816. His output during the remaining five years of his life represents some of the most exquisite poetry written in English. He died while living in Italy in 1821 at the age of twenty-six. "Ode to Autumn" was written in 1818, Keats' most productive year as a poet. What kinds of thoughts and feelings do different seasons trigger in you? Do you tend to take stock of your life more at one time of the year than at another? If so, why? How do your feelings about autumn compare with those of Keats? ■

Ode to Autumn

John Keats

Season of mists and mellow fruitfulness!
Close bosom-friend of the maturing sun;
Conspiring with him how to load and bless
With fruit the vines that round the thatch-eaves run;
To bend with apples the mossed cottage-trees,
And fill all fruit with ripeness to the core;
To swell the gourd, and plump the hazel shells
With a sweet kernel; to set budding more,
And still more, later flowers for the bees,
Until they think warm days will never cease,
For Summer has o'erbrimmed their clammy cells.

Who hath not seen thee oft amid thy store?
Sometimes whoever seeks abroad may find
Thee sitting careless on a granary floor,
Thy hair soft-lifted by the winnowing wind;
Or on a half-reaped furrow sound asleep,
Drowsed with the fume of poppies, while thy hook
Spares the next swath and all its twined flowers;
And sometimes like a gleaner thou dost keep
Steady thy laden head across a brook;
Or by a cider-press, with patient look,
Thou watchest the last oozings, hours by hours.

Where are the songs of Spring? Ay, where are they?
Think not of them, thou hast thy music too,—
While barred clouds bloom the soft-dying day
And touch the stubble-plains with rosy hue;
Then in a wailful choir the small gnats mourn
Among the river sallows, borne aloft
Or sinking as the light wind lives or dies;
And full-grown lambs loud bleat from hilly bourn;
Hedge-crickets sing, and now with treble soft
The redbreast whistles from a garden-croft;
And gathering swallows twitter in the skies.

THE
LAKE
ISLE OF
INNISFREE

LEARNING FOCUS

- Use technology to create a visual representation.
- Incorporate literary techniques into an original work.

CONTEXT A playwright, a poet, and later a politician of the newly independent Irish Free State, William Butler Yeats is one of the most highly regarded Irish writers of the last century. Born in 1865 in Dublin and raised in an artistic household, Yeats was initially interested in painting but turned to literature in his early twenties. He dedicated himself to the establishment of a national Irish theatre and celebrated Irish culture through the use of myths and legends in his work. Yeats' prolific career spanned four decades, and he was awarded the Nobel Prize for Literature in 1923. He died in 1939. Yeats wrote "The Lake Isle of Innisfree" after a visit to London. What images and ideas do the words "rural" and "urban" bring to your mind? In what ways does this poem deal with the differences between rural and urban life? Based on what you read in this poem, what do you think Yeats, as a poet, would make of large cities in the twenty-first century? ■

The Lake Isle of Innisfree

William Butler Yeats

I will arise and go now, and go to Innisfree,
And a small cabin build there, of clay and wattles made:
Nine bean-rows will I have there, a hive for the honey-bee,
And live alone in the bee-loud glade.

And I shall have some peace there, for peace comes dropping slow,
Dropping from the veils of the morning to where the cricket sings;
There midnight's all a glimmer, and noon a purple glow,
And evening full of the linnet's wings.

I will arise and go now, for always night and day
I hear lake water lapping with low sounds by the shore;
While I stand on the roadway, or on the pavements grey,
I hear it in the deep heart's core.

NOTES

linnet a small bird in the finch family

throstle a bird in the oscine family that is a type of thrush known for its beautiful song

vernal of, relating to, or occurring in the spring; from the Latin word *vērnālis*, from *vērnus*, from *vēr*, meaning "spring"

ANALYZE AND INTERPRET

1. Write a response to the poem focusing on these lines: "Come forth into the light of things, / Let Nature be your Teacher." In your response, describe the knowledge that Wordsworth believes we can gain from nature and not from books; then reflect on your own learning experiences in the natural world. What further lessons do you think humans need to learn from nature?

2. Create a collage to represent visually the ideas in this poem. Give your collage a title. Share your work with a group, invite the members' reactions, and explain why you chose the images and words you did.

MORE TO EXPLORE

Themes: Friends, Rebels, Nature, Europe, Journeys

Elements: metre, pathetic fallacy, quatrain, rhyme, thesis

Ode to Autumn   John Keats

NOTES

thatch-eaves roof made of reeds or fronds woven together

winnowing separating the chaff from the grain by the means of blowing air

wailful mournful

ANALYZE AND INTERPRET

1. a) In a group of three, assign one of the three stanzas to each member. b) Read the stanza you are responsible for, making jot notes to help you understand its structure and content. c) Rewrite the stanza line by line using plain or everyday speech, but maintaining 10 syllables per line. d) With the other members of your group, read your version of the ode. e) Listen to another group's version. Do you prefer the ode in a plain-language version or in Keats' Romantic style? Discuss your preference with the group.

2. On the Internet, find another ode written by Keats, and print it out. In a chart, compare and contrast this new ode with "Ode to Autumn." Points of comparison could include subject, tone, style, rhythm, imagery, theme, and overall effectiveness. Use direct quotations from the odes to support your points. Then, using the chart, write a comparison essay of the two works.

MORE TO EXPLORE

Themes: Loss, Rural Life, Nature, Europe

Elements: alliteration, formal language, iambic pentameter, motif, personification, rhyme, second-person point of view

---

The Lake Isle of Innisfree   William Butler Yeats

NOTES

Innisfree name of a lake near Yeats' ancestral home of Sligo, Ireland

wattles poles interwined with twigs, reeds, or branches for use in the construction of walls or fences

linnet a small brown finch, the male of which has a beautiful song

ANALYZE AND INTERPRET

1. Create a drawing or other visual, to accompany the poem, that depicts Innisfree as seen by the narrator. Use electronic tools, such as a scanner or publishing program, to merge the image and the text. As you present your product, describe how such electronic tools can be used to enhance the content of various types of writing.

2. In your journal, list some qualities you would seek in the perfect place to "escape from it all." Then decide whether you would prefer to use poetry or prose to write about this place. Create the description of this ideal get-away spot— your own "Innisfree"—using figurative language and vivid imagery to develop the sensory details of your piece of writing.

MORE TO EXPLORE

Themes: Self, Rural Life, Urban Life, Nature, Europe, Journeys

Elements: alliteration, metaphor, metre, quatrain, rhyme

FALLING SONG

LEARNING FOCUS

- Use a graphic organizer to record and compare responses.
- Interpret the relationship between a literary work and its title.

CONTEXT Daniel David Moses is best known as a playwright, but he is also a poet and an anthologist. Born in 1952, Moses is a Delaware Indian from the Six Nations Reserve on the Grand River in Ontario. He graduated from York University in Toronto and from the University of British Columbia. Moses now lives in Toronto, where he writes full-time and works with both Aboriginal and cross-cultural organizations. Moses received the James Buller Award for Excellence in Aboriginal Theatre for his play *The Medicine Show*. In 1990, he was shortlisted for a Governor General's Award for his play *Coyote City*. In "Falling Song," the natural and urban worlds are juxtaposed. Do you know of any other works in which this juxtaposition also happens? If so, how do they present the natural and urban worlds? ■

Falling Song

Daniel David Moses

There was the sweet but reedy
honking of geese coming down
this morning with rain over
rush hour streets, coming
through like bells that celebrate.

I got right up, pushing up
close to the sooty window
pane. I peered out and up through
the weather, imagining
that that line of winged dots would

be shifting as if waves moved
easily through them, as if
waves floated them south. I wanted
to catch them riding, spots on
the wake of the wind, marking

the certain direction of
their migration. But I got
no satisfaction. Mist kept
them mysterious, quickly
dampening their call. Leaning

over the sill, I gaped at
a window shade dull sky, at
a hollow city, and felt
like I'd missed a parade I
would have wanted to follow.

MY SONG

Marble flower inlay in the Red Fort, Delhi, India

LEARNING FOCUS

- Use questions to prompt a journal-entry response.
- Build consensus and research similar artistic works.

CONTEXT Rabindranath Tagore, one of the most renowned writers in modern Indian literature, was born in Calcutta in 1861 into a prominent family. Tagore wrote novels, short stories, and plays, and composed hundreds of popular songs as well. He wrote in Bengali, one of South Asia's many languages, and translated most of his works into English himself. Internationally, Tagore stressed the need for the East and the West to unite, and travelled widely in his attempts to spread his ideals. Politically active in India, he was a supporter of Mahatma Gandhi, the pacifist who helped to lead the country to independence. Tagore was awarded the Nobel Prize for Literature in 1913. He died in 1941. Why might Tagore have referred to this poem as a "song"? What other poems or songs can you compare it with? ■

My Song
Rabindranath Tagore

This song of mine will wind its music around you, my child,
    like the fond arms of love.
This song of mine will touch your forehead like a kiss of blessing.
When you are alone it will sit by your side and whisper in your ear,
    when you are in the crowd it will fence you about with aloofness.
My song will be like a pair of wings in your dreams,
    it will transport your heart to the verge of the unknown.
It will be like the faithful star overhead when dark night
    is over your road.
My song will sit in the pupils of your eyes, and will carry your sight
    into the heart of things.
And when my voice is silent in death, my song will speak in your
    living heart.

YOU WALKED GENTLY TOWARDS ME

CONTEXT Ben Okri established a successful career as a poet, novelist, and short-story writer even before he had graduated from university. Born in 1959 in a small town in Nigeria, Okri moved to England to complete his education at the University of Essex, and continues to make Britain his home. In 1987, he won the Commonwealth Prize for his first short-story collection. He later achieved international recognition by winning the Booker Prize, England's foremost literary award, for his third novel, *The Famished Road*. The poem "You Walked Gently Towards Me" invites us into the speaker's memory of a specific evening while helping us to recall similar moments in our own lives. Those moments are often so vivid that we remember what the weather was like or what we were wearing. Think of past events in your own life about which you remember very specific details. Is there a common element in these events that makes them so memorable? ■

You Walked Gently Towards Me

Ben Okri

You walked gently towards me
In the evening light
And brought silence with you
Which fell off when
I touched your shoulder
And felt the rain on it.

We went through the city
Up the roaring streets
Full of many lights
And we sought a place
To be alone
And found none.

The evening was merciful
On your smile.
Your laughter touched
The hungry ghosts
Of passing years.

You moved smoothly
On the waters
Your shadow sounded of silk
You led me to places
Full of mellow darkness
Secret coves where they
Didn't let us in
And under the rain
You bid me kiss you with
Your silent and uncertain eyes.

We walked home
And the rain laughed around us
With its insistent benediction
And your hair was strung with
     Diadems
Your face with glittering dreams
And my eyes were wet
      With your luminous spirited joy.

ANALYZE AND INTERPRET

1. Reread the poem, using a word web to record the dominant emotion you feel as you read each stanza in turn. For each feeling, list the words that most powerfully call it to mind. Then compare opinions with a partner and together try to reach a consensus. How do these feelings contribute to the mood of the poem as a whole?

2. With a partner, discuss the title of the poem. What do you think "falling" refers to? Why might Moses have called this poem a song? Make jot notes of your discussion. Then have a class discussion in which you compare your ideas.

MORE TO EXPLORE

Themes: Self, Loss, Urban Life, Nature, Aboriginal Cultures, Canada

Elements: analogy, assonance, description, empathy, tone

ANALYZE AND INTERPRET

1. In your journal, describe your immediate response upon reading this poem by considering the following questions: a) What pictures formed in your mind as you read? b) What emotions does the poem evoke in you? c) What do you think the poet's purpose was in writing this poem? d) How would you describe the type of language the poet uses? e) Why do you think he chose this title? After you have completed your response, discuss your reactions with a small group.

2. In a small group, try to achieve a consensus on the tone and mood of the poem. Then think of a popular song that expresses the same tone and mood. If possible, find a recording of this song to play for the class. Afterward, explain the reasons for your choice and invite comments on whether your classmates agree with it.

MORE TO EXPLORE

Themes: Childhood, Family, Asia, Journeys, Creativity

Elements: alliteration, archetype, first-person point of view, personification, simile

Notes

benediction a blessing; from the Latin word *benedictiō*, from *bene*, meaning "well," and *dīcere*, meaning "to speak"

Diadems a crown or cloth headband signifying royalty; from the Greek word *diadein*, from *dia*, meaning "across," and *de*, meaning "to bind"

Analyze and Interpret

1. Okri has used imagery to great effect in this poem. Choose your favourite three images and, in a few sentences, jot down what makes these images so powerful. Then exchange papers with a partner and discuss the similarities and differences in your choices.

2. This poem expresses romantic love. Using the library or Internet resources, find another poem that conveys romantic love. In an outline, compare and contrast the two poems in terms of one of the following elements: setting, language choice, imagery, or tone. In several paragraphs, analyze this element in the two poems.

More to Explore

Themes: Romance, Urban Life, Africa

Elements: description, dramatic monologue, mood, personification, setting, symbol

UNTITLED (VANCOUVER)

Molly Lamb Bobak

c. 1941, oil on canvas, 76.5 x 56.0 cm

CONTEXT Molly Lamb Bobak was born in Vancouver, British Columbia, in 1922, and later studied at the Vancouver School of Art. In 1942, she joined the Canadian Women's Army Corps, and in 1945 was appointed as the first female Canadian war artist. After the war, Bobak returned to her hometown where she taught at the Vancouver School of Art and began a career as a radio and television broadcaster. After studying in Europe on a Canada Council Fellowship, she moved to New Brunswick in 1960. There, she taught art both at the University of New Brunswick and on a television program. Bobak has received numerous honorary degrees, and is a member of the Royal Canadian Academy of Arts. Much of Bobak's work focuses on the dignity and significance of ordinary events in our everyday lives. If you were asked to paint or sketch a recent event in your own life, which one would you choose? Why? What details would you include to highlight the significance of the situation?

ANALYZE AND INTERPRET

1. In a group, discuss the artist's use of light and shadow. Identify all the sources of light in the painting. How would you describe the tonal quality of the light? How does the lighting contribute to the mood of the painting? How does Bobak use light to delineate the focal point of the work? Where in the painting is the light used realistically, and where does the artist take liberties with light? Record your discussion and share your notes with the rest of the class.

2. In an interview, Molly Lamb Bobak once said, "Sometimes I worry if I have anything to say, truly, because I see something and I paint it, without thinking beyond the visual thing, the movement of the people and the colour and so on." As a class, discuss "Untitled" in terms of Bobak's statement. Do you think that a painting needs to say something in order to be good? What is most important to you about a painting?

MORE TO EXPLORE

Themes: Peers, Urban Life, Canada, Journeys

Elements: mood, motif, setting, visual composition, visual scale

CONTEXT It has been said that Margaret Atwood, born in Ottawa in 1939, may be the most famous living Canadian writer. Her early writing focuses on our relationship with the often harshly beautiful Canadian landscape. Atwood is an immensely prolific writer, having published short stories, novels, and collections of poetry and essays throughout her forty-year career. She has received many honorary degrees and many awards, including the Booker Prize in 2000 for her novel *The Blind Assassin*. Atwood's work often meditates on the tension between the inner and outer lives of her characters and on gender relations. In the poem "Up," what does the first line suggest about what is to come in this poem? Does the tone of this poem surprise you? Why or why not? ■

UP

Margaret Atwood

You wake up filled with dread.
There seems no reason for it.
Morning light sifts through the window,
there is birdsong,
you can't get out of bed.

It's something about the crumpled sheets
hanging over the edge like jungle
foliage, the terry slippers gaping
their dark pink mouths for your feet,
the unseen breakfast—some of it
in the refrigerator you do not dare
to open—you will not dare to eat.

What prevents you? The future. The future tense,
immense as outer space.
You could get lost there.
No. Nothing so simple. The past, its density
and drowned events pressing you down,
like sea water, like gelatin
filling your lungs instead of air.

Forget all that and let's get up.
Try moving your arm.
Try moving your head.
Pretend the house is on fire
and you must run or burn.
No, that one's useless.
It's never worked before.

Where is it coming from, this echo,
this huge No that surrounds you,
silent as the folds of the yellow
curtains, mute as the cheerful

Mexican bowl with its cargo
of mummified flowers?
(You chose the colours of the sun,
not the dried neutrals of shadow.
God knows you've tried.)

Now here's a good one:
you're lying on your deathbed.
You have one hour to live.
Who is it, exactly, you have needed
all these years to forgive?

POETRY

LEARNING FOCUS

- Use a literary text to prompt reflection on the writing process.
- Compare literary texts to assess and discuss their effectiveness.

CONTEXT Sally Ito is a poet, translator, and fiction writer with an M.A. degree from the University of Alberta. A Japanese Canadian, she was born and raised in Alberta, and has lived and worked in Japan. Her book *Frogs in the Rain Barrel*, which was published in 1995, was first runner-up in the Milton Acorn People's Poet of Canada Award competition. Ito also won the Howard O'Hagan Award for Short Fiction. Another of her books, *Floating Shore*, was published in 1998. Ito currently lives in Edmonton and teaches writing at King's University College. In "Poetry," what is Sally Ito saying about where poems come from? What do you think inspires poets to write? ■

Poetry
Sally Ito

Waves that sigh
are best recorded in dreams
where their meaning is
not obscure.
Still we continue
chiselling words in sand,
have them washed away by Leviathan,
only to begin again.
But comes the day we drop the chisel
and grope after the silvery tail
disappearing into the sea
and oh, what of the scales left in our hands!
opalescent bits of glass
through which our Self may be mirrored,
darkly, darkly,
as the night from which
this monster came.

A FLOWER OF WAVES

CONTEXT Lady Ise was born in Japan in approximately 875 CE. Ise grew up in a family of prominent scholars and poets, which helped to raise her profile in the court in which she lived. During Japan's Heian period (794–1185 CE), it was considered essential for men and women of culture to be able to compose beautiful poetry. As well as an accomplished poet, Ise was known as a first-rate musician. She died in 938 CE. "A Flower of Waves" is an example of tanka, a thirty-one syllable form of poetry dating back at least 1,300 years. Generally, tanka poems evoke a moment or mark an occasion with concision and musicality. In the best tanka, the images often flow seamlessly into one thought. What single thought might you want to express in a tanka, haiku, or other short poem? How might you express that thought in a form other than writing? ■

A Flower of Waves

Lady Ise

TRANSLATED BY ETSUKO TERASAKI WITH
IRMA BRANDEIS

A flower of waves
blossoms in the distance
and ripples shoreward
as though a breeze had quickened
the sea and set it blooming.

ANALYZE AND INTERPRET

1. **a)** With a partner, determine whether this poem is written from the first-, second-, or third-person point of view, and list every word in the poem that reveals this point of view. **b)** With your partner, discuss why Atwood might have chosen the point of view she did. **c)** Next, rewrite the poem from one of the other points of view. **d)** Make jot notes about whether your rewrite affects the story line, tone, or message of the poem. **e)** Find a pair that chose a different point of view for its rewrite, and compare and contrast the effects of each of your versions.

2. Using the Internet and poetry anthologies in the school library or resource centre, work in a small group to compile an anthology of poems about sleep and waking. Write an introduction to each poem that comments on its theme and tone. Select or create illustrations. Compile your anthology in the form of a small booklet.

MORE TO EXPLORE

Themes: Self, Personal Challenges, Canada, Journeys

Elements: antithesis, dramatic monologue, rhyme, rhythm, tone

NOTES

Leviathan a huge sea animal, or a huge ship, or any great and powerful person or thing; from the Hebrew word for dragon

ANALYZE AND INTERPRET

1. Writing poetry can be challenging. With a partner, discuss how writing poetry makes you feel. What are some of the difficulties you face? What insights into yourself has writing poetry facilitated? After your discussion, reread "Poetry," comparing your feelings about expressing yourself in poetic form with those expressed in this poem.

2. With a small group, find at least two other poems, by other poets, with themes similar to that of "Poetry." As a group, discuss how these poets deal with the issues you've identified. In your discussion, you may wish to consider the following questions: Which poet portrays the theme most effectively, and why? Which poetic devices have these poets chosen to use, and how effective are they? Present the poems to your class and discuss your analysis.

Themes: Self, Personal Challenges, Nature, Canada, Journeys

Elements: allusion, metaphor, metre, mood, personification, symbol

A Flower of Waves

Lady Ise

ANALYZE AND INTERPRET

1. As you read this poem, try to visualize the images Lady Ise creates. Then sketch your mental images. Next, share your sketches with a small group and discuss how the group's images are alike and different. As a group, list the words and phrases in the poem that you find particularly powerful.

2. This poem was originally written in Hiragana, a writing system of 50 sound symbols used by Japanese women in approximately 1,000 CE. Work with a partner or small group to research the importance of this writing system and how it contributed to the poetic history of Japan. Present your findings in the form of an imaginary interview with Lady Ise or another Japanese female poet.

MORE TO EXPLORE

Themes: Nature, Asia, Creativity

Elements: description, metaphor, mood, setting, third-person point of view

ODE TO MY SOCKS

LEARNING FOCUS

- Record, evaluate, and summarize the uses of a literary device.
- Use existing literary texts as a model for creating your own.

CONTEXT Pablo Neruda is the pen name adopted by Neftalí Ricardo Reyes Basoalto, a Chilean poet and diplomat. Neruda was born in 1904, and as a young adult he joined the foreign service, in which he developed a distinguished career. His travels before and after World War II took him around the globe and helped shape his Marxist perspective and commitment to workers' rights. Neruda published widely and in 1971 was awarded the Nobel Prize for Literature. Committed to fighting for the rights of the poor in Chile, Neruda was instrumental in the failed attempt to bring a more compassionate Chilean leader to power in the 1970s. He died in 1973. How does "Ode to My Socks" play on the traditional purpose and style of an ode? What theme is Neruda exploring in this poem? How do the tone and mood of the poem relate to this theme? ■

Ode to My Socks

Pablo Neruda
TRANSLATED BY ROBERT BLY

Maru Mori brought me
a pair
of socks
which she knitted herself
with her sheepherder's hands,
two socks as soft
as rabbits.
I slipped my feet
into them
as though into
two
cases

knitted
with threads of
twilight
and goatskin.
Violent socks,
my feet were
two fish made
of wool,
two long sharks
sea-blue, shot
through
by one golden thread,
two immense blackbirds,
two cannons,
my feet
were honored
in this way
by
these
heavenly
socks.
They were
so handsome
for the first time
my feet seemed to me
unacceptable
like two decrepit
firemen, firemen
unworthy
of that woven
fire,
of those glowing
socks.

Nevertheless
I resisted
the sharp temptation
to save them somewhere

as schoolboys
keep
fireflies,
as learned men
collect
sacred texts,
I resisted
the mad impulse
to put them
in a golden
cage
and each day give them
birdseed
and pieces of pink melon.
Like explorers
in the jungle who hand
over the very rare
green deer
to the spit
and eat it
with remorse,
I stretched out
my feet
and pulled on
the magnificent
socks
and then my shoes.

The moral
of my ode is this:
beauty is twice
beauty
and what is good is doubly
good
when it is a matter of two socks
made of wool
in winter.

HISTORY LESSON

Mask representing sun, c. 1870, artist unknown, Nuxalk First Nation

CONTEXT Jeannette C. Armstrong was born in 1948 on the Penticton Indian Reserve in British Columbia. A speaker of both Okanagan and English, she is considered to be one of the first Aboriginal female novelists in North America. Along with fiction, she writes poetry, essays, and children's literature. She is also a teacher, an artist, a sculptor, and an activist. Armstrong received a traditional education from Okanagan elders and, in 1978, she obtained a degree from the University of Victoria. She is the first director of the En'owkin International School of Writing, a creative writing school organized by and for Aboriginal peoples. Her interest in music combined with poetry is reflected in her poem/song "Grandmothers" on the compact disc entitled *Word Up!* In "History Lesson," she offers a version of the past 500 years of North American history, beginning with the arrival of Christopher Columbus. How does her perspective of that history compare with your understanding of what happened? What do you think is the "lesson" that the reader is meant to learn from the poem? ■

History Lesson

Jeannette C. Armstrong

Out of the belly of Christopher's
ship
a mob bursts
Running in all directions
Pulling furs off animals
Shooting buffalo
Shooting each other
left and right

Father mean well
waves his makeshift wand
forgives saucer-eyed Indians

Red coated knights
gallop across the prairie
to get their men
and to build a new world

Pioneers and traders
bring gifts
Smallpox, Seagrams
and Rice Krispies

Civilization has reached
the promised land.

Between the snap crackle pop
of smoke stacks
and multi-coloured rivers
swelling with flower powered zee
are farmers sowing skulls and bones
and miners
pulling from gaping holes
green paper faces
of smiling English lady

The colossi
in which they trust
while burying
breathing forests and fields
beneath concrete and steel
stand shaking fists
waiting to mutilate
whole civilizations
ten generations at a blow.

Somewhere among the remains
of skinless animals
is the termination
to a long journey
and unholy search
for the power
glimpsed in a garden
forever closed
forever lost.

THE PROFILE OF AFRICA

Detail from *Marika*, 1988, David Woods

LEARNING FOCUS

- Evaluate and cite evidence in identifying a perspective.
- Explore the aural and written effects of a literary device.

CONTEXT Maxine Tynes is a seventh-generation Nova Scotian who has never moved away from her province. Born in Dartmouth in 1949, Tynes is an Africadian, a descendant of a group of American slaves who escaped to the Maritimes in hope of a better life. In 1987, Tynes published a collection of poetry titled *Borrowed Beauty* for which she won the Milton Acorn People's Poet of Canada Award the following year. Primarily a poet, she has also worked as a high school English teacher and freelance broadcaster with CBC Radio. Tynes is the first Africadian to be appointed a member of the Board of Governors of Dalhousie University. "The Profile of Africa" evokes the tradition of black artists whose work harks back to an Africa of the imagination and the spirit. For Maxine Tynes, Africa represents a kind of lost paradise. Most Canadians are in one way or another newcomers with roots in other places. What, if any, connection do you have to your ancestral community? ■

The Profile of Africa
Maxine Tynes

we wear our skin like a fine fabric
we people of colour
brown, black, tan coffeecoffee cream ebony
beautiful, strong, exotic in profile
flowering lips
silhouette obsidian planes, curves, structure
like a many-shaded mosaic
we wear our skin like a flag
we share our colour like a blanket
we cast our skin like a shadow
we wear our skin like a map
chart my beginning by my profile
chart my beginning by my colour
read the map of my heritage in
my face
my skin
the dark flash of eye
the profile of Africa.

ANALYZE AND INTERPRET

1. Make a list of the metaphors and similes that the speaker of the poem uses to describe his socks. Do you think they are effective choices? Why? How do these comparisons contribute to the tone and theme of the poem? Write a paragraph summarizing your ideas.

2. Choose an object that is personally important to you, and write an ode to it. You may wish to begin by examining other odes, such as those by John Keats, to determine the most suitable structure for your poem. When finished, read your ode to the class, using tone of voice and body language to create a dramatic effect.

MORE TO EXPLORE

Themes: At Work, South America, Humour, Creativity

Elements: metaphor, rhyme, rhythm, simile

NOTES

Christopher's ship a reference to the landing of Christopher Columbus' Spanish-sponsored expedition; his three ships, the *Niña*, the *Pinta*, and the *Santa Maria*, first reached land, it is generally believed, at San Salvador, an island in the Bahamas, on October 12, 1492

the promised land a biblical allusion; the land to which God promised to lead the Jewish people after their flight from Egypt in the thirteenth century BCE

colossi the plural form of *colossus*, meaning a gigantic person or thing; the original Colossus, a huge statue built between 294 and 282 BCE on the Greek island of Rhodes, is one of the seven wonders of the world

garden a biblical allusion to the Garden of Eden, a place of perfect peace and harmony

ANALYZE AND INTERPRET

1. In a small group, discuss what themes are introduced by the historical events described in the first verse. How are these themes developed through the rest of the poem? Reread the last verse of the poem and, as a group, make jot notes about what you think the poet is saying. Do you agree with her conclusions? Why or why not? Individually, write a short paragraph summarizing your group's ideas about the theme of the poem.

2. With a partner, discuss how the poet is being ironic in these lines: "Civilization has reached / the promised land." What other examples of irony can you find in the poem? Have a class discussion on how effective the author's use of irony is in conveying her message of social criticism.

MORE TO EXPLORE

Themes: Self and Culture, Stereotypes, Loss, Aboriginal Cultures, Canada, Moral Questions, Eye on the Past

Elements: allusion, characterization, irony, sarcasm, satire, third-person point of view

The Profile of Africa   Maxine Tynes

NOTES

obsidian volcanic glass

ANALYZE AND INTERPRET

1. In a small group, try to determine the attitude of the speaker. Identify specific words and phrases of the poem that contribute to your understanding of the speaker's attitude. Have one member make notes during your discussion. Then compare your notes with another group's, and discuss the similarities and differences.

2. a) With a partner, list every word that is repeated in this poem. b) Discuss with your partner some of the effects that these repeated words have. c) Tape the two of you reading the poem several times. d) Play back your "draft" readings, noting places for improvement. e) Analyze how the poet's use of repeated words affected your interpretation, and how the tone of the poem changed with each reading.

MORE TO EXPLORE

Themes: Self and Culture, Stereotypes, Canada, Africa, Eye on the Past

Elements: first-person point of view, idiom, simile, symbol

IN THE MORNING (27 MAY)

LEARNING FOCUS

- Adapt a literary text into a different medium.
- Consider and explore an alternative perspective.

CONTEXT Elizabeth Brewster was born in New Brunswick in 1922. Brewster has lived in Ontario, Saskatchewan, Alberta, British Columbia, England, and the United States. In 1972, she joined the Department of English at the University of Saskatchewan. Over the past fifty years, she has received many poetry awards. What moment like the one described in this poem has impressed itself on you recently? What was it about this moment in time that made it so memorable? ■

In the Morning (27 May)
Elizabeth Brewster

Didn't know I had robins:

there's a large one now
drinking from a pool of water
left by my sprinkler,
then tugging a small swatch
of grass left last night by the lawnmower,
wheeling himself across the yard,
head swivelling
to both sides.

He's observing me,
trying, I think,
to decide if I'm harmless

maybe meditates
poems about humans,
their occasional usefulness
to birds.

BEAUTIFUL SUMMER

LEARNING FOCUS

- Use a graphic organizer to help you create a comparison of texts.
- Use oral prompts to help you in the creation of an original text.

CONTEXT Anne Hébert was born in Sainte-Catherine-de-Fossambault, Québec, in 1916. Until her mid-thirties, she studied and lived in Québec City, where she worked on Radio-Canada broadcasts and wrote scripts for the National Film Board. In 1954, she received a scholarship to go to Paris, France, where, by 1967, she lived full-time until her death in 2000. A novelist, short-story writer, dramatist, and screenwriter, as well as a poet, Hébert garnered many prizes in her lifetime, including the Prix David, the Prix France-Québec, the Prix Femina, and three Governor General's Awards. Two of her novels were made into films, and several of her books are considered modern classics of Québec literature. Much of Hébert's work explores the concept of freedom; a prevalent theme is the need to escape from both society's, and our own, restrictive viewpoints and behaviours. What images come to your mind when you try to imagine this theme of escape to freedom? To what extent does the poem "Beautiful Summer" deal with this theme? ■

Beautiful Summer
Anne Hébert
TRANSLATED BY
LOLA LEMIRE TOSTEVIN

Sun shouts
On the sea at noon
Spears of gold
Scorching madness
I glide under green water
In search of the fire's soul
Gleaming among the algae.

HORSE-FLY BLUE

LEARNING FOCUS

- Use a discussion as a prompt to elaborate on and revise a response.
- Explore the relationships among form, meaning, and tone in a literary text.

CONTEXT Métis writer Marilyn Dumont was born in Alberta in 1955. One of her first jobs was in video production. Later she studied creative writing at the University of British Columbia while teaching English to First Nations adults. Dumont now teaches full-time in British Columbia and writes poetry and prose. Her work has been widely anthologized, and in 1997 she received the Gerald Lampert Memorial Award for her collection of poetry *A Really Good Brown Girl*. "Horse-Fly Blue" is a poem in the form of a conversation. Why might Dumont have chosen to write this conversation in poetic form rather than as a dialogue in a script or in a short story? Have you ever had, or listened to, a conversation like this one? If so, in what ways are the conversations similar? ■

Horse-Fly Blue
Marilyn Dumont

'…d'you believe in god?,' I ask
       he says, he 'doesn't
       know,
       care'
'But,' I say,
'can't you see that this sky
is the colour of the Greek Mediterranean,
and won't last?'

       although I've never seen the Mediterranean
       I have faith

'Can't you see that this light,'
      'what light?' he says

is the same as all those other afternoons when
the light was receding like
our hairlines, when it shone through
our winter skin and we
awoke from a long nap and
it was light all the time we were sleeping?

'Doesn't this light remind you of all those other times
you looked up from your reading
and weren't expecting to see
change and nothing
did change except the way
you looked, the way you met the light,
greeted it at the door as a friend
or smiled at it from a distance as your lover?

Can't you see that the sky is
horse-fly blue?
I swear I've seen this light before;
before I was born,
I knew the colour of the sky.
When I was five
the yard I played in
had a sky this colour,' I say   'what colour?' he says.

ANALYZE AND INTERPRET

1. Rewrite the poem as a narrative paragraph, making any necessary alter-ations. Then create a new title. Share your paragraph with a partner and, together, note the style and approach of both paragraphs. In what ways do they differ? In a short journal entry, explain which paragraph you prefer and why.

2. Imagine that you are the robin and meditate a "poem about humans." Explore the robin's attitude toward humans and their "occasional usefulness." Share the poems in a group and display them on a bulletin board.

MORE TO EXPLORE

Themes: At Play, Nature, Canada

Elements: description, first-person point of view, irony, narration, personi-fication

---

ANALYZE AND INTERPRET

1. Research to locate the poem entitled "Oread" by the American poet H.D. (Hilda Doolittle). First, create a chart or other graphic organizer to help you plan a paragraph comparing "Oread" with "Beautiful Summer." Consider such elements as subject, theme, images, language, poetic devices, and mood in your discussion. Share your paragraph with a group.

2. Write a poem about a beautiful moment in summer using this poem as your model. Concentrate on creating a mood with simple, clear images. When you are proofreading your work, read your poem out loud and consider how your choice of words contributes to the aural quality of your poem. Share your poem with a group, and ask your classmates to comment on the effectiveness of your word choice.

MORE TO EXPLORE

Themes: Self, Nature, Canada, Journeys

Elements: alliteration, description, personification, setting, symbol

ANALYZE AND INTERPRET

1. Write your initial response to the poem, including your interpretation of the relationship between the two speakers. What does their conversation reveal about their relationship? Share and compare your response in a group of three. After the discussion, revise and elaborate on your initial response using ideas from the discussion and any new insights you have had. At the end of your response, write a short note evaluating how the discussion contributed to your understanding and response.

2. In a small group, discuss the fact that Dumont wrote this poem in the form of a conversation. How does the form of a poem affect your understanding of and response to it? What other form could she have chosen? As part of your discussion, experiment with ways of presenting the same words using different punctuation and spacing, and talk about how your variations affect the tone and meaning.

MORE TO EXPLORE

Themes: Friends, Nature, Aboriginal Cultures, Canada, Moral Questions

Elements: dialogue, irony, rhetorical question, simile

'OUT, OUT—'

LEARNING FOCUS

- Use evidence to support an interpretation.
- Use technology to help you adapt one genre into another.

CONTEXT Poet Robert Frost was more than a critical success; he was also one of the most popular American poets of the twentieth century. Frost was born in California in 1874 and raised in Massachusetts. His short, subtle lyric poems, as well as his longer dramatic monologues and narratives, dramatize the hard life of rural New England. Within these poems, he mixes practical wisdom with a keen awareness of the tragic side of human life. Frost died in 1963. The title of this poem is a direct literary allusion. Do you recognize the origin of this line? How does this allusion relate to the theme of the poem? ■

'Out, Out–'
Robert Frost

The buzz saw snarled and rattled in the yard
And made dust and dropped stove-length sticks of wood,
Sweet-scented stuff when the breeze drew across it.
And from there those that lifted eyes could count
Five mountain ranges one behind the other
Under the sunset far into Vermont.
And the saw snarled and rattled, snarled and rattled,
As it ran light, or had to bear a load.
And nothing happened: day was all but done.
Call it a day, I wish they might have said
To please the boy by giving him the half hour
That a boy counts so much when saved from work.

His sister stood beside them in her apron
To tell them 'Supper.' At the word, the saw,
As if to prove saws knew what supper meant,
Leaped out at the boy's hand, or seemed to leap—
He must have given the hand. However it was,
Neither refused the meeting. But the hand!
The boy's first outcry was a rueful laugh,
As he swung toward them holding up the hand
Half in appeal, but half as if to keep
The life from spilling. Then the boy saw all—
Since he was old enough to know, big boy
Doing a man's work, though a child at heart—
He saw all spoiled. 'Don't let him cut my hand off—
The doctor, when he comes. Don't let him, sister!'
So. But the hand was gone already.
The doctor put him in the dark of ether.
He lay and puffed his lips out with his breath.
And then—the watcher at his pulse took fright.
No one believed. They listened at his heart.
Little—less—nothing!—and that ended it.
No more to build on there. And they, since they
Were not the one dead, turned to their affairs.

THE JOB OF AN APPLE

LEARNING FOCUS

- Demonstrate an understanding of a text structure by using it as a model for an original work.
- Assess how your preparatory work contributed to your participation in a group.

CONTEXT Ronna Bloom is an artist with wide-ranging interests. Born in Montreal in 1961 and educated at the Slade School of Art in London, England, she now works in Toronto as a poet, performer, videographer, and photographer. In addition, Bloom is a trained psychotherapist and educator. A collection of her poetry entitled *Fear of the Ride* was published in 1996, and her second book of poetry, *Personal Effects: Poems*, appeared in 2000. As you read "The Job of an Apple," consider what poetic devices Bloom uses, and how they contribute to the mood of the poem. Could Bloom have achieved a similar effect if instead she had written a short story about the job of an apple? ■

The Job of an Apple

Ronna Bloom

The job of an apple is to be hard,
to be soft, to be crisp, to be red,
yellow, and green. The job of an apple is to be pie,
to be given to the teacher, to be rotten.
The job of an apple is to be bad
and good, to be peeled, cored, cut,
bitten, and bruised. The job
of an apple is to pose for painters,
roll behind fridges, behind grocery aisles,
to be hidden, wrapped in paper,
stored for months, brought out in the dry heat
of India and eaten like a treasure.
The job of an apple is to be
handed over in orchards, to be wanted
and forbidden. The job of an apple is to be Golden
Delicious, Granny Smith, and crab. The job
of an apple is to be imported, banned, and confiscated
going through customs from Montreal to New York.
The job of an apple is to be round. Grow. Drop.
To go black in the middle when cut. To be thrown
at politicians. To be carried around for days. To change
hands, to change hands, to change hands.
The job of an apple is to be a different poem in the mouth
of every eater. The job of an apple is to be juice.

A NARROW
FELLOW IN
THE GRASS

- Interpret an aspect of a poem in an oral presentation.
- Research other works by an author to extend your knowledge and understanding.

CONTEXT Emily Dickinson was born in Amherst, Massachusetts, in 1830. Although she was described as outgoing and personable by her fellow students both at Amherst Academy and later at Mount Holyoake College, her later life was marked by an acute sense of privacy. Never highly regarded as a poet in her lifetime, she described herself as an author of "Barefoot Rank"—unschooled and unaccomplished. Only seven poems in nearly two thousand were published during her career, and, after her death in 1886, hundreds of her poems were found stashed away throughout her home. Today, Emily Dickinson is considered an innovator whose imagery, diction, and themes are both powerful and original. Do you know of any other innovative writers who were not recognized in their own lifetime? Why did this happen? What is innovative or unconventional about the following poem? What effects does an artist like Dickinson achieve by being innovative or unconventional? ■

A Narrow Fellow in the Grass
Emily Dickinson

A narrow Fellow in the Grass
Occasionally rides—
You may have met Him—did you not
His notice sudden is—

The Grass divides as with a Comb—
A spotted shaft is seen—
And then it closes at your feet
And opens further on—

He likes a Boggy Acre
A Floor too cool for Corn—
Yet when a Boy, and Barefoot—
I more than once at Noon

Have passed, I thought, a Whip lash
Unbraiding in the Sun
When stooping to secure it
It wrinkled, and was gone—

Several of Nature's People
I know, and they know me—
I feel for them a transport
Of cordiality—

But never met this Fellow
Attended, or alone
Without a tighter breathing
And Zero at the Bone—

NOTES

ether in this instance, a liquid used for medicinal purposes as an anaesthetic

ANALYZE AND INTERPRET

1. In a group, discuss your response to and interpretation of the ending of the poem. In the second-last line, who does "they" refer to? Do you think that the narrator is overly cynical about human nature or simply realistic?

2. Rework the content of this poem as a story for a local radio news report. **a)** With a partner, record and listen to several news reports, and discuss how the information in each story is organized. **b)** Write your news story with details of the event as described in the poem; be sure to answer the questions Who? What? Where? When? Why? and How? **c)** Record your news story. **d)** Join another pair, and listen to both recordings. **e)** Assess what was most effective about each story and its presentation.

MORE TO EXPLORE

Themes: Childhood, Loss, Family, At Work, Rural Life, Crisis

Elements: alliteration, allusion, climax, dénouement, dramatic monologue, pathos, rhythm, tragedy

---

The Job of an Apple   Ronna Bloom

ANALYZE AND INTERPRET

1. One of the jobs of a *poet* is to help the reader see familiar things through new eyes. Has this poem made you think differently about an apple? Another job of the poet is to help the reader make connections between things. What associations has the poet made you aware of? What other "poetic jobs" do you think Bloom has accomplished in this work? Make jot notes as you consider these questions. Then create a poem about the different jobs of a poet, using "The Job of an Apple" as your model.

2. **a)** Research to locate the poem "Thirteen Ways of Looking at a Blackbird" by Wallace Stevens, and consider the ways in which it is similar to and different from "The Job of an Apple." **b)** Take notes to prepare for a group discussion comparing the two poems. Try using the two overlapping circles of a Venn diagram to organize your ideas. **c)** After the group discussion, assess how your preparatory note taking affected your participation.

MORE TO EXPLORE

Themes: Nature, Canada, Intrigue, Humour, Creativity

Elements: description, hyperbole, metaphor, personification, third-person point of view

---

A Narrow Fellow in the Grass   Emily Dickinson

ANALYZE AND INTERPRET

1. With a partner, choose one of the following three topics for discussion: **a)** Who or what do you think is the subject of this poem? What clues lead you to your conclusion? **b)** What qualities of Dickinson's subject are represented through the technique of personification? **c)** How is the narrator's attitude displayed through the poem's diction and imagery? With your partner, use your discussion as the basis for a five-minute oral presentation on the topic you chose.

2. With a partner, use the library or the Internet to find several other poems by Dickinson. Read these poems together and discuss ways in which Dickinson presents nature in them. Do you find that her depiction of nature is consistent throughout these poems? Have a class discussion in which you reveal what you discovered, and compare and contrast your discoveries with those of others.

MORE TO EXPLORE

Themes: Self, Rural Life, Nature, Humour

Elements: alliteration, assonance, metre, page layout, quatrain

SCHOONER

LEARNING FOCUS

- Analyze the diction and syntax of a text to gain insight into its structure.
- Use an excerpt as a prompt for a creative response.

CONTEXT Kamau Brathwaite is one of the Caribbean's best-known authors. He was born in Bridgetown, Barbados, in 1930, and has maintained strong ties with his homeland ever since. In England, he studied at Cambridge University and at the University of Sussex, where he received his Ph.D. He worked as an education officer in Ghana, West Africa, after which he returned to the Caribbean and then taught at the University of the West Indies in Jamaica for thirty years. He currently divides his time between Barbados and New York City. A prominent theme of Brathwaite's work is the African roots of Caribbean culture. Through his poetry, he explores the historical links and events that form a Caribbean identity. Coming from a strong oral tradition, Brathwaite has made numerous recordings in which he reads his work. He is also known for the "jagged line," in which he breaks up a word over two lines of a poem; his purpose may be to emphasize the different roots of each part of the word, reflecting the divergent ancestry of Caribbean people. In your view, what is the story that the poem "Schooner" is trying to tell? What is the effect of the poem's "jagged lines"? ■

Schooner
Kamau Brathwaite

A tossed night between us
high seas
and then in the morning
sails slack
rope flapping the rigging
your schooner came in

on the deck, buttressed
with mango boxes, chicken-
coops, rice: I saw you:
older than I would wish you
more tattered than my pride
could stand

you saw me
moving reluctant to the quay-
side, stiff as you knew me
too full of pride.
but you had travelled
braved the big wave
and the bilge-swishing stomach,
climbed the tall seas
to come to me

ship was too early
or was I too late?

walking still slowly
(too late or too early?)
saw you suddenly turn

ropes quickly cast off from the capstan
frilled sails were unfurled
water already between your hull and the harbour

too late too late
or too early?

running now
one last rope stretched
to the dockside
tripping over a chain—
chink in my armour—

but the white bows were turning
stern coming round squat in the water

and I
older now
more torn and tattered than my pride
could stand
stretch out my love to you across the water
but cannot reach your hand

FROM THE TITANIC

CONTEXT Edwin John Pratt was born in 1882 into a religious household in Western Bay, Newfoundland. Pratt's father was a Methodist minister who preached in different communities throughout Canada. Pratt himself became a preacher before returning to school, eventually receiving his Ph.D. in theology from the University of Toronto in 1917. He joined the English Department at Victoria College, University of Toronto, and remained there until 1953. Although Pratt left Newfoundland as a young boy, he was always fascinated with its history. His first book of poetry was, in fact, titled *Newfoundland Verse*. The sinking of the *Titanic* captured Pratt's imagination and became the subject of just one of many long narratives he wrote during his lengthy career. Pratt, like many poets before him, chose to tell the story of the sinking of a mighty ship using a structured and traditional form. What is the effect of using this form? Are poets today likely to use structured, traditional forms to tell stories? Why or why not? ■

From The Titanic

E.J. Pratt

Out on the water was the same display
Of fear and self-control as on the deck—
Challenge and hesitation and delay,
The quick return, the will to save, the race
Of snapping oars to put the realm of space
Between the half-filled lifeboats and the wreck....

Aboard the ship, whatever hope of dawn
Gleamed from the *Carpathia*'s riding lights was gone,
For every knot was matched by each degree
Of list. The stern was lifted bodily
When the bow had sunk three hundred feet, and set
Against the horizon stars in silhouette
Were the blade curves of the screws, hump of the rudder.
The downward pull and after buoyancy
Held her a minute poised but for a shudder
That caught her frame as with the upward stroke
Of the sea a boiler or a bulkhead broke.

Climbing the ladders, gripping shroud and stay,
Storm-rail, ringbolt or fairlead, every place
That might befriend the clutch of hand or brace

Of foot, the fourteen hundred made their way
To the heights of the aft decks, crowding the inches
Around the docking bridge and cargo winches.
And now that last salt tonic which had kept
The valour of the heart alive—the bows
Of the immortal seven that had swept
The strings to outplay, outdie their orders, ceased.
Five minutes more, the angle had increased
From eighty on to ninety when the rows
Of deck and porthole lights went out, flashed back
A brilliant second and again went black.
Another bulkhead crashed, then following
The passage of the engines as they tore
From their foundations, taking everything
Clean through the bows from 'midships with a roar
Which drowned all cries upon the deck and shook
The watchers in the boats, the liner took
Her thousand fathoms journey to her grave....

And out there in the starlight, with no trace
Upon it of its deed but the last wave
From the *Titanic* fretting at its base,
Silent, composed, ringed by its icy broods,
The grey shape with the palaeolithic face
Was still the master of the longitudes.

THE
BEAR
ON THE
DELHI
ROAD

CONTEXT A major figure in Canadian literature, Earle Birney was born in Calgary, Alberta, in 1904. He pursued his post-secondary education at the University of British Columbia, the University of Toronto, and universities in California and London, England. His studies centred on Old and Middle English, with a focus on the writer Geoffrey Chaucer. Birney twice won the Governor General's Award for books of poetry, *David* (1942) and *Now Is Time* (1945), and was awarded the Stephen Leacock Medal for the novel *Turvey* (1949). Throughout his career, he was considered an experimental poet who combined encyclopedic knowledge with a fascination with the mechanics of language. Birney also had a successful career as a playwright, a novelist, and an editor. He taught at several universities, including the University of British Columbia, where he founded the first department of creative writing in Canada. Birney died in Toronto in 1995. Much of Birney's poetry reflects his interest in the natural world. What other poets do you know who are also interested in nature? How does their portrayal of nature compare with Birney's in this poem? ■

The Bear on the Delhi Road

Earle Birney

Unreal tall as a myth
by the road the Himalayan bear
is beating the brilliant air
with his crooked arms
About him two men bare
spindly as locusts leap

One pulls on a ring
In the great soft nose His mate
flicks flicks with a stick
up at the rolling eyes

They have not led him here
down from the fabulous hills
to this bald alien plain
and the clamorous world to kill
but simply to teach him to dance

They are peaceful both these spare
men of Kashmir and the bear
alive is their living too
If far on the Delhi way
around him galvanic they dance
it is merely to wear wear
from his shaggy body the tranced
wish forever to stay
only an ambling bear
four-footed in berries

It is no more joyous for them
in this hot dust to prance
out of reach of the praying claws
sharpened to paw for ants
in the shadows of deodars
It is not easy to free
myth from reality
or rear this fellow up
to lurch lurch with them
in the tranced dancing of men

ANALYZE AND INTERPRET

1. The relationship between the two people changes halfway through the poem. At what specific point does this change occur? In a group, discuss how the poet uses the following elements to reinforce the differences in the two parts of the poem: **a)** parallel structure and repetition; **b)** diction; **c)** line length. Take notes during your discussion and compare your ideas with those of another group.

2. Write a narrative or poem related to the poet's refrain of "too late or too early?" based on an experience in your life. Next, make revisions to your work by paying attention to how effectively your narrative illustrates the theme. Then ask a classmate to proofread the rough draft of your work to identify errors in spelling and usage.

MORE TO EXPLORE

Themes: Self, Loss, Romance, Canada, Caribbean, Journeys

Elements: alliteration, dramatic monologue, metaphor, rhetorical question

From The Titanic   E.J. Pratt

NOTES

Carpathia this ship, named after an eastern European mountain range, raced to the scene and took aboard survivors from lifeboats

bulkhead one of the upright partitions dividing a ship into compartments to prevent leakage or spread of fire

winches hoisting mechanisms

fathoms units of length equal to six feet (1.8 m)

palaeolithic the historical period dating back approximately 750,000 years; from the Greek words *palaios*, meaning "ancient," and *lithos*, meaning "stone"

longitudes angular distances measured on a map or globe

ANALYZE AND INTERPRET

1. After reading this poem excerpt, create a chart. In one column, list examples of specific words Pratt has used to elicit either pity or fear in the reader. In the second column, list specific images he has created for the same purpose. As a class, discuss the extent to which the language and images create an emotional response in the reader.

2. Prepare to audiotape a dramatic oral reading of this poem excerpt. Rehearse with other students in order to improve your confidence in your delivery. After recording your version, listen to your interpretation and note what was most effective about your presentation.

MORE TO EXPLORE

Themes: Loss, Nature, Canada, Science and Technology, Crisis

Elements: alliteration, archetype, couplet, epic, metre, narration, personification, rhyme

---

The Bear on the Delhi Road   Earle Birney

NOTES

Kashmir a region on the northern border of India and northeast Pakistan

Delhi a territory in north central India containing the cities of Old and New Delhi

deodars cedar trees native to India

ANALYZE AND INTERPRET

1. **a)** Work with a partner to create a copy of the poem in a computer file. **b)** Take turns reading the poem aloud several times. Pay close attention to the way you group the words into units of thought as you speak. **c)** Mark up your copy of the poem with commas, periods, and capital letters to reflect your understanding of the meaning. **d)** Compare your visual organization of the poem first with that of another group, and then with the poet's original presentation. **e)** Discuss how the visual organization helps to convey the meaning of the poem.

2. In your imagination, try to recreate the scene the poet witnessed that inspired him to write this poem: the setting, the people, the animal, the sounds, and the smells. Next, list the characters in the scene. Then choose one character, and write a poem retelling the story from his or her point of view. In your poem, focus on creating strong images: the sights, sounds, smells, and feelings that affect your character. Share your poem with a group, and invite comments on your use of sensory imagery.

MORE TO EXPLORE

Themes: Self and Culture, At Play, Rural Life, Nature, Canada, Asia

Elements: assonance, description, page layout, rhythm, setting, simile, third-person point of view

MOTHER
AND CHILD

Oshuitoq Peesee

1956, carved stone, L. 20.3 cm

CONTEXT Oshuitoq Peesee was an Inuk sculptor born in 1913 on Dorset Island off the south coast of Baffin Island, in what is now Nunavut. He was a member of the Cape Dorset (Kingait) Inuit artistic community. Oshuitoq's work emerged in the contemporary period of Inuit art that began in the late 1940s, when the federal government assisted the Inuit with the development of artistic communities. Approximately thirty communities were established, each developing its own specific subjects and distinctive sculptural styles. Oshuitoq died in 1979. Artists such as Oshuitoq carved not only in soapstone, but in other stones as well. In fact, soapstone, a soft talc steatite, is not used nearly as much as harder stones such as serpentine, argillite, dolomite, and quartz. What materials have been used for creating sculptures you are familiar with? If you were to sculpt, what material might you choose, and why? ■

NOTES

Oshuitoq the surname, or family name, of the sculptor; in some Aboriginal cultures, when a person's full name is used, the family name precedes the given name

ANALYZE AND INTERPRET

1. In a group, discuss some of the choices the artist made in the composition of this sculpture. Consider the following questions: **a)** What is the focal point of the sculpture? **b)** Why are the arms and hands of the mother so large? **c)** Why do you think the mother is not looking down at the child? **d)** How much detail does the sculptor include? How might the level of detail the sculptor has used have an impact on the viewer?

2. Write a poem that reflects the mood and emotional tone of this sculpture. Keep in mind the importance of the sounds of the words you use and the rhythm you create in establishing mood. Ask several classmates to listen to your poem and comment on whether the various elements of your poem work together to create a single mood. Use their suggestions to revise your work.

MORE TO EXPLORE

Themes: Childhood, Self and Culture, Family, Rural Life, Aboriginal Cultures, Canada

Elements: archetype, characterization, visual composition, visual scale

MOTHER

LEARNING FOCUS

- Extend your understanding by using imagery as a model to create your own image.
- Follow a procedure to create a well-developed final product.

CONTEXT Nagase Kiyoko was born in Kumayama, Japan, in 1906. After living in other parts of Japan, including Osaka and Tokyo, she returned, at the age of thirty-nine, to the town of her birth. There, she worked as a farmer, but continued to write poetry at night. During her professional career, Nagase also wrote essays and received many literary awards. Much of Nagase's work, including this poem, was translated into English by the well-known American poet and scholar Kenneth Rexroth, who introduced the works of many Japanese writers to English-speaking countries. How would you explain the effect that the mother in the poem has had on her child, the speaker? Which metaphor or simile in the poem do you consider the most powerful? Why? How would you compare this poem with other poems about mothers you have read? ■

Mother

Nagase Kiyoko
TRANSLATED BY KENNETH REXROTH
AND IKUKO ASSUMI

I am always aware of my mother,
ominous, threatening,
a pain in the depths of my consciousness.
My mother is like a shell,
so easily broken.
Yet the fact that I was born
bearing my mother's shadow
cannot be changed.
She is like a cherished, bitter dream
my nerves cannot forget
even after I awake.
She prevents all freedom of movement.
If I move she quickly breaks,
and the splinters stab me.

MACAVITY: THE MYSTERY CAT

LEARNING FOCUS

- Research and use oral techniques to assist you in comparing and contrasting literary texts.
- Use discussion to help you refine a dramatic reading of a literary text.

CONTEXT Thomas Stearns Eliot was born in St. Louis, Missouri, in 1888. He attended Harvard University, after which he moved to England in 1914. It was there that the well-known poet Ezra Pound helped him to get his early poems published. Though Eliot wrote poetry throughout his life, and was awarded the Nobel Prize for Literature in 1948, he is perhaps best known for his poem "The Waste Land," written when he was thirty-four years old. He also established himself as a first-rate literary critic. In his lifetime, Eliot published some 600 articles and reviews, as well as numerous books of poetry. In 1939, Eliot wrote *Old Possum's Book of Practical Cats* for a friend's child. In the 1970s, the book was adapted into the spectacularly successful musical *Cats*, which ran for many years on Broadway in New York, and was staged in many cities throughout the world. Eliot was known as both an extremely serious poet and a very witty one. Can you think of a piece of writing that is humorous but also carries a serious message? Does "Macavity" fit into this category? Why or why not? ■

Macavity: The Mystery Cat

T.S. Eliot

Macavity's a Mystery Cat: he's called the Hidden Paw—
For he's the master criminal who can defy the Law.
He's the bafflement of Scotland Yard, the Flying Squad's despair:
    For when they reach the scene of crime—*Macavity's not there!*

Macavity, Macavity, there's no one like Macavity,
He's broken every human law, he breaks the law of gravity.
His powers of levitation would make a fakir stare,
And when you reach the scene of crime—*Macavity's not there!*
You may seek him in the basement, you may look up in the air—
But I tell you once and once again, *Macavity's not there!*

Macavity's a ginger cat, he's very tall and thin;
You would know him if you saw him, for his eyes are sunken in.
His brow is deeply lined with thought, his head is highly domed;
His coat is dusty from neglect, his whiskers are uncombed.
He sways his head from side to side, with movements like a snake;
And when you think he's half asleep, he's always wide awake.

Macavity, Macavity, there's no one like Macavity,
For he's a fiend in feline shape, a monster of depravity.
You may meet him in a by-street, you may see him in the square—
But when a crime's discovered, then *Macavity's not there!*

He's outwardly respectable. (They say he cheats at cards.)
And his footprints are not found in any file of Scotland Yard's.
And when the larder's looted, or the jewel-case is rifled,
Or when the milk is missing, or another Peke's been stifled,
Or the greenhouse glass is broken, and the trellis past repair—
Ay, there's the wonder of the thing! *Macavity's not there!*

And when the Foreign Office finds a Treaty's gone astray,
Or the Admiralty lose some plans and drawings by the way,
There may be a scrap of paper in the hall or on the stair—
But it's useless to investigate—*Macavity's not there!*
And when the loss has been disclosed, the Secret Service say:
"It *must* have been Macavity!"—but he's a mile away.
You'll be sure to find him resting, or a-licking of his thumbs,
Or engaged in doing complicated long division sums.

Macavity, Macavity, there's no one like Macavity,
There never was a Cat of such deceitfulness and suavity.
He always has an alibi, or one or two to spare:
And whatever time the deed took place—MACAVITY WASN'T
    THERE!
And they say that all the Cats whose wicked deeds are widely
    known
(I might mention Mungojerrie, I might mention Griddlebone)
Are nothing more than agents for the Cat who all the time
Just controls their operations: the Napoleon of Crime!

SONNET

La corde à linge, 1965, Sindon Gécin

CONTEXT Anne Clifford is a Canadian poet. Although her contemporary poem is an amusing satire, it follows the traditional form of the Shakespearean sonnet. Clifford uses both old-fashioned and modern diction in her sonnet. What is Anne Clifford satirizing in this poem? What message does the final couplet express? If you were writing a sonnet, satirical or otherwise, what subject would you choose? ■

Sonnet
Anne Clifford

O whitest wash, that rivals e'en the snow
In shining radiance, enzyme cleansed and free
From grime and grease and filth of human flow,
How deep my neighbours' envying of thee!
O blankets that blaze forth a purity
That puts the shabby snowdrop in the shade,
O drip dry sheets, that offer surety
Of whiteness that can never melt or fade,
To thee the mighty phosphate bows its head,
And foaming at the mouth to do thy will
Enriches thy magnificence in bed,
Content alone to serve thee with its skill.
Though for thy glory lakes and rivers die
No price for such perfection is too high.

NOTES

Nagase the surname, or family name, of the poet; in many Asian cultures, when a person's full name is used, the family name precedes the given name

ANALYZE AND INTERPRET

1. Choose the image in "Mother" that is most powerful to you and explain to a partner how this image contributes to your understanding of the poem as a whole. Next, come up with another image that is in keeping with the images Nagase has used. Share this new image with a partner, and explain why you created it.

2. Use this poem as a model to write your own poem about your relationship with someone in your immediate or extended family. **a)** Consider how you feel about your subject; this feeling will set the tone for your poem. **b)** Freewrite words, phrases, and images that come to mind. **c)** Read these words aloud to get a feel for where you want to make your line breaks. **d)** Evaluate your draft by asking the following questions: What is the main idea I want my poem to communicate? What is the emotional impact of my poem? Does everything in my poem contribute to the effect I want to achieve? **e)** Rework your poem until you are satisfied that your message is conveyed effectively.

MORE TO EXPLORE

Themes: Self, Adolescence, Family, Asia

Elements: metaphor, mood, paradox, simile

Macavity: The Mystery Cat   T.S. Eliot

NOTES

Scotland Yard the detective department of the metropolitan police agency in London, England

Flying Squad a police unit trained to respond quickly to emergencies

fakir in this instance, a mystic who practises levitation as an act of devotion

larder a place where food is stored, such as a pantry

Peke refers to the Pekinese breed of dog

Mungojerrie, Griddlebone refers to two other cats that appear in Eliot's *Old Possum's Book of Practical Cats*

ANALYZE AND INTERPRET

1. Read the poem aloud with a partner. How do the rhyme and rhythm contribute to the tone of the poem? Locate and read poems by other writers of light verse such as Edward Lear and Lewis Carroll. Using these poems, make a list of some of the identifying features of light verse. Refer to elements such as subject, diction, tone, wit, rhyme, and rhythm.

2. Work with a group to prepare a dramatic reading of the poem. Discuss how you might make use of some of the following to add interest and atmosphere to your presentation: lighting, costumes, masks, music, gestures, and movement. When all the groups in your class have presented, compare the various techniques used to interpret the material both visually and aurally, and discuss which were most effective.

MORE TO EXPLORE

Themes: Rebels, Europe, Intrigue, Humour

Elements: alliteration, metre, parody, rhyme, satire

Sonnet   Anne Clifford

NOTES

Shakespearean sonnet a poem whose 14 lines are built on an internal structure of three quatrains (three sets of four lines) with alternating rhymes (ABAB CDCD EFEF) and a final rhyming couplet (GG). Its iambic pentameter rhythm (five feet per line, each foot having one lightly accented and one heavily accented syllable) is also the basic metre of Shakespeare's plays.

ANALYZE AND INTERPRET

1. In a small group, discuss what you know about the sonnet form. Next, as a group use a dictionary or reference guide to find out more about the different types of sonnets. With your group, determine which features of the sonnet are evident here.

2. With a partner, rewrite the sonnet using contemporary language, including slang. Be sure to maintain the form of a sonnet in your new version. Compare the similarities and differences between your version and another group's version.

MORE TO EXPLORE

Themes: Civic Responsibility, Nature, Canada, Humour, Eye on the Past, Science and Technology

Elements: alliteration, cliché, hyperbole, iambic pentameter, parody, rhyme, satire, sonnet

IN A REMOTE KOREAN VILLAGE

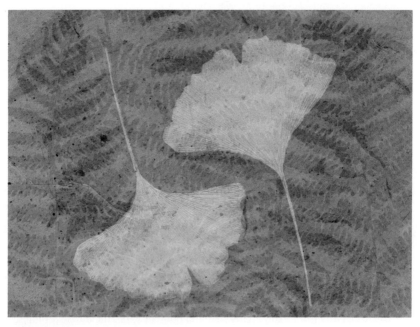

Gingko leaves

CONTEXT Chang Soo Ko was born in Korea in 1934. He studied in the United States. He eventually served as his country's consul general in Seattle, Washington, and as its ambassador to Ethiopia and to Pakistan. Ko has published numerous original volumes of poetry in Korean. He has also written and published books of poetry in English, including *Seattle Poems*. Ko is well known as an English translator of Korean poetry, and has won prizes for both translation and poetry. As a multilingual writer and translator, he has the advantage of translating his own works from Korean into English and vice versa. What difficulties might crop up when the person translating a poem is *not* also the writer of it? How might he or she resolve some of these difficulties? ■

In a Remote Korean Village

Chang Soo Ko

All autumn long,
the gingko tree in the garden,
like a peacock spreading its feathers,
showed off its golden leaves.
One day the gentle gardener,
standing on a branch in the center of the tree,
shook it with a strange passion.
Silhouetted against the sun,
the gardener looked like a black magician.
The tree must have shed most of its leaves.

For many a day,
whether I listened to music or walked the streets,
the leaves fell endlessly
into the lost river of my existence.
At autumn's end the stiff boughs of the tree
spread over me like a spiderweb.

A few leaves rustled in the wind;
the boughs shivered feebly against the overcast sky.
In the invisible wind,
a few birds perched on the boughs,
looking as if they would fly off any moment.

Winter winds blew;
the landscape changed with the snow's rhythm.
And the tree began to dance with its dark boughs.
After a while,
the bare branches
glowed again with golden leaves.
I could not see the gardener anywhere.

NEIGHBOUR

Bonfire with Beggar Bush, 1989, Mary Pratt

CONTEXT Christine Churches was born in 1945 in the small farming town of Keith in the southeast of South Australia. She has written that when she was in primary school, "at the end of a baking summer day, our teacher read poems aloud to distract us from the heat." After raising a family, Churches enrolled as a mature student at the University of Adelaide, where she received a Ph.D. in history in 1991 and stayed on as a research fellow. She is the co-author of several books of history. Churches has said that "'Neighbour' is a poem about my father, and unspoken warfare." What are the benefits and drawbacks of having neighbours? How would you describe the ideal neighbour? ■

Neighbour
Christine Churches

I know him only as a man of Sunday afternoon, and a
                     backyard fire burning.
There, by the flame-tree, the man is stooping and brooding;

He feeds on the flames and the armfuls of smoke
which he can create with his old bent hoe;
he is content, and she is silent; enough that he is working.

There, by the flame-tree;
smoke sulks and powders from the parasite flame,
greys and ashes the hard-muscled tree;
the man is stooping and bending:
dull, pleasing pokes of the hoe,
the flame clings hold of the stubborn leaves.
He suns his thoughts,
there, by the flame-tree,
with the flowers of filleting scarlet,
too soon unjoined from the flowing branches;
raking up the leaves and the loosely jointed twigs,
and burning them, stubbornly, with those of his mind.

I know him only as a man of Sunday afternoon, and a
                     backyard fire burning;
so who shall ever know him, and all his unburnt thoughts;
which the good-wife watching from the window
                     must never know or see?

THE HIDDEN FENCE

LEARNING FOCUS

- Seek consensus on the significance of a text's title.
- Evaluate how the structure of a text affects meaning.

CONTEXT Rita Joe, a member of the Mi'kmaq First Nation, was born in 1932 on the Whycocomagh Reserve in Cape Breton, Nova Scotia. Rita Joe was five years old when her mother died. She then lived in a series of foster homes, and spent four years in a residential school. She began her writing career when she was in her late thirties, first by contributing humorous columns to a Mi'kmaq-language newspaper. Today, Joe is the author of numerous books of verse, as well as an autobiography titled *Song of Rita Joe: Autobiography of a Mi'kmaq Poet* (1996). In it, she expresses the view that her life story is a moral tale in which each difficulty hides a lesson. What types of circumstances do you think hold hidden lessons? What kinds of lessons might people learn in such situations, and how can these lessons change the world around us? ■

The Hidden Fence
Rita Joe

Once upon a time I was in spaces free
I trod the lane of the rainbow road
My identity my own
And all the earth and sky my friend.
In barricaded fences of rescue
Submission becoming my prison
Now slowing to a trickle.
My stride becoming a shuffle
The feathers hanging limp as I signed the X

The spaces are still there for me to follow
In the wide open range
I teach you my culture
I want to teach you about me

Let me.

NOTES

gingko tree also spelled "ginkgo"; an ornamental or shade tree with fan-shaped leaves and yellow fruit, native to numerous Asian countries; from the Japanese word *ginkyo*, from the Chinese word *yinxing*, meaning "silver apricot"

ANALYZE AND INTERPRET

1. Poets often use images from nature to express an emotional state. With a partner, identify several specific nature images in this poem. Discuss what feeling each image represents or evokes. Then compare and contrast your interpretations with those of others in a class discussion.

2. **a)** In your journal, create a web of words, phrases, and images that you associate with trees. You will use this web to create a lyric poem modelled on "In a Remote Korean Village." **b)** First, decide what the dominant emotional tone of your poem will be. **c)** Then consider what images you will use to support these emotions, and what message or theme you will explore. **d)** After writing a draft, read your poem aloud to a partner and discuss whether the impact of the poem might be enhanced by changing the order of the images. **e)** Revise your poem to create a polished final draft.

MORE TO EXPLORE

Themes: Self, Rural Life, Nature, Asia, Journeys

Elements: description, metaphor, personification, setting, simile

ANALYZE AND INTERPRET

1. In your journal, write down what you consider to be the key line of the poem and explain why you chose it. Then share your line with a group. Compare the lines chosen and discuss why you chose the one that you did.

2. **a)** Do a close reading of the poem to gather impressions of the neighbour. What conclusions can you draw about his age, his personality, his relationship with his wife, and his attitude toward his task? **b)** Create a monologue that reveals the inner thoughts of the neighbour. **c)** Perform your monologue for a group of classmates using props such as a hoe and crumpled, used paper for leaves. **d)** Afterwards, discuss your interpretations of the neighbour's character. Be prepared to defend your ideas with references to the poem.

| The Hidden Fence | Rita Joe |

ANALYZE AND INTERPRET

1. In a group, discuss the significance of the title of this poem. What do you think the fence represents for the author? In what sense is the fence hidden? How might different people respond to this fence? Try to achieve a consensus on these questions, then choose a spokesperson to report your views to another group.

2. With a partner, discuss how the content of the poem is supported by the way the poet has divided it into stanzas. How might she have divided the first stanza into two parts? Why do you think she chose to keep these two parts together? How does the second stanza both reinforce and expand on the ideas introduced in the first stanza? What is the effect of isolating the last two words of the poem? Make notes summarizing your discussion, and share your ideas with another group.

MORE TO EXPLORE

Themes: Self and Culture, Aboriginal Cultures, Canada, Moral Questions, Eye on the Past

Elements: first-person point of view, parable, symbol, tone

Wrap-Up

1. Make a copy of any poem you have not previously studied. Place it on a large sheet of paper, and write an annotated response that documents the reading strategies you use to understand and interpret this poem. Your strategies might include identifying the poem's speaker, listening as the poem is read aloud, and paraphrasing lines in your own words. Share and discuss your strategies with the class.

2. Poems can project an attitude toward life. On a piece of paper, create a visual continuum showing two opposite attitudes, such as optimism versus pessimism, rebellion versus compliance, action versus passiveness, attachment versus alienation, or rejection versus acceptance. Then place ten poems you read in this unit along this continuum. Beside each title, write two or three sentences in which you explain your choices.

3. Choose one poem from this unit, and find a piece of instrumental music that reflects its overall rhythm, tone, and mood. Then make a colour copy of a piece of artwork from the Internet or in a book, or else purchase a poster or postcard, that captures the essence of your poem. Post the artwork and, while playing your background music, do a dramatic reading of the poem for the class. Afterward, explain your choices and invite feedback on how effectively you have pulled together the elements of your presentation.

4. Choose a poem from this unit that caused you to think in a new way about an idea or experience. Write a letter to the poet in which you express your reactions to her or his poem. Be sure to begin your letter by explaining your purpose in writing. Develop and support reasons for your reactions. Then review the word choice and tone in your letter, considering how the poet might react to it. Make any necessary revisions.

5. Free verse allows a poet to use whatever rhythms and line lengths are appropriate to what he or she is saying. Choose one free verse poem from this unit to analyze in a formal essay. Consider the following questions when planning and writing your essay: Why is free verse an appropriate form for this poem? How might the effect of the poem have been different if the writer had used rhyming stanzas? How does the poem achieve unity of form and theme?

6. Poetry is thought to have emerged from the oral tradition of the ballad, a song that tells a story. Ballads generally use dialogue, rhyme, and repeated stanzas to create a dramatic, detached effect. With a partner, research the two main types of ballads, folk and literary, and find an example of each. Which poem in this unit strikes you as the most ballad-like, and why? Address the use of dialect, colloquial language, and repetition in the three poems. Share your research and comparisons with another pair of classmates.

"There's a world of difference between truth

and facts. Facts can obscure truth." ◼ Maya Angelou

Within your lifetime, there have been phenomenal changes in the amount and accessibility of information. When you were born, most published information came from books, magazines, and newspapers. Today, more and more of it comes through electronic sources. What, then, is the role of non-fiction in this information age? Quite simply, understanding non-fiction helps you deal effectively and creatively with an increasingly complex world. This unit will help you discover everything that non-fiction can do—inform, persuade, provoke, surprise, amuse, and enrich. The unit explores non-fiction in all its major forms. You will read literary memoirs and essays. Along the way, you will encounter a profile, photographs, and an eyewitness report. You will also enter some compelling debates. This unit highlights the powerful role of media in our lives. Media texts as they appeared in their original format will demonstrate how design elements enhance and communicate ideas. This unit will show you how the many forms of non-fiction work. This experience may well inspire you to write, script, design, film, photograph, draw, and produce your own statements about the world around you.

MY OLD NEWCASTLE

David Adams Richards

LEARNING FOCUS

- Generate ideas for writing.
- Communicate in small groups to debate an issue.
- Use language to create a distinct voice.

CONTEXT Author David Adams Richards was born in Newcastle, New Brunswick, in 1950. He graduated from St. Thomas University in Fredericton, New Brunswick. Richards has made the people and the landscape of the Miramichi River Valley the subject of his fiction. He published his first novel in 1974, and reviewers agreed that his storytelling "captures the sardonic humour and desperation of small-town life." In 1988, he won the Governor General's Award for *Nights Below Station Street*, the first novel in a trilogy. This novel was also produced as a television drama, which won a Gemini award. Richards won the Governor General's Award a second time for a work of non-fiction, *Lines on the Water: A Fisherman's Life on the Miramichi*, described as "a testament to nature and humanity revealed through the delicate art of fly-fishing." His recent novel *Mercy Among the Children* won the Giller Prize in 2000. Richards now lives in Toronto. What are some of the reasons people write memoirs? What reasons do people have for reading them? What are the differences between what we can learn from someone's memoir and what we can learn from a biography of that person written by someone else? Which do you prefer reading? Why? ■

I n Newcastle, New Brunswick, which I call home, we all played on the ice floes in the spring, spearing tommy–cod with stolen forks tied to sticks. More than one of us almost met our end slipping off the ice.

All night the trains rumbled or shunted their loads off to Halifax or Montreal, and men moved and worked. To this day I find the sound of trains more comforting than lonesome. It was somehow thrilling to know of people up and about in those hours, and wondrous events taking place. Always somehow with the faint, worn smell of gas and steel.

The Miramichi is a great working river.

There was always the presence of working men and women, from the mines or mills or woods; the more than constant sound of machinery; and the ore covered in tarps at the side of the wharf.

But as children, sitting in our snowsuits and hats and heavy boots on Saturday afternoons, we all saw movies that had almost nothing to do with us. That never mentioned us as a country or a place. That never seemed to know what our fathers and mothers did—that we went to wars or had a flag or even a great passion for life.

As far as the movies were concerned, we were in a lost, dark country, it seemed. And perhaps this is one reason I write. Leaving the theatre on a January afternoon, the smell of worn seats and heat and chip bags gave way to a muted cold and scent of snow no movie ever showed us. And night came against the tin roofs of the sheds behind our white houses, as the long spires of our churches rose over the town.

Our river was frozen so blue then that trucks could travel from one town to the other across the ice, and bonfires were lit by kids skating; sparks rose upon the shore under the stars as mothers called children home at nine o'clock.

All winter long the sky was tinted blue on the horizon, the schools we sat in too warm; privileged boys and girls sat beside those who lived in hunger and constant worry. One went on to be a Rhodes scholar, another was a derelict at 17 and dead at 20. To this day I could not tell you which held more promise.

Spring came with the smell of mud and grass burning in the fields above us. Road hockey gave way to cricket and then baseball. The sun warmed, the ice shifted, and the river was free. Salmon and sea trout moved up a dozen of our tributaries to spawn.

In the summer the ships came in, from all ports to ours, to carry ore and paper away. Sailors smoked black tobacco cigarettes, staring down at us from their decks; blackflies spoiled in the fields beyond town, and the sky was large all evening. Cars filled with children too excited to sleep passed along our great avenues lined with overhanging trees. All down to the store to get ice cream in the dark.

Adolescent blueberry crops and sunken barns dotted the fields near the bay, where the air had the taste of salt and tar, and small spruce trees seemed constantly filled with wind; where, by August, the water shimmered and even the small white lobster boats smelled of autumn, as did the ripples that moved them.

In the autumn the leaves were red, of course, and the earth, by Thanksgiving, became hard as a dull turnip. Ice formed in the ditches and shallow streams. The fields became yellow and stiff. The sounds of rifle shots from men hunting deer echoed faintly away, while women walked in kerchiefs and coats to seven o'clock mass, and the air felt heavy and leaden. Winter coming on again.

Now the town is three times as large, and fast-food franchises and malls dot the roadside where there were once fields and lumberyards. There is a new process at the mill, and much of the wood is clear-cut so that huge acres lie empty and desolate, a redundancy of broken and muted earth. The river is opened all winter by an ice-breaker, so no trucks travel across the ice, and the trains, of course, are gone. For the most part the station is empty, the tracks fiercely alone in the winter sun.

The theatre is gone now, too. And those thousands of movies showing us, as children filled with happy laughter someplace in Canada, what we were not are gone as well. They have given way to videos and satellite dishes and a community that is growing slowly farther and farther away from its centre. Neither bad nor good, I suppose—but away from what it was.

tommy-cod small saltwater fish related to cod

Rhodes scholars students chosen to receive a prestigious scholarship to attend Oxford University in England; British statesman Cecil Rhodes (1853–1902) set up the scholarships

ANALYZE AND INTERPRET

1. With a partner, discuss the definition of "nostalgia." Choose an object, a photograph, or a piece of music that makes you feel nostalgic. What memories and emotions does it awaken in you? Write a journal entry in which you reflect on the significance of this item to you.

2. Twice in the essay, the author talks about the movie theatre and movies. Why do movies figure so prominently in his thoughts about his hometown? In a group, discuss your reaction to this statement about movies: "They have given way to videos and satellite dishes and a community that is growing slowly farther and farther away from its centre." Based on this statement, what do you think is the author's view on the effect of videos and satellite dishes? Would life be better without them? Have an informal group debate on the effect of television and videos on people's sense of community.

3. Do you think that everyone in Newcastle shares the author's ideas about how the town has changed over the years? What factors would affect their reactions? In a group, prepare a voice play entitled "My Newcastle" featuring monologues by various people in town. a) Assign each group member a character role, such as a police officer, retired railway worker, social worker, gas station owner, elementary school student, or fisher. b) Together write a first draft. c) Read your work aloud to other members of your group to get feedback on whether you have succeeded in creating a believable individual with a distinct voice. d) Use these comments when working on your final draft. e) Present your voice play to the rest of the class.

MORE TO EXPLORE

Themes: Childhood, Self and Culture, Loss, Friends, At School, Canada, Eye on the Past, Science and Technology

Elements: comparison, description, first-person point of view, mood, simile

CANADIAN PIONEERS— A NEW DEFINITION OF AN OLD IDEA

Janine Beach

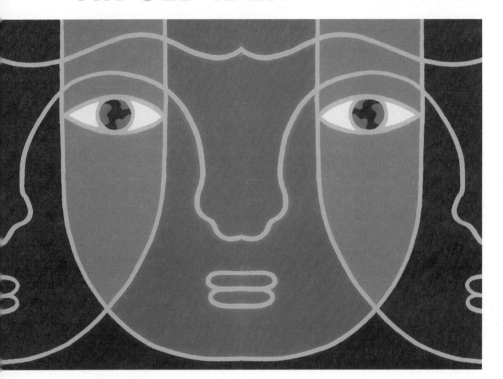

LEARNING FOCUS

- Use anecdotes to support a position.
- Communicate in a group to clarify an issue.
- Respond to a social issue.

CONTEXT Janine Beach was studying at McGill University in Montreal when she wrote this personal essay. Describing herself as a middle-class African-Canadian student of Trinidadian heritage, she tackles the subject of cultural stereotyping and discrimination in Canada from her viewpoint and that of her peers. Have you had the experience of feeling misunderstood in the classroom or in your community? What factors led to this misunderstanding? In her essay, why does Beach describe herself and her friends as "cultural pioneers"? Do you think her feelings, in the end, are positive, negative, or both? Why? ■

On my final day of university last year, I was called something that I had never been called before while I sat waiting for my appointment with my academic advisor to begin. My advisor peered at me over his bifocals and after a few seconds he leaned forward and asked, "Where are you from?" "Ontario," I replied. "No," he persisted, "I mean, where are you *from*?" "Oh," I said, understanding. "My parents are from Trinidad." He smiled knowingly. "So, you're a pioneer."

Until that moment, my definition of pioneer had been limited to British settlers or activist types. However, I have started to realize my friends and I are pioneers of a different sort. We have neither cultivated lands nor established cities. We have never lobbied for fundamental rights. Instead, we have developed something that is perhaps more integral to survival. We have established a unique identity, one that bridges two disparate homelands.

I am a member of a tiny, yet tenacious, group that boasts a significant West Indian population. This group is the black middle class. Until I was 18, I lived in a small town with tree-lined streets and old homes, a congenial community, where people care about their neighbours. My parents' support propelled me toward valuable experiences in academics and the arts. Along the way, I gained equally valuable lessons in the realities of discrimination in Canada.

Sociologists are correct when they describe Canadian discrimination as subtle. In keeping with this country's reputation for understatement, the discrimination I have experienced has been limited to the quiet, underhanded kind: the kind that leaves me surprised at some times, and suspicious at others.

The day after my family moved into our house, our neighbour's black lawn jockey mysteriously disappeared. After greeting canvassers, my mother is often asked whether or not the lady of the house is available. My surname, which is five letters long and begins with the letter B, has been mistaken for "Black" more times than I care to remember. My mother, a school principal, has also been mistaken—for the school's cleaning lady. Perhaps most interesting is the general confusion that people experience when they first meet me. Invariably, they are stunned that I am, well, not white.

One of my born-in-Trinidad friends hypothesizes the reason for this surprise is that I do not sound "black" on the telephone. But what does black sound like? It may not sound like the Queen's English, but I do not think that it sounds like a music video on Black Entertainment Television.

When I ask my friends about similar experiences the list is long and varied. Most have endured racial slurs in the classroom and on the playing field. Some have been stopped by police in their own neighbourhoods and questioned. They are viewed as spokespersons for their race rather than individuals with unique perspectives. While at a Toronto high school, one of my girlfriends (who had an A average) was advised to transfer to general-level courses. The administration felt that she would feel more comfortable with students more like herself. She will feel *most* comfortable when she attends Harvard University this fall.

One of my male friends, a medical student, says he has grown accustomed to the frightened glances of white women when he passes them on city streets. They clutch their purses a little bit more tightly. To many, he is a potential thief, not a potential doctor.

When I decided to research the cultural perception of the black middle class, many of my classmates were incredulous. One remarked, "I didn't know that that group even existed." Well, we certainly do.

Our parents are well-educated and have embraced a work ethic. They are doctors, teachers, social workers, accountants, and administrators. They have instilled pride in our cultural heritage and have solidified it with a value system. As Canadians, we are also proud of our native country and are strong advocates of its social democracy and generosity. We are gifted with a distinct combination of Canadian ideas and West Indian ideals.

We have been taught that education and perseverance will create opportunity. Most importantly, we have been encouraged to aim high and to never allow others to underestimate us simply because of our race. For us, blackness is associated with ingenuity and strength. In reality, these perceptions of blacks are few and far between.

As we embark on adult lives, my friends and I are aware that we will often be regarded as black first, and intelligent or qualified second. It is an unfortunate reality that we must endure, as surely as we must grapple with our positions as cultural pioneers. Perhaps it is not our skin colour that truly unifies us, but our experiences.

NOTES

discrimination the act of treating people differently because of their race, gender, age, appearance, religious beliefs, economic means, or lifestyle

sociologist an academic person, often a university professor, who studies human society—how and why groups of people behave as they do

hypothesizes theorizes; offers a possible explanation

ANALYZE AND INTERPRET

1. Have you ever been treated unfairly by someone because she or he had preconceived ideas about your gender, age, race, appearance, clothing, or something else about you? In your journal, record your feelings about this event. What connections can you make between your experiences and those of the author?

2. Janine Beach develops her essay around a series of anecdotes. How does she use each one to make a point about her themes of prejudice, discrimination, and racial stereotyping? In a small group, discuss which anecdote you think is the most effective, and why.

3. The author's purpose in writing her essay is to raise public awareness about specific issues. Make a list of the issues she raises. Then work with a group to brainstorm ways in which you think these issues should be addressed. Share your ideas with the class.

MORE TO EXPLORE

Themes: Self and Culture, Stereotypes, Urban Life, Canada

Elements: anecdote, first-person point of view, irony

REACTION–
INTERACTION

Diane Kenyon

CONTEXT Diane Kenyon is a freelance lecturer, tutor, and writer. She was born with partial hearing but is now profoundly deaf. In 1972, she was the co-founder of BREAKTHROUGH, a self-help movement that is administered by people with hearing impairments. She has also worked with the LINK program for people with disabilities. Kenyon is married to a person with a profound hearing disability, and she is particularly interested in the experience of being a deaf parent. Have you ever had the experience of meeting a person with a hearing impairment? How did you communicate with each another? Judging from the title, what do you think the focus of this essay will be? ■

Most hearing people perceive deafness as a medical problem to be cured, but the pill has their name on it!

Such a little pill, compounded of improved communication skills, attitudes and knowledge, a dose of visual awareness, and a sprinkling of sensitivity and confidence.

I smile as I begin my daily patter. "Could you speak more slowly please, and move your lips, as I am deaf. This will help me to understand what you are saying." This smile is not conjured up to sell my deafness. I am a naturally cheerful person; I have a confident approach to my disability.

I am deadly serious about my directive. I expect people to listen to my request and try to comply. This is the only stance that I can take if we are to communicate on the level that comes after *"Pleased to meet you."* If we cannot negotiate a channel whereby our minds can make contact, then these people simply move on, deftly passing me by in some socially acceptable way. For me, there is no one to move on to.

Speech sounds are meant to be heard with ears, not seen by eyes. Yet eyes to *hear with* are what deaf people have.

Whenever I jar up against another human being, it is useless just to tell them that I am deaf. I have to hunt for ways of explaining that their method of communication thrusts me into isolation. Although my body and its clothing are in the room of life, I the person am not. My participation is stunted by their immobile lips, hands, and attitudes.

I see myself as a warm person; human contact is life to me. I am always working to assure people that I understand their difficulties in adapting their mode of verbal communication to give me access. I am an optimist: I always hope that when we meet next, they will *remember* my needs. Usually they have forgotten. I don't want to be thought of as a nuisance. I don't want always to prompt and remind.

Reactions to my declaration of deafness are verbal, so once again I am disadvantaged. Using my hearing aids and much guesswork, I strain to understand their handicapping responses.

I give a talk at a lunch club. The first man I mention my deafness to cups his hand behind his ear, saying, "What? What?"

A mousetrap kind of reaction to cover his embarrassment. He does not mean to be offensive: his behaviour is that of an elephant who stands on your foot, totally unconscious of the effect.

Another man, with enormous relish, relates a joke about hearing aids.

He delivers the lines with the confidence of the totally ignorant, expecting it to give as much pleasure to me as to the assembled others. I do not know that he is telling a joke, let alone a joke about deafness. Later a friend tells me. It feels as if someone is speaking about me in a foreign language, laughingly telling a group of strangers something very private.

My stoical front temporarily recedes and, needing a bit of empathy, I share a couple of moans about deafness.

"Yes, Diane, but we all have our problems," delivered with a finger-wagging, reprimanding look suggesting that I am caught up too much with my disability. All my efforts to constantly and anxiously balance the problems and distractions that people have with my own communication needs get me nowhere.

"I'm no good at all this 'mouthing' lark," referring to speaking clearly.

A statement which cleanly slices through any link between us. No "But how can I improve?" No meeting me halfway.

Someone thrashes their hands at me and asks, "Do you do all this stuff then?" meaning signing/fingerspelling.

THIS STUFF? It's my ramp, my wide door entry to human culture. This stuff! Illuminating fingers forming alphabet letters that make sense of mouth movements.

"My cousin was deaf, no problems at all. She could understand me fine."

Pressed further it is revealed that this paragon had only the edge off her hearing, and "understanding" meant nodding her head at all times.

"Isn't the deaf MP wonderful? He manages so well, doesn't he?"

I must bear up, be undemanding, and accept my lot.

"Can't they operate?"

Then I can be cured and they won't have to be perturbed by me.

"Ah, but you heard me when I offered you a gin and tonic, didn't you?"

You only hear when you want to. Likewise "My grandfather was deaf, put it on though."

"Can she understand me?"

To a friend, turning immediately away from me. Sometimes in the form of nervous half laughs, along with, "What do I do now?"

"No problem, no problem, I've worked with the deaf. I'm used to such people." Shouted at me through rigid lips eclipsed by a tatty moustache.

An "on the ball, I've got it taped" kind of attitude.

"Is your daughter with you? I could speak to her instead."

From people who panic at my first "Pardon?"

Silence whilst they fight for composure, followed by a politely distancing comment.

I can't retaliate because I can't hear it!

The deafness which alienates and dehumanizes is caused by inaccessible words. To be denied access to language which takes liberties with you is an assault on your control over your life. The human contact deaf people need is what causes us the greatest unhappiness.

It feels good to be with other deaf people and have relaxed and fluent conversation. But I live in this world and, like anyone else, I want access to the widest spectrum of human life. I am determined to achieve this for myself, and the new generation of deaf people.

Notes

stoical in this instance, means "self-controlled." Originally, a Stoic was a follower of Zeno, a philosopher of ancient Greece who taught people that to live the good life, they should become indifferent to both pleasure and pain.

Analyze and Interpret

1. With a partner, discuss how the author introduces, develops, and sums up her ideas by considering the following questions: How are the first two paragraphs an effective opening for the selection? Why do you think Kenyon used both italics and normal typeface in the central section? How does this combination affect your understanding of the piece? Share your ideas with another pair and note down any new insights.

2. Working in a small group, create and role-play a conversation into which you incorporate some of the "reactions/interactions" described by Diane Kenyon. Present your dramatization to the class and invite their comments.

3. Basing your ideas on the points Kenyon makes in this essay, in a chart draw up a list of "do's and don'ts" that can guide the hearing in their interactions with the deaf. Present your material in the form of a leaflet with a title. Use a word processor to create visual appeal, and include illustrations. Display your final products in the classroom.

More to Explore

Themes: Personal Challenges, Stereotypes, Peers, Role Models

Elements: anecdote, conflict, dialogue, persuasion, satire

THE CARTOGRAPHY OF MYSELF

Al Purdy

LEARNING FOCUS

- Compare an author's experience with your own.
- Write about a Canadian travel experience.
- Use information from print and electronic sources.

CONTEXT Al Purdy, considered by many to be Canada's "unofficial" poet laureate, died in 2000 at the age of 82. Though his career spanned over half a century, Purdy once admitted to coming of age as a writer only in the 1960s when he settled down in a house he himself built in southern Ontario. It was there that he began to use the speech patterns of everyday life in his writing as he reflected on his youthful experiences. Purdy was educated at a small college in Belleville, Ontario, but later steeped himself in both classical and modern poetry while travelling and working across Canada. One example of Purdy's precise, concrete imagery in this personal essay is the title itself. What does the title mean? What metaphor could you use to describe yourself? ■

I n early summer, 1965, I was coasting along in a Nordair DC8, bound for Frobisher Bay, Baffin Island. It was about four a.m. and most of the other passengers were asleep, but I was peering from the window watching the small reflection of our airplane skimming over the blue water and floating ice of Frobisher Bay, several thousand feet down. Low hills on either side of us were patched with snow, like Jersey cows. The water was so blue that the colour looked phony; the sun had been up for about an hour.

Far beneath the noisy DC8, ice floes reeled away south. Black-and-white Arctic hills surrounded us. This was the first time I had been to the Arctic, and I was so excited that I could hardly sit still. In Cuba,

England, France, and other countries I'd felt like a stranger; but here, I'd never left home. And I thought what an odd feeling it was in a region that most people think is desolate and alien. But I felt that the Arctic was just a northern extension of southern Canada.

Baffin Island:
>   A club-shaped word
>   a land most unlike Cathay or Paradise
>   but a place the birds return to
>   a name I've remembered since childhood
>   in the first books I read—
>   ("The Turning Point")

I have this same feeling of enjoyment, of being at home, all over Canada. Maybe part of the reason comes from an earlier feeling of being trapped forever in the town of Trenton, Ontario, when I was a child; then the tremendous sense of release when I escaped, riding the freight trains west during the Depression. Also, I take a double view of history, for then and now merge somewhat in my mind. Winnipeg is also Fort Garry and Seven Oaks. Adolphustown, not far from where I live in Prince Edward County, is the spot where the United Empire Loyalists landed nearly 200 years ago. The restored fortress of Louisbourg in Cape Breton makes me feel like a living ghost, especially when looking at the tombstone of Captain Israel Newton who died there, a member of the colonial army from New England. And driving along Toronto's Don Valley Parkway, I think of the old Indian trails that take the same route under black asphalt. In cities everywhere, grass tries to push aside the concrete barriers of sidewalks.

I think especially of people in connection with places. Working on a highway near Penticton, British Columbia, with a fellow wanderer named Jim, shovelling gravel atop boiling tar: a speeding car ignored warning signs and nearly killed us; the big road foreman blistered that driver's hide until his face turned dull red.

And walking through the Okanagan Valley with my friend, picking cherries from orchards for food, sleeping wherever we could: sometimes in vacant sheds, and once buried in the pungent shavings of a sawmill. Then going to work for two weeks on a mountain farm, for a man whose name sounded like "Skimmerhorn." I got five dollars for those two weeks, cutting down trees with Jim and splitting them with wedges. At night, we listened to John McCormack sing "The Far Away Bells Are Ringing" on a wind-up phonograph. Jim stayed behind to work for a stake, but I gave up and rode the freights west to Vancouver. I never saw him again.

One of my favourite Canadian places is the area around Hazelton and Woodcock on the big bend of the Skeena River in British Columbia. I was stationed at Woodcock in 1943, helping to build a landing field as part of the defences for an expected Japanese invasion. Snow-covered mountains surrounded the barracks sheds, with the Skeena River racing down the green valley on its way to Prince Rupert. Sometimes there were eagles, circling overhead nearly as high as the sun. And on weekend passes, airmen from the base would hop freight trains to Hazelton or Smithers to drink beer and terrorize pleasurably the local female population.

In 1960 I went back to the big bend of the Skeena to do some writing about the Tsimshian Indians around Hazelton and Kispiox. I was driving a '48 Pontiac that coughed its way up and down the mountain roads, threatening to expire at any minute. But I managed to reach Kispiox on the Indian reservation, with its carved house fronts and rotting totem poles. The place seemed entirely deserted, so I drove past the village and down to the Kispiox River. Standing in the shallows, wearing hip waders and baseball caps, were some 20 American fishermen with station wagons parked nearby.

There are other places stored on my mind's memory tapes. Places where I feel comfortable, at home: the battlefield at Batoche, in Saskatchewan, where I camped in a trailer; the highline tracks of the CPR near Field, British Columbia, where I'd walked after a cop kicked me off a freight at Golden, then became a CPR labourer on a landslide blocking passage east for 48 hours, then rode in legal luxury to Calgary on a work train. And once there was a mile-long Arctic island, my home for three weeks of summer: I lay with my ear flat against the monstrous stone silence of the island, listening to the deep core of the world—silence unending and elemental, leaked from a billion-year period before and after the season of man.

I think back to all the places I've been, the people I've met, and the things I've done. Having written and edited some 20 books, I hope to write a dozen more—to follow all the unknown roads I have not explored, until they branch off and become other roads in my mind....

There is a map in my head that I've carried there ever since I left school, and I connect it, oddly, with Leo Tolstoy. He wrote a short story called "How Much Land Does a Man Need," in which a man was given title, free and clear, to as much land as he could encircle on foot between sunup and sundown. The man was too greedy for land, tried to walk around too much of it, and died of exhaustion just before the sun went down.

But I have as much land as I need right now. There is a tireless runner in my blood that encircles the borderlands of Canada through the night hours, and sleeps when day arrives. Then my mind awakes and the race continues. West with the long and lamentably undefended American border; north along the jagged British Columbia coast to the whale-coloured Beaufort Sea and the Arctic Islands; south again past Baffin and Newfoundland to the Maritimes and sea lands of the Grand Banks. This is the map of myself, what I was and what I became. It is a cartography of feeling and sensibility: and I think the man who is not affected at all by this map of himself that is his country of origin, that man is emotionally crippled.

My own country seems to me not aggressive, nor in search of war or conquest of any kind. It is exploring the broken calm of its domestic affairs. Slowly it investigates its own somewhat backward technology, and sets up committees on how not to do what for whom. My country is trying to resolve the internal contradictions of the Indian and French-Canadian nations it contains. In rather bewildered and stupid fashion it stares myopically at the United States, unable to assess the danger to the south—a danger that continually changes in economic character, and finally confronts us from within our own borders.

This is the map of my country, the cartography of myself.

NOTES

Nordair DC8 a type of passenger aircraft operated by Nordair Airlines, which serviced northern Canada in the mid-twentieth century

Cathay an old-fashioned name for China; refers to the Mongol people who ruled in Beijing from 936–1122 CE

Fort Garry a Hudson's Bay Company post established in 1822 that became the city of Winnipeg

Seven Oaks the place that later became Fort Garry and then Winnipeg, where in 1816 a fierce battle took place between the fur-trading rivals of the North West Company and the Hudson's Bay Company; the incident is referred to as the massacre of Seven Oaks

United Empire Loyalists those people born or living in the American colonies during the American Revolution who supported England's royal cause

Louisbourg the eighteenth-century fortified capital of the French colony of Ile Royale on Cape Breton Island

CPR Canadian Pacific Railway; the transcontinental railway created as a condition of entry for British Columbia into Confederation in 1871; in 1967 it merged with Canada's other national railway, CN (Canadian National Railways)

Leo Tolstoy Russian writer (1828–1910) whose novels include *War and Peace*

ANALYZE AND INTERPRET

1. Reread the selection carefully with a small group. In a chart, in one column isolate the words and phrases that suggest that Purdy is knowledgeable about Canada's history. In a second column, list the words and phrases indicating that Purdy is proud to be Canadian. In a personal reflection, evaluate the extent to which you share his views on Canada. Exchange texts with a partner and comment on each other's points of view.

2. Based on your own travels in Canada, or on the travelling you would like to do, create your own "cartography" of yourself in Canada. Use this selection as a model. Indicate what you have seen or wish to see, and its meaning for you. Be sure to include a personal, as well as a geographic and historical, perspective.

3. Find and read a selection of poems by Al Purdy, making sure that some of them deal with places in Canada. Select the poem that you most enjoyed, print it, and create or find an appropriate illustration for it. As an introduction, write a paragraph that explains why you liked this poem.

MORE TO EXPLORE

Themes: Self, Nature, Canada, Journeys, Creativity

Elements: anecdote, description, first-person point of view, flashback, metaphor, mood, setting

ALBERT EINSTEIN

Yousuf Karsh

1948, black–and–white print

LEARNING FOCUS

- Analyze how an author creates mood.
- Create an effective photograph.
- Analyze and discuss the relationship between a photograph and a viewer.

CONTEXT Born in Armenia in 1908, Yousuf Karsh came to Canada in 1924. He lived with his uncle, a photographer, and later apprenticed under photographer John H. Garo of Boston. From him, Karsh learned how to make dramatic use of lighting—a technique that has become his trademark. He opened his own studio in Ottawa in 1932, quickly gaining a reputation for his portraits of famous people. His photograph of British wartime prime minister Winston Churchill is one of the most widely reproduced portraits in the history of photography. Karsh took this portrait of Albert Einstein, the best known physicist of all time, in 1948. After the photo session, Karsh wrote, "I found Einstein a simple, kindly, almost childlike man. One did not have to understand his science to feel the power of his mind or the force of his personality." How does a photographic portrait convey personality differently from a written or televised profile of a person, or from a painted portrait or sculpture of that person? Think of a public personality you are familiar with: what medium—visual or otherwise—do you think would be most effective for portraying that person? Why? ■

ANALYZE AND INTERPRET

1. Examine the portrait closely, and write a report of it based on the following questions: What impression of the subject do you think Yousuf Karsh wished to create? What mood did he wish to convey? What techniques did he call upon to convey this impression and mood? After you have written a rough draft of your report, exchange it with another student's for editing.

2. Create your own photographic portrait of a classmate, friend, family member, or person of interest to you. For a backdrop, choose a setting that will interest viewers. Decide on both lighting and a camera angle that will effectively communicate a mood.

3. Research to find other examples of Karsh's portraiture. Select one portrait that you find particularly interesting or compelling. Present the portrait to a small group, explaining why it attracted you.

MORE TO EXPLORE

Themes: Self, Role Models, Canada, Eye on the Past, Science and Technology

Elements: characterization, mood, visual composition

WHERE THE WORLD BEGAN

Margaret Laurence

Untitled (from *Prairie Dreams*), Courtney Milne

LEARNING FOCUS

- Support your interpretations with quotations.
- Show how personal values are reflected in writing.
- Write a personal essay about a place.

CONTEXT Margaret Laurence was born in Neepawa, Manitoba, in 1926, and began writing stories at the age of seven. After graduating from university, she worked as a reporter for the *Winnipeg Citizen*. She published her first books while living in Africa. She later returned to Canada, moving to Lakefield, Ontario. Laurence became famous for her novels and short stories that were set in the fictional prairie town of Manawaka, including *The Stone Angel* (1964) and *The Diviners* (1974). She was honoured with two Governor General's Awards. Laurence also wrote children's books and worked actively for world peace. She died in 1987. If, like Laurence, you have left your place of birth, where would you say your roots are? Is it possible to have more than one place you can consider to be "home"? Why or why not? ■

A strange place it was, that place where the world began. A place of
incredible happenings, splendours and revelations, despairs like
multitudinous pits of isolated hells. A place of shadow-spookiness,
inhabited by the unknowable dead. A place of jubilation and of
mourning, horrible and beautiful.

It was, in fact, a small prairie town.

Because that settlement and that land were my first and for many
years my only real knowledge of this planet, in some profound way they
remain my world, my way of viewing. My eyes were formed there. Towns
like ours, set in a sea of land, have been described thousands of times as dull,
bleak, flat, uninteresting. I have had it said to me that the railway trip
across Canada is spectacular, except for the prairies, when it would be
desirable to go to sleep for several days, until the ordeal is over. I am
always unable to argue this point effectively. All I can say is—well, you really
have to live there to know that country. The town of my childhood could
be called bizarre, agonizingly repressive or cruel at times, and the land in
which it grew could be called harsh in the violence of its seasonal changes.
But never merely flat or uninteresting. Never dull.

In winter, we used to hitch rides on the back of the milk sleigh, our
moccasins squeaking and slithering on the hard rutted snow of the
roads, our hands in ice-bubbled mitts hanging onto the box edge of the
sleigh for dear life, while Bert grinned at us through his great frosted
moustache and shouted the horse into speed, daring us to stay put.
Those mornings, rising, there would be the perpetual fascination of
the frost feathers on windows, the ferns and flowers and eerie faces
traced there during the night by unseen artists of the wind. Evenings,
coming back from skating, the sky would be black but not dark, for you
could see a cold glitter of stars from one side of the earth's rim to the
other. And then the sometime astonishment when you saw the
Northern Lights flaring across the sky, like the scrawled signature of
God. After a blizzard, when the snowploughs hadn't yet got through,
school would be closed for the day, the assumption being that the
town's young could not possibly flounder through five feet of snow
in the pursuit of education. We would then gaily don snowshoes and
flounder for miles out into the white dazzling deserts, in pursuit of a
different kind of knowing. If you came back too close to night, through

the woods at the foot of the town hill, the thin black branches of poplar and chokecherry now meringued with frost, sometimes you heard coyotes. Or maybe the banshee wolf-voices were really only inside your head.

Summers were scorching, and when no rain came and the wheat became bleached and dried before it headed, the faces of farmers and townsfolk would not smile much, and you took for granted, because it never seemed to have been any different, the frequent knocking at the back door and the young men standing there, mumbling or thrusting defiantly their requests for a drink of water and a sandwich if you could spare it. They were riding the freights, and you never knew where they had come from, or where they might end up, if anywhere. The Drought and Depression were like evil deities which had been there always. You understood and did not understand.

Yet the outside world had its continuing marvels. The poplar bluffs and the small river were filled and surrounded with a zillion different grasses, stones, and weed flowers. The meadowlarks sang undaunted from the twanging telephone wires along the gravel highway. Once we found an old flat-bottomed scow, and launched her, poling along the shallow brown waters, mending her with wodges of hastily chewed Spearmint, grounding her among the tangles of yellow marsh marigolds that grew succulently along the banks of the shrunken river, while the sun made our skins smell dusty-warm.

My best friend lived in an apartment above some stores on Main Street (its real name was Mountain Avenue, goodness knows why), an elegant apartment with royal-blue velvet curtains. The back roof, scarcely sloping at all, was corrugated tin, of a furnace-like warmth on a July afternoon, and we would sit there drinking lemonade and looking across the back lane at the Fire Hall. Sometimes our vigil would be rewarded. Oh joy! Somebody's house burning down! We had an almost-perfect callousness in some ways. Then the wooden tower's bronze bell would clonk and toll like a thousand speeded funerals in a time of plague, and in a few minutes the team of giant black horses would cannon forth, pulling the fire wagon like some scarlet chariot of the Goths, while the firemen clung with one hand, adjusting their helmets as they went.

The oddities of the place were endless. An elderly lady used to serve, as her afternoon tea offering to other ladies, soda biscuits spread with peanut butter and topped with a whole marshmallow. Some considered this slightly eccentric, when compared with chopped egg sandwiches, and admittedly talked about her behind her back, but no one ever refused these delicacies or indicated to her that they thought she had slipped a cog. Another lady dyed her hair a bright and cheery orange, by strangers often mistaken at 20 paces for a feather hat. My own beloved stepmother wore a silver fox neckpiece, a whole pelt, *with the embalmed (?) head still on.* My Ontario Irish grandfather said, "sparrow grass," a more interesting term than asparagus. The town dump was known as "the nuisance grounds," a phrase fraught with weird connotations, as though the effluvia of our lives was beneath contempt but at the same time was subtly threatening to the determined and sometimes hysterical propriety of our ways.

Some oddities were, as idiom had it, "funny ha ha"; others were "funny peculiar." Some were not so very funny at all. An old man lived, deranged, in a shack in the valley. Perhaps he wasn't even all that old, but to us he seemed a wild Methuselah figure, shambling among the underbrush and the tall couchgrass, muttering indecipherable curses or blessings, a prophet who had forgotten his prophesies. Everyone in town knew him, but no one knew him. He lived among us as though only occasionally and momentarily visible. The kids called him Andy Gump, and feared him. Some sought to prove their bravery by tormenting him. They were the medieval bear baiters, and he the lumbering bewildered bear, half blind, only rarely turning to snarl. Everything is to be found in a town like mine. Belsen, writ small but with the same ink.

All of us cast stones in one shape or another. In grade school, among the vulnerable and violet girls we were, the feared and despised were those few older girls from what was charmingly termed "the wrong side of the tracks." Tough in talk and tougher in muscle, they were said to be whores already. And may have been, that being about the only profession readily available to them.

The dead lived in that place, too. Not only the grandparents who had, in local parlance, "passed on" and who gloomed, bearded or bonneted, from the sepia photographs in old albums, but also the uncles, forever 18 or 19, whose names were carved on the granite family stones in the cemetery, but whose bones lay in France. My own young mother lay in that graveyard, beside other dead of our kin, and when I was 10, my father, too, only 40, left the living town for the dead dwelling on the hill.

When I was 18, I couldn't wait to get out of that town, away from the prairies. I did not know then that I would carry the land and town all my life within my skull, that they would form the mainspring and source of the writing I was to do, wherever and however far away I might live.

This was my territory in the time of my youth, and in a sense my life since then has been an attempt to look at it, to come to terms with it. Stultifying to the mind it certainly could be, and sometimes was, but not to the imagination. It was many things, but it was never dull.

The same, I now see, could be said for Canada in general. Why on earth did generations of Canadians pretend to believe this country dull? We knew perfectly well it wasn't. Yet for so long we did not proclaim what we knew. If our upsurge of so-called nationalism seems odd or irrelevant to outsiders, and even to some of our own people (*what's all the fuss about?*), they might try to understand that for many years we valued ourselves insufficiently, living as we did under the huge shadows of those two dominating figures, Uncle Sam and Britannia. We have only just begun to value ourselves, our land, our abilities. We have only just begun to recognize our legends and to give shape to our myths.

There are, God knows, enough aspects to deplore about this country. When I see the killing of our lakes and rivers with industrial wastes, I feel rage and despair. When I see our industries and natural resources increasingly taken over by America, I feel an overwhelming discouragement, especially as I cannot simply say "damn Yankees." It should never be forgotten that it is we ourselves who have sold such a large amount of our birthright for a mess of plastic Progress. When I saw the War Measures Act being invoked in 1970, I lost forever the vestigial remains of the naive wish-belief that repression could not happen here, or would not. And yet, of course, I had known all along in the deepest and often hidden caves of the heart that anything can happen anywhere, for the seeds of both man's freedom and his captivity are found everywhere, even in the microcosm of a prairie town. But in raging against our injustices, our stupidities, I do so *as family*, as I did, and still do in writing about those aspects of my town which I hated and which are always in some ways aspects of myself.

The land still draws me more than other lands. I have lived in Africa and in England, but splendid as both can be, they do not have the power to move me in the same way as, for example, that part of southern Ontario where I spent four months last summer in a cedar cabin beside a river. "Scratch a Canadian, and you find a phony pioneer," I used to say to myself in warning. But all the same it is true, I think, that we are not yet totally alienated from physical earth, and let us only pray we do not become so. I once thought that my lifelong fear and mistrust of cities made me a kind of old-fashioned freak; now I see it differently.

The cabin has a long window across its front western wall, and sitting at the oak table there in the mornings, I used to look out at the river and at the tall trees beyond, green-gold in the early light. The river was bronze; the sun caught it strangely, reflecting upon its surface the near-shore sand ripples underneath. Suddenly, the crescenting of a fish, gone before the eye could clearly give image to it. The old man next door said these leaping fish were carp. Himself, he preferred muskie, for he was a real fisherman and the muskie gave him a fight. The wind most often blew from the south, and the river flowed toward the south, so when the water was wind-riffled, and the current was strong, the river seemed to be flowing both ways. I liked this, and interpreted it as an omen, a natural symbol.

A few years ago, when I was back in Winnipeg, I gave a talk at my old college. It was open to the public, and afterward a very old man came up to me and asked me if my maiden name had been Wemyss. I said yes, thinking he might have known my father or my grandfather. But no. "When I was a young lad," he said, "I once worked for your great-grandfather, Robert Wemyss, when he had the sheep ranch at Raeburn." I think that was a moment when I realized all over again something of great importance to me. My long-ago families came from Scotland and Ireland, but in a sense that no longer mattered so much. My true roots were here.

I am not very patriotic, in the usual meaning of that word. I cannot say "My country right or wrong" in any political, social, or literary context. But one thing is inalterable, for better or worse, for life.

This is where my world began. A world which includes the ancestors—both my own and other people's ancestors who become mine. A world which formed me, and continues to do so, even while I fought it in some of its aspects, and continue to do so. A world which gave me my own lifework to do, because it was here that I learned the sight of my own particular eyes.

NOTES

banshee in Gaelic folklore, a female spirit whose wailing forewarns of a death in the family

Depression known as the Great Depression; the worldwide collapse of the economy that began in 1929 and had a particularly devastating effect on Canada. One in five Canadians became dependent on government relief before World War II broke out in 1939.

Goths a Germanic people who invaded the Roman Empire in the early centuries of the Common Era (nearly 2,000 years ago)

effluvia unpleasant odours; waste

Belsen a German village that was the site of a Nazi concentration camp during World War II

Uncle Sam a man symbolizing the United States; often shown on armed services recruiting posters sporting a white beard and a tall hat decorated with the stars and stripes of the American flag. This term originated in Troy, New York, in about 1812, where a local resident known as Uncle Sam sold army supplies labelled "U.S."; townspeople began substituting "Uncle Sam" for U.S.

Britannia an image of a woman, who is bearing a helmet, shield, and trident, used to symbolize Britain; it appears on items such as coins. The name comes from the Latin *Britanni*, meaning "the Britons."

Damn Yankees a phrase used to refer to and insult those from New England or a northern state; it dates from the U.S. Civil War between the Union (the North) and the Confederacy (the South) from 1861–1865

War Measures Act Canadian statute giving the federal government emergency powers, usually during wartime, to search and arrest citizens. It was invoked by Prime Minister Pierre Trudeau in October 1970, after two high-profile kidnappings by the separatist FLQ (Front de Libération du Québec).

ANALYZE AND INTERPRET

1. In your journal, write a response to "Where the World Began." Consider the following questions when framing your response: What feelings did the essay evoke in you? Which parts touched you most deeply? How has the essay affected the way you look at the place where you live? Which of Laurence's beliefs do you share? Read over your work, considering how effectively you used quotations from the text to support your ideas.

2. The author reveals a great deal about herself in this essay. Make a list of words and phrases that describe her. How are her personal values reflected in her writing? Discuss your ideas with a group of classmates.

3. Where is the place where your world began? Write a personal essay about it, in which you include answers to the following questions: What are your most vivid memories about your life there? Who are the people you most strongly associate with this place? How do you think this place will influence the way you see the world as you grow older? Share your essay with a group of classmates, and ask them to comment on how you used descriptive details to evoke a sense of place.

MORE TO EXPLORE

Themes: Childhood, Self and Culture, Nature, Canada, Creativity

Elements: allusion, description, first-person point of view, metaphor, setting

THE OPEN CAR

Thomas King

Thomas King

- Compare ideas, values, and perspectives.
- Analyze structure and purpose.
- Examine the relationship between media and audience.

CONTEXT Born in 1943, Thomas King was raised in California by parents of Aboriginal and Greek ancestry. He obtained his Ph.D. at the University of Utah and has taught in the Native Studies programs of a number of North American universities. King's writing encompasses short stories, novels, poetry, children's books, and non-fiction. In much of his work, King is interested in the nature of memory, especially its uncertainty or unreliability. Can you remember a time when your memory of an event was quite different from a friend's or family member's? How do we at times shape our memories in convenient ways? ■

My brother and I grew up in a small town in central California. My mother ran a beauty shop out of our house. She worked long hours, and what I remember most was that we were the only family in the neighbourhood who didn't have a television or a car.

That's what my mother wanted. A car. A convertible. When we got a car, she told Christopher and me, we could put the top down and get away. We could go on a trip. We could travel.

Three weeks ago, I had to go from Toronto to New York, and because I had some time before and after my meetings, I persuaded Helen that we should travel by train. I pointed out that a train trip would give us a chance to relax and see the countryside. She reminded me that I was simply terrified of flying and would do anything to stay off a plane.

Which is true.

Nonetheless, I prevailed on her generous spirit and bought two rail tickets for New York. It was a 12-hour trip, and Helen was skeptical.

"What are we going to do for food?"

"They have food on the train," I told her. "It's got to be as good as anything you get on a plane."

Helen packed apples, grapes, ham and cheese sandwiches, water, juice, cookies, yogurt, crackers into two plastic bags, lugged them on the train, and arranged them like small pillows around our feet. Just as the train pulled away from Union Station, she remembered we had to cross a border.

"We have to eat all the apples before we get to Niagara."

"How many do we have?"

"Eight."

My mother believed that travelling was broadening, that by visiting other people and other places you became more tolerant and understanding. And she believed that travel was magic.

I ate two apples. Helen ate one. When we arrived at Niagara Falls, and the American border guards came on the train, we still had five apples.

The border is the part of the trip that Helen doesn't like. Leaving Canada and crossing to the States. She is a staunch nationalist, and the only pleasure she takes in going from one country (home) to the other (the evil empire) is in telling the guards (when they ask) that she is Canadian. She was hardly in a mood to give up five perfectly good apples, I can tell you that.

Outside the train, two station wagons pulled up with German shepherds in the back seat. These were not pets. At the time, I supposed that they were drug-sniffing dogs, but I wasn't sure, and I wasn't going to ask.

The guards worked their way through the train in twos, coming along the aisles slowly, checking passports, asking questions. There was a young black man sitting in front of us. He was, from the sound of his voice, from the Caribbean, and when they got to him, the guards stopped.

My mother travelled through her music. Every Sunday morning, she would stack records on the phonograph spindle, and, when they had all dropped onto the turntable, she would lift them off, turn them over, and begin again. They were musicals, for the most part, and operas—*Carmen, La Traviata, The Desert Song, South Pacific.*

There was a globe in the living room, and while the music played and my mother sang along with each piece, Christopher would find Spain and Italy and Arabia and Tahiti on the map.

One of the guards began asking the man a series of questions—where he was from, where he was going, how long he was going to stay.

And more questions.

Did he have any cigarettes. Any liquor. Any drugs. How much money was he carrying. Did he have a job. The guard asked the man about marijuana several times, each time hooking his lips around his fingers and sucking on an imaginary joint with practised ease to demonstrate exactly what they were looking for.

The man's responses were low and flat, so much so that neither Helen nor I could hear the answers even though we leaned forward in our seats on the pretext of looking out the window.

Evidently, the first guard couldn't hear the man either, for he became irritated and then angry. The man continued in his low, patient way, until finally the guard stopped him and motioned for him to stand up.

"Get your bags and your identification," the guard told the man, "and see immigration in the open car."

The man got his duffel bag from the overhead, smiled at the guard, and walked slowly toward the back of the train. The guard watched the man go. Then he took two steps forward and leaned in to Helen and me. Helen settled into her seat and locked her feet around the food.

"Citizenship?"

"Canadian."

"Canadian."

"Where are you going?"

"New York."

"New York."

The guard smiled at Helen as if she had just told him she thought he looked spiffy in his uniform and then he tipped his hat, just the way the sheriff always did in the Westerns I saw as a kid.

"Have a nice day," he said.

That was it. No liquor, no cigarettes, no drugs, no money, no job. No apples. No open car. As the guard stood by our seats, just before he moved on to the next person, I had two competing emotions.

First, I was appalled that they had not taken us to the open car, where Helen could have told them what they could do with our five apples. And, second, I was relieved.

We stayed at the border for about an hour. Just before the train rolled out of the station, the black man returned to his seat. He was still smiling as he slung his bag into the overhead. He sat down next to the window, put his head against the glass, and went to sleep.

I was about 15 when my mother got her first car. It was a pink Plymouth Fury convertible with enormous fins and a cutaway at the headlights that made it look a little like a shark. My mother was proud of that car. On days when she finished work early, she would put the top down and drive it around town, slowly, as if she were in a parade. She always wore dark glasses and a long yellow scarf that floated above the back seat.

Just as soon as the car was broken in properly, my mother told us, we would pack up our stuff and go on a trip.

New York was fun. Not as clean as Toronto and a little scarier—and Helen pointed these differences out to me—but fun. Even Helen had a good time, though she was not unhappy when we got back on the train to come home.

We did not take much food with us on this part of the trip. Helen forgot about it until all the stores near our hotel had closed. We walked around the area, but nothing was open.

We were reduced to boarding the train early the next morning with nothing more than a pitiful bag of bran muffins, four little bottles of orange juice, and six bananas.

About six months after she got the car, my mother announced that we were going to take a trip. She got a road map from the gas station and laid it out on the table. Christopher and I watched as she worked her way down the coast and through the mountains, circling places as she went. Later, she took a ruler and measured out the distance, converted it into miles, and figured out how much the gas would cost to get there and back.

Then she folded the map up and put it away.

When we got to the border at Niagara for the second time, we were met by Canadian border guards.

"Watch this," Helen told me as the guards came on the train.

Actually, the Canadian guards looked pretty much the same as the American guards.

"Look around," Helen said. "Do you see any dogs?"

There were no dogs, at least none that I could see. But there were people standing on the platform taking pictures of the train.

"Maybe they can't afford dogs."

Why do we travel? Obviously, because we can afford to. Time. Money. Time and money. Perhaps it is a particular inclination—curiosity, romance, distraction. Perhaps it is nothing more than that.

I have friends who travel regularly, and when they say travel, they mean trips that involve great crossings—oceans, continents, hemispheres—and visits to great cities—Paris, Rome, Bombay, Tokyo, London. They leave home with vaccinations and visas and return with colour slides and colds.

As I recall, the Canadian guards had guns. Helen disputes this vigorously. In any case, they came through the train in twos, asking the same questions that the Americans had asked. And when they got to an East Indian couple, they stopped.

Every week, on Saturday (as long as the weather was good), we would get up early and wash the car. We washed it twice with detergent and then rinsed it gently with the garden hose, so we wouldn't get water on the upholstery or hurt the finish. Christopher and I crawled around under the seats, picking up twigs and leaves, little stones, lint, and pieces of a bubble-gum wrapper, while my mother took an SOS pad to the whitewalls and scrubbed them until they glowed.

We told her we'd like to go to Donner Lake or to the ocean, and my mother said that that was a great idea.

The East Indian man told the border guard that he and his wife were Canadian citizens.

"Do you have any proof of citizenship?"

The man smiled and nodded his head and handed the guard two passports. The first guard looked at the passports for a moment and then handed them to his partner, who flipped through the pages, looking at each one in great detail.

"What's the purpose of your visit?"

"We live in Toronto."

"How much liquor are you bringing back into Canada?"

"None."

"Cigarettes?"

"No."

"Presents?"

"Nothing."

The first guard turned to his partner. Then he turned back to the couple.

"Get all your bags and your identification," the guard said, "and take them to immigration in the open car."

One day, my mother walked over to my aunt's house and left the car sitting in the carport. I grabbed the keys from the hook and Christopher got the map and we jumped in the car and put the top down, just the way we had seen Mom do it.

Then I started the car, left it in park, and revved the engine a couple of times. It was exciting sitting there behind the wheel, with the top down, Christopher calling out the towns we were passing and the towns we were coming to.

We had only been driving for about five minutes, when the car suddenly shuddered, coughed a couple of times, and died. I tried starting it, but it was no use. Christopher and I got out of the car and put the top back up. I hung the keys back up on the hook and Christopher put the map away.

The next day, my mother tried to start the car, but nothing happened. Later Mr. Santucci came by. He poured some gas into the tank and tinkered around under the hood, and in about an hour the car was running just fine.

When the guard got to us, I was ready for him.

"Citizenship?"

"Canadian."

"Do you have any cheese?"

I must admit, the question threw me, and had I had my wits about me, I am certain I could have come up with a clever response.

"No," I said.

"Have a nice day," said the guard.

My mother never travelled. She stayed home. I think she would have liked to travel, but she had my brother and me and the beauty shop. My father travelled. He started travelling just after Christopher was born and never came back. Perhaps he is still travelling.

Customs cleared the train, and the East Indian couple returned to their seats. As we pulled away from Niagara, I went back to the open car to see what we had missed, which, as it turned out, wasn't much. The open car was a cramped affair with a bar off to one side where you could get frozen hot dogs, pizza, hamburgers, nachos (microwaved while you waited), and a variety of drinks.

It had all the ambience of a small bus station. There were no tables or chairs, nothing convenient for an intimate conversation or an interrogation. Whatever you wanted to eat or do had to be managed standing, and I wondered what the immigration people could have done to the black man and the East Indian couple in a room like this.

When I got back to my seat, I told Helen about the open car.

"Did they have any yogurt?"

"They had pizza."

"Salads?"

"Hot dogs."

My mother no longer wants to travel. At least that's what she tells me. When Helen and I went to New York, my mother flew to Toronto to watch the kids. Have a good time, she told us. If you want to stay a few extra days, don't worry about anything.

So I told her about the car and what Christopher and I had done. When I finished the story, she looked at me and shook her head. The Plymouth was a hardtop, she said. The Pontiac was a convertible. And the Plymouth hadn't run out of gas, it had been a problem with the alternator. John Varris fixed that, she told me, not Mr. Santucci. If you're going to tell a story, she insisted, at least get the facts right.

We waited and ate when we got back to Toronto. A nice little restaurant on Queen. As we sat there waiting for the server, Helen began to laugh.

"What do you think the Americans would have done to us if they had found the oranges?"

"You mean apples."

"What apples?"

After we ordered, Helen slid a guidebook across the table. "We should go there next," she said, and she spread a map of Ireland out across the table and began running the coastline with her finger, stopping here and there to read a description from the book.

My mother was right. The Pontiac was the convertible.

Notes

Niagara refers to the Ontario town of Niagara Falls

staunch firm or steadfast

ambience atmosphere or mood of the immediate environment

Queen here, referring to Queen Street West, one of Toronto's restaurant districts

Analyze and Interpret

1. In a group, discuss your reaction to the two border crossing incidents in the essay. How would you have felt if you had been present? What would you have wanted to do? What do you think would have happened if the author and his companion, Helen, had spoken up to protest the treatment of the young black man or the East Indian couple? Discuss racist incidents you have personally witnessed. What is your responsibility as a witness? Make a list of some things that you can do in your school and community to combat racism.

2. This essay is structured by interweaving events from the author's past and present. Create a chart that summarizes the essay by documenting these two strands. Write a paragraph that explores the effectiveness of this structure. Share your paragraph in a group and comment on one another's ideas.

3. Study the articles and ads in several travel magazines and the weekend travel sections of the newspaper. What assumptions have the editors and advertisers made about the reasons why most people travel? Create a collage that reflects your response to the question "Why do we travel?" Write captions for the images you have chosen. In your captions, explore ideas on aspects of the travel industry, and the benefits and drawbacks of these travel destinations to the local residents.

More to Explore

Themes: Stereotypes, Family, Urban Life, Aboriginal Cultures, Canada, Journeys

Elements: dialogue, flashback, informal language, narration, symbol

WRONG ISM

J.B. Priestley

LEARNING FOCUS

- Analyze and express a viewpoint on a thesis.
- Identify and present similarities between two pieces of writing.
- Debate and defend a position on an issue.

CONTEXT John Boynton Priestley was born in 1894 in Yorkshire, England. After serving in World War I, he studied at Cambridge University. Priestley gained international popularity in 1929 with his novel *The Good Companions*. He also wrote approximately fifty plays, several of which have enjoyed revivals at the Shaw Festival in Ontario. During World War II, as a patriotic radio broadcaster, Priestley gained fame second only to Britain's prime minister at the time, Winston Churchill. A prolific writer, Priestley published over 120 books. He died in 1984. Priestley wrote this persuasive essay in the 1960s, and yet the topic is still applicable today. What does the term "regionalism" mean to you? What are some recent events that have resulted from nationalism? How does Priestley's view of internationalism compare with current views of globalization? ■

There are three isms that we ought to consider very carefully—regionalism, nationalism, internationalism. Of these three the one there is most fuss about, the one that starts men shouting and marching and shooting, the one that seems to have all the depth and thrust and fire, is of course nationalism. Nine people out of ten, I fancy, would say that of this trio it is the one that really counts, the big boss. Regionalism and internationalism, they would add, are comparatively small, shadowy, rather cranky. And I believe all this to be quite wrong. Like many another big boss, nationalism is largely bogus. It is like a bunch of flowers made of plastics.

The real flowers belong to regionalism. The mass of people everywhere may never have used the term. They are probably regionalists without knowing it. Because they have been brought up in a certain part of the world, they have formed perhaps quite unconsciously a deep attachment to its landscape and speech, its traditional customs, its food and drink, its songs and jokes. (There are of course always the rebels, often intellectuals and writers, but they are not the mass of people.) They are rooted in their region. Indeed, without this attachment a man can have no roots.

So much of people's lives, from earliest childhood onwards, is deeply intertwined with the common life of the region, they cannot help feeling strongly about it. A threat to it is a knife pointing at the heart. How can life ever be the same if bullying strangers come to change everything? The form and colour, the very taste and smell of dear familiar things will be different, alien, life-destroying. It would be better to die fighting. And it is precisely this, the nourishing life of the region, for which common men have so often fought and died.

This attachment to the region exists on a level far deeper than that of any political hocus-pocus. When a man says "my country" with real feeling, he is thinking about his region, all that has made up his life, and not about that political entity, the nation. There can be some confusion here simply because some countries are so small—and ours is one of them—and so old, again like ours, that much of what is national is also regional. Down the centuries, the nation, itself, so comparatively small, has been able to attach to itself the feeling really created by the region. (Even so there is something left over, as most people in Yorkshire or Devon, for example, would tell you.) This probably explains the fervent patriotism developed early in small countries. The English were announcing that they were English in the Middle Ages, before nationalism had arrived elsewhere.

If we deduct from nationalism all that it has borrowed or stolen from regionalism, what remains is mostly rubbish. The nation, as distinct from the region, is largely the creation of power-men and political manipulators. Almost all nationalist movements are led by ambitious frustrated men determined to hold office. I am not blaming them. I would do the same if I were in their place and wanted power so badly. But nearly always they make use of the rich warm regional feeling, the emotional dynamo of the movement, while being almost untouched by it themselves. This is because they are not as a rule deeply loyal to any region themselves. Ambition and a love of power can eat like acid into the tissues of regional loyalty. It is hard, if not impossible, to retain a natural piety and yet be for ever playing both ends against the middle.

Being itself a power structure, devised by men of power, the nation tends to think and act in terms of power. What would benefit the real life of the region, where men, women, and children actually live, is soon sacrificed for the power and prestige of the nation. (And the personal vanity of presidents and ministers themselves, which historians too often disregard.) Among the new nations of our time innumerable peasants and labourers must have found themselves being cut down from five square meals a week to three in order to provide unnecessary airlines, military forces that can only be used against them and nobody else, great conference halls and official yachts and the rest. The last traces of imperialism and colonialism may have to be removed from Asia and Africa, where men can no longer endure being condemned to a permanent inferiority by the colour of their skins; but even so, the modern world, the real world of our time, does not want and would be far better without more and more nations, busy creating for themselves the very paraphernalia that western Europe is now trying to abolish. You are compelled to answer more questions when trying to spend half a day in Cambodia than you are now travelling from the Hook of Holland to Syracuse.

This brings me to internationalism. I dislike this term, which I used only to complete the isms. It suggests financiers and dubious promoters living nowhere but in luxury hotels; a shallow world of entrepreneurs and impresarios. (Was it Sacha Guitry who said that impresarios were men who spoke many languages but all with a foreign accent?) The internationalism I have in mind here is best described as world civilization. It is life considered on a global scale. Most of our communications and transport already exist on this high wide level. So do many other things from medicine to meteorology. Our astronomers and physicists (except where they have allowed themselves to be hush-hushed) work here. The UN special agencies, about which we hear far too little, have contributed more and more to this world civilization. All the arts, when they are arts and not chunks of nationalist propaganda, naturally take their place in it. And it grows, widens, deepens, in spite of the fact that for every dollar, ruble, pound, or franc spent in explaining and praising it, a thousand are spent by the nations explaining and praising themselves.

This world civilization and regionalism can get along together, especially if we keep ourselves sharply aware of their quite different but equally important values and rewards. A man can make his contribution to world civilization and yet remain strongly regional in feeling: I know several men of this sort. There is of course the danger—it is with us now—of the global style flattening out the regional, taking local form, colour, flavour, away for ever, disinheriting future generations, threatening them with sensuous poverty and a huge boredom. But to understand and appreciate regionalism is to be on guard against this danger. And we must therefore make a clear distinction between regionalism and nationalism.

It is nationalism that tries to check the growth of world civilization. And nationalism, when taken on a global scale, is more aggressive and demanding now than it has ever been before. This in the giant powers is largely disguised by the endless fuss in public about rival ideologies, now a largely unreal quarrel. What is intensely real is the glaring nationalism. Even the desire to police the world is nationalistic in origin. (Only the world can police the world.) Moreover, the nation-states of today are for the most part far narrower in their outlook, far more inclined to allow prejudice against the foreigner to impoverish their own style of living, than the old imperial states were. It should be part of world civilization that men with particular skills, perhaps the product of the very regionalism they are rebelling against, should be able to move easily from country to country, to exercise those skills, in anything from teaching the violin to running a new type of factory to managing an old hotel. But nationalism, especially of the newer sort, would rather see everything done badly than allow a few non-nationals to get to work. And people face a barrage of passports, visas, immigration controls, labour permits; and in this respect are worse off than they were in 1900. But even so, in spite of all that nationalism can do—so long as it keeps its nuclear bombs to itself—the internationalism I have in mind, slowly creating a world civilization, cannot be checked.

Nevertheless, we are still backing the wrong ism. Almost all our money goes on the middle one, nationalism, the rotten meat between the two healthy slices of bread. We need regionalism to give us roots and that very depth of feeling which nationalism unjustly and greedily claims for itself. We need internationalism to save the world and to broaden and heighten our civilization. While regional man enriches the lives that international man is already working to keep secure and healthy, national man, drunk with power, demands our loyalty, money, and applause, and poisons the very air with his dangerous nonsense.

NOTES

man, men in this instance, refers to humanity generally; a traditional use of the masculine to refer to both males and females

Yorkshire, Devon counties in England with their own distinctive regional character

impresarios those who sponsor or produce entertainment

Sacha Guitry a witty Russian-born actor, director, playwright, and screenwriter (1885–1957) who came of age in Paris and is today considered a trailblazer for French avant-garde cinema

ANALYZE AND INTERPRET

1. In a group, discuss your understanding of the author's views on regionalism, nationalism, and internationalism. What reasons does he give for calling nationalism "bogus"? What is your opinion of his thesis?

2. Select a newspaper article about a political situation that you think reflects some of the issues Priestley raises in this essay. Prepare to present the article to a group of classmates by taking brief notes on the issues it explores. In your presentation, explain why you chose this article, making reference to at least two quotations from the essay in your analysis.

3. Have an informal class debate on this proposition: "We need internationalism to save the world and to broaden and heighten our civilization." In preparation for the debate, make a list of arguments for or against the proposition and do research to find information to support your position. After the debate, write a journal entry assessing your participation. Consider how clearly you expressed your point of view. Also evaluate whether you were able to clarify and extend the ideas of your classmates during the debate.

MORE TO EXPLORE

Themes: Self and Culture, Civic Responsibility, Europe, Moral Questions, Science and Technology

Elements: definition, persuasion, rhetorical question, simile, thesis

"WHERE DO YOU GET YOUR IDEAS FROM?"

Ursula K. Le Guin

LEARNING FOCUS

- Analyze and use organizational structures.
- Explore the relationship between the writer and reader.
- Prepare, organize, and present a short story review.

CONTEXT Born in 1929 in Berkeley, California, Ursula K. Le Guin is the daughter of an anthropologist and a children's book author. She grew up immersed in the legends and myths of her Nordic ancestry. Le Guin attended Radcliffe College and Columbia University, and later studied in France. After five attempts at getting her first novel, *Rocannon's World*, published, Le Guin succeeded in 1964, and went on to write many books, including her 1974 novel *The Dispossessed*, which won two major science-fiction awards. She also won a National Book Award in 1972 for her children's story *The Farthest Shore*. How would you answer the title question for yourself? To what extent do your ideas come from "inside" you? To what extent from the "outside"? What particular strategies or skills do you use to trigger ideas both in your everyday life and in your school work? ■

Whenever I talk with an audience after a reading or lecture, somebody asks me, "Where do you get your ideas from?" A fiction writer can avoid being asked that question only by practising the dourest naturalism and forswearing all acts of the imagination. Science-fiction writers can't escape it, and develop habitual answers to it: "Schenectady," says Harlan Ellison. Vonda N. McIntyre takes this further, explaining that there is a mail order house for ideas in Schenectady, to which writers can subscribe for 5 or 10 or (bargain rate) 25 ideas a month; then she hits herself on the head to signify remorse, and tries to answer the question seriously. Even in its most patronizing form— "Where do you get all those crazy ideas from?"—it is almost always asked seriously: the asker really wants to know.

The reason why it is unanswerable is, I think, that it involves at least two false notions, myths, about how fiction is written.

First myth: There is a secret to being a writer. If you can just learn the secret, you will instantly be a writer; and the secret might be where the ideas come from.

Second myth: Stories start from ideas; the origin of a story is an idea.

I will dispose of the first myth as quickly as possible. The "secret" is skill. If you haven't learned how to do something, the people who have may seem to be magicians, possessors of mysterious secrets. In a fairly simple art, such as making pie crust, there are certain teachable "secrets" of method that lead almost infallibly to good results; but in any complex art, such as housekeeping, piano-playing, clothes-making, or story-writing, there are so many techniques, skills, choices of method, so many variables, so many "secrets," some teachable and some not, that you can learn them only by methodical, repeated, long-continued practice—in other words, by work.

Who can blame the secret-seekers for hoping to find a shortcut and avoid all the work?

Certainly the work of learning any art is hard enough that it is unwise (so long as you have any choice in the matter) to spend much time and energy on an art you don't have a decided talent for. Some of the secretiveness of many artists about their techniques, recipes, etc., may be taken as a warning to the unskilled: what works for me isn't going to work for you unless you've worked for it.

My talent and inclination for writing stories and keeping house were strong from the start, and my gift for and interest in music and sewing were weak; so that I doubt that I would ever have been a good seamstress or pianist, no matter how hard I worked. But nothing I know about how I learned to do the things I am good at doing leads me to believe that there are "secrets" to the piano or the sewing machine or any art I'm no good at. There is just the obstinate, continuous cultivation of a disposition, leading to skill in performance.

So much for secrets. How about ideas?

The more I think about the word "idea," the less idea I have what it means. Writers do say things like "That gives me an idea" or "I got the idea for that story when I had food poisoning in a motel in New

Jersey." I think this is a kind of shorthand use of "idea" to stand for the complicated, obscure, un-understood process of the conception and formation of what is going to be a story when it gets written down. The process may not involve ideas in the sense of intelligible thoughts; it may well not even involve words. It may be a matter of mood, resonances, mental glimpses, voices, emotions, visions, dreams, anything. It is different in every writer, and in many of us it is different every time. It is extremely difficult to talk about, because we have very little terminology for such processes.

I would say that as a general rule, though an external event may trigger it, this inceptive state or story-beginning phase does not come from anywhere outside the mind that can be pointed to; it arises in the mind, from psychic contents that have become unavailable to the conscious mind, inner or outer experience that has been, in Gary Snyder's lovely phrase, composed. I don't believe that a writer "gets" (takes into the head) an "idea" (some sort of mental object) "from" somewhere, and then turns it into words and writes them on paper. At least in my experience, it doesn't work that way. The stuff has to be transformed into oneself, it has to be composed, before it can grow a story.

The rest of this paper will be an attempt to analyze what I feel I am actually working with when I write, and where the "idea" fits into the whole process.

There seem to be five principal elements to the process:

> **1.** The patterns of the language—the sounds of words.
> **2.** The patterns of syntax and grammar; the ways the words and sentences connect themselves together; the ways their connections interconnect to form the larger units (paragraphs, sections, chapters); hence, the movement of the work, its tempo, pace, gait, and shape in time.
>
> (Note: In poetry, especially lyric poetry, these first two kinds of patterning are salient, obvious elements of the beauty of the work—word sounds, rhymes, echoes, cadences, the "music" of poetry. In prose the sound patterns are far subtler and looser and must indeed avoid rhyme, chime, assonance, etc.,

and the patterns of sentencing, paragraphing, movement, and shape in time may be on such a large, slow scale as to escape conscious notice; the "music" of fiction, particularly the novel, is often not perceived as beautiful at all.)

3. The patterns of the images: what the words make us or let us see with the mind's eye or sense imaginatively.

4. The patterns of the ideas: what the words and the narration of events make us understand, or use our understanding upon.

5. The patterns of the feelings: what the words and the narration, by using all the above means, make us experience emotionally or spiritually, in areas of our being not directly accessible to or expressible in words.

All these kinds of patterning—sound, syntax, images, ideas, feelings—have to work together; and they all have to be there in some degree. The inception of the work, that mysterious stage, is perhaps their coming together: when in the author's mind a feeling begins to connect itself to an image that will express it, and that image leads to an idea, until now half-formed, that begins to find words for itself, and the words lead to other words that make new images, perhaps of people, characters of a story, who are doing things that express the underlying feelings and ideas that are now resonating with each other....

If any of the processes get scanted badly or left out, in the conception stage, in the writing stage, or in the revising stage, the result will be a weak or failed story. Failure often allows us to analyze what success triumphantly hides from us. I do not recommend going through a story by Chekhov or Woolf trying to analyze out my five elements of the writing process; the point is that in any successful piece of fiction, they work in one insoluble unitary movement. But in certain familiar forms of feeble writing or failed writing, the absence of one element or another may be a guide to what went wrong.

For example: Having an interesting idea, working it up into a plot enacted by stock characters, and relying upon violence to replace feeling may produce the trash-level mystery, thriller, or science-fiction story; but not a good mystery, thriller, or science-fiction story.

Contrariwise, strong feelings, even if strong characters enact them, aren't enough to carry a story if the ideas connected with those feelings haven't been thought through. If the mind isn't working along with the emotions, the emotions will slosh around in a bathtub of wish fulfillment (as in most mass-market romances) or anger (as in much of the "mainstream" genre) or hormones (as in porn).

Beginners' failures are often the result of trying to work with strong feelings and ideas without having found the images to embody them, or without even knowing how to find the words and string them together. Ignorance of English vocabulary and grammar is a considerable liability to a writer of English. The best cure for it is, I believe, reading. People who learned to talk at two or so and have been practising talking ever since feel with some justification that they know their language; but what they know is their spoken language, and if they read little, or read schlock, and haven't written much, their writing is going to be pretty much what their talking was when they were two. It's going to require considerable practice. The attempt to play complicated music on an instrument which one hasn't even learned the fingering of is probably the commonest weakness of beginning writers.

A rarer kind of failure is the story in which the words go careening around bellowing and plunging and kicking up a lot of dust, and when the dust settles you find they never got out of the corral. They got nowhere, because they didn't know where they were going. Feeling, idea, image, just got dragged into the stampede, and no story happened. All the same, this kind of failure sometimes strikes me as promising, because it reveals a writer revelling in pure language—letting the words take over. You can't go on that way, but it's not a bad place to start from.

The novelist-poet Boris Pasternak said that poetry makes itself from "the relationship between the sounds and the meanings of words." I think that prose makes itself the same way, if you will allow "sounds" to include syntax and the large motions, connections, and shapes of narrative. There is a relationship, a reciprocity, between the words and the images, ideas, and emotions evoked by those words: the stronger that relationship, the stronger the work. To believe that you can achieve meaning or feeling without coherent, integrated patterning of the sounds, the rhythms, the sentence structures, the images, is like believing you can go for a walk without bones.

Of the five kinds of patterning that I have invented or analyzed here, I think the central one, the one through which all the others connect, is the imagery. Verbal imagery (such as a simile or a description of a place or an event) is more physical, more bodily, than thinking or feeling, but less physical, more internal, than the actual sounds of the words. Imagery takes place in "the imagination," which I take to be the meeting place of the thinking mind with the sensing body. What is imagined isn't physically real, but it *feels as if it were:* the reader sees or hears or feels what goes on in the story, is drawn into it, exists in it, among its images, in the imagination (the reader's? the writer's?) while reading.

This illusion is a special gift of narrative, including the drama. Narration gives us entry to a shared world of imagination. The sounds and movement and connections of the words work to make the images vivid and authentic; the ideas and emotions are embodied in and grow out of those images of places, of people, of events, deeds, conversations, relationships; and the power and authenticity of the images may surpass that of most actual experience, since in the imagination we can share a capacity for experience and an understanding of truth far greater than our own. The great writers share their souls with us—"literally."

This brings me to the relationship of the writer to the reader: a matter I again find easiest to approach through explainable failure. The shared imaginative world of fiction cannot be taken for granted, even by a writer telling a story set right here and now in the suburbs among people supposed to be familiar to everybody. The fictional world has to be created by the author, whether by the slightest hints and suggestions, which will do for the suburbs, or by very careful guidance and telling detail, if the reader is being taken to the planet Gzorx. When the writer fails to imagine, to *image,* the world of the narrative, the work fails. The usual result is abstract, didactic fiction. Plots that make points. Characters who don't talk or act like people, and who are in fact not imaginary people at all but mere bits of the writer's ego got loose, glibly emitting messages. The intellect cannot do the work of the imagination; the emotions cannot do the work of the imagination; and neither of them can do anything much in fiction without the imagination.

Where the writer and the reader collaborate to make the work of fiction is perhaps, above all, in the imagination. In the joint creation of the fictive world.

Now, writers are egoists. All artists are. They can't be altruists and get their work done. And writers love to whine about the Solitude of the Author's Life, and lock themselves into cork-lined rooms or droop around in bars in order to whine better. But although most writing is done in solitude, I believe that it is done, like all the arts, for an audience. That is to say, with an audience. All the arts are performance arts, only some of them are sneakier about it than others.

I beg you please to attend carefully now to what I am not saying. I am not saying that you should think about your audience when you write. I am not saying that the writing writer should have in mind, "Who will read this? Who will buy it? Who am I aiming this at?"—as if it were a gun. No.

While *planning* a work, the writer may and often must think about readers; particularly if it's something like a story for children, where you need to know whether your reader is likely to be a 5-year-old or a 10-year-old. Considerations of who will or might read the piece are appropriate and sometimes actively useful in planning it, thinking about it, thinking it out, inviting images. But once you start writing, it is fatal to think about anything but the writing. True work is done for the sake of doing it. What is to be done with it afterwards is another matter, another job. A story rises from the springs of creation, from the pure will to be; it tells itself; it takes its own course, finds its own way, its own words; and the writer's job is to be its medium. What a teacher or editor or market or critic or Alice will think of it has to be as far from the writing writer's mind as what breakfast was last Tuesday. Farther. The breakfast might be useful to the story.

Once the story is written, however, the writer must forgo that divine privacy and accept the fact that the whole thing has been a performance, and it had better be a good one.

When I, the writer, reread my work and settle down to reconsider it, reshape it, revise it, then my consciousness of the reader, of collaborating with the reader, is appropriate and, I think, necessary. Indeed I may have to make an act of faith and declare that they will exist, those unknown, perhaps unborn people, my dear readers. The blind, beautiful arrogance of the creative moment must grow subtle, self-conscious, clear-sighted. It must ask questions, such as: Does this say what I thought it said? Does it say all I thought it did? It is at this stage that I, the writer, may have to question the nature of my relationship to my readers, as manifested in my work. Am I shoving them around, manipulating them, patronizing them, showing off to them? Am I punishing them? Am I using them as a dump site for my accumulated psychic toxins? Am I telling them what they better damn well believe or else? Am I running circles around them, and will they enjoy it? Am I scaring them, and did I intend to? Am I interesting them, and if not, hadn't I better see to it that I am? Am I amusing, teasing, alluring them? Flirting with them? Hypnotizing them? Am I giving to them, tempting them, inviting them, drawing them into the work *to work with me*—to be the one, the Reader, who completes my vision?

Because the writer cannot do it alone. The unread story is not a story; it is little black marks on wood pulp. The reader, reading it, makes it live: a live thing, a story.

A special note to the above: if the writer is a socially privileged person—particularly a white or a male or both—his imagination may have to make an intense and conscious effort to realize that people who don't share his privileged status may read his work and will not share with him many attitudes and opinions that he has been allowed to believe or to pretend are shared by "everybody." Since the belief in a privileged view of reality is no longer tenable outside privileged circles, and often not even within them, fiction written from such an assumption will make sense only to a decreasing, and increasingly reactionary, audience. Many women writing today, however, still choose the male viewpoint, finding it easier to do so than to write from the knowledge that feminine experience of reality is flatly denied by many potential readers, including the majority of critics and professors of literature, and may rouse defensive hostility and contempt. The choice, then, would seem to be between collusion and subversion; but there's no use pretending that you can get away without making the choice. Not to choose, these days, is a choice made. All fiction has ethical, political, and social weight, and sometimes the works that weigh the heaviest are those apparently fluffy or escapist fictions whose authors declare themselves "above politics," "just entertainers," and so on.

The writer writing, then, is trying to get all the patterns of sounds, syntax, imagery, ideas, emotions, working together in one process, in which the reader will be drawn to participate. This implies that writers do one hell of a lot of controlling. They control all their material as closely as they can, and in doing so they are trying to control the reader, too. They are trying to get the reader to go along helplessly, putty in their hands, seeing, hearing, feeling, believing the story, laughing at it, crying at it. They are trying to make innocent little children cry.

But though control is a risky business, it need not be conceived in confrontational terms as a battle with and a victory over the material or the reader. Again, I think it comes down to collaboration, or sharing the gift: the writer tries to get the reader working with the text in the effort to keep the whole story all going along in one piece in the right direction (which is my general notion of a good piece of fiction).

In this effort, writers need all the help they can get. Even under the most skilled control, the words will never fully embody the vision. Even with the most sympathetic reader, the truth will falter and grow partial. Writers have to get used to launching something beautiful and watching it crash and burn. They also have to learn when to let go of control, when the work takes off on its own and flies, farther than they ever planned or imagined, to places they didn't know they knew. All makers must leave room for the acts of the spirit. But they have to work hard and carefully, and wait patiently, to deserve them.

NOTES

naturalism in this instance, it is used to mean extreme realism

Schenectady a city and industrial centre in New York State; in this instance, used derisively to mean a provincial and unimportant or distant place

syntax the way in which words are put together to form sentences; the rhythm of one's writing

scanted in this instance, skimped on; given short shrift

schlock a Yiddish term meaning something of inferior quality

careening lurching or swerving in an uncontrolled manner

didactic referring to a person who is inclined to lecture or moralize too much

collusion a secret agreement between individuals for a deceitful purpose

subversion the act of overthrowing or undermining

ANALYZE AND INTERPRET

1. With a partner, carefully reread the essay. Pay attention to the structure the writer has used to organize her main ideas. First, decide how this article could be divided into sections based on these separate ideas. Then create subheadings for each section to signal that a new idea is being introduced. Make a photocopy of the article and prepare a new layout that incorporates your subheadings. Consider how breaking up the text of the essay in this way helps the reader understand the material presented in it.

2. When discussing the relationship between the writer and the reader, the author says: "Where the writer and the reader collaborate to make the work of fiction is perhaps, above all, in the imagination. In the joint creation of the fictive world." Consider how this statement applies to a short story or novel you admire. What is the fictive world that the author has created? How does the author facilitate your entry into that world? What do you bring to this collaboration of the imagination? Record your ideas in a journal entry.

3. Read a short story by Ursula K. Le Guin. You will write a review of it based on some of the criteria she sets out in this article. **a)** Before you begin, read several professional book reviews in newspapers or magazines to study their style and tone. **b)** In your review, briefly introduce the story and analyze its strengths and weaknesses according to her criteria. **c)** End with a recommendation on whether your audience should read the story.

MORE TO EXPLORE

Themes: Personal Challenges, Peers, Role Models, At Work, Creativity

Elements: classification, comparison, first-person point of view, persuasion, thesis, voice

MARILYN BELL— THE FRIGHTENING NIGHT AND THE TERRIBLE DAY

June Callwood

CONTEXT June Callwood is a renowned Canadian journalist, author, and activist. Born in 1924 in Chatham, Ontario, she first worked as a newspaper reporter. During her lengthy career, she has taken a particular interest in women's issues and has been an outspoken activist for a variety of causes. In this piece, she tells the story of young Marilyn Bell and her heroic swim across Lake Ontario in 1954. Bell's story is set against the backdrop of the 1950s, when feats of this nature by women were uncommon. How do you think a writer would cover a feat like this today? Do you think a present-day writer would emphasize the same or different aspects of the story? How might mass media, such as television or the Internet, cover such an event? ■

L ady athletes are a special case. The tendency among stout-hearted males is to regard them as a contradiction in terms, and to ignore them. This has never been easy. The most exciting performance by a Canadian athlete at the 1960 Winter Olympics was a lady's—Ann Heggtveit, of Ottawa, won Canada's first gold medal in skiing. Before her, Ethel Catherwood, Saskatoon, had leaped higher than any other woman in the world at the 1928 Olympics. That was the year when Canada's four-girl team of sprinters won a gold medal in the 400-metre relay. Later on, Barbara Ann Scott became a three-word synonym for figure-skating, and still later little Marlene Stewart defeated the world's best women golfers. But there was one lady athlete who had a season of glory so intense that no one, male or female, could ignore her altogether. She was Marilyn Bell, 16 years old the night she swam across Lake Ontario, in September of 1954.

Marilyn looked like somebody's babysitter, blue-eyed and honey-haired, shy and soft of speech. Yet she endured a more punishing test than any that several generations of male stoics had been able to withstand before her. At the turn of the century, boxing bouts that lasted 30 and 40 rounds were not uncommon, and hockey and lacrosse players were almost all 60-minute men. In the 1930s, again, endurance was once more a prime athletic quality. In some foot races in the 1930s the contestants eventually stopped running and started walking in the manner of somnambulists with hives; one of the characteristic spectacles of the era was a coast-to-coast walkathon called the Bunion Derby.

Long-distance swimming and six-day bike races and even marathon flagpole sitting flourished for a decade, and then they died.

More and more, sport came to stress speed and downgrade stamina, as the nature of the games changed and 60-minute men became extinct. Endurance for its own sake had been long out of style by the time Marilyn Bell, a solemn, freckle-faced schoolgirl of five-feet-two and 119 pounds, won international acclaim for the most remarkable feat of endurance in the history of Canadian sport.

The ordeal of Marilyn Bell began in the flat black waters of Lake Ontario 53 minutes before midnight on September 8, 1954. Ahead of her lay perhaps 30 miles of numbing cold, semi-consciousness, and self-denying courage. And, of course, ahead of her lay a lasting achievement as well.

It is the achievement that surmounts the years; forgotten except by the girl herself, and perhaps by the handful of people in a few boats who spent 20 hours and 59 minutes in her wake, are the frightening night and the terrible day in the water.

The swim traversed the lake from Youngstown, New York, at the mouth of the Niagara River, to the Canadian National Exhibition breakwater at Toronto. The course lay across 21 miles of water. In the shifting winds that turned the lake from calm to choppy to heavily swelled and back again, the girl in the water was blown many uncharted miles from a direct course, perhaps as many as 10, and although there were at least four times when it seemed she could not possibly survive another stroke, she persevered one way and another and beat the ungiving waters.

The swim began as a lure for the CNE. It involved Florence Chadwick, a 34-year-old marathon swimmer from California, who was offered $2,500 by the CNE to tackle the lake and $7,500 more if she beat it. Uninvited, Marilyn and Winnie Roach Leuszler, a girl of 28 from St. Thomas, Ontario, challenged Miss Chadwick. *The Toronto Telegram*, co-sponsor with the CNE of the Chadwick promotion, refused to recognize the challenge, and a nice little newspaper war was in the making. It burgeoned into a front-page story, with six-inch banner headlines, when *The Toronto Star* underwrote the challengers' expenses, and rented boats to accompany them across the lake.

At this moment, very little was known of Marilyn Bell except within the shallow confines of marathon swimming, a phenomenon that briefly raised its soggy head each July at Atlantic City and each September at Toronto's Exhibition. The name of Marilyn Bell had flickered across the sports pages in July 1954, when she was seventh at Atlantic City and the first female to finish a 26-mile race open to both sexes.

Still, in September, officials of the CNE pleaded with the *Star* to withdraw the support it had offered Marilyn. As the CNE sports director, George Duthie, put it: "That lake is no place for a youngster." The Star refused, presumably because of the battle its headline writers were now waging against the *Telegram*. "She sold more newspapers than any news event since the war," a *Star* circulation man said after the swim, noting that both papers sold 30,000 more copies than usual on the day of the swim and the day after it.

Because of Marilyn's youth and the comparative obscurity of marathon swimming, neither the newspapers nor the CNE officials were aware that Marilyn had been an accomplished swimmer for at least six years. She was born in Toronto on October 19, 1937, and her father, a spare, retiring clerk-accountant for a food chain, taught her to swim when she was four. Six years later he bought her a season ticket to an outdoor pay-as-you-swim pool. By the next summer Marilyn had won her first swimming award, a medal for stroking a mile in 42 minutes. The coach at the pool, Alex Duff, asked her to join a group of junior swimmers called the Dolphinettes, who put on demonstrations to raise money for the Community Chest. Through Duff, Marilyn met Gus Ryder, a tough-minded, white-haired swimming coach who ran classes at the Lakeshore Memorial Pool. Ryder invited her to join his swimming club which, between meets, taught disabled children to swim.

"She was the most charming kid, thoughtful and eager," Ryder later recalled. "She had a sort of deep well, a kind of reservoir, and a tremendous loyalty."

When Marilyn was 13 she began giving swimming lessons to the disabled children. At 14 she was a professional instructor.

This was the background, then, of young Marilyn Bell when she drove to Youngstown, New York, with Ryder and Joan Cooke, a blond, vibrant friend who was also an instructor at Ryder's Lakeshore Memorial Pool. Bad weather delayed the swim for two days during which Marilyn, her parents, Ryder, and some *Star* reporters and photographers moved aboard *Mona IV*, a boat chartered by the *Star*. Marilyn dozed and read, or left the boat for long walks. She said then that two things concerned her: a gnawing distaste for swimming in the dark, and a loathing of eels and lampreys fastening to her skin. As it turned out, her apprehensions were fully realized.

At a little after nine on the night of September 8 a rainstorm broke over Youngstown. Ninety minutes later it passed, leaving the lake mirror calm. Word reached the *Mona IV* that Florence Chadwick was preparing to take off. Then, as the American swimmer moved out through the black water, Marilyn threw off her dark red blanket, kissed her parents, walked to the edge of the lawn in front of the U.S. Coast Guard building, and plunged off the retaining wall. It was seven minutes past 11.

Ahead, in the 24-foot lifeboat *Mipepa,* Gus Ryder shone a flashlight to guide her. In these early moments Marilyn refused to let her mind dwell on the dark mystery around her. She recalled that in the water at Atlantic City she had hummed *O Canada* and *The Happy Wanderer.* For now, she confined her thoughts to overtaking Miss Chadwick. After a few hours, a sucking sensation prickled high on her thigh—a lamprey. Shuddering, but forcing herself to be calm, she knocked it away with her fist. Three more times before dawn, eels, sucking, attached themselves to her flesh. Each time she knocked them away, without hysteria.

Marilyn caught Florence Chadwick three miles out, and drummed ahead, crawling as purposefully as a fireman skinning up a ladder. Far back, Winnie Roach Leuszler had become separated from her pilot boat; she climbed aboard a press launch, returned to Youngstown, removed her grease, and went to bed. She slept until six in the morning, then plunged into the lake again. Her second attempt was doomed; near nightfall, still nine miles from the Canadian side, she was hauled from the water like an exhausted sailfish, sobbing and only half conscious.

The wind rose toward dawn, building foam-flecked waves 12 feet high. They made Miss Chadwick ill, but she stifled her nausea for another hour. Then, exhausted and half-drowned, she too was lifted from the water. She had managed 12 miles.

Now Marilyn was facing her own crises, treading water glassy-eyed. Ryder, impassive, passed the bewildered girl a cup of corn syrup on the end of a long stick. She took it and stared vaguely as it spilled into the tossing water. Ryder extended another cup. She sipped it, listless as a child with fever, then rolled over and began the endless, staggered rhythm of her stroke.

Full light showed her haggard and gaunt. Pain probed her arms and legs, her stomach throbbed. Her breathing and her stroke had lost their co-ordination, and she gulped unwanted water from the lake. She began to cry. Ryder extended liniment on the stick for her dragging legs. She slowly sank her head, forced her legs above the surface, and rubbed on the liniment. Then she plodded on.

Ryder used Miss Chadwick's capitulation as a psychological device. At 10:30, as Marilyn faltered again, he scrawled on a blackboard, FLO IS OUT. At noon he wrote, DON'T LET THE CRIPPLED KIDS DOWN. By early afternoon, she was dozing. She had not been to bed now for 30 hours. The Toronto Harbour Commissioners, fearing she might drown, dispatched two lifeboats to flank her. In mid-afternoon Ryder summoned Joan Cooke, who swam fully clothed to the *Mipepa* from a nearby launch.

At five in the afternoon, with Marilyn seemingly lifeless, Ryder sent Miss Cooke into the water. In pants and a bra, she swam alongside and shrilly wakened her wallowing friend. Then she pulled away in a brisk crawl and Marilyn, woodenly revived but groggy, gave chase.

The wind died, and now crosscurrents underwater played tricks with her course. For every few hundred yards she swam, she drifted half that many from her true line. After an hour and a half of this, she wearily stilled her arms and turned her pale, pathetic face to the pilot boat. Streaks of oil and dirt creased her cheeks, broken by the crooked paths of tears. Her father, aboard the *Mona IV,* ordered her out. Ryder gave no hint he had heard; he raised his blackboard—IF YOU QUIT I QUIT.

The words registered dully. She drew a long breath, her legs and arms responded to some deep and distant message, and the grim employment began anew…stroke…stroke…stroke. Some well of reserve, some channel of reflex kindled her. She never faltered again. She stopped once, to take the last of the syrup and some pablum. Then, a water-logged automaton, she crawled toward the distant, glittering fairgrounds.

In the gathering dusk ahead, tens of thousands of people, caught up by the breathless newscasts and the bizarre headlines, welcomed the approach of Marilyn's white cap, a tiny periscope inching to the break-water. During her hours in the black water she had become a talis-man of courage for the city and for people far beyond it. The hope and the tension were contagious—as the sun sank, her partisans clogged every approach to the shoreline she was straining toward, and for these few hours, elsewhere in Canada, radio was once again the supreme bringer of the word. At six minutes past eight her left hand touched the concrete wall. She hung there a moment, gasping for air, and then Ryder and a reporter pulled her into the *Mipepa*. Dazed and discon-nected as a punch-drunk fighter, she struggled against their hands, reflexively resisting help. Indeed, it wasn't until Joan Cooke leaped into an ambulance beside her, crying, "Oh, Marilyn, you did it! You did it!" that she knew all the lake was behind her.

NOTES

lady in this instance, refers to a female; since the 1970s, this usage is gen-erally considered inappropriate, either because it minimizes the power of a woman and is therefore patronizing, or because it implies that only a woman with a high social standing can be called a "lady" and is therefore elitist

stoics in this instance, persons with endurance and bravery who are impas-sive in the face of pain

Canadian National Exhibition (CNE) known as "the Ex," the world's largest annual exhibition, based in Toronto; originated as a travelling agricultural fair in the Canadian West in the 1840s. Its focus shifted from agriculture to indus-try, and by the 1960s the fair had evolved into primarily a consumer market and amusement park.

lampreys elongated fish characterized by a jawless sucking mouth

liniment a lotion applied to the skin for medicinal purposes

crippled in this instance, an old-fashioned term used to refer to people who do not have full use of their limbs; by the 1980s, this usage was considered to have a negative connotation by placing undue emphasis on the limitations of a person with disabilities

pablum any substance that gives nourishment; in this instance, a bland-tasting prepared food that is easy to digest. "Pablum" with the first letter capitalized is the trademark brand name for a soft cereal for infants that was originally developed at the Hospital for Sick Children in Toronto.

automaton a person who behaves in a mechanical, stilted fashion

periscope an instrument that permits observation from a position displaced from the direct line of sight, as in a submarine

talisman a charm or object with magical powers; originally from the Greek *telos*, meaning "result"

ANALYZE AND INTERPRET

1. In a small group, discuss the topic of heroism. What is a hero? Why do you think people have heroes? Do you think it is especially important for young people to have heroes? Who are your heroes, and why do you admire these people? Make a list of heroic qualities. Compare your list with that of another group.

2. Prepare an oral presentation about a person whom you admire. Gather information about this person from at least three different sources. Which achievements and values of this person will you focus on? How has your admiration for this person influenced your life? Choose anecdotes and quotations that will bring this person to life for your listeners.

3. Do an Internet search to locate information about a current female swimmer, as well as further information about Marilyn Bell. Write a newspaper opinion piece in which you consider differences between Marilyn Bell's circumstances and the current situation for today's swimmer. What details of each swimmer's era will you want to include in your comparison? What information from your Internet search will you use to support your position? Share your first draft with a partner, and invite comments on whether your language and tone are appropriate for newspaper readers.

MORE TO EXPLORE

Themes: Personal Challenges, Role Models, At Work, Nature, Canada, Journeys

Elements: chronological organization, description, narration, persuasion, thesis, third-person point of view

VICTORY!

Stan Behal

1996

- Compare your responses to a photograph with those of others.
- Analyze the effect of camera shots.
- Use a visual to generate ideas for writing.

CONTEXT Stan Behal obtained degrees in history and political science, but decided to follow his passion for photography instead. He began his career working as a freelancer for Canadian Press and *Maclean's,* and has been with *The Toronto Sun* since 1982. In this picture, he captures Donovan Bailey winning the 100-metre dash at the Olympic Games in 1996. Why do you think a professional photographer might be attracted to covering sports events? If you had to choose, which sports would you photograph? Which would you videotape? Which would you present on audio? Why? ■

ANALYZE AND INTERPRET

1. In a group, discuss occasions in your life when you felt a sense of victory. Consider the following questions: **a)** How does a victory make you feel? **b)** Do all victories feel the same? **c)** Can a victory ever feel like a defeat? **d)** Does a victory always involve competition against someone else? **e)** Is the winner always the victor? **f)** How have your ideas of victory changed from when you were a child?

2. The apparent distance between the subject and the camera is usually described as a close-up, a medium shot, or a long shot. This photo is a medium shot which allows you to see the main subject and some of the background. Why do you think the photographer chose a medium shot for this picture? How would the effect have been different if he had chosen a close-up or long shot? With a group of classmates, find other photographs on the sports pages of the newspaper, identify the type of shot for each, and assess the photos' effectiveness.

3. Use this photograph as a starting point for a poem about the subject of victory. **a)** First, give yourself 15 minutes to freewrite your ideas. During this time, record any words and phrases that come to mind. **b)** When the time is up, read over your notes to discover a dominant mood or theme. **c)** Start to shape your notes into a rough draft of your poem. **d)** Share your draft with a partner and invite comments on how clearly you have expressed your ideas. **e)** Polish your poem and share it with your classmates.

MORE TO EXPLORE

Themes: Personal Challenges, Role Models, At Work, Canada

Elements: mood, narration, page layout, visual composition, visual scale

JAPANESE AIR AND SUBMARINE ATTACK SINKS HMS *PRINCE OF WALES* AND HMS *REPULSE*

SINGAPORE, 10 DECEMBER 1941

Cecil Brown

LEARNING FOCUS

- Reflect on your response to a text.
- Use cultural and historical sources to enrich your understanding.
- Work with others to create a timeline.

CONTEXT Born in Pennsylvania in 1907, Cecil Brown became a radio and news correspondent for the Columbia Broadcasting System (CBS) at a young age. He went on to develop a reputation for daring and bravery, broadcasting reports on early conflicts of World War II, including the German invasion of Yugoslavia and the British campaign in Libya. His print journalism was later collected in the book *Suez to Singapore*. In this eyewitness report, Brown lives through and then details the sinking of the HMS *Repulse*, a British warship attacked by the Japanese in 1941. What other eyewitness reports have you read or seen? To what extent did they strike you as objective? In what circumstances is it appropriate to include subjective material in a news report? ■

Two months after this naval disaster, Singapore fell to the Japanese, 15 February 1942.

The torpedo strikes the ship about 20 yards astern of my position. It feels as though the ship has crashed into dock. I am thrown four feet across the deck but I keep my feet. Almost immediately, it seems, the ship lists.

The command roars out of the loudspeaker: "Blow up your lifebelts!"

I take down mine from the shelf. It is a blue-serge affair with a rubber bladder inside. I tie one of the cords around my waist and start to bring another cord up around the neck. Just as I start to tie it the command comes: "All possible men to starboard."

But a Japanese plane invalidates that command. Instantly there's another crash to starboard. Incredibly quickly, the *Repulse* is listing to port, and I haven't started to blow up my lifebelt.

I finish tying the cord around my neck. My camera I hang outside the airless lifebelt. Gallagher already has his belt on and is puffing into the rubber tube to inflate it. The effort makes his strong, fair face redder than usual....

Captain Tennant's voice is coming over the ship's loudspeaker, a cool voice: "All hands on deck. Prepare to abandon ship." There is a pause for just an instant, then "God be with you."

There is no alarm, no confusion, no panic. We on the flag deck move toward a companionway leading to the quarterdeck. Abrahams, the Admiralty photographer, Gallagher, and I are together. The coolness of everyone is incredible. There is no pushing, but no pausing either. One youngster seems in a great hurry. He tries to edge his way into the line at the top of the companionway to get down faster to the quarterdeck.

A young sub-lieutenant taps him on the shoulder and says quietly, "Now, now, we are all going the same way, too."

The youngster immediately gets hold of himself....

The *Repulse* is going down.

The torpedo-smashed *Prince of Wales*, still a half to three-quarters of a mile ahead, is low in the water, half shrouded in smoke, a destroyer by her side.

Japanese bombers are still winging around like vultures, still attacking the Wales. A few of those shot down are bright splotches of burning orange on the blue South China Sea.

Men are tossing overboard rafts, lifebelts, benches, pieces of wood, anything that will float. Standing at the edge of the ship, I see one man (Midshipman Peter Gillis, an 18-year-old Australian from Sydney) dive from the Air Defence control tower at the top of the main mast. He dives 170 feet and starts to swim away.

Men are jumping into the sea from the four or five defence control towers that segment the main mast like a series of ledges. One man misses his distance, dives, hits the side of the *Repulse*, breaks every bone in his body, and crumples into the sea like a sack of wet cement. Another misses his direction and dives from one of the towers straight down the smokestack.

Men are running all along the deck of the ship to get further astern. The ship is lower in the water at the stern and their jump therefore will be shorter. Twelve Royal Marines run back too far, jump into the water, and are sucked into the propeller.

The screws of the *Repulse* are still turning. There are five or six hundred heads bobbing in the water. The men are being swept astern because the *Repulse* is still making way and there's a strong tide here, too.

On all sides of me men are flinging themselves over the side. I sit down on the edge of the *Repulse* and take off my shoes. I am very fond of those shoes. A Chinese man made them for me just a few days ago in Singapore. They are soft, with a buckle, and they fit well. I carefully place them together and put them down as you do at the foot of your bed before going to sleep.

I have no vision of what is ahead, no concrete thoughts of how to save myself. It is necessarily every man for himself. As I sit there, it suddenly comes to me, the overwhelming, dogmatic conviction. I actually speak the words: "Cecil, you are never going to get out of this."

I see one man jump and land directly on another man. I say to myself, "When I jump, I don't want to hurt anyone."

Down below is a mess of oil and debris, and I don't want to jump into that either. I feel my mind getting numb. I look across to the *Wales*. Its guns are flashing and the flames are belching through the greyish-black smoke.

My mind cannot absorb what my eyes see. It is impossible to believe that these two beautiful, powerful, invulnerable ships are going down. But they are. There's no doubt of that.

Men are sliding down the hull of the *Repulse*. Extending around the edge of the ship is a three-inch bulge of steel. The men hit that bulge, shoot off into space and into the water. I say to myself, "I don't want to go down that way. That must hurt their backsides something terrible."

About eight feet to my left there is a gaping hole in the side of the *Repulse*. It is about 30 feet across, with the plates twisted and torn. The hull of the *Repulse* has been ripped open as though a giant had torn apart a tin can. I see an officer dive over the side, dive into the hold underneath the line, dive back inside the ship.

I half turn to look back on the crazy-angled deck of the ship. The padre is beside one of the pom-poms, administering the final rites to a gunner dying beside his gun. The padre seems totally unconcerned by the fact that the *Repulse* is going down at any moment....

The jump is about 20 feet. The water is warm; it is not water, but thick oil. My first action is to look at my stopwatch. It is smashed at 12:35, one hour and 20 minutes after the first Japanese bomb came through 12,000 feet to crash into the catapult deck of the *Repulse*.

It doesn't occur to me to swim away from the ship until I see others striking out. Then I realize how difficult it is. The oil soaks into my clothes, weighting them, and I think underwater demons are tugging at me, trying to drag me down. The airless lifebelt, absorbing oil too, tightens and tautens the preserver cords around my neck. I say to myself, "I'm going to choke to death, I'm going to choke to death."

Next to confined places, all my life, I've been afraid of choking to death. This is the first moment of fear.

I have a ring on my left hand which Martha bought for me on the Ponte Vecchio in Florence when we were on our honeymoon. It is rather loose on my finger. With oil on my hands, I'm afraid I will lose it. I clench my fist so that it won't slip off.

I start swimming away with the left hand clenched. With my right hand I make one stroke, tug at the cord around my neck in a futile effort to loosen it, then make another stroke to get away from the ship.

That ring helps save my life. Something like it must have helped save the lives of hundreds of men. Your mind fastens itself on silly, unimportant matters, absorbing your thoughts and stifling the natural instinct of man to panic in the face of death.

I see a life preserver 18 inches long and four inches thick. It is like a long sausage and I tuck it to me. A small piece of wood appears inviting and I take that too. A barrel comes near, but I reject that because the oil prevents me getting a grip on it. All around me men are swimming, men with blood streaking down their oil-covered faces.

The oil burns in my eyes as though someone is jabbing hot pokers into the eyes. That oil in the eyes is the worst thing. I've swallowed a bit of oil already, and it's beginning to sicken me.

Fifty feet from the ship, hardly swimming at all now, I see the bow of the *Repulse* swing straight into the air like a church steeple. Its red underplates stand out as stark and as gruesome as the blood on the faces of the men around me. Then the tug and draw of the suction of 32,000 tons of steel sliding to the bottom hits me. Something powerful, almost irresistible, snaps at my feet. It feels as though someone were trying to pull my legs out by the hip sockets. But I am more fortunate than some others. They are closer to the ship. They are sucked back.

When the *Repulse* goes down it sends over a huge wave, a wave of oil. I happen to have my mouth open and I take aboard considerable oil. That makes me terribly sick at the stomach.

Notes

lists (as a verb) inclines to one side, tilts

serge tightly woven wool, usually used in suits; from the Middle English word *sarge*, from the Latin word *sçrica* (*vestis*), meaning "silken (clothing)," from the Greek word *serikos*, meaning "of the Seres" (a people of eastern Asia)

starboard; port; astern right side; left side; and at the back of a ship

dogmatic describes a person who rigidly clings to a series of authoritative principles

pom-poms automatic anti-aircraft cannons

tautens strains or tenses up

Ponte Vecchio legendary bridge in Florence, Italy, built across the Arno River in 1350 and still standing today; in Italian, *ponte* means "bridge" and the literal translation of *vecchio* is "old man"

Analyze and Interpret

1. The writer enables the reader to relate more closely to the sinking of the *Repulse* by focusing on the experiences of individual sailors. Select an incident that you find particularly engaging and, in the voice of the person involved, write an interior monologue in which you react to the disaster unfolding around you.

2. Drawing your information from this selection and from other print and electronic resources, write a newspaper report of the events described by Cecil Brown. Remember to follow the structure of a news story, considering who, what, when, where, why, and how. Use a computer to create the appearance of an actual newspaper article. Then find a news story from 1942 that deals with the event, and compare it with your story.

3. Working in a group of six, use print and electronic resources to research an aspect of World War II that took place in Asia, such as the fall of Singapore, the fall of Hong Kong, or the bombing of Hiroshima. As a group, create a timeline of events by having each person contribute the information for one event in the form of an illustration and a brief written outline. Display the timelines in the classroom.

More to Explore

Themes: Personal Challenges, Journeys, Eye on the Past, War and Peace

Elements: chronological organization, description, first-person point of view, narration, specialized terms, tone

OFF TO WAR

Claude P. Dettloff

1940

- Revise a response to strengthen ideas.
- Practise using correct punctuation in written dialogue.
- Design a pictorial gallery.

CONTEXT Claude P. Dettloff was a Canadian photographer and photo essayist. For years, as a freelancer, Dettloff contributed a regular visual column to the *Winnipeg Tribune* called "Meandering Candid Camera." Each of these photo essays depicted four or five Winnipeg scenes, with captions written by Dettloff. By 1939, Dettloff had settled in Vancouver, where he eventually became a staff photographer for the Vancouver *Province*. This famous photograph, taken in New Westminster, British Columbia, in June 1940, captures a moment of poignancy brought about by war. Who is the focal point of the image, and why? How would you describe the narrative taking place? What clues lead you to your conclusions? Consider your interpretation of this photograph: which elements in the photo make it so powerful? Do you think a ten-second video clip of the moment would have had more or less impact than this photo? Why or why not? ■

ANALYZE AND INTERPRET

1. **a)** After examining the photograph, spend about 10 minutes freewriting your response. **b)** In a group of three, share and compare your responses, making notes during your discussion. **c)** Amplify your initial response according to any new ideas that result from the discussion.

2. Write a narrative to accompany this photograph. **a)** First, decide on an appropriate voice and level of language, depending on the point of view you wish to adopt. **b)** As you write, use the correct format for punctuating and structuring dialogue. **c)** Share your narratives in a round-table reading.

3. Research to find other examples of war photography. Create a pictorial gallery to demonstrate the different impressions of war captured by various photographers. Write a caption to accompany each photograph that expresses the impression created by the image.

MORE TO EXPLORE

Themes: Childhood, Family, Civic Responsibility, Canada, War and Peace

Elements: pathos, setting, visual composition

ON VETERANS

Jean Chrétien

LEARNING FOCUS

- Analyze the use of rhetorical devices.
- Consider the effect of language on an audience.
- Analyze how a film conveys meaning.

CONTEXT Jean Chrétien was born in 1934 in Shawinigan, Québec. After high school, he enrolled in law school at Laval University. Always a strong Canadian federalist, he first won a seat as a Liberal Member of Parliament under Prime Minister Lester Pearson in 1963. After 1968, he held many portfolios in Pierre Trudeau's government. Calling himself "the little guy from Shawinigan," Chrétien was first elected Prime Minister of Canada in 1993. In this formal, prepared speech, he addresses veterans of World War II who have returned to France to commemorate the fiftieth anniversary of the landing on Normandy. What clues can you find that this text was first delivered as spoken language? What are some of the devices that Chrétien, with his speech writer, has used to make this speech effective for both the veterans and the wider media audience? Why do we as a society regularly mark important occasions with speeches such as this one? ■

We are gathered here, on this calm and peaceful day, to remember a very different day 50 years ago.

We are reunited on this calm and peaceful day to commemorate a very different day, 50 years ago, when the winds of freedom swept these beaches.

On the beach behind us, Canadians gave their lives so the world would be a better place. They gave their lives so we—all of us, Canadians and Europeans—could live free, decent lives. Free of fear and oppression.

Who were these young men? They are buried not far from here.

On their graves you will find names like McMillan and Nillson and Cormier and Freedman. Names like Cherulli and Bergeron and Osborne. Names like Silverberg and Topolnitski. Names like Sigurdson and May and Chartrand and Stinson.

The men in these graves came from towns like Estevan and Galt and Rivière-du-Loup and Corner Brook and Prince George and the Rama First Nation Reserve. They came from every region. From every province.

Some were not even born in Canada. They were Canadians by choice. And they died on the beaches of the continent they had left behind, fighting for the country they adopted—the country they loved.

There are some who would say these men had nothing in common. Not geography. Not language. Not background. Not religion. Or ethnicity. Or colour.

But they had one thing very much in common. They were all part of a young nation. A new kind of nation. Where the ancient hatreds of the past were no match for the promise of the future. Where people believed they should speak different languages, worship in different ways, and live in peace.

They died on the shores and in the fields of a Europe consumed by hate and terror. A Europe under the yoke of evil. A Europe in which whole races were being wiped out, where freedom and dissent were crushed.

Three hundred and fifty-nine of them died on these beaches the first day alone, 50 years ago today. In the days and weeks that followed, during the battle of Normandy, more than 5,000 of them died in the fields and countryside around us. And many more died before Europe was finally liberated.

They did not die as anglophones or francophones, as Easterners or Westerners, as Christians or Jews, as immigrants or natives. They died as Canadians.

Today we honour these men and what they died for. And we thank their comrades—the thousands who fought and triumphed and lived. The veterans who were here on the Longest Day 50 years ago. And who are with us today.

The men who cradled and comforted their fallen comrades. Who buried them. And who fought on. With courage and determination.

Today you are showing a new courage. Many of you are retracing your steps of 50 years ago. Reliving the great adventure and the great horror.

This is *your* day. And on behalf of the people of Canada, I say *thank you*.

Thank you for your sacrifices half a century ago. And thank you for your greatest achievement of all—your legacy.

Your efforts here on these beaches, along with your comrades from the other allied countries, helped turn the tide of war.

You liberated the people of this region. You helped them rebuild their lives and their communities. And you began the liberation of this continent after a long and brutal nightmare.

You helped secure not just a historic victory, but—even more important—a lasting, solid peace.

Your other accomplishment was just as remarkable. You gave birth to the modern Canada.

A small nation of 12 million people, our country took on challenges and responsibilities out of all proportion with our small size. One million men and women served in uniform. Millions more served at home—in industry, at home, on farms. Canada became a major fighting force and an important arsenal of democracy.

And here on Juno Beach, we began the liberation of Europe not under an imperial flag, not commanded by foreign officers—but as Canadians.

In this, the greatest invasion the world has ever known, Canada was a full partner with our allies the United States and Great Britain.

Not one of 30 nations, not one of 20 nations, but one of three.

So that day 50 years ago was not only a turning point in the war. It was a turning point in our development as a proud, independent nation. It was our coming of age.

Canada entered the war as a young nation, barely out of its infancy. We emerged from the war as an adult nation—a major industrial power and a force for peace in the world.

Today, we recall a valiant victory. We join the people of Normandy and France in celebrating the triumph of justice over injustice, of freedom over its foes. We pay tribute to the brave efforts of all our allies and our friends.

We also thank the people of Normandy for their warmth and their generosity over the years to the thousands of our veterans and their families who have returned. Your hospitality now recalls the smiles and the support our soldiers saw on that day long ago.

Half a century of peace and security. A modern, robust nation that is the envy of people all over the world. *This* is the debt we owe to the Canadians who came ashore 50 years ago.

Of course, it is a debt we can never completely repay. But it is one we must remember every day of our lives.

We have the obligation to strive for tolerance, understanding, and generosity at home. We can never become complacent about democracy and freedom.

That is the best monument we could build to the heroes of D-Day. A society that lives up to the ideals and values that they fought and died for.

To those of you who fought here 50 years ago, to your comrades who died in battle and the ones who are no longer with us, *you* won a great and lasting peace.

It is our solemn pledge to you that as Canadians—at home and abroad—we will continue to *earn* that peace.

NOTES

D-Day June 6, 1944; the day when the Allies landed in France during World War II; here, "D" is an abbreviation for "Designated"

ANALYZE AND INTERPRET

1. In your journal, respond to the following question: Is this speech effective in instilling a sense of national pride in the audience? In a small group, share and compare your responses. In what ways do perspectives on this issue differ within the group? What factors contribute to these differences?

2. Many of the phrases in this speech are sentence fragments. **a)** Work with a partner to identify and list these sentence fragments. **b)** Next, describe and evaluate their intended effect. **c)** Determine whether the effect of these fragments is different in an oral delivery than in a written form. **d)** With the whole class, present and discuss your findings.

3. **a)** In groups of four or five, select and watch a film that deals with the subject of war. **b)** Analyze your film's portrayal of the war experience. Consider the following questions as you organize your analysis: What opinion or attitude toward war is expressed? In what way is this attitude evident? How does the representation of war reflect the beliefs and values of society at the time the movie was made? What audience might this film be geared toward? **c)** Combine two groups, and have members present aspects of their analysis as part of a panel discussion on the representation of war in films you have seen.

MORE TO EXPLORE

Themes: Role Models, Civic Responsibility, Canada, Europe, Moral Questions, Eye on the Past, War and Peace

Elements: oral tradition, pathos, persuasion, tone

FROM ANIMATION 101

John Lasseter

CONTEXT Born in Hollywood, California, in 1957, John Lasseter fell in love with cartoons and the art of animation during his first year of high school. That same year, he wrote to the Walt Disney Company to ask advice on how to develop his new passion. Later, at the recommendation of the Walt Disney Company, he enrolled in the animation program at the California Institute of the Arts. There he won two Student Academy Awards. Lasseter directed the first feature-length computer animated film, *Toy Story*, which was the highest grossing film of 1995. Do you also have a passion for developing some specific skill? Where might you find guidance and help in pursuing your passion? Does the *Toy Story* animation studio, depicted in the photograph on this page, look like a place where you would like to work? Why or why not? ▪

In 1937, Bill Tytla, who animated and directed the beautiful "A Night on Bald Mountain" sequence in *Fantasia* said, "There is no particular mystery to animation. It is quite simple and like anything that is uncomplicated, it is about the hardest thing in the world to do!"

I have always had a passionate interest in animation, especially computer animation. While at the California Institute of Arts in the late 1970s, I produced two animated films, *Lady and the Lamp* and *Nitemare*, each winners of the Student Academy Award for Animation. In the mid-nineties, while vice-president of Creative Development at Pixar, an independent production company, I got to direct my first animated feature, *Toy Story*, the first such film to be produced entirely with computers. *Toy Story* went on to receive a Special Achievement Oscar.

Computer animation is an artistic medium which has grown out of science. But most of the images and animation created in this new medium were produced by the scientists who wrote the software tools, which is something like having all the paintings in the world created by the chemists who made the paint.

The most important thing to understand, in my opinion, is that computer animation is not an art form unto itself. Animation is the art form. The computer is merely another medium within this art form, as are pencils, clay, sand, and puppets. In fact, I think of the computer as a big, expensive pencil which uses electricity. Sometimes it takes several people to operate the pencil. But until it is grasped by the hand of an artist, it is as useless as a pencil. Computer animation is not accomplished by computers any more than clay animation is created by clay.

Animation is not only an art form; rather, it is a method of communication and a means of entertainment, an art form wherein ideas must be visually communicated. To communicate ideas clearly by visual means, one must first learn the fundamentals of graphic design, which is the vocabulary and grammar of graphic communication.

You must design your image so that it communicates your idea clearly. But visually communicating an idea is not enough. It should also be interesting and entertaining. Once this is achieved, you can be sure that your idea will have far more impact and the audience will both absorb and retain it.

As soon as an image starts to move, the principles of animation take effect. In the computer animation industry, one might think that to animate means to move an object from point A to point B. But the dictionary definition of the verb animate is "to give life to." In order to give life to movement, one cannot just move an object without reason. Every movement in an animated scene must have a reason for being. That is the basis for character animation. One must learn animation's fundamental principles, such as timing, staging, anticipation, flow through, squash and stretch, overlapping action, slow in and slow out, etc.

So often in the computer animation field, people with little animation experience will sit in front of a computer merely moving a few objects around and in doing so, consider themselves to be animators. Whether the artist draws by hand or computer, the success of character animation lies in the personality of the characters. Without an underlying conviction, the actions of a character are merely a series of unrelated motions. But with a thought process to connect them, actions bring a character to life. Strong characters and a compelling story, rather than technological advances, are what make an animation project great. It was Chuck Jones who said, "All great cartoon characters are based on the human behaviour we recognize in ourselves."

With all four of my short films, I strived to integrate human characteristics into the objects I chose as my subjects. In *Luxo Jr.*, a little lamp steals the spotlight with his playful antics. *Red's Dream* reveals what a lonely unicycle dreams about. In *Knickknack,* a glass-domed snowman is undone by his machinations to join a lively crowd.

I believe that *Tin Toy* was the first computer animated film to win an Academy Award because Tinny, the wind-up toy, managed to humorously and poignantly convey so many human emotions. All of the objects in the films have their own personalities and raison d'être, which serve to propel those films and make them memorable.

The principles of filmmaking, or film grammar, are vital to movies as a whole. How the story is constructed, the staging and pacing of action as well as the editing, are just some of the principles involved. If an idea does not further the story, no matter how compelling it may be, it should not be there. Everything within a single frame of film, the characters, the objects, the background, even the space around the objects, should be there for a purpose.

Computer animation is unique in that it combines the techniques of graphic design, animation, story writing, live-action filmmaking, and computer science. But as with any artistic medium, the most vital element is creativity.

NOTES

machinations secret, crafty schemes; cunning, artful designs, often with an evil purpose

raison d'être from the French language, meaning literally "reason for being"; justification

ANALYZE AND INTERPRET

1. Consider why the author chose the title that he did for this expository essay. What did you learn about computer animation from reading it? Create a three-columned chart: in the first column, list what you learned; in the second, list questions; and in the third, list sources. Share your chart with a small group.

2. With a partner, view a computer-animated film, such as *Toy Story,* as well as a film made using traditional animation, such as *Snow White.* Discuss the differences between these two animation techniques. Do you think the animation style affects the content of the film? Discuss which film you prefer and why.

3. Lasseter quotes animator Chuck Jones: "All great cartoon characters are based on the human behaviour we recognize in ourselves." Choose a familiar cartoon character and write an essay discussing her or him in terms of this quote. Focus on several aspects of human behaviour that the character exhibits. Give examples of each and tell how these behaviours apply to you.

MORE TO EXPLORE

Themes: At Work, Creativity, Science and Technology

Elements: camera angle, classification, exposition, graphics, special effects, specialized terms, visual composition

WILLIAM GOLDING

M.T. Kelly

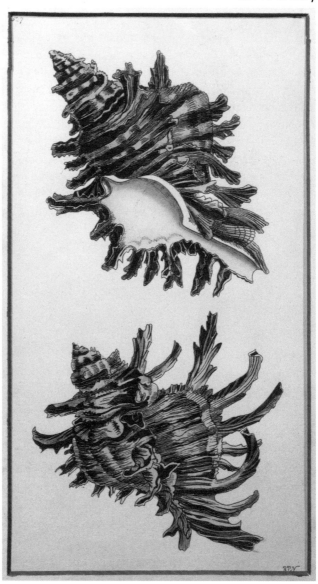

Conch Shell, c. 1790–1820, Richard Polydore Nodder

CONTEXT Few authors are so widely associated with one work as William Golding is with *Lord of the Flies*. Rejected by twenty-one publishing houses, the novel was finally published in 1954 and has been translated into more than twenty languages. Born in England in 1911, Golding wrote many other successful novels and was awarded the Nobel Prize for Literature in 1983. He died in 1993. The following television interview with Golding was conducted by author M.T. Kelly, who was born in Toronto, Ontario, in 1946. Kelly has worked at such occupations as a high-school teacher, journalist, novelist, poet, and playwright in places including Toronto and Sudbury, Ontario; Moose Jaw, Saskatchewan; and Scotland. Consider the challenge presented to the interviewer faced with an author who casts such a large shadow. What sort of questions would you have asked this person? How might Kelly's knowledge and experience either help or hinder his interviewing style? How might interviewers frame their questions in order to uncover something as yet unknown about their subject? ■

The interview took place in a windowless suite at the Harbour Castle Hilton in downtown Toronto, at about 10 in the morning, during the International Authors' Festival. Sir William seemed tired, cranky, and somehow smaller than he had three years before when I had spent a day with him at the Woodlands Indian Cultural Centre near Brantford, Ontario. Although he came by himself, it seemed he was being directed into the room, and he sighed as he sat down, ready to do his duty, grey-faced, a little lost in the chair. As the interview progressed, he livened up. His first response, to the questions about Lord of the Flies, *seemed one that he had given many times before, part of the evasive arsenal of a Nobel Laureate. After that, his interest became real and the smile I remembered returned, as did his warmth and energy.*

M.T. Kelly

KELLY   For over 30 years, *Lord of the Flies* has been taught in high-school English classes and read by millions of people. How do you feel now about the book?

GOLDING   To begin with, I've mostly forgotten it as a book. People sometimes ask me detailed questions and I don't know what the relevance of the question is because I've forgotten the background, which you would need to know. I'm much more in the position of someone who, whenever he travels around the world, comes across it in a different guise. [gazes thoughtfully upward] I do remember one theme in it, which is the conch. The conch shell. When I wrote that book I did not know that in India the conch is supposed to be that instrument which, when sounded, calls the gods into convocation. Now the point is that a Hindu would read the *Lord of the Flies* and see an almost entirely different picture. Almost on page one, his panorama would be vast and have absolutely nothing to do with the hard-working schoolmaster who actually wrote the book. In China, on the other hand, one who plays the conch is said to be one who makes great and absurd religious claims. In Mexico, I came across a temple to the *plumed* conch. Heaven only knows what the Aztecs would make of the conch. But you see what I mean, it has become a worldwide phenomenon, as far as literacy goes, and has therefore really got away from me.

KELLY   Your books are very serious, difficult, complex works, but they are extremely popular. They've sold millions of copies. How have you managed to combine the two?

GOLDING   Well, I didn't know I had. When you say they're popular and they're serious and complex, I would take issue with you over complex. I would think they're fairly simple. They have a straightforward story line, and the thing which is perhaps difficult for some people about them is that they're usually set in unusual circumstances, not circumstances you would normally come across.

KELLY   Well, sometimes symbols are in a man's work whether he's aware of them or not. Your books seem to be quite full of symbols.

GOLDING   May I substitute for the word symbol, the word levels? That you can have not just a story with a subtext, that is to say another story running along underneath it—Hemingway knew this one and used it. But you can also have what you might call a story with a supertext, or supratext, a story running above the other one almost as though moral considerations are operations going on in heaven, and therefore affecting the story which is going on in the physical world, and there might even be a hell underneath. Now that sounds Christian and I don't mean it that way. I mean it as a concept of how to write a story and give it these levels and dimensions.

KELLY   But Hemingway also said that when very good books are popular, they're popular for the wrong reasons. On the surface level, as you would call it, do you think the people who read your books see the marriage of heaven and hell that occurs?

GOLDING   That's a good phrase. Familiar to me. Some do, some don't. I think far more people experience the supra- and subtexts than are even aware of what they are doing. They call it getting into a book, being absorbed in it, and so on.

KELLY   Your last three novels, *The End of the Earth* trilogy, used the setting of a nineteenth-century ocean voyage to play out themes of human cruelty. What appealed to you about that setting?

GOLDING   Well, I am a sailor and have been one more or less all my adult life, either in terms of sailing my own boat or being in the Navy.

KELLY   Much has been made of the fact that you were present at the sinking of the *Bismarck* when you were serving in the Navy in World War II, but for the record, tell me a little bit about that story.

GOLDING   Well, I was on a cruiser at the time and we were chasing the *Bismarck* and I used to tell the story that I was the seaman in the crow's nest when we failed to sight the *Bismarck*. But I usually didn't add to that remark that she was more than 40 miles ahead so I couldn't have seen her anyway. But what I do remember is being on lookout on the bridge, and we were the flagship on this squadron. We were escorting an aircraft carrier on her way to attack *Bismarck* and we were revving up to full speed to go forward and I remember hearing the admiral saying to the captain, "If they don't get her, I'll go in and deliver a torpedo attack," and I thought, Doesn't he know who he's got with him? This is preposterous. That would've been a one-way trip.

KELLY   You've dealt with the battle between good and evil. This might seem like a rather apocalyptic way of putting it, but do you believe in good and evil and how has your view changed over the years?

GOLDING   I think I believed very simply in good and evil when I was a young man. I've come to realize that I do believe in it but the situation is much more complex than I'd thought [laughs] and I have no explanations. I've experienced evil in people—I did live through the Second World War and anyone who survived that and could still think that man hasn't got something in him which seems almost to drive him, to use an absurd phrase, to antisocial behaviour.... I mean an antisocial attitude in the largest sense, whether it is stealing from somebody or whether it is burning him.

KELLY   Are you an optimist or a pessimist?

GOLDING   Oh, ha ha ha, who knows? The answer, I think, is I don't know. I'm sometimes optimistic and very occasionally pessimistic, but I'm more optimistic than I was.

KELLY   Why are you now more of an optimist?

GOLDING   Fundamentally, I think because I'm old enough to realize how little I know. And therefore this allows the spring of a human being to come out and he is optimistic, otherwise he wouldn't be able to live through till tomorrow. We have in us this spring of optimism which is part of our nature, and history sometimes fights against it, but when you're old, you just let the spring run.

KELLY   How has the work of other writers affected your writing?

GOLDING   Well, I have to bring enormous great names into the field with works by people like Homer, Shakespeare, Milton....

KELLY   Some of these great books you mention are about journeys. Were you conscious of that when you did your sea trilogy?

GOLDING   Well now, you're thinking of *The Odyssey*? Yeah. During the war when I was at sea I was reading *The Iliad*, which was Homer's enormous war poem. It was very odd to be fighting an actual war and reading about another one. And I thought there was something rather *plus ça change* about the whole situation.

KELLY   Well, Monty Python once did a very funny take-off on Dylan Thomas saying, "I'm just a craftsman, a cabinet-maker." And I'm not saying you did this but you have said, "I'm against the picture of the artist as the starry-eyed visionary. I'd prefer the word craftsman." [grins] I *don't* think so.

GOLDING   You see these other things would be an enormous claim—to be anything more than a craftsman. A craftsman is a jolly good thing to be. And I think I would stick by that. I would call myself a craftsman.

KELLY   Not a priest?

GOLDING   [wags his finger] Now you add that to me. That's your word, not mine. I wouldn't call myself a priest. Perhaps an elder in the congregation. Well, I'm certainly an elder, but not in the wisdom stakes.

KELLY   Well, I don't know, but I believe that literature, art, music—all these things in a subliminal way have to do with religion.

GOLDING   Oh, well then, you and I are right on the same line. I would agree absolutely with this in all my experience throughout the arts. I mentioned Shakespeare, Homer, and Milton—with all these there is an interconnection and you can't put your finger on it. We might call it religion if we like, but that's a large word, isn't it?

KELLY   I don't think we should be afraid of using it.

[pause while the camera operator changes the video]

KELLY   What does the sea mean to you?

GOLDING   An image of our unconscious, perhaps? That is what I would think of it now. I see it in poetic terms mostly. I think of it one way as Shelley's crystalline streams, you know? Or I think of Shakespeare in a storm, "What care these roarers for the name of King?" And so on. It is not only part of my life as a fact, as something I've sailed on, fought on, swum in, dived in, and so on. It is also a part of literature and this great symbol of the unconscious. And after that, all I can say is rhubarb, rhubarb, rhubarb.

KELLY   Well, I wondered, would you like to be buried in the sea or in the sweet earth?

GOLDING   I don't want to be buried at all! Granted that this melancholy ceremony has to—I think cremation is the thing and then scatter my ashes wherever. I sometimes think I'd like them scattered in a busy street. Most people think that if they get scattered on a hillside, they're going to become a part of nature. I'd sooner be part of a town I think.

Notes

plumed decorated with feathers

the Bismarck a German battleship, named after the first chancellor of the German Empire, Otto Eduard Leopold von Bismarck (1815–1898), and launched in 1939; before it was sunk in battle two years later, it was the world's largest and most powerful warship

apocalyptic pertaining to a prophetic revelation, but used colloquially here to mean extreme or profoundly serious

plus ça change part of a French expression, "*plus ça change, plus c'est la même chose,*" meaning "nothing changes"

subliminal something that is below the threshold of conscious perception or awareness; "sub" from the Latin word *sub*, meaning "under," and "liminal" from the Latin word *līmen*, meaning "threshold"

Analyze and Interpret

1. Many students have read and studied *Lord of the Flies*. In a short report, explain how the information in this interview might influence or enhance one's understanding of that novel. Cite specific information from the interview, using the correct format for integrating quotations into a piece of writing.

2. Use the information in the interview to construct a character analysis of Golding. In your analysis, consider what he says, as well as the way he structures his responses and the tone created by his comments.

3. Create a bibliography of William Golding's work. Then, in a small group, identify the research tools that you used to find this information, and assess the reliability of each tool.

More to Explore

Themes: Self and Culture, At Work, Canada, Journeys, Creativity

Elements: anecdote, archetype, dialogue, empathy

Movie Review

SURF'S UP

Rick Groen

CONTEXT Rick Groen is the film critic for *The Globe and Mail* newspaper. Groen was born in 1947 in Toronto, where he later received his B.A. and M.A. in English literature at the University of Toronto. His first literary essay was published in the late 1970s in *Canadian Forum* magazine, and literature remains his first love. Since joining the *Globe* in 1980, he has covered many aspects of arts and entertainment, including television and theatre. He received the National Newspaper Award for Criticism in 1991. Can you find evidence in this movie review of *The Perfect Storm* that Groen studied literature? What characteristics do you look for in a movie review? In what ways are these characteristics the same as or different from what you would expect from a book, theatre, or restaurant review? ■

LEARNING FOCUS

- Explain the effect of an author's use of literary devices.
- Formulate and support an argument.
- Create a storyboard based on research.

F inally, the first really good film of the summer. *The Perfect Storm* may fall shy of perfection, but it gets a damn sight closer than any of the hot-weather rivals to date. The secret lies in its versatility. Not many movies can seem terrifically modern and touchingly old-fashioned in the same frame. How? Well, this is a state-of-the-art action flick that nevertheless aspires to the look and feel of documentary realism. It's also a traditional sea tale that taps into our current taste for true-life adventure—think of something with the heart and soul of a Conrad yarn, yet buttressed by very special effects and shrewdly packaged for devotees of the Outdoor Living Network.

Based on Sebastian Junger's non-fiction book, the movie recounts the tragedy of the *Andrea Gail*, a commercial fishing boat that, in the fall of 1991, headed out for a final catch and steamed straight into a meteorological monster. Narratively, that might seem to make for a thin and predictable story: Small boat + big storm = bad news. Indeed, the Hollywood temptation must have been to flesh out the script in one of two conventional ways—either crank up the visual gimmickry to gale-force volume or lay on a mawkish subplot for melodramatic effect. Or do both—you know, *Twister* meets *Titanic*.

To his everlasting credit, director Wolfgang Petersen does neither. And that's an unexpected surprise. Since migrating from his native Germany to the studios of California, Petersen has turned out a string of pictures all in the competent-to-mediocre range—*Outbreak, Air Force One, In the Line of Fire.* But he's consistently failed to duplicate the quality of *Das Boot,* the submarine sizzler that first earned him the Hollywood invite. Failed until now, that is. Apparently, Wolfgang just has a feel for the water—he does great boat pic.

Actually, he starts us off on land, shooting on location in the Massachusetts fishing port of Gloucester. His camera scans a stone memorial honouring sailors lost to the deep—the town boasts a 300-year history of ancient mariners—and then closes in on a fleet of returning vessels, safely in harbour after weeks at sea. For some, the fishing has been lucrative, yet not for Captain Billy Tyne (George Clooney) of the *Andrea Gail.* His luck is on the wane and his ship's hold is half-empty. A revealing little sequence shows him and his disappointed crew lining up at the paymaster's hall—the total cheque is slim, their cut even slimmer. A rival captain (Mary Elizabeth Mastrantonio) offers her sympathy but nothing else—she's on a hot streak and knows it won't last.

Like this incident with the paymaster, the establishing scenes that follow have a similarly perceptive, near-documentary quality. We're allowed to linger over the faded yet functional ruggedness of the town and its docks and the waterfront bar, where Springsteen blares from the jukebox and the women view their men with a mixture of love and resentment—love of their blue-collar swagger and resentment of their prolonged absences. Or maybe, deep down, it's just the reverse. After all, these are not the sort of guys who typically make for ideal husbands and fathers. Captain Tyne has two daughters somewhere in Florida; veteran Murph (John C. Reilly) is devoted to his son yet estranged from his wife; rookie Bobby (Mark Wahlberg) is in love with a single mom, but the sea holds him in a tighter grip.

So the fish beckon them out for one last try late in the season. Again, Petersen treats us to an insider's peek at the day-to-day mechanics of a working boat. The environment is spartan—the quarters cramped, the comforts non-existent. And disasters, small or large, lurk everywhere. Even marooned on deck, a stunned shark can still bite, and the ship's heavy machinery has its own geared teeth. But when the lines are set in the predawn hours, and the anticipated strike happens, there's a tremendous high in the subsequent frenzy. Then, the fishermen are literally in business, pulling money straight from the sea.

Headed by Clooney and Wahlberg (reteamed after *Three Kings*), the principal male cast is uniformly impressive, capturing the salt in the sailors without sentimentalizing or mythologizing them. Their characters are intriguing enough to keep taking us aback. For example, as the storm gathers, the men must choose between waiting it out in relative safety while their catch spoils, or racing right through it toward a huge payday. Their immediate response is to risk their lives for their livelihood. It's an easy decision that goes with the job—essentially, they made the choice a long time ago. And when the storm finally pounces, their reaction is a fascinating blend of respectful fear alternating with undisguised excitement.

At this blustery point, Petersen shifts into white-knuckle mode. Intermittently, to maintain the suspense, he cuts away from the *Andrea Gail* to an equally imperilled sailboat further south in the Atlantic. Obviously, we don't have the same feelings invested in this crew's dire predicament; instead, it serves as a kinetic subplot, a means of further ratcheting up the action by introducing an air-to-sea rescue squad. However, once more, the film veers away from stagey heroics to focus on the nitty-gritty reality. Even the act of refuelling the chopper in mid-journey is fraught with treachery.

Meanwhile, back on the *Andrea Gail*, the surrounding seas are mountainous, looming with the size and force of high-rise buildings poised to topple. Here, the effects are special indeed, as cinematographer John Seale (the eye behind *The English Patient*) teams with the computer whizzes to produce a continuing torrent of convincing visuals, punctuated when the captain, eyes ablaze, turns to confront a killer wave—riding up, obsessively up, he's Ahab atop the whale. The only falter appears at the climax: the soundtrack goes silent and Billy summons a rapturous vision of his landlocked sweetheart. Some might find this a moving tableau; to me, it crossed over into the maudlin.

Much better is the quiet dénouement, where nature's raging cathedral gives way to man's stained-glass version and, beyond its holy windows, the widows in their weeds gather to gaze upon the now-placid waters—the ocean so tranquil and grave. *The Perfect Storm* comes to a peaceful end, and proves its versatility anew—how wonderfully rare for an action picture to pack an emotional punch.

NOTES

Das Boot a German movie released in the U.S. in 1982; the English translation of its title is "The Boat"

ancient mariners a reference to the poem entitled "The Rime of the Ancient Mariner" by the English Romantic poet Samuel Taylor Coleridge (1772–1834)

"he's Ahab atop the whale" a reference to *Moby Dick*, the novel by nineteenth-century American author Herman Melville, in which Captain Ahab obsessively pursues a great white whale

ANALYZE AND INTERPRET

1. A distinctive feature of this movie review is its use of numerous literary devices. **a)** With a partner, use your dictionary or a reference guide to define "literary device." **b)** Then, with your partner, identify and list all the literary devices in the review you can find. **c)** As a class, create a group list and discuss how the author's use of these devices adds to or detracts from his analysis.

2. If possible, view this movie. Afterwards, write a letter to Rick Groen in which you agree or disagree with his review. Use examples from the movie to support your opinion.

3. **a)** Work with a partner to research another catastrophic incident, perhaps one that took place in your area. **b)** With your partner, use the information you have gathered to create a point-form outline for a storyboard of one scene from a film production of this event. **c)** In your outline, consider the elements that make a good story, such as rising action, climax, and dénouement. **d)** With your partner, create the storyboard. **e)** Exchange storyboards with another pair, and invite comments on the believability and appeal of the scene you have depicted.

MORE TO EXPLORE

Themes: At Work, Canada, Creativity, Science and Technology

Elements: allusion, description, first-person point of view, metaphor, synopsis

GARBAGE 101: A SURVEY COURSE

Hilary Sircom

LEARNING FOCUS

- Determine a thesis and supporting arguments.
- Analyze the effect of rhetorical devices.
- Evaluate the techniques of oral argument.

CONTEXT Hilary Sircom was born in Berkshire, England, in 1933 and immigrated to Nova Scotia in 1958. When Sircom wrote this short article, recycling was about to be implemented in her neighbourhood, and, as a good citizen, she felt that she was about to undergo an important test. Why does Sircom use humour in this piece? What tone does it create, and how does it contribute to what her purpose might be in writing the piece? Under what circumstances would you choose to use humour to make a point? ■

It's coming soon, that very special day—the day that will separate the men from the boys, the sheep from the goats, and the rest of us from our garbage.

This is the day of testing—the first day of the rest of our recycled lives. This is the day we're tested on what we learned in Garbage 101, and it's a test everyone will be required to pass to earn a place on the curb in the next millennium.

In our municipality in Nova Scotia, this traumatic experience has come upon the unsuspecting and law-abiding citizens sooner than most of us would have dreamed. In fact, even now, as we bite our nails and turn ashen, the Trashman cometh—on every other Wednesday, on our side of the street.

We have been studying the text (the latest updated edition). The basic requirements may vary slightly in the different counties or municipalities but the 3 Rs are a constant refrain—Reduce, Recycle, Reuse. We have our crib notes posted on the fridge.

We have acquired the tools of our trade—the black bags, the blue bags, the green bags, the clear bags, the grocery bags, the twizzlers. We have a garbage barrel, a green bucket, a green cart. Students in advanced classes have…THE CONE!

The Cone is a green plastic cone-shaped…thing for making compost, that fine nutrient-rich dirt that's full of all manner of castings and tailor-made for reducing garbage output and fertilizing garden output.

Now is the moment of truth. Do we really know how to add newspapers, envelopes, magazines, flyers, and telephone books, subtract plastic windows and staples, divide soiled from clean, multiply milk cartons and egg crates, and carry to the end of the driveway?

Have we mastered Elementary Plastics? Do we recognize the common denominator when asked to factor in HDPE2 and 5, PETE1, and LDPE4? Can we differentiate between tetra packs and mini-sips? Do we know how crinkly is crinkly? ("Note: Crinkly grocery bags, LDPE2, and vinyl, and HDPE3 are NOT acceptable.")

Do we have a chance of being found proficient in the manual arts department? Have we mastered the skills required to flatten, fold, and tie into bundles ("2' × 2' × 1'") our corrugated cardboard ("the type with wavy lines sandwiched between two layers")?

Compost is a dirty word in many households. We tremble at the thought of THE CONE which has all the mystery of a miniature pyramid and as much myth and mystique as a tomb of the Pharaohs. It awaits our ministrations behind the barn. This is where our most intimate secrets are to be buried. The elected handmaiden will be sneaking out after dark with our fragrant offerings. Should we…can we…actually put these fresh mackerel guts in there? Will last week's ham bone be accepted—or reproach us in the years to come? Only time and the wildlife—raccoons and skunks are lurking—can tell.

There is a system of rewards and punishments built into this garbage examination. Widows and orphans weep and even strong men (like Eliza Doolittle's father, used to this way of life) quake at the thought of failure. If we get it wrong, there will be penalties—red rejection stickers on garbage that is truly beyond the pale, the contempt of the neighbours, maybe even a request to call at the Municipal Office.

However, the rewards for achievers are dazzling. If we get it right, there is a clean sweep and we can be certain that there will still be, twice a year, a Special Garbage Day, when we can dispose of larger items such as couches and bedsteads. Finally, after months of tireless adherence to the instructions, those who receive Honours may merit an invitation to Hazardous Waste Day ("time and place to be announced") featuring those classic disposal problems, old paint and dead batteries.

Notes

the Trashman cometh a twist (pun) on the title of a play by American play-wright Eugene O'Neill entitled *The Iceman Cometh*

Eliza Doolittle's father refers to a character in the 1956 stage musical *My Fair Lady*, based on George Bernard Shaw's play *Pygmalion*; Alfred Doolittle (father of the main character, Eliza) is a dustman, or garbage collector

Analyze and Interpret

1. **a)** With a partner, identify the purpose of this essay. **b)** Explain your conclusion, and your reasoning behind it, to another pair. **c)** With your partner, write down, in your own words, the author's thesis. In a list, identify the significant points she uses to support it. **d)** Exchange papers with a different pair, and discuss the similarities and differences between your analyses.

2. Identify the author's use of the following literary techniques: hyperbole, rhetorical questions, sarcasm, and humour. Explain, in a well-developed paragraph or two, how these techniques contribute to the tone of the essay.

3. As a class, divide into two groups and hold a debate on the following resolution: "Recycling and composting should be required by law." **a)** As a class, review various techniques of effective argumentative and rhetorical speech. **b)** With your group, prepare your position in point form. **c)** Designate two debaters for each side, and conduct the debate. **d)** As a class, evaluate the effectiveness of the arguments that were presented.

More to Explore

Themes: Personal Challenges, Urban Life, Civic Responsibility, Nature, Canada, Humour, Eye on the Future, Science and Technology

Elements: allusion, first-person point of view, sarcasm, satire

Roz Chast

HOW TO TURN A CLOSED-DOWN NUCLEAR REACTOR INTO A THEME RESTAURANT:
A MASTER PLAN

First, come up with a snappy name.

Then plan a theme menu.

Have the waiters dress in protective gear, just for fun.

And, best of all, the food just cooks *itself*.

■ Analyze a media product.
■ Create an original satire.
■ Explain the use and effect of satire.

CONTEXT Born in 1954 in Brooklyn, New York, Roz Chast studied art at the Rhode Island School of Design. Chast is currently a popular *New Yorker* magazine staff cartoonist, having come to the craft after unprofitable attempts at full-colour illustration. Chast has published several collections of cartoons. As you read and view this cartoon, consider the visual and verbal ways in which she has created humour. What point might Chast be trying to make, and why would she use humour to do it? ■

Notes

meltdown the uncontrolled burning of the fuel core of a nuclear reactor

fission a nuclear reaction in which atoms are split, producing energy

mushroom cloud the atmospheric result of a thermo-nuclear explosion

Analyze and Interpret

1. Use your glossary in this anthology and your dictionary or other reference tools to define the terms "tone" and "mood." What are some of the differences between these two terms? In a small group, discuss whether the tone and mood of this piece are the same or different, and why. What feelings do the tone and mood of the piece evoke in you?

2. In a small group, plan to write the menu for a "nuclear café." **a)** Use the Internet or library to research terms and locations associated with nuclear power. **b)** Using satire, name and write a description of each dish. **c)** Use a computer's page layout or word-processing program to design and print your menu.

3. Find and create a collection of five cartoons that use satire to illustrate a serious point. Present your collection to a small group, explaining the satire in each cartoon. Then, as a class, discuss the value of satire in criticizing society and its flaws. Be prepared to defend your beliefs.

More to Explore

Themes: Civic Responsibility, Nature, Humour, Eye on the Future, Science and Technology

Elements: caption, graphics, hyperbole, specialized terms, visual composition

Editorial

FEAR OF SCIENCE AND LOVE OF THE LAND

The Globe and Mail

LEARNING FOCUS

■ Analyze and interpret a position taken by an author.

■ Assess the validity of arguments and evidence.

■ Plan, draft, revise, and edit a written argument.

CONTEXT This editorial from a Canadian newspaper is not signed, which, by tradition, indicates it is meant to represent the collective opinion of the editorial board. The subject is genetically modified (GM) foods, which at the time of writing were very controversial in Europe, but much less so in Canada. In fact, Canada's research scientists and farmers were leaders in developing and experimenting with such foods. The newspaper editorialist musters arguments to counteract the hostility from Europe and to forestall public opposition at home. Which of the arguments do you find most persuasive? Which arguments are unconvincing? If you were to write a letter to the editor, how would you respond to the arguments in the editorial? ■

The case of a Saskatchewan farmer battling Monsanto Co. about the use of genetically altered canola seeds and the chemical herbicide that goes with them will deepen suspicions among many people about biotechnology in agriculture. Genetically modified (GM) foods have precipitated opposition in Europe to the point that consumers are forcing supermarkets to certify that no GM foods exist within their stores. Attitudes in North America are less hostile, but the great potential of GM foods to increase productivity in agriculture could be threatened by public opinion in the absence of effective answers to broadly unfounded fears.

Last month, the European Union rejected a ruling from the World Trade Organization requiring the EU to eliminate barriers to the import of North American beef that has been treated with growth hormones. There is no evidence that growth hormones in cows change the nature of beef consumed by humans, but Europeans exploit such fears to justify trade barriers that protect their own beef producers. The spectre of "Frankenstein foods" is raised in Europe to restrict imports of everything from steaks to tomatoes.

The Canadian government fell prey to similarly inchoate fears and specific interests when it rejected the use of a hormone that increases milk production in dairy cows last year. In a Canadian supply-management system already plagued with overproduction of milk, higher productivity in dairy cows threatens the status quo. Because no evidence could be found that human health was at risk, Ottawa relied on claims that cow health might be affected, despite the absence of any such significant problems in the United States.

General hostility to technologically grounded increases in food productivity also applies to irradiation, which kills rotting agents and prolongs the shelf life of many foods. The sound of "radiation" is enough, apparently, to scare many consumers away.

The Europeans are considering a total ban on the use of antibiotics in animal feed on grounds that antibiotic residues may contribute to the growth of so-called superbugs that "use" low doses to become resistant. In fact, the *Wall Street Journal* reported that "EU officials concede that they lack clear scientific evidence to link the use of antibiotics in animal feed to growing antibiotic resistance in humans." Nevertheless the officials invoke a "precautionary principle" to give enormous benefit to any doubt in these cases. Productivity in agriculture is the cost.

Dennis Avery of the Hudson Institute argues in the July issue of *World Link Magazine* that "neither population growth, urban sprawl, nor global warming pose nearly as great a threat to the world's wildlands as the energetic plows of the low-yield farmers....Without the higher crop yields achieved with hybrid seeds, chemical fertilizers, irrigation, and modern pest control, the world would already have plowed another 40 million square kilometres of wildlands to produce today's food supply." GM foods must be the source of another revolution in agricultural productivity if we are to prevent the loss of vastly more natural land.

Fear of new technology fed by low-productivity agricultural interests operating behind high trade barriers threatens not only the supply, quality, and affordability of food in coming years, but the global environment. It is not enough to decry public opposition to genetically altered foods and related innovations; rational doubts require convincing assurances from public and private authorities lest the growing power of science be sadly hobbled in expanding fields.

NOTES

biotechnology biology combined with technology; the use of living organisms to make agricultural, medical, or industrial products

"Frankenstein foods" monstrous; likely to cause the ruin of their inventors; based on Mary Shelley's nineteenth-century novel in which Dr. Frankenstein creates a monster out of stolen body parts

inchoate having just begun, unformed

ANALYZE AND INTERPRET

1. **a)** How does the author of this editorial portray people who are opposed to biotechnology? Do you think that this is a fair portrayal? **b)** What do you think was the writer's purpose in writing this editorial? With a partner, discuss whether or not the editorial will achieve its purpose.

2. An effective piece of persuasive writing supports the opinion being put forward with logical arguments, facts, statistics, examples, and expert opinions. In a group, examine each of the issues the author raises and assess the argument made to support it. Do you feel that the author's points are argued clearly and logically? What do you think of the evidence presented to support the arguments? Share your ideas with your classmates.

3. Plan to write an editorial that supports the other side of the biotechnology debate. **a)** Use the Internet to find information that opposes biotechnology. **b)** Make an outline that lists your key ideas with supporting details. **c)** Submit your outline to several classmates, inviting them to comment on how logically you have organized your ideas and how effectively you have argued your position. **d)** Decide which of their comments you wish to act on, and then make changes in your outline. **e)** After writing your editoral, consider submitting it to a local newspaper.

MORE TO EXPLORE

Themes: At Work, Nature, Canada, Europe, Eye on the Future, Science and Technology

Elements: formal language, persuasion, thesis

ENGINEERED FOOD

The Globe and Mail

■ Analyze and assess ideas and
  arguments.
■ Explain how a writer creates
  and uses tone.
■ Generate and express ideas for
  a personal essay.

CONTEXT The following four letters to the editor were written in response to the previous selection in this anthology, "Fear of Science and Love of the Land." The "Letters to the Editor" section of a newspaper provides a print forum for the general public to react to local and larger issues such as genetically modified foods. In these letters, each writer puts forward a different argument to contradict the opinions expressed in the original editorial. How would you summarize each writer's argument? Which one made the biggest impression on your thinking? Are there other media through which members of the public like you can express opinions? Might these means be more effective than a newspaper? Why or why not? ■

Dear Editor:

Your editorial concerning genetically modified food did not acknowledge the concern of many Canadians, myself included, that we have no choice when it comes to what we ingest. Genetically altered food is all around us and already in much of the food we eat. It is being forced upon the public by an industry concerned with its own interests, not that of the global community and its ability to produce food.

This is not just a health issue but a moral issue. Many vegetarians choose their diet because they have a moral objection to eating animals, and they are thankfully accommodated. I object to having to eat genetically modified food against my will, whether it comes from the grocery, a restaurant, or prepared food. Canadians should be up in arms over this and demand better labelling of food.

G. Parro, Whitby, Ont.

■ ■ ■

Dear Editor:

Your editorial implies that genetic engineering is going to increase agricultural productivity, feed the world, save farmers, and preserve wildlands from the plows of "low-yield agriculture." Thank goodness Monsanto Co. is a caring, conscientious corporate citizen, who provides such a glowing example of environmental concern and human caring. All citizens and farmers should be eternally grateful that Monsanto and a handful of other "life science" corporations are busily trying to patent and rearrange the genes of food and fibre crops for the benefit of the planet and humankind.

No doubt Monsanto is tirelessly working to increase farmers' income and save those darn burrowing owls to boot.

It's just unfortunate that North Americans can't force Europeans to eat our genetically engineered crops and hormone-laced beef.

Ian Chuson, Oxbow, Sask.

■ ■ ■

Dear Editor:

Stating that "fear of new technology" is the reason the public is opposed to genetically modified food or bovine-growth hormone is nonsense. It is fear of the Monsanto Co. These folks who produced Agent Orange and DDT would have us believe their genetically modified seeds and their animal-growth hormones are for our own good. Monsanto's only motivation is profit and not safety.

Pamela Connolly, Ottawa, Ont.

■ ■ ■

Dear Editor:

The editorial perpetuates the myths associated with food production and world hunger. The truth is that the world produces enough food for all of its citizens. The problem is that it isn't distributed in any way resembling equity, fairness, or efficiency.

Genetically modified food is the wrong answer to the wrong question.

Slade McCormick, Ponoka, Alta.

■ ■ ■

NOTES

burrowing owls this endangered species, found in western North America, has become a symbol of the threat that habitat loss poses to wildlife, through such acts as clear-cutting

Agent Orange a toxic chemical dropped on the jungle by the American military during the Vietnam War. It stripped the trees of their foliage, allowing the Americans to destroy enemy hiding places.

DDT a long-lasting, poisonous chemical that was once widely used as an insecticide in North America. Rachel Carson's book *The Silent Spring* helped to get it banned.

ANALYZE AND INTERPRET

1. In a group, discuss the arguments against biotechnology presented in these letters. Then, individually, summarize in a sentence or two the main point of each letter. Which letter do you think is most persuasive? Do any of them reflect your thoughts on this issue?

2. With a partner, discuss the tone of the second letter. Identify words and phrases that create the tone. Why do you think the letter writer chose this particular tone? How does the tone affect your response to the letter? Rewrite the letter using a different tone. Share your letter with another pair and ask them to describe the tone.

3. In the last letter, Slade McCormick says, "Genetically modified food is the wrong answer to the wrong question." **a)** What do you think is the "right" question McCormick has in mind? With your class, discuss both the question and some possible answers to it. **b)** Do research to find organizations that deal with the topic you have identified. Gather information on your topic from at least three different sources. **c)** Synthesize these ideas into a personal essay that expresses your thoughts on this issue.

MORE TO EXPLORE

Themes: Nature, Canada, Moral Questions, Eye on the Future, Science and Technology

Elements: conflict, first-person point of view, sarcasm

THE "TALKING" MACE

National Post

- Explore design elements.
- Explore implicit and explicit messages in media works.
- Research and analyze an art form.

CONTEXT In the photograph on this page, taken in the year 2001, Nicole Latour-Theede, sergeant-at-arms of the legislature of the Northwest Territories, holds a mace. Maces are ceremonial staves displayed in legislatures as a symbol of the authority of those elected bodies. A collective of First Nations and Métis artisans designed and created this particular mace. To celebrate its creation, the *National Post* in January 2000 ran the annotated graphic that appears on the following two pages. Consider the content and layout of the graphic. In what types of situations do you view and read at the same time? In which of these situations is viewing more important than reading, and in which is reading more important? Why? In which is there a balance between the two? How is this balance achieved? ◼

Snowflake crown on top of mace: because no two snowflakes are alike, these symbolize the diversity of the people of the N.W.T. The crown shape recognizes respect for the monarchy.

Carved head of mace: made of stromatolitic marble from the shore of the east arm of Great Slave Lake. On it are six high-relief panels inlaid in silver depicting northern scenes, culture, and wildlife. Stromatolite is a fossil comprised of layered mounds of algae called cyanobacteria, one of the first life forms on Earth that appeared between 4 billion and 2.5 billion years ago.

Golden orb nestled in snowflake crown: symbolizes the globe and represents northern images such as the midnight sun and the circle of life.

Silver crosspiece on top of orb: the crosspiece forms an ulu (a scraping knife), a teepee, and a house, representing the Inuvialuit, Dene, Métis, and non-Aboriginal cultures.

Words beneath snowflake crown engraved on band of silver: "One land, many voices." The phrase is written in the 10 languages of the N.W.T.: Chipewyan, Cree, Dogrib, Gwich'in, North Slavey, South Slavey, Inuvialuktun, Inuinnaqtun, English, and French.

Diamond on crosspiece: 1.31 carat from Ekati diamond mine, Canada's first diamond mine. The diamond is one of the first cut from the Ekati mine.

Beadwork: in the Delta braid pattern typical of the Inuvialuit of the Mackenzie Delta near Inuvik. Beadwork is a Dene/Métis art form and Delta braid is a traditional fabric art of the Inuvialuit. Beadwork was created by Rosie Firth, an elder from Fort McPherson.

Shaft of mace, a bronze cast of a stylized narwhal tusk: although narwhal is found mainly in Nunavut, the tusk replicates seal tusks used in the original N.W.T. mace and was included to honour the history of the Legislature and the N.W.T.'s ties with Nunavut.

T he mace unveiled on January 14, 2000, in the Northwest Territories Legislative Assembly makes a "talking" sound. Length: 1.5 metres. Weight: 12 kilograms. Insured value: $500,000. Primary composition: silver and bronze. Other adornments: a 1.31 carat diamond, 33 gold nuggets, a fossilized marble head, and a display stand made of white marble adorned with clusters of the oldest rocks on Earth.

Porcupine quillwork (lower on shaft): created by Sarah Hardisty, an elder from Jean Marie River.

Sound of mace: tiny pebbles collected from the 33 communities in the N.W.T. cascade down the shaft and collect here. When the mace is moved, the pebbles make a sound similar to a rainstick. The sound is meant to represent the united voices of the people. To achieve the sound, the interior of the foot is divided into five compartments, and the shaft is embedded with 12 bronze spikes specially set at 30-degree angles to achieve maximum tone.

Bottom of mace: six-sided foot of silver carved in shallow relief depicting the endless landscape of the North.

orb a sphere

ANALYZE AND INTERPRET

1. In a small group, discuss whether you have ever come across a similarly structured text before. What was its subject and purpose? Consider how this labelling format would compare with a written description that is followed by a graphic. In a group of four, determine which of these two methods is more effective for this subject matter.

2. In a small group, design a symbol or emblem that communicates ideas about your community. Label the features of the symbol, explaining the design elements you have included and what they symbolize.

3. Do research to find a piece of art or architecture that uses its form and elements to communicate ideas. Use a labelling technique to indicate the parts of the piece you have selected. Then write a paragraph in which you reflect on your research, and note ideas for improvement in future research.

MORE TO EXPLORE

Themes: Civic Responsibility, Nature, Aboriginal Cultures, Canada, Creativity

Elements: caption, page layout, visual composition, visual scale

Internet Report
Summary

REFLECTIONS OF GIRLS IN THE MEDIA

Children Now

LEARNING FOCUS

- Analyze and evaluate information.
- Synthesize information for communication.
- Use critical thinking to consider reliability and bias.

CONTEXT Children Now is a California-based organization that joins with community groups, parents, businesses, and government to provide advocacy and support for children and families. This organization uses the Internet to disseminate information and promote action on behalf of children. "Reflections of Girls in the Media" is a statistical study of the way female roles are depicted in six different media: TV programming, movies, magazines, music videos, TV commercials, and print ads. Why are statistical studies important when we wish to analyze social trends? Why is it necessary to not accept statistical data at face value? How can people who create surveys ensure that their findings will be accurate? How can readers of statistics develop "statistical literacy skills" in order to evaluate the credibility of statistical findings? ■

Overview: A Two-Part Study

As they move from childhood to adolescence, both girls and boys begin to redefine themselves, a complex process which includes developing moral and ethical codes, coping with emerging sexuality, constructing a new self-image, clarifying gender role conceptions, and preparing for future occupational roles. Adolescents look to many sources for guidance throughout this process. Research has shown that the media play a powerful role in shaping children's beliefs, attitudes, and perceptions.

From an early age girls are active participants in the media community, watching over 20 hours of television a week, seeing 20,000 advertisements a year, listening to radio and CDs, watching music videos, reading fashion magazines and newspapers, and playing video games. Researchers have suggested that the cumulative impact of these media may make it one of the most influential forces in the adolescent community.

This is the first study ever to examine messages sent to adolescent girls across a range of media: television, movies, magazines, music videos, television commercials, and magazine advertisements. It looks across these media at several messages sent to girls—motivations, priorities, appearances, and behaviours—analyzing the extent to which these messages are reinforced across the different media.

The results of the study illustrate the dual role media play. The media offer girls many positive role models, women shown being self-reliant and using intelligence, honesty, and efficiency to achieve their goals. The study also shows, however, that the media often contain stereotypical messages about appearance, relationships, and priorities. Most importantly, the findings show that all of these media do send girls similar messages—both positive and negative—increasing their influence through repetition.

Key Findings

Media often offer girls strong, positive role models.

- In the media favoured by teenage girls, women are often portrayed as strong positive characters—offering girls role models to emulate and imitate.

- Women in the media are often shown as independent, depending first upon themselves to solve their own problems, and to achieve their goals.

- In TV programs studied, 35% of women and 32% of men rely on themselves to solve their problems, and more women (39%) and men (38%) depend on themselves to achieve their goals.

- In the movies 35% of women and 49% of men solve their own problems, while 62% of women and 67% of men depend on themselves to achieve their goals.

- And 29% of commercials targeted at women appealed to them "being in control" compared with 2% directed at men. 28% of magazine articles emphasize self-reliance. Very few articles encouraged young women to seek the help of men or their male romantic partners.

Women are shown as honest, direct, and intelligent and frequently use their intelligence to achieve their goals.

- On television 46% of women and 52% of men are frequently shown acting in an honest and direct way, while in the movies 58% of women and 47% of men are seen acting this way.

- 34% of women and 30% of men on TV are shown using their intelligence. Furthermore, 24% of women use their intelligence to achieve their goals, compared to 14% of men. In movies, 69% of women and 71% of men are seen as behaving with intelligence.

Media Often Reinforce Female Stereotypes

This research also demonstrated that the media favoured by teenage girls often send them limiting messages about their priorities and potential. The media reinforce troubling stereotypes about the relative importance of appearance and relationships to women while stressing that careers are more important for men than women.

Women continue to be underrepresented in most media, which limits opportunities to portray women in a full range of roles.

- TV has the highest representation of women, with 55% men and 45% women; movies have 63% men and only 37% women; television commercials have 58% men and 42% women; and music videos have 78% men and 22% women (although this is largely due to the composition of music groups).

- Only magazines directed at teen girls have more women than men, with 70% women and 30% men in articles and 82% women and 18% men in advertisements.

Women are most often portrayed in the context of relationships. Men, on the other hand, are most often seen in the context of careers.

- More women than men are seen dating across a range of media—on TV 23% of women compared to 17% of men, in movies 27% of women compared to 16% of men, and in commercials 9% of the women compared to 4% of the men.

- In contrast, men are seen spending their time "on the job" far more often than women in all media—on TV 41% of men compared to 28% of women, in movies 60% of men and 35% of women, in commercials 17% of men and 9% of women.

- Women are also more likely to be motivated by the desire to have a romantic relationship—on TV 32% of women and in the movies 35% of women, compared to 20% of men in each instance.

- In contrast, on TV 32% of men are motivated by the desire to get or succeed in a job compared to 24% of women.

- In movies 53% of men were motivated by their career compared to 31% of women. Magazine articles reinforce this message by focusing much more on "dating" (35% of their articles) than they do on subjects like "school" or "careers" (12%).

Media's female portrayals send girls messages emphasizing a woman's ideal appearance and the importance of this appearance to their lives.

- Across media, between 26 and 46% of women are portrayed as "thin" or "very thin" (compared to between 4 and 16% of men).

- Women are much more likely than men to make or receive comments about their appearance in all three media—on TV 28% of women compared to 10% of men, in movies 58% of women compared to 24% of men, and in commercials 26% of women compared to less than 1% of men.

- Women are seen spending their time in appearance-related activities such as shopping and grooming. On TV 10% of women compared to only 3% of men can be seen "grooming" or "preening." In movies, this grows to 31% of women and 7% of men. In TV commercials, it's 17% of women to 1% of men.

- 37% of the articles in teen magazines included a focus on appearance.

A Content Analysis Across Six Media

A survey of 10- to 17-year-olds found that young people today are getting conflicting messages when it comes to how women are portrayed both personally and professionally in television shows. They see women frequently portrayed as good role models—acting with confidence, independence, and intelligence. However, kids are also very aware of the messages girls receive about appearance as well as of the ways television relies on gender stereotypes.

Key Findings

Kids believe television provides positive role models and messages about gender.

- 52% of girls and 53% of boys say there are enough good role models for girls today in television, although more girls (44%) than boys (36%) say there are too few.

- Older girls ages 16 to 17 are less likely (46%) than younger girls ages 10 to 12 (56%) to think there are enough good role models for girls.

- Majorities of 10- to 17-year-olds also say there are enough good role models for boys in television (56% of girls and 64% of boys).

- Girls and boys think television shows the importance of having a career or job for both women (67% and 68% respectively) and men (73% and 72% respectively).

- Kids also think television shows boys and girls as equals (57% of girls and 61% of boys agree), although over one-third of boys and girls disagree.

- Majorities of both girls and boys say qualities such as confidence, problem solving, intelligence, and wanting to be in a relationship are equally likely to be displayed by male as female television characters.

Kids are also very aware of ways in which television reflects and may reinforce some gender stereotypes.

- Both girls (61%) and boys (53%) say the female characters they see on television are thinner than women in real life, but that male characters on television are about the same weight as the men in real life (61% of girls and 58% of boys).

- Older girls (71% of girls ages 16 to 17) are more likely to think women television characters are thinner than women they know in real life than do younger girls (51% of girls ages 10 to 12).

- Kids notice an emphasis on attractiveness, especially for women and girls, in television shows: 57% of girls and 59% of boys say the female characters in the television shows they watch are "better looking" than the women and girls they know in real life.

- Worrying about appearance or weight, crying or whining, weakness, and flirting are all qualities both girls and boys say they associate more with a female character on television than a male character.

Playing sports, being a leader, and wanting to be kissed or have sex, on the other hand, are thought of as characteristics displayed more often by male characters.

- Both girls (62%) and boys (58%) say the female characters they see on television usually rely on someone else to solve their problems, whereas male characters tend to solve their own problems (53% of girls and 50% of boys agree).

Girls want to look like the characters they see on television.

- 7 out of 10 (69%) girls—and 40% of boys—say they have wanted to look like, dress, or fix their hair like a character on television.

- Furthermore, almost 31% of girls and 22% of boys say they have changed something about their appearance to be more like a television character.

- And 16% of girls and 12% of boys say they have dieted or exercised to look like a television character.

More girls than boys, in particular, think the kids on television are like them and their friends.

- 59% of girls and 46% of boys believe the girls they see on television are like them and their friends, while 52% of girls and 49% of boys believe that the boys they see on television are like them and their friends.

- Among girls and boys who think television characters that are about their age are not like themselves, the majority say it is because they behave differently (51%).

Girls turn often to many types of media.

- Girls between 10 and 17 spend most of their time listening to CDs and tapes (50% very often), listening to the radio (46% very often), and watching television programs (32% very often).

- In a middle tier, girls are watching movies on the VCR (24% very often), reading fashion magazines (24% very often), going to the movies (15% very often), reading magazines other than fashion magazines (12% very often), and playing video or computer games (11% very often).

Conclusion

As girls leave childhood, enter adolescence, and begin to develop into the women they will become, they look to many sources including the media for guidance. In this period of change, they will determine their goals and priorities for the future. This study demonstrates that the messages sent in even one television show, or movie, or magazine, or advertisement, or music video do not stand alone. They become part of a larger sphere of influence in girls' lives and thus have the power to reinforce—or the potential to challenge—all other messages girls are sent. Our hope is that this study—by highlighting media's potential to offer girls role models and showing how well it is sometimes done—will encourage the creation of even more positive female portrayals throughout media.

Content Analysis Methodology

Dr. Nancy Signorielli of the University of Delaware conducted the analysis. She examined six types of media that are among the most heavily used by teenage girls. In order to get an accurate sense of the total messages girls receive during a specific period, the media were sampled during the month of November 1996 to the greatest extent possible. The sample of media included:

Top 25 television shows favoured by girls 12 to 17 for two weeks in November 1996; top 15 movies released in 1995 seen by girls 12 to 17 in movie theatres [available for rental in November 1996]; four issues each of the top four teen magazines [September to December 1996]; top 20 music videos ranked on MTV for the first three weeks of November 1996; television commercials shown before, during, and after the sample of television shows; and magazine advertisements from the sample of teen magazines.

Whenever possible, the same coding guidelines were used to code each of the samples. Coders underwent rigorous training to ensure reliability.

ANALYZE AND INTERPRET

1. Working with a small group, on the Internet find other examples of formal reports such as annual reports of charitable or business organizations. **a)** Discuss with the group the following questions: Why do you think an organization might choose to publish a report or a summary of a report on the Internet? What are the advantages of doing so? Are there any disadvantages? **b)** Select whichever Internet report you have found that you think is presented most effectively. Explain why in a group presentation to the class, using visual aids as needed.

2. Consider the following quotation from this selection: "…the media play a powerful role in shaping children's beliefs, attitudes, and perceptions." Write a persuasive essay in which you argue for or against this statement.

3. With a group of classmates, discuss how readers can evaluate the reliability of the information contained in a report. For example, what does this article say about how the data was obtained? Talk about how factors such as the following might influence the results: **a)** the number of subjects polled; **b)** the questions asked; **c)** the socioeconomic background of the subjects. Present a summary of your group's viewpoints to the rest of the class.

MORE TO EXPLORE

Themes: Adolescence, Self and Culture, Stereotypes, Peers, Role Models, Media Impact

Elements: classification, comparison, definition, heading, subheading, synopsis, third-person point of view

LEARNING FOCUS

- Reflect upon the connections between language and cultural values.
- Work with a partner to design a poster.
- Explain choices made in the design of a media work.

CONTEXT This poster announces an annual conference of the Assembly of First Nations (AFN). The AFN is the national representative and lobby organization of the First Nations in Canada, representing over 630 First Nations communities. Its purpose is to represent the First Nations in such areas as Aboriginal and treaty rights, economic development, education, justice, land claims, and many other important issues. What tone do we expect from an informational poster? How much information should this type of poster contain, and how should it be presented? What might be the purpose of an informational poster's slogan or title? Why do you think the creators of this poster chose the title "Living Languages, Lasting Cultures"? ■

ANALYZE AND INTERPRET

1. With the class, discuss why some posters are considered to be works of art. Cite reasons for your viewpoint.

2. With your class, brainstorm ways in which you think language and culture are linked. How is the survival of both interdependent? Reflect on your own experiences and those of people you know. Write an essay on this subject to share with your classmates.

3. With a partner, you will design a poster for a community or school event. a) Begin by brainstorming ideas for the slogan and visual elements. b) Work together to create a rough layout showing the general placement of type and illustration. You might try sketching out the main elements on separate pieces of paper and moving these around to explore different designs. c) Choose the medium, such as paint, collage, or coloured marker, and create your poster.

MORE TO EXPLORE

Themes: Self and Culture, Peers, Role Models, At Work, Civic Responsiblility, Aboriginal Cultures, Canada

Elements: exposition, graphics, page layout, visual composition

Living Languages
Lasting Cultures

21ˢᵗ Annual General Assembly

July 11-13, 2000 · Lansdowne Park, Ottawa, Ontario

AFN 2000 Election

ASSEMBLY OF FIRST NATIONS
One Nicholas Street, Suite 1002
Ottawa, Ontario K1N 7B7
Tel: (613) 241-6789
Fax: (613) 241-5808
Website: www.afn.ca

For information, please contact the
following individuals (613) 241-6789

Conference Coordinator: Bonny Maracle (ext. 297)
Registration: Art Dedam (ext. 237)
or Charlene Martin (ext. 232)
Events/Social: Judy Whiteduck (ext. 231)
or Sharon Fraser (ext. 330)
PGI/Golf Tournament: Louise Lahache (ext. 250)
or Iain Phillips (ext. 386)
Tradeshow: Brad Kelly (ext. 399)
or Nita (1-800-337-7743)
Elections: Bob Johnson (ext. 303)

LEARNING FOCUS

- Evaluate and categorize media works according to specific criteria.
- Analyze a media text through comparison.
- Choose a position and write a persuasive essay.

CONTEXT The United Way is a volunteer service organization dedicated to improving the lives of children and families throughout the world. What are the aims of public appeal posters such as this one? Are these aims different from those of other types of posters? What tone do you think is typical of public appeal posters, and why is this tone effective? In this poster, what mood do the image and caption create, and what impact might the mood have on viewers? ◼

ANALYZE AND INTERPRET

1. Working with a partner, make a list of any slogans that you can recall from print and non-print advertisements. Identify three or four key criteria that make these slogans effective. Would you rewrite any of the slogans to make them more powerful? If so, why and in what ways? Does the United Way poster meet your criteria?

2. Working with a small group, collect a variety of posters. Decide which posters should be grouped together to show similarities in such categories as similarity of purpose, audience, or design. Try to find enough posters to be able to have at least two groupings. Display your posters, explaining your groupings to the class.

3. Write a short persuasive essay in which you either support or refute the United Way poster's contention that children need lessons in the arts in order to "grow."

MORE TO EXPLORE

Themes: Childhood, At Play, Civic Responsibility, Canada, Media Impact, Creativity, Eye on the Future

Elements: caption, metaphor, page layout, visual composition, visual scale

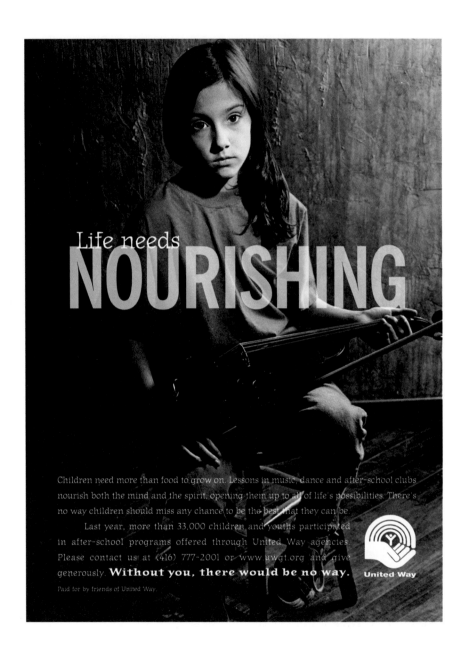

Life needs
NOURISHING

Children need more than food to grow on. Lessons in music, dance and after-school clubs nourish both the mind and the spirit, opening them up to all of life's possibilities. There's no way children should miss any chance to be the best that they can be.

Last year, more than 33,000 children and youths participated in after-school programs offered through United Way agencies. Please contact us at (416) 777-2001 or www.uwgt.org and give generously. **Without you, there would be no way.**

Paid for by friends of United Way.

United Way

CONTEXT Margaret Wente is an accomplished Canadian journalist. Born in 1950 in Evanston, Illinois, she began her career at *Canadian Business Magazine* and worked for two years as a senior editor on the CBC television show "Venture." Since 1986, she has been at *The Globe and Mail*, recently as the columnist for Counterpoint, where she presents her opinion pieces. In 1980, Wente received the National Magazine Award for Business Writing. How does an opinion piece differ from an editorial? Are the two forms similar in any way? How? What would be the equivalent of an opinion piece on television or on the radio? ■

NOTES

orgy excessive indulgence in any activity

benign harmless

ostracism exclusion from a group

pathologizing attributing behaviour to illness or disease

ANALYZE AND INTERPRET

1. In a logbook, use jot notes to create a list of the ideas raised in this opinion piece. Then, in your journal, write a paragraph that summarizes these ideas. Trade paragraphs with a partner. Is it possible to determine the organizational pattern of this opinion piece by reading these summaries? Share your ideas with a small group.

2. As a class, discuss the purpose of having regular columns in print media such as a newspaper. What might the readership be looking for in a regular column?

3. With a partner, do research to find advertisements for products marketed to boys. Discuss how the advertising has been directed at the target market, and whether features of the product reinforce male stereotypes.

MORE TO EXPLORE

Themes: Adolescence, Self and Culture, Stereotypes, Family, Peers, Rebels, Canada

Elements: exposition, headline, informal language, irony, paradox, tone

On Boy Trouble

MARGARET WENTE
COUNTERPOINT

They are tormented by unattainable ideals, constantly assaulted by commercial images of physical perfection that drive them to strive obsessively for the right look. They hate their bodies. They are riddled with self-loathing and crippling psychological debilities. They are objectified by the opposite sex, who only care about looks. Many of them live in constant fear of physical attack.

They are ruthlessly constrained by sex-role stereotyping that channels them into a stifling narrow band of conventional behaviour. They are damaged by their own parents, who try to mould them to fit society's gender expectations. They are short-changed in school by a system that favours the other sex. Their cries for help go unheard; they are silenced.

We're not talking girls here. We've done girls to death. We're all sick of girls, who will, in any event, be fine. The victims du jour are—you guessed it—boys.

In the unforgiving hierarchy of boy culture, only the handsome jocks have status. Everyone else—nerd, geek, Goth, or plain, unlabelled loser—is subject to emotional abuse whose scars may last a lifetime.

"The Troubled Life of Boys," says the cover of the latest New York Times magazine, which devotes most of its issue to the miseries of male adolescence. (Villain Number One turns out to be G.I. Joe, whose biceps, if life-sized, would measure an astonishing 32 inches.) Books with titles like *Real Boys*, *Raising Cain*, *Wonder of Boys*, and *Lost Boys* are flying off the shelves. Forget *Reviving Ophelia*. It was Hamlet who had the real problems.

The lost boys industry has been given a huge boost from the shootings in Littleton, Colo., and other schools, which have produced an orgy of introspection about how a seemingly benign middle-class culture could have produced such monsters. Experts like William Pollack (*Real Boys*) claim not to be surprised. "I think we have a national crisis of boys in America," he told the American Psychological Association last week. "It's boys who are doing this because of this code about what they can say and can't say, how they feel about their body self, how they feel about their self-image, how they feel about themselves in school." (Some people might quibble that we have a crisis of guns in America, but that's another subject.)

Some of the most sought-after experts on masculinity in crisis are, oddly, feminists. Among the most-hyped books of the fall is Susan Faludi's *Stiffed*, which will explain how men "are at the mercy of social forces distorting their lives." It promises to be as big as her last book, *Backlash*, which explained how a patriarchal society wages war on women.

All of these experts paint a picture of a boy's world so bleak and cheerless, so soulless and lethal, it could come straight out of *Lord of the Flies*. The weak are endlessly bullied by the strong, beaten up, pushed around, and taunted. Any sign of difference is an excuse for ostracism, and any sign of emotion or sensitivity is cruelly ridiculed. In the unforgiving hierarchy of boy culture, only the handsome jocks have status. Everyone else—nerd, geek, Goth, or plain, unlabelled loser—is subject to emotional abuse whose scars may last a lifetime. Worst of all: they can't share their pain. The culture demands that they suppress it.

If much of this sounds eerily familiar, it is. What we have here is the pathologizing of normal adolescence—just as we had in those phenomenally popular books of a decade ago delineating the tragedy of teenage girls. The dreary truth is that modern adolescence is, for nearly everyone, an excruciating time when peer pressure reigns supreme, self-esteem vanishes, hormones rage, sex roles are exaggerated, and the struggle for identity begins in earnest. So what else is new?

The experts propose various contradictory remedies for the malady of adolescent boyhood. Some of them say we need to encourage boys to act more like girls: to express their feelings, to openly care and share. Others think we need to help them be more like men used to be, back in the days when every man could hold a good honest job and a good honest place in family life. Take your pick. Either way, consider yourself warned. Your son needs help, and lots of it. ■

LEARNING FOCUS

■ Compare, analyze, and
evaluate media works.

■ Use research as the basis for
writing an adaptation.

■ Use audience feedback to
improve oral communication.

CONTEXT In this feature article, author Mike Randolph offers his own peculiar twist on the increasingly common Canadian occurrence of close encounters with bears. Have you heard any stories about meeting bears, cougars, or other potentially dangerous animals in the wilderness? Do you think the wilderness experience is worth the risk? What sort of information should hikers or canoe-trippers become aware of in order to ensure their own safety? Where might they find that information? ■

ANALYZE AND INTERPRET

1. Working with a small group, collect samples of newspapers and magazines. Find examples in these print publications of "hard news stories" and "feature articles." What is similar and different in these two forms of journalistic writing? Why do you think "Some Paws for Concern" has been labelled and formatted here as a feature article? Compare your group's thoughts with those of other groups. Would you change any of your thinking as a result of this comparison? Why?

2. Rewrite "Some Paws for Concern" as a hard news story, taking into account the characteristics you have identified as typical of hard news, and inventing any information that you think is necessary to make a good news story.

3. Produce an audio reading of "Some Paws for Concern," using tone of voice, pauses, and inflection to create dramatic effect. Play your reading for classmates, and invite comments and criticism of your reading.

MORE TO EXPLORE

Themes: Personal Challenges, At Play, Nature, Canada, Journeys, Humour

Elements: deck, hyperbole, informal language, pun, rhetorical question

SOME PAWS FOR CONCERN

Forget Yogi and Boo Boo. When you head into grizzly bear country to explore the wild, there is a minuscule chance your visit will be met with open arms and sharp teeth. Should you play dead, run, make noise, or pray?

Mike Randolph

The wilderness is, after all, wild. It's wild *because* of the bears. You could stay away from wilderness altogether, but what kind of alternative is that?

O ur mission was not to attract a grizzly bear— quite the opposite, really—so finding a large hunk of bloody moose meat stuffed in with our gear at the beginning of a week-long canoe trip through grizzly bear country was not a discovery that you might call pleasant. In fact, quite the opposite.

Andy and I had already witnessed the considerable powers of attraction that raw moose meat holds for grizzly bears a week before, back at the lodge. One of the hunters had shot a moose, a young bull, and had quartered it and hung the meat to dry in the shed near the float plane. That night, one of the Yukon's many grizzlies came a

calling. It didn't go in through the door.

It went through the wall. Tore the cedar boards off as though it were peeling a banana and climbed right on in, then ambled away with a rear haunch, 100 kilos worth of midnight snack.

The moose meat stuffed in our gear was from that same animal. See, our pilot, the one who had just dropped us off in the middle of bear country, was planning on visiting a trapper who lived in a cabin near a lake on the way back. The meat was a gift. Had it wrapped up in brown butcher's paper and everything, although the blood soaked through in places not too long after. When we had landed on our lake to unload the canoe and our packs, somehow it got mixed up with everything else.

There is an old saying about bears, about their sense of smell, actually. It goes like this: "A pine needle fell. The eagle saw it. The deer heard it. The bear smelled it." I got that from a book called *Bear Attacks, Their Causes and Avoidance,* by an Alberta biologist named Stephen Herrero.

That's not a book that you want to read before going into grizzly bear country, although you probably should, which is why I did.

In that book you will learn a lot about bear attacks, although not, unfortunately, what everyone wishes they could know— the one foolproof way to avoid them. Just doesn't exist. But that shouldn't surprise anyone. The wilderness is, after all, wild. It's wild *because* of the bears. You could stay away from wilderness altogether, but what kind of alternative is that?

The book does have some helpful hints, though. For instance, grizzly bears usually concentrate their attacks around the area of the head. Neck and face, mostly. Playing dead works in some cases, but not in others— bit of a crapshoot. Also, it depends on how well you can play the part—it may require some real commitment. Essentially, the technique involves lying face down with your hands clasped over your neck, fingers intertwined. The idea here is that a bear can crush your face, so you want to cover that. The ground works best for this, although your elbows help a little, too. And your fingers go around your neck because, well, it'd be nice to hang on to those fingers but they're not essential, whereas your neck is. The only thing left exposed in this position is your head, but if you're 18 or older, you've got one advantage here.

Without much difficulty, grizzly bears can crush the leg bone of an elk to get at the marrow inside and your skull is a lot softer than an elk bone, *but* the average adult human's head is just a little too big even for a grizzly bear. They can open up their jaws wide, real wide, but not quite wide enough.

Unfortunately, however, hungry bears are often quite persistent and resourceful. What they'll often do is gnaw on your head for a spell. When they clamp down on a strip of scalp, they just pull. Generally, it tears away in long strips. You might think it's impossible to lie there playing dead when a 300-kilo

blur of teeth and claws is tearing your scalp off, but it's been done before—and some of those people survived.

With that in mind, my vote was to toss the moose meat in the lake and get the hell out of there, but Andy had a better idea. (Actually it was his second idea that was better; his first plan was to take the meat with us and have an open-fire feast that night, but I issued some convincing scalp-related arguments against this.) His second idea, the good one, was to unwrap the meat and leave it out in the open and *then*

seen a large sow and cubs in this area before.

Yes, we knew about her. But landing on that lake was the only way to get to the headwaters of the river we wanted to canoe down. And it was such a pretty river. Tumbling through the low Selwyn Mountains, clear green glacial water running over round, multicoloured boulders.

We took a compass bearing on the closest bend in the river while we could still see it, then entered the willows. After two hours of sweaty thrashing and hauling through the scrub, we

"A pine needle fell. The eagle saw it. The deer heard it. The bear smelled it."

to get the hell out of there. After all, we were carrying a week's worth of food with us anyway, so why not use the meat as a decoy?

Whatever, good or bad, that was our plan. Ahead of us, there was a two-kilometre portage down to the river and it was getting late. We'd have to cross a jungle of willow bushes, two to three metres high. The books say that willow thickets such as the ones we were about to wade through are good bear habitat. But we had even more convincing testimony. The pilot knew this lake quite well and he had

made it to the water. Set up camp on a gravel bed.

Finally, with nothing else to do, we could relax beside the river. We sat on the gravel, which was the colour of ivory. Smooth to the touch. It was late, but the Yukon sun was still strong enough to backlight the dark blue mountain peaks and cast a dusky glow over the rest of the valley. Like a never-ending evening.

As I said before, if you want to eliminate the possibility of a bear attack altogether, there is a way. But I'd rather take my chances. ■

LEARNING FOCUS

- Make inferences based on evidence.
- Establish criteria as a basis for evaluation.
- Identify links among elements of a text.

CONTEXT The growth of the environmental movement in the late 1960s gave impetus to the idea that a way must exist for us to balance the needs and desires of human beings with the finite resources of the environment. The term "sustainable development," coined at the United Nations' first conference on the human environment, has come to refer to development that meets the needs of the present without compromising the ability of future generations to meet their own needs. Do you think we are moving toward the kind of balance that promotes sustainable development? If not, what are the obstacles we face? In what ways can an interactive Web site such as this have an impact on environmental issues? Are there negative as well as positive implications to these sites? If so, what might they be? ▪

ANALYZE AND INTERPRET

1. With a small group, view and respond to the overall format of this Web site. Consider what the primary purpose of the site might be, as well as characteristics of the audience for this site. Are you able to infer anything about the designers of this site based on its design? Assign one member of the group to take notes on your discussion, and then compare your findings with those of other groups.

2. Work in a group of four to establish criteria for evaluating Web sites, considering such aspects of a site as layout, colour, clear language, and number and type of links. Then, individually, visit this Web site or another dealing with sustainable development and evaluate it based on your established criteria. Meet with your group to compare your evaluations, and to consider ways to refine your criteria.

3. Select and visit two links provided by a sustainable development Web site. In a chart, summarize the content of each link. Then write a paragraph in which you evaluate each link in terms of its relationship to the main site, and the effectiveness of its content and design. With the class, discuss whether you can pinpoint criteria for creating effective Web site links.

MORE TO EXPLORE

Themes: Role Models, Civic Responsibility, Nature, Canada, Moral Questions, Media Impact, Eye on the Future, Science and Technology

Elements: graphics, heading, page layout, specialized terms, visual composition, visual scale

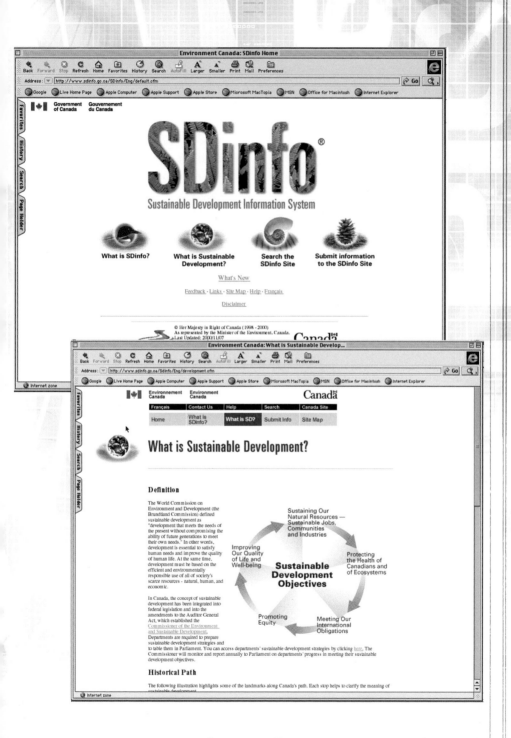

- Explain the effect of design decisions on consumers.
- Analyze how visual elements communicate meaning.
- Discuss the social responsibilities of advertisers.

CONTEXT The initial impression given by a print advertisement is key to its impact. Its visual appeal, the atmosphere it creates, its tone, and the point it tries to make to a target audience all contribute to our immediate response. What is the main focal point of this ad? How are the visual components arranged, and how does minimal use of colour contribute to the impact? Consider the text component of this ad, and look for a product name or logo. Often specific visual and text components in an ad are linked in some way. Do you see any links between components here? What might the purpose of these links be? ■

ANALYZE AND INTERPRET

1. With the class, discuss whether or not advertisers have a responsibility to society. If so, what might it be?

2. Which current print advertisements do you like? Which do you dislike? Why? With a group, discuss how you are affected by advertising, considering the following questions: a) To what extent do ads and billboards influence what you buy? b) What makes an ad persuasive? c) How do you feel about purchasing products that carry prominently displayed logos and brand names? d) What do you think of the way teens, women, and men are represented in ads? e) Do you think ads exert a positive or negative influence on society? Summarize your ideas and share them with the rest of the class.

3. With a partner, study this ad for a few minutes and write down five questions you would like to ask the designer about it. Consider the headline, the visuals, and the body copy when formulating your questions. With another group, share your questions and discuss possible answers. Then work by yourself to write a paragraph analyzing the visual and informational elements.

MORE TO EXPLORE

Themes: Canada, Media Impact, Eye on the Future, Science and Technology

Elements: idiom, informal language, pun, visual composition, visual scale

e-phobia?

Getting started in electronic commerce on the Web can be pretty scary stuff if you're not talking to the right people. At Ericsson, our Professional Services group has already launched e-businesses for lots of Canadian companies. We can show you Internet solutions your competitors have never dreamed of. And we've got a crack team of 1500 specialists who can explain it all without the technospeak. Give us a call. Or drop by our website.

ERICSSON

1 800 661-4201   www.ericsson.com/ca   Make yourself heard.

CONTEXT Allan Maki was born in Thunder Bay, Ontario, in 1955 and graduated from the Ryerson School of Journalism in 1977. He went on to work as a sports reporter and columnist at the *Calgary Herald* for nineteen years before joining *The Globe and Mail* in 1997. Besides covering every Grey Cup since 1980, he has written about sporting events ranging from the Olympic Games to the Calgary Stampede. What images and ideas come to mind when you read or hear the phrase "the life of a sports writer"? What experiences or views have prompted these associations for you? ■

NOTES

running of the bulls at Pamplona an annual test of bravery in a northern Spanish town involving a daredevil run through the narrow streets alongside a herd of raging bulls

ANALYZE AND INTERPRET

1. With a small group, locate a regular column in a newspaper or magazine and consider the following questions: In what section of the publication, and how regularly, does this column appear? How is the column formatted, or laid out, on the page? What do you like or dislike about the subject matter, tone, and design of the column?

2. Read the selection silently. Then, working in a small group, practise reading it aloud so that each reader's tone of voice, volume, and vocal emphases contribute to an auditory understanding of the piece. Present a section of the selection orally to the whole class, and invite reactions and comments.

3. Much of this selection's impact depends on the author's use of exaggeration. Find and explain three examples that you find particularly effective and, in one sentence each, state what the reality of the situation would be.

MORE TO EXPLORE

Themes: Stereotypes, Peers, At Work, Canada, Humour, Media Impact

Elements: caption, classification, headline, hyperbole, irony, oxymoron, sarcasm

Life of a Sports Writer Isn't All Fun and Games

Allan Maki

Let me start off by saying that being a sports writer is a good life.

You don't always have to get up early in the morning and join the rush-hour drive to work. You don't have to go to the office every day. And as Red Smith of The New York Times once wrote, "You don't have to lift anything heavy."

The only really bad part about being a sports writer is that as soon as people find out what you do for a living, they inevitably get that far-away look in their eyes and say things such as, "Boy, that's a great job. I'd love to be paid for going to hockey games."

They always say "going to hockey games." They never say "working at hockey games." In other words, they don't get it. They think that when sports writers go to the Stanley Cup final, it's a two-week, all-expenses paid vacation with a set of luggage thrown in as a going away gift.

Nothing could be further from the truth. In fact, the truth is not particularly glamorous and not what people want to hear. The truth is that we sports writers work long days, sweat two pints of blood on deadline, write without ever seeing the winning goal scored live, and sometimes can't get within earshot of the player who scored the winning goal because he is surrounded by a media clot so thick you couldn't cut through it with a police escort.

Not that I'm complaining. I'm just giving you the facts. Here are a few more from the Dallas Stars–Buffalo Sabres Stanley Cup final: in most National Hockey League arenas, the reporters don't sit in the press box; there are just too many of us. We sit in a designated work area deep in the bowels of the building. Sometimes, if we're lucky, we're still in the same area code as the actual game.

This means we end up watching everything on television. It's the strangest deal: we travel from thousands of miles away to be at the event only to watch it on TV. At least we have a table, electrical

RYAN REMIORZ/CP PICTURE ARCHIVE

Buffalo Sabres' Geoff Sanderson moves around Dallas Stars' goaltender Ed Belfour to score the first goal during first period NHL action in game four of the Stanley Cup finals in Buffalo, Tuesday, June 15, 1999.

outlets, and a phone for our laptops and we can see replays of the winning goal so we can rewrite our stories.

In Dallas, the work area is as crowded as a morning subway train. Three hundred print journalists sit side by side in a sweltering non-air-conditioned room while TVs blare and deadlines approach. Overtime, as you may have guessed, is not a joyous moment for someone who has to produce 800 words as soon as the horn sounds to end the game.

And when the game ends, that's when things really turn ugly. The rush to the dressing room can best be compared to the running of the bulls in Pamplona. Getting inside is no problem. Getting close to a player is simply unheard of. They hide in a special off-limits section of their dressing room. The few who come out say as little as possible before running off like frightened farm animals.

If you're lucky, you can grab a few quotes and escape without getting smashed in the head by a guy carrying a TV camera who can't see where he's going. Then comes the rush back to the work area, where the temperature is now hotter than on Mars and everyone is frantically rewriting their stories for their newspaper's final edition.

Yes, it's a wonderful life being a sports writer. Little wonder that we collapse onto our beds at the end of the day, exhausted yet eager for another bright and hopeful morning that begins at 6:45 a.m. when the construction crew starts its jack-hammering outside the hotel.

Not that I'm complaining.

1. Non-fiction's variety and flexibility are partly created by the wide range of purposes it serves. With a group, choose six pieces from this unit. Using chart paper, create a graphic organizer to evaluate the main purpose of each, considering the relationships between the intended audience, author's intent, and main topic, as well as how the choice and use of words reveal the author's attitude. Find other groups that analyzed one or more of the same texts, and prepare a presentation in which you compare your results.

2. Authors choose a variety of sentence beginnings, structures, and lengths to create engaging prose. Select two pieces from this unit. Use "The Talking Mace" as a model for your own annotated graphic that analyzes and documents features of the sentences in each. In your analysis, consider how various sentence beginnings might emphasize a mood, action, or idea. Have the authors used shorter sentences to emphasize important points? Have they used a combination of declarative, exclamatory, and interrogative sentences to create variety? Post your graphic in the classroom.

3. With a partner, select a piece of your own writing or one of the articles in this unit to lay out as a formatted magazine feature article. You will need to brainstorm possible visuals and pull-quotes. Consider how the typeface and type size you choose will affect a reader's first impression. How might your choice of colour have an impact on readers? When you have planned your presentation, use a computer and scanner to lay out your formatted article.

4. The selections "My Old Newcastle," "Canadian Pioneers," "Where the World Began," "William Golding," and "Living Languages, Lasting Cultures" all depict situations in which individuals or groups discover more about themselves and their relationships to their culture. Write a formal essay about the interaction between self and culture, using excerpts from these selections to support your thesis.

5. In a group, plan a multimedia presentation that examines one issue about science and technology raised in this unit. Brainstorm which aspect of the topic you will focus on. Incorporate specific information from the selections into your content. Be sure to include images and video clips, and consider interviewing people involved with this issue. Create a flowchart that indicates what will be said, shown, and played during each point of your presentation.

6. Choose a form of non-fiction that appears in this unit, and find an example of it that is at least 100 years old. Within the piece, identify three words or phrases you are familiar with, and three more that are not familiar to you. In a short newspaper article, provide background information on the selection. Then explain the following: How might the familiar words have changed in meaning since the selection was written? What is the definition of each unfamiliar word? How would you describe the etymologies, or histories, of all six words?

Lights…characters…sets…dialogue…conflict…plot.…With these essential elements, the living spectacle that is drama unfolds, drawing audiences into imaginative worlds where characters play out ideas and issues. Drama is about action: look up the origin of the word *drama* in any dictionary, and you will find that it originates from the Greek word meaning "do." Essentially, drama communicates, on stage or set, to an audience—through spoken language, gesture, expression, costumes, props, backdrops, lighting, and music. As you will soon discover, drama can amuse, enthrall, inspire, and offer new ways of perceiving the world. Included in this unit are many dramatic forms, among them stage plays, a monologue, a television comedy sketch, and a screenplay excerpt. The selections provide a taste of drama from different countries across the centuries, helping you to appreciate drama's long and rich tradition. As you read these scripts and explore such timeless themes as patriotism, ethics, gender bias, and racial prejudice, remember that you also, working collaboratively with others to develop dramatic performances, can bring the writers' works to life for an audience.

From Henry V: "Once more unto the breach"

William Shakespeare

Battle of Agincourt, 1415, late 15th century, from *St. Alban's Chronicle*

LEARNING FOCUS

- Analyze how auditory devices contribute to meaning.
- Infer meaning and extend your vocabulary by exploring a context.
- Write a comparison essay.

CONTEXT Generally considered to be the greatest dramatist in history, William Shakespeare was born in 1564 in Stratford-upon-Avon, England. Although the exact number is disputed by modern scholars, Shakespeare wrote approximately thirty-eight plays, which were widely popular in his day. He also wrote 154 sonnets. He died in 1616. This monologue constitutes all of Act III, Scene 1, of the history play *Henry V*. The speech is delivered by Henry himself, the young warrior king, as he leads his troops into battle in France, a kingdom to which he laid claim in the early fifteenth century. Have you read or heard other monologues in literary works? Why do you think writers might choose to use this form of expression instead of another? ■

Act III, Scene 1

KING HENRY: Once more unto the breach, dear friends, once more;

    Or close the wall up with our English dead!

    In peace there is nothing so becomes a man

    As modest stillness and humility:

    But when the blast of war blows in our ears,

    Then imitate the action of the tiger;

    Stiffen the sinews, summon up the blood,

    Disguise fair nature with hard-favoured rage:

    Then lend the eye a terrible aspect;

    Let it pry through the portage of the head

    Like the brass cannon; let the brow o'erwhelm it

    As fearfully as doth a galled rock

    O'erhang and jutty his confounded base,

    Swilled with the wild and wasteful ocean.

    Now set the teeth, and stretch the nostril wide;

    Hold hard the breath, and bend up every spirit

    To his full height! On, on, you noble English,

    Whose blood is fet from fathers of war-proof!

    Fathers that, like so many Alexanders,

    Have in these parts from morn till even fought,

    And sheathed their swords for lack of argument.

    Dishonour not your mothers; now attest

    That those whom you called fathers did beget you!

    Be copy now to men of grosser blood,

    And teach them how to war! And you, good yeomen,

    Whose limbs were made in England, show us here

    The mettle of your pasture; let us swear

That you are worth your breeding: which I doubt not;

For there is none of you so mean and base,

That hath not noble lustre in your eyes.

I see you stand like greyhounds in the slips,

Straining upon the start. The game's afoot:

Follow your spirit; and, upon this charge,

Cry "God for Harry, England, and Saint George!"

NOTES

breach in this instance, a gap in a fortification through which troops will pass to enter battle

portage in this instance, portholes, referring here to eyes

doth an archaic word meaning "does"

galled in this instance, worn

jutty to jut over, project beyond

fet in this instance, derived

Alexanders refers to leaders such as Alexander the Great (356–323 BCE), a general, conqueror, and king of Macedonia (an ancient kingdom of northern Greece)

copy in this instance, an example

yeomen assistants or subordinates to higher-ranking military officers; from the Middle English word *yoman*, probably meaning "young" plus "man"

slips in this instance, refers to leashes by which dogs are temporarily restrained

Harry a nickname for King Henry V

Saint George the patron saint of England

ANALYZE AND INTERPRET

1. This speech is written in iambic pentameter. Copy out the first six lines of the speech. Read these lines aloud, beating out the rhythm with your hand. Mark the beats on your copy. Then read the lines aloud in normal speech. What do you notice? How does the rhythm of the words help to emphasize the seriousness of Henry's message? Write a brief summary of your thoughts, and then compare your notes with a classmate's.

2. Read the selection over again and list all the words that are unfamiliar to you. With a partner, discuss the words you identified and try to determine their meaning from the context. You may need to look up some of the words in the dictionary. Then work together to paraphrase the speech; you do not need to account for every word of the original in your paraphrase. Share your work with another pair, and discuss any differences in your interpretations.

3. **a)** Work with a group to create a two-column chart. In the first column, list personal qualities and values that are important in everyday life, beginning with the traits that King Henry identifies at the beginning of this speech when he says, "In peace there is nothing so becomes a man as modest stillness and humility." In the second column, list the qualities that are required by soldiers, beginning with those that King Henry describes for "when the blast of war blows in our ears." **b)** Individually, write a short essay discussing the discrepancies between the two sets of traits: How do you think humans overcome their peacetime natures when they are required to fight in a war? How do you think you would manage in that situation? **c)** Share your essay with the group, and invite members to comment on the evidence you used to support your ideas.

MORE TO EXPLORE

Themes: Self and Culture, Role Models, At Work, Civic Responsibility, Europe, Eye on the Past, War and Peace

Elements: analogy, archetype, blank verse, dramatic monologue, hyperbole

Television Sketch

Shakespearean Baseball Game

Wayne and Shuster

CONTEXT Wayne and Shuster were the comedy team of John Louis Wayne, born in 1918, and Frank Shuster, born in 1916. Both were from Toronto, Ontario, where they met and collaborated in comedy revues during high school. They both studied at the University of Toronto, and while doing graduate work there, they were conscripted and sent overseas at the onset of World War II. During their military service, Wayne and Shuster again collaborated in a comedy revue called *The Army Show*. After the war, they worked together in radio, and by 1946 they had their own radio show on CBC. In the 1950s, Wayne and Shuster broke into television, appearing as guests on various American programs, such as Ed Sullivan's popular variety show. Their skits, which relied heavily on sets and props, combined vaudevillian slapstick, pantomime, visual tricks, and literary allusion. Resisting the lure of more exposure and money in the United States, Wayne and Shuster remained in Canada. Johnny Wayne died in 1990. What is it about slapstick, or physical humour, that can make it so funny? Do you know of any contemporary comedians who use physical humour as part of their routine? Do you prefer this form of humour to verbal wit? In what ways can the two forms of humour work together? ■

(A heraldic device background over which to super titles. It is crossed baseball bats and a catcher's mask.)

(Orchestra: fanfare.)

(Zoom in Super: THE ROYAL WAYNE AND SHUSTER FESTIVAL PLAYERS)

ANNOUNCER: *(voice over)* The Royal Wayne and Shuster Festival Players present…

(Lose Super. Zoom in: A COMEDY OF HITS, RUNS AND ERRORS)

ANNOUNCER: A comedy of hits, runs and errors.

(Dissolve to: graphic of baseball stadium or crowd on tape. Super: BOSWORTH FIELD, A BASEBALL STADIUM NEAR STRATFORD)

ANNOUNCER: *(voice over)* Enter, two Umpires.

(Dissolve to dugout set empty. Two umpires enter from either side. Orchestra: fanfare.)

First: Hail, Bernardo…

Second: I give you greetings, Antonio.

Thou hast the line-ups?

First: Aye…The batting orders duly

Signed by managers both.

Second: 'Tis well…what o'clock is it?

First: 'Tis at the stroke of two.

(Music: short modal fanfare.)

Second: Hark…The players come. To our appointed places

Shall we go. You at first and I behind the plate.

First: 'Tis done. *(He turns and* Second *takes his arm.)*

Second: This game depends on how you make your call.

Farewell until you hear me cry Play Ball.

(They exit. Music: big fanfare to herald entrance of baseball team. They enter Stratford style, with a flourish.)

Frank: My excellent good friends, may fortune smile upon

our enterprise today. As manager of this most valiant club,

I swear by all that's holy in our game,

I shall not rest until the pennant over Stratford flies.

Cast: *(Cheer.)*

Richard: Most noble manager…

Frank: Who calls?

Richard: 'Tis I…Richard.

Frank: Speak, oh faithful Richard.

Richard: I pray you tell us how doth the starting line-up go?

Frank: *(takes out card)* 'Tis as it was before. With Harry,

Joe and Pete out in the field. Rusty?

Rusty: Sire?

Frank: Thou the shortstop spot will play.

And you three guarding your accustomed bags.

Sam, the First; Bill, the Second; and Richard, the Third.

(To pitcher, rubs up ball.)

And as for you, most noble Sandy,

Hie thee to the bull-pen.

So that if our pitcher from his box is knocked,

you shall go upon the mound and take his place.

(Flips him ball.)

SANDY: I go. *(He picks up jacket and exits.)*

FRANK: *(follows him)* For this relief much thanks.

PEEWEE: Most noble manager…a word.

FRANK: Speak, oh Peewee.

PEEWEE: Where is the Captain of our Team? The mighty Rocky.

The man whom all the sports reporters call…

The noblest catcher of them all.

FRANK: *(sadly)* Alas, the mighty Rocky sits and mopes in

yon locker-room. And well he might,

for in these last ten games he has not hit the ball.

Not even once. Yes, hitless has he gone,

and twenty times has been called out on strikes.

(Orchestra: entrance music. Sad modal.)

PEEWEE: But soft, he comes.

(Cut to JOHNNY's entrance. Cut back to FRANK.)

FRANK: To think he led the league in RBIs…

And now he reads the record book and cries.

(Orchestra: soliloquy background.)

JOHNNY: *(enters reading record book)*

Oh, what a rogue and bush-league

slob am I…

Is it not monstrous that this player here,

But in a fiction, in a dream of passion,

Should gaze upon the record book and find

That he has ten games hitless gone…

Oh, cursed fate…

That I who led the league

Should now bat 208.

A hit…A hit…My kingdom for a hit.

Once more to hear that welcome crack of bat upon the ball…

And then to run from first to second then to third.

And then to dig for home.

To slide…slide…slide…

Aye, there's the rub.

There's a divinity that shapes our ends.

FRANK: *(moves to him)* Most noble Rocky.

JOHNNY: Who speaks?

FRANK: *(bends down)* 'Tis I, the mentor of your team.

JOHNNY: Ah, sweet, my manager. Gaze not upon my face.

This is the poison of deep grief

and springs from a batting slump.

FRANK: *(puts hands on his shoulders)* Take heart, Gentle Rocky

For today your batting slump will end.

JOHNNY: What say you?

FRANK: I have devised a plan wherein you will bat five for five.

JOHNNY: A hit for every time I go to bat?

FRANK: 'Tis so.

JOHNNY: Angels and ministers of grace, defend us.

(Crosses right, to players.) He has gone bananas.

FRANK: Here is the instrument of your success…Bat boy, hither.

(Enter bat boy with bat on velvet cushion.)

JOHNNY: 'Tis but a bat.

FRANK: Not but a bat.

JOHNNY: Not but a bat?

FRANK: But a special bat. A Louisville slugger that once

   To Babe Ruth did belong.

JOHNNY: Thou puttest me on.

FRANK: I put thee not on. A slugger with which

   The mighty Bambino sixty home runs did hit.

   (Orchestra: low background as JOHNNY kneels.)

JOHNNY: Is this a slugger…which I see before me?

   The handle toward my hand.

   Come let me clutch thee.

   And with this mighty staff of Birnam Wood

   shall I win the day.

FIRST UMPIRE: *(off stage)* Play ball!

FRANK: The game begins!

   (Orchestra: fanfare.)

CAST: *(Cheer. Go for gloves.)*

JOHNNY: Pitchers, catchers, shortstops, lend me your ears.

   The game begins and we must win—

FRANK: And win we shall. All hail Stratford.

CAST: All hail Stratford. *(They all kneel.)*

FRANK: A manager's blessing upon you all…

   And as for your Captain, Noble Rocky, give me your hand.

JOHNNY: 'Tis gladly given.

FRANK: Play well, valiant Captain. And remember,

   this game is being televis-ed.

JOHNNY: Televis-ed?

FRANK: And the TV will record each passing play.

    (Orchestra: mod background up and fade.)

JOHNNY: TV or no TV, that is not the question.

    We shall play with might and main. *(Cheer.)*

    Where is my battery mate? The pitcher, the mighty Burford.

    (He enters.) Art thou prepared to take thy place

    upon the mound?

BURFORD: *(thick Southern accent)* Marry Sire, I am.

    I shall do everything thou dost desire.

    I shall throw a goodly mixture of curves, sliders

    and changes of pace that will cause them

    to saw the air mightily with their bats.

    And on the scoreboard

    there will be a giant goose egg for all to see.

    Farewell, y'all.

JOHNNY: He is indeed a southpaw.

    His Paw is from the South.

FRANK: And now, sweet Rocky—lead your players to the fray!

CAST: *(Cheer.)*

JOHNNY: To our appointed places shall we go.

    Before this evening sun is set,

    we'll win the day for Stratford—and Gillette!

    (Music: flourish into lapse of time music. Montage of baseball shots and crowds—batters hitting, sliding into base, pitching, etc. Sound: crowd up and down. Dissolve to scoreboard: ninth inning, 1:0.)

RUSTY: How goes the game?

FRANK: Not well…'Tis the bottom of the ninth

    with one away,

    and they do lead us by the score

of One to Nothing. *(Crosses right.)*

Who's next to bat?

MACDUFF: 'Tis I…Macduff. Ready am I to do thy bidding, Sire.

FRANK: Then take thou thy bat…

and hie thee to the plate.

MACDUFF: I go. *(He exits.)*

P.A.: Now batting, Macduff.

(Sound: crowd up.)

JOHNNY: *(enters)* How goes it, cousin?

FRANK: Our chances dim with every pitch.

'Tis one away…

Macduff is at the plate.

JOHNNY: Lay on Macduff. And watch out for that breaking stuff.

(Sound: crack of bat and cheer. Cut to crowd cheering on tape. Back to FRANK.)

FRANK: *(walks left as he follows ball)* A hit…a very palpable hit.

UMPIRE: *(off)* FOUL BALL!!!

CROWD: Ohhhhhhhhh!

FRANK: Foul ball…He called it foul?

A plague upon him. That ball was fair.

JOHNNY: Fair, it was indeed. You, sirrah…

(Walks forward to umpire.) That ball was fair.

SECOND: That ball was foul.

JOHNNY: So fair a foul I have not seen.

Accursed knave with heart

as black as the coat you wear upon your back.

Get thee a pair of glasses.

Get thee to an optometrist.

SECOND: *(Snarls long gibberish at him.)*

JOHNNY: I would the gods had made thee more poetical.

SECOND: *(Snarls again. He exits.)*

JOHNNY: Thou art a robber and a crook.

Thy name should be in Jim Bouton's book.

FRANK: Calm thyself.

JOHNNY: And foiddermore...

FRANK: Calm thyself, sweet Rocky.

(Yells.) Come on—Macduff—

Take thou a cut at it.

SECOND: *(voice over)* Strike three!

(Sound: crowd groans.)

JOHNNY: That was the unkindest cut of all.

(MACDUFF enters and sadly heads for dugout.)

FRANK: Now is the summer of our discontent.

That was our second out.

One more time at bat do we have to win the game.

(Crosses left.) Who's next?

JOHNNY: 'Tis I.

FRANK: 'Tis you.

JOHNNY: Marry, 'tis.

FRANK: Then go, my friend, with aid divine

And hit that Pepsi-Cola sign.

(Bat boy brings a bat and baseball helmet. JOHNNY goes to plate. Split screen. Cut to FRANK and RUSTY.)

RUSTY: See how the valiant Rocky stands at the plate,

like some mighty colossus,

the bat resting gently on his shoulder.

FRANK: But soft...Here is the windup, here is the pitch.

(Sound: beanball on head.)

CROWD: (Groans.)

FRANK: No…(Turns away.) I cannot look…

The sight doth sear my eyes.

RUSTY: The ball did strike his head. The pitcher bean-ed him.

FRANK: He comes this way…I cannot look!

(Orchestra: business. Cut to JOHNNY singing.)

JOHNNY: Take thou me to the ball game,

Take thou me to the park.

Buy me some peanuts and crackerjack,

Wash it all down with a flagon of sack.

FRANK: Oh, what a noble mind is here o'erthrown.

JOHNNY: (picks up catcher's mask) Ahh…Alas, Poor Durocher,

I knew him…A man of infinite lip.

(Sees FRANK. Picks up bats.)

Ah, greetings to you, sweet nymph.

I would have brought you violets but they withered.

(Hands him bats.)

FRANK: (turns to camera) Oh horror. Not only hitless, but witless.

JOHNNY: Two outs damned spot—

Life's but a walking shadow,

a poor player that hits and bunts his weary hour

upon the field, and then is heard no more.

It is a tale told by an umpire,

full of sound and fury, signifying one–nothing…

(JOHNNY passes out.)

(Orchestra: undertone background.)

FRANK: (kneels) Now cracks a noble head.

Goodnight, sweet catcher.

Flights of shortstops sing thee to thy rest.

(He rises sadly.) Let four bonus players bear Rocky,

like a soldier, to the dugout. *(They lift him.)*

(Orchestra: snare drum.)

FRANK: No more will Stratford watch him play ball.

I'm trading the bum to Montreal.

(Super: exeunt with a flourish of bat boys.)

(Orchestra: Up Dead March to finish.)

(Silhouette lighting.)

Super: THE END

NOTES

super in this instance, means "superimpose," indicating that text will be overlaid on a backdrop

RBIs baseball terminology for "runs batted in"

bat 208 a baseball statistic referring to a batter's ratio of the number of hits for every 500 times at bat

rub in this instance, an obstacle or impediment

Babe Ruth, Bambino two nicknames for George Herman Ruth (1895–1948), an American baseball player who hit 714 career home runs and held 54 major league records

Birnam Wood the setting for part of Shakespeare's *Macbeth*

marry an archaic term used as an exclamation of surprise or emphasis; from the Middle English word *Marie*, referring to the Virgin Mary, originally from the Hebrew word *Miryâm*

southpaw slang for a left-handed baseball pitcher; from the Old English word *sûth*, meaning "south," and from the Middle English word *pawe*, originally from Old French *powe*, meaning "foot of an animal"

Gillette refers to the Gillette Corporation, suggesting that Gillette is a corporate sponsor of this ball game

Jim Bouton a major-league baseball pitcher who played in the 1960s and 1970s, primarily for the New York Yankees

foiddermore the phonetic spelling for the word "furthermore" when pronounced with a classic New York City accent

flagon a large vessel with a spout, a handle, and often a lid, used for holding liquids such as wine

Durocher a major-league baseball infielder, and later manager, Leo Ernest Durocher (1905–1991) was known as "The Lip" because of his controversial commentaries

exeunt stage direction indicating that two or more people exit; from the Latin third-person plural of *exire,* meaning "they go out"

ANALYZE AND INTERPRET

1. a) In a small group, brainstorm examples of what makes you laugh, using a word web to record your thoughts. b) Use this word web to create a list of questions for a survey on what makes people laugh. c) Have each member conduct the survey on five or more people. d) With the group, take a tally of your responses, using a graphic organizer to record the responses you gathered. e) With a partner, watch two current television sitcoms and a comedy show, making notes on what you find funny in them. f) Report your findings to the group, comparing what you found funny in the shows with the survey results.

2. a) Assign a person to each role in this television sketch. b) Continuing in the role of the character you were assigned, role-play what the next scene in this sketch might be. Have one person use a video camera to record the entire sketch in one continuous action. c) Watch the videotape and think about the effectiveness of the camera angles and movements. d) With your group, use the continuous-action video as a basis for creating a shot-by-shot storyboard for the sketch. e) Display your storyboards in the classroom.

3. With a group, brainstorm a list of potentially funny situations, such as a hockey game, a workout at the gym, a family dinner, or a blind date. As a group, write a radio or stage script that conveys the humour of the situation. Perform it for the class as a "first draft," or workshop production. After the performance, discuss with the class what revisions might be needed to make the production more effective.

MORE TO EXPLORE

Themes: Peers, At Play, Canada, Humour, Eye on the Past

Elements: allusion, camera angle, caricature, comedy, dialogue, props, satire, set design, sound effects, sound track, voice over

Branta Canadensis

Ellen Peterson

Flight Stop, 1982, Michael Snow

LEARNING FOCUS

- Explore uses of a literary device to extend understanding.
- Use a response journal to explore and share insights.
- Adapt one genre into another to create a performance.

CONTEXT Ellen Peterson was born in 1963 in Kitchener, Ontario. Her family later moved to Winnipeg, where she has lived ever since. Peterson's career in theatre has included acting, writing, teaching, directing, and doing a stint as an improvisation comedian. She has commented that when she began writing *Branta Canadensis*, she envisioned a satirical play in which geese behaved as people might. Peterson's original idea involved a committee of geese who bicker so much that nothing gets done. However, this approach did not feel right to her because, on reflection, she concluded that "Geese in some ways are much smarter than humans—they mate for life and go south for the winter...." Can you think of a time as a creative writer when your original idea didn't feel right in the end? What were some of the indications you had that the piece of creative writing wasn't "working"? What strategies did you use to deal with this type of block? ◼

Characters

Female Canada Geese:	Male Canada Geese:
ONE	NINE
THREE	SEVEN
FOUR	TEN
SIX	TWO
EIGHT	FIVE
ELEVEN	TWELVE

The Males and Females are mates in the order given: NINE with ONE, SEVEN with THREE, and so on. The Geese are dressed identically in black, shades of grey and brown, and white, in derby hats and old suits.

Setting

The sky.

(In darkness, the sound of geese in flight. Lights up. Twelve actors stand in a V-formation, with the apex of the V farthest downstage. They stand with arms outstretched, occasionally, randomly, raising or lowering their arms for a moment, to suggest flight without flapping. Characters TWO through ELEVEN may stand in any order, but number ONE stands at the apex, and TWELVE is slightly out of formation at the rear. The sound of the geese gradually dissolves into speech.)

ONE: South.

THREE: Still.

FOUR: Again.

TWO: Wind.

NINE: Still.

EIGHT: Again.

SIX: On…

SEVEN: On…

TEN: Still…

NINE: Again…

ONE: …South.

TWO through ELEVEN: *(Answering.)* South…south…south…

ONE: Everybody with us?

TWO through ELEVEN: *(Answering.)* Yes…here…all here…

THREE: Oh, oh dear…

SEVEN: Are you all right?

THREE: Well…

SEVEN: You'll be all right.

THREE: I'm so tired.

FIVE: So tired.

TEN: Tired?

THREE: So tired.

EIGHT: Still.

TWO: Keep going.

ONE: Still south?

FIVE: Bearing west.

ONE: And everyone…

> *(In unison, they stand on one foot, lower and raise their arms, and pivot ninety degrees to stage right, then pivot back to face downstage. They put their feet down and continue flying.)*

TEN: I thought we were going too west.

FOUR: It's the clouds.

SIX: Storm coming.

ONE: Still all right?

ONE through TWELVE: Yes…yes…all right…fine…

FIVE: Tired? I can lead.

ONE: I'm fine.

FOUR: My gosling, you're lagging behind.

TWELVE: Mother…

FOUR: Yes?

TWELVE: How high are we?

FOUR: Very high now.

TWELVE: It's beautiful!

NINE: Beautiful.

TEN: Beautiful?

TWELVE: Mother do you see the river?

FOUR: Yes dear, don't fall behind.

TEN: Isn't it long enough for today?

(The others laugh, honking.)

ELEVEN: I don't think so.

SEVEN: Not nearly.

THREE: No?

NINE: Not nearly.

TWO: Oh, no, not yet…

FIVE: So much farther still to go.

ONE: South.

TWELVE: South.

SIX: South…

THREE: I'm so tired.

FIVE: Only natural.

SEVEN: Very tired?

ELEVEN: How much farther?

TWO: Days.

SEVEN: Try not to think about it.

TWELVE: Mother, what is it like, south?

FOUR: Warm.

NINE: Warm.

SIX: Warm.

TEN: And there is food.

TWELVE: How do we get there?

(Several laugh.)

TWO: We fly.

TWELVE: But how do we know? Which way?

TEN: We know.

EIGHT: The stars.

TWELVE: How do we know when?

FIVE: We know.

TWO: When the sky is white.

TEN: And cold.

SEVEN: Cold.

FOUR: The north goes under the white sky.

EIGHT: The white sky covers the north…

NINE: It falls on the north in pieces.

THREE: Cold pieces.

SIX: The north falls asleep under the cold white…

FOUR: …and we fly out from under the white sky…

SEVEN: …into the warm…

TEN: …blue…

FIVE: …south.

ALL: (Answering.) South…south…south…

SEVEN: We feed with the sun on the green south.

FOUR: The sun eats until it is warmer again.

TWO: More south.

FIVE: More south, not east.

ONE: More south and everyone…

(They execute a turn as before, to stage left.)

Well done.

Four: The river gets hungry and swallows all the pieces of the white sky. And the sun…

Ten: Warm sun.

Six: Warm.

Five: Puts us on her back to fly us home.

Twelve: When?

Eight: In time.

Eleven: Is south soon?

Five: Soon.

One: Soon enough, keep flying. Can you lead?

Five: I can lead.

> (*Five takes the position at the apex, while the others change places within the ranks according to an apparent pattern.*)

Twelve: I want to be south.

Seven: Patience.

Three: I'm very tired.

Nine: Soon south; patience.

Two: Almost time to rest.

Four: Watch. Down there is rough.

Six: Forest.

Eight: Small when you fly…

Nine: Tall when you stand.

One: Golden and not green.

Five: Miles and miles unbroken rough golden—

Six: Rough forest or the fields and grey scarred places…

Seven: Full of noise and creatures.

Ten: Not safe!

Five: Not safe there.

Seven: Until…

THREE: When wings ache…

SEVEN: The sun shines back from below.

ONE: Laughing at itself, reflection—

TWO: In the flat blue shining—

FIVE: Water there, look!

FOUR: Water is rest when you are tired.

EIGHT: And we have flown enough for this day…

FIVE: Now rest.

(Stretching and raising their arms, bending their knees, they land and settle in a random group, each goose with his or her mate, except for ELEVEN and TWELVE. ELEVEN is standing with two couples, and speaks with the females.)

ELEVEN: Everyone has a partner?

EIGHT: Each chooses for their whole life.

ELEVEN: Why is one chosen?

EIGHT: Only the other can ever know.

FOUR: The choosing needs to happen.

EIGHT: Carefully. It is simple when it is time.

(TWELVE walks toward them. ELEVEN separates herself from the group and walks away with TWELVE. They perform a tentative courtship ritual, circling one another and then touching noses.)

TWELVE: This is for my whole life.

ELEVEN: My whole life, all south…

TWELVE: All north.

ELEVEN: All flying?

TWELVE: All flying and all resting.

ELEVEN: My whole life.

FIVE: Danger here!

TEN: Danger.

ELEVEN: What is it?

ONE: Fly!

(They leap to flight, rapidly trying to return to the V-formation.)

SIX: Fly!

THREE: Hurry!

(There is a very loud explosion, and SEVEN wheels out of control and into the darkness behind the group.)

He is on the ground!

EIGHT: Fly!

TEN: Fly!

THREE: He is on the ground.

FOUR: I know. Fly.

TWO: Fly.

THREE: Oh…my whole life…

SIX: Hurry.

EIGHT: Faster, don't look back…

ELEVEN: Oh, hurry, what is it?

TWELVE: Mother?

THREE: My whole life, all south…

FOUR: All north, I know.

THREE: All flying, all resting, all gone.

ONE through TEN: I know…I know…

ONE: Higher…

TEN: Safe?

NINE: Safe.

SIX: Safe?

THREE: He is on the ground.

EIGHT: I know.

FOUR: There will be another choosing.

THREE: I know.

FOUR: For your whole life.

TWELVE: Why?

FOUR: That is no question. Keep flying.

TEN: Who leads?

TWELVE: I can lead.

(They re-arrange the formation with TWELVE leading.)

South.

NINE: Too north!

FIVE: Not north, not north.

TWELVE: And everyone…

(They execute a 180 degree turn, and end facing upstage.)

South.

ONE: Again.

FIVE: Still.

ALL: South…south…south…

(As the lights fade the sound of geese calling returns, rises, and fades into the distance. The end.)

NOTES

gosling a young goose

ANALYZE AND INTERPRET

1. Think about an animal, a bird, or another creature that holds symbolic sig-nificance for you. In your journal, jot down what this creature symbolizes to you, and what characteristics about it might trigger this symbolism. In a small group, talk about what Peterson's view of Canada geese might be. Is she using the geese to symbolize something? Then, with the entire class, dis-cuss the use of symbolism in general: Do you think a symbol always rep-resents the same thing to every reader of a text? To what extent, if any, do our own associations affect how we interpret the symbol?

2. With your response journal in hand, reread the play. While reading, on the left side of the page, jot down speeches, phrases, and descriptions that catch your attention. Include your favourite parts, as well as those that presented difficulties for you. On the right side, record your responses to each item on the left. Exchange responses with a partner, and read each other's work. Discuss your ideas about the play in a group.

3. Create a poem for two voices in which you explore one aspect of the life of a Canada goose. Choose appropriate lines from the play and adapt them for your poem. Rehearse your poem with a partner and record it. Consider using a second tape recorder to incorporate background music or sound effects to add atmosphere to your poem. You might also try using sounds made by your voice or with your body. Play your poem for your classmates, and ask them to comment on how your use of sounds complemented the poem.

MORE TO EXPLORE

Themes: Peers, Nature, Canada, Journeys

Elements: connotation, mood, motif, personification, setting, sound effects, symbol, voice over

King Kong

RKO Radio Pictures

- Analyze how time period affects the content of a visual text.
- Use research to explore techniques of advertising.
- Create a speech to appropriately convey meaning and to persuade.

CONTEXT Part adventure, part fantasy, part horror, *King Kong* was released in 1933 and has endured as a classic in the history of cinema. The movie, about a young woman and a gigantic ape-monster, is a retelling of the archetypal Beauty and the Beast fable. *King Kong* uses techniques, such as stop-action animation sequences, that were technical breakthroughs at the time. The movie's narrative involves a company of filmmakers working on site on the fictional Skull Island. The filmmakers battle for supremacy over nature, symbolized by the beast, King Kong. They then put the creature on display in New York City, where it struggles against the restrictions of urban civilization. Movie posters are one way to introduce the public to cinematic stories. What is your favourite type of movie? How do movie posters try to grab your attention? In what ways might techniques used in movie posters be similar to or different from techniques used in other print advertisements? ■

ANALYZE AND INTERPRET

1. This poster was created around the time of the movie's release. With the class, discuss what features of the poster indicate that it is not contemporary. If you were asked to create a poster for the film with a contemporary feel, which elements would you include, and which would you leave out?

2. With a partner, research on the Internet or in a video store to find one movie poster that appeals to you and a second one that is unappealing. With your partner, use a graphic organizer to list which features of each poster contributed to your reactions. Next, present the two posters to a group. See if they can guess which poster you liked and which you disliked. Then explain the reasons for your choices, and invite the reactions of group members.

3. Take the role of a design executive who has to present this poster to the moviemakers for their advertising campaign. Develop a speech in which you pitch your design. What overall feeling have you tried to communicate in the poster? Which design elements contribute to this feeling? Rehearse and then perform your speech for a group of classmates and invite their comments.

MORE TO EXPLORE

Themes: Self and Culture, Urban Life, Nature, Intrigue, Crisis

Elements: antithesis, archetype, conflict, graphics, headline, special effects, visual composition, visual scale

Screenplay

From Sense and Sensibility

Adapted by Emma Thompson
from the novel by Jane Austen

Sense and Sensibility director Ang Lee with actor Kate Winslet

LEARNING FOCUS

- Analyze screenplay elements.
- Examine how structure affects characterization and tone.
- Use a text as a model for writing an adaptation.

CONTEXT Jane Austen was born in 1775 in Steventon, Hampshire, England. She was tutored at home, which provided her with a broader education than most girls received in her era. A groundbreaking writer, Austen is considered a major pioneer of the modern novel due to her finely ironic fiction about domestic life. She died in 1817. Emma Thompson, who won an Academy Award for her screenplay adaptation of Austen's novel *Sense and Sensibility*, was born in 1959 in Paddington, England. At Cambridge University, she studied English literature and became involved in the theatre. Today she is a highly accomplished actor, director, screenwriter, and producer for stage and screen. For a film production, what might be some of the advantages and disadvantages of having the screenwriter or director also be an actor in the movie? For a film, which role—such as leading actor, director, screenwriter, producer—would most interest you? Why? ■

ABBREVIATIONS

CAM	camera
cont.	continued
CU	close-up
ECU	extreme close-up
EVE	evening
EXT	exterior
INT	interior
POV	point of view
V/O	voice over

0 EXT. OPEN ROADS. NIGHT. TITLE SEQUENCE.

A series of travelling shots. A well-dressed, pompous-looking individual (JOHN DASHWOOD, 35) is making an urgent journey on horseback. He looks anxious.

1 EXT. NORLAND PARK. ENGLAND. MARCH 1800. NIGHT.

Silence. Norland Park, a large country house built in the early part of the eighteenth century, lies in the moonlit parkland.

2 INT. NORLAND PARK. MR. DASHWOOD'S BEDROOM. NIGHT.

In the dim light shed by candles we see a bed in which a MAN (MR. DASHWOOD, 52) lies—his skin waxy, his breathing laboured. Around him two silhouettes move and murmur, their clothing susurrating in the deathly hush. DOCTORS. A WOMAN (MRS. DASHWOOD, 50) sits by his side, holding his hand, her eyes never leaving his face.

> **MR. DASHWOOD** *(urgent)*
> Is John not yet arrived?

> **MRS. DASHWOOD**
> We expect him at any moment, dearest.

MR. DASHWOOD *looks anguished.*

MR. DASHWOOD
The girls—I have left so little.

MRS. DASHWOOD
Shh, hush, Henry.

MR. DASHWOOD
Elinor will try to look after you all, but make sure she finds a good husband. The men are such noodles hereabouts, little wonder none has pleased her.

They smile at each other. MRS. DASHWOOD *is just managing to conceal her fear and grief.*

MRS. DASHWOOD
But Marianne is sure to find her storybook hero.

MR. DASHWOOD
A romantic poet with flashing eyes and empty pockets?

MRS. DASHWOOD
As long as she loves him, who*ever* he is.

MR. DASHWOOD
Margaret will go to sea and become a pirate so we need not concern ourselves with her.

MRS. DASHWOOD *tries to laugh but it emerges as a sob. An older* MANSERVANT (THOMAS) *now enters, anxiety written on every feature.*

THOMAS
Your son is arrived from London, sir.

MR. DASHWOOD *squeezes his wife's hand.*

MR. DASHWOOD
Let me speak to John alone.

She nods quickly and he smiles at her with infinite tenderness.

MR. DASHWOOD
Ah, my dear. How happy you have made me.

MRS. DASHWOOD *makes a superhuman effort and smiles back. She allows*

THOMAS *to help her out. She passes* JOHN DASHWOOD *as he enters, presses his hand, but cannot speak.* JOHN *takes her place by the bed.*

JOHN
Father…

MR. DASHWOOD *summons his last ounces of energy and starts to whisper with desperate intensity.*

MR. DASHWOOD
John—you will find out soon enough from my will that the estate of Norland was left to me in such a way as prevents me from dividing it between my families.

JOHN *blinks. He cannot quite take it in.*

JOHN
Calm yourself, Father. This is not good for you—

But MR. DASHWOOD *continues with even greater determination.*

MR. DASHWOOD
Norland in its entirety is therefore yours by law and I am happy for you and Fanny.

JOHN *looks torn between genuine distress and unexpected delight.*

MR. DASHWOOD
But your stepmother—my wife—and daughters are left with only five hundred pounds a year, barely enough to live on and nothing for the girls' dowries. You must help them.

JOHN*'s face is a picture of conflicting emotions. Behind them is the ominous rustling of parchments.*

JOHN
Of course —

MR. DASHWOOD
You must promise to do this.

A brief moment of sincerity overcomes JOHN*'s natural hypocrisy.*

JOHN
I promise, Father, I promise.

MR. DASHWOOD *seems relieved. Suddenly his breathing changes.* JOHN *looks alarmed. He rises and we hear him going to find the* DOCTOR.

JOHN
Come! Come quickly!

But it is we who share the dying man's last words.

MR. DASHWOOD
Help them...

3 EXT. JOHN AND FANNY'S TOWN HOUSE. LONDON. DAY.

Outside the house sits a very well-to-do carriage. Behind it waits another open carriage upon which servants are laying trunks and boxes.

FANNY (V/O)
"Help them?"

4 INT. JOHN AND FANNY'S TOWN HOUSE. DRESSING ROOM. DAY.

JOHN is standing in mourning clothes and a travelling cape. He is watching, and obviously waiting for, a pert WOMAN (FANNY DASHWOOD) who is standing by a mirror looking at him keenly.

FANNY
What do you mean, "help them"?

JOHN
Dearest, I mean to give them three thousand pounds.

FANNY goes very still. JOHN gets nervous.

JOHN
The interest will provide them with a little extra income. Such a gift will certainly discharge my promise to my father.

FANNY slowly turns back to the mirror.

FANNY
Oh, without question! More than amply...

JOHN
One had rather, on such occasions, do too much than too little.

A pause as FANNY turns and looks at him again.

JOHN
Of course, he did not stipulate a particular sum...

5 INT. LAUNDRY. NORLAND PARK. DAY.

A red-eyed MAID (BETSY) *plunges a beautiful muslin frock into a vat of black dye.*

6 INT. NORLAND PARK. MRS. DASHWOOD'S BEDROOM. DAY.

MRS. DASHWOOD *is rushing about, mourning ribbons flapping, putting her knick-knacks into a small valise. The room is in chaos. A young* WOMAN (ELINOR DASHWOOD) *looks on helplessly.*

> **MRS. DASHWOOD**
> To be reduced to the condition of visitor in my own home! It is not to be borne, Elinor!

> **ELINOR**
> Consider, Mamma! We have nowhere to go.

> **MRS. DASHWOOD**
> John and Fanny will descend from London at any moment, followed no doubt by cartloads of relatives ready to turn us out of our rooms one by one—do you expect me to be here to welcome them? Vultures!

She suddenly collapses into a chair and bursts into tears.

> **ELINOR**
> I shall start making enquiries for a new house at once. Until then we must try to bear their coming.

7 INT. JOHN AND FANNY'S CARRIAGE. DAY.

JOHN *and* FANNY *are on their way out of London.*

> **JOHN**
> Fifteen hundred then. What say you to fifteen hundred?

> **FANNY**
> What brother on earth would do half so much for his real sisters—let alone half-blood?

> **JOHN**
> They can hardly expect more.

> **FANNY**
> There is no knowing what they expect. The question is, what can you afford?

8 Int. Norland Park. Drawing Room. Day.

A beautiful young Woman (Marianne Dashwood) *is sitting at the piano playing a particularly sad piece.* Elinor *enters.*

> ELINOR
>
> Marianne, cannot you play something else? Mamma has been weeping since breakfast.

Marianne *stops, turns the pages of her music book and starts playing something equally lugubrious.*

> ELINOR
>
> I meant something less mournful, dearest.

9 Ext. Roadside Inn. Day.

John *and* Fanny *are waiting as the* Ostlers *make the final adjustments to their carriage. The* Landlord *hovers, waiting for a tip.*

> JOHN
>
> A hundred pounds a year to their mother while she lives. Would that be more advisable? It is better than parting with the fifteen hundred all at once.

He displays some coins in his hand. Fanny *removes one and nods.*

> FANNY
>
> But if she should live longer than fifteen years we would be completely taken in. People always live forever when there is an annuity to be paid them.

John *gives the coins to the* Landlord.

10 Ext. Norland Park. Margaret's Tree-House. Day.

Elinor *comes to the foot of a large tree from which a small staircase issues.*

> ELINOR
>
> Margaret, are you there? Please come down. John and Fanny will be here soon.

A pause. Elinor *is about to leave when a disembodied and truculent young voice stops her.*

(left to right): Emma Thompson as Elinor Dashwood, Kate Winslet as Marianne Dashwood, and Gemma Jones as Mrs. Dashwood

MARGARET (V/O)

Why are they coming to live at Norland? They already have a house in London.

ELINOR

Because houses go from father to son, dearest—not from father to daughter. It is the law.

Silence. ELINOR *tries another tack.*

ELINOR

If you come inside, we could play with your atlas.

MARGARET (V/O)

It's not my atlas any more. It's their atlas.

CU on ELINOR *as she ponders the truth of this statement.*

11 INT. JOHN AND FANNY'S CARRIAGE. DAY.

JOHN *and* FANNY *joggle on.*

JOHN

Twenty pounds now and then will amply discharge my promise, you are quite right.

FANNY

Indeed. Although to say the truth, I am convinced within myself that your father had no idea of your giving them money.

JOHN

They will have five hundred a year amongst them as it is—

FANNY

—and what on earth can four women want for more than that? Their housekeeping will be nothing at all—they will have no carriage, no horses, hardly any servants and will keep no company. Only conceive how comfortable they will be!

12 INT. NORLAND PARK. SERVANTS' HALL. DAY.

The large contingent of SERVANTS *who staff Norland Park are gathered in gloomy silence as* ELINOR *addresses them.*

ELINOR

As you know, we are looking for a new home. When we leave we shall be able to retain only Thomas and Betsy.

CAM *holds on* THOMAS *and* BETSY, *a capable woman.*

ELINOR (**cont.**)

We are very sorry to have to leave you all. But we are certain you will find the new Mrs. Dashwood a fair and generous mistress.

13 EXT. NORLAND PARK. DRIVE. DAY.

JOHN *and* FANNY'*s carriage approaches Norland.*

FANNY (V/O)

They will be much more able to give *you* something.

14 INT. JOHN AND FANNY'S CARRIAGE. DAY.

JOHN *and* FANNY *are about to get out.*

JOHN

So—we are agreed. No money—but the occasional gift of game and fish in season will be very welcome.

FANNY

Your father would be proud of you.

NOTES

susurrating murmuring, whispering; this onomatopoeic word comes from the Latin word *susurrus,* meaning "whisper"

dowries money or property provided by the bride's family for the wedded couple in some cultures

parchments in this instance, legal documents

lugubrious mournful, dismal, or gloomy, often to an exaggerated degree

annuity the annual payment of either an income or returns on an investment

truculent disposed to fighting or destructiveness

ANALYZE AND INTERPRET

1. Reread Scene 2, paying close attention to the stage directions as well as to the dialogue. Consider the following questions: How does the scene serve as an introduction to the story? How does it establish the characters and their relationships? What conflicts does it introduce? What indirect reference to the title can you find? How does this scene fulfill the screenwriting adage "Always start the story at the last possible moment"? Write your ideas down in point form, and then discuss them with a partner.

2. On their way to Norland, John and Fanny talk about his financial responsibilities toward his stepmother and stepsisters. The screenwriter, Emma Thompson, made the decision to break up their conversation into six short scenes. With the class, discuss what you think her reasons were for doing this. How does breaking it up this way contribute both humour and tension to the conversation? How does it reflect the relationship between the husband and wife?

3. In a group of six, choose a story from the fiction section of this anthology that you think lends itself to being rewritten as a screenplay. Divide into pairs; each pair will write a different version of the first scene of the screenplay. Use the format of the excerpt from "Sense and Sensibility" as your model. As you write, pause often to role-play or read aloud your dialogue to help you to evaluate whether it conveys the personality of the characters and whether it sounds like authentic speech. When you have completed the opening scenes, take turns reading them to the other two pairs. Discuss the similarities and differences in your interpretations.

MORE TO EXPLORE

Themes: Self and Culture, Loss, Family, Rural Life, Europe, Moral Questions, Eye on the Past

Elements: adaptation, camera angle, characterization, dialogue, irony, set design, sound track, voice over

Trifles

Susan Glaspell

CONTEXT Susan Glaspell was born in Davenport, Iowa, in 1876. She studied philosophy at Drake University in Des Moines, Iowa, after which she worked as a staff journalist for the *Des Moines Daily News*. She later gave up her journalism career to concentrate on fiction and drama. In 1915, she co-founded the Provincetown Players in Cape Cod, Massachusetts, which became an influential theatrical troupe. She lived in New York City and in Greece, writing and participating in progressive political causes. In 1930 she became the second woman to win a Pulitzer Prize for drama, for *Alison's House*, a play loosely based on the life of Emily Dickinson. By the time of her death in Provincetown in 1948, she had written over fifty short stories, fourteen plays, and nine novels. *Trifles* is often referred to as a "classic" of modern drama. When thinking about written texts, what do you understand the term "classic" to mean? In your view, how are the characteristics of a classic text different from those of a text that is not generally considered a classic? ■

Characters

COUNTY ATTORNEY

MRS. PETERS

SHERIFF

MRS. HALE

HALE

Setting

The kitchen in the now-abandoned farmhouse of JOHN WRIGHT, *a gloomy kitchen, and left without having been put in order—the walls covered with a faded wallpaper. Downstage right is a door leading to the parlour. On the right wall above this door is a built-in kitchen cupboard with shelves in the upper portion and drawers below. In the rear wall at right, up two steps, is a door opening onto stairs leading to the second floor. In the rear wall at left is a door to the shed and from there to the outside. Between these two doors is an old-fashioned black iron stove. Running along the left wall from the shed door is an old iron sink and sink shelf, in which is set a hand pump. Downstage of the sink is an uncurtained window. Near the window is an old wooden rocker. Centrestage is an unpainted wooden kitchen table with straight chairs on either side. There is a small chair downstage right. Unwashed pans under the sink, a loaf of bread outside the breadbox, a dish towel on the table—other signs of incompleted work. At the rear the shed door opens and the* SHERIFF *comes in followed by the* COUNTY ATTORNEY *and* HALE. *The* SHERIFF *and* HALE *are men in middle life, the* COUNTY ATTORNEY *is a young man; all are much bundled up and go at once to the stove. They are followed by the two women—the* SHERIFF'S *wife,* MRS. PETERS, *first; she is a slight wiry woman, a thin nervous face.* MRS. HALE *is larger and would ordinarily be called more comfortable looking, but she is disturbed now and looks fearfully about as she enters. The women have come in slowly, and stand close together near the door.*

COUNTY ATTORNEY: *(at stove rubbing his hands)* This feels good. Come up to the fire, ladies.

MRS. PETERS: *(after taking a step forward)* I'm not—cold.

SHERIFF: *(unbuttoning his overcoat and stepping away from the stove to right of table as if to mark the beginning of official business)* Now, Mr. Hale, before we move things about, you explain to Mr. Henderson just what you saw when you came here yesterday morning.

COUNTY ATTORNEY: *(crossing down to left of the table)* By the way, has anything been moved? Are things just as you left them yesterday?

SHERIFF: *(looking about)* It's just the same. When it dropped below zero last night I thought I'd better send Frank out this morning to make a fire for us—*(Sits right of centre table.)* no use getting pneumonia with a big case on, but I told him not to touch anything except the stove—and you know Frank.

COUNTY ATTORNEY: Somebody should have been left here yesterday.

SHERIFF: Oh—yesterday. When I had to send Frank to Morris Center for that man who went crazy—I want you to know I had my hands full yesterday. I knew you could get back from Omaha by today and as long as I went over everything here myself—

COUNTY ATTORNEY: Well, Mr. Hale, tell just what happened when you came here yesterday morning.

HALE: *(crossing down to above table)* Harry and I had started to town with a load of potatoes. We came along the road from my place and as I got here I said, "I'm going to see if I can't get John Wright to go in with me on a party telephone." I spoke to Wright about it once before and he put me off, saying folks talked too much anyway, and all he asked was peace and quiet—I guess you know about how much he talked himself; but I thought maybe if I went to the house and talked about it before his wife, though I said to Harry that I didn't know as what his wife wanted made much difference to John—

COUNTY ATTORNEY: Let's talk about that later, Mr. Hale. I do want to talk about that, but tell now just what happened when you got to the house.

HALE: I didn't hear or see anything; I knocked at the door, and still it was all quiet inside. I knew they must be up, it was past eight o'clock. So I knocked again, and I thought I heard somebody say, "Come in." I wasn't sure, I'm not sure yet, but I opened the door— this door *(Indicating the door by which the two women are still standing.)* and there in that rocker—*(Pointing to it.)* sat Mrs. Wright. *(They all look at the rocker downstage left.)*

COUNTY ATTORNEY: What—was she doing?

HALE: She was rockin' back and forth. She had her apron in her hand and was kind of—pleating it.

COUNTY ATTORNEY: And how did she—look?

HALE: Well, she looked queer.

COUNTY ATTORNEY: How do you mean—queer?

HALE: Well, as if she didn't know what she was going to do next. And kind of done up.

COUNTY ATTORNEY: *(takes out notebook and pencil and sits left of centre table)* How did she seem to feel about your coming?

HALE: Why, I don't think she minded—one way or other. She didn't pay much attention. I said, "How do, Mrs. Wright, it's cold, ain't it?" And she said, "Is it?"—and went on kind of pleating at her apron. Well, I was surprised; she didn't ask me to come up to the stove, or to set down, but just sat there, not even looking at me, so I said, "I want to see John." And then she—laughed. I guess you would call it a laugh. I thought of Harry and the team outside, so I said a little sharp: "Can't I see John?" "No," she says, kind o' dull like. "Ain't he home?" says I. "Yes," says she, "he's home." "Then why can't I see him?" I asked her, out of patience. "'Cause he's dead," says she. "*Dead?*" says I. She just nodded her head, not getting a bit excited, but rockin' back and forth. "Why—where is he?" says I, not knowing what to say. She just pointed upstairs—like that. *(Himself pointing to the room above.)* I started for the stairs, with the idea of going up there. I walked from there to here—then I says, "Why, what did he die of?" "He died of a rope round his neck," says she, and just went on pleatin' at her apron. Well, I went out and called Harry. I thought I might—need help. We went upstairs and there he was lyin'—

COUNTY ATTORNEY: I think I'd rather have you go into that upstairs, where you can point it all out. Just go on now with the rest of the story.

HALE: Well, my first thought was to get that rope off. It looked... *(Stops, his face twitches.)*...but Harry, he went up to him, and he said, "No, he's dead all right, and we'd better not touch anything." So we went back downstairs. She was still sitting that same way. "Has anybody been notified?" I asked. "No," says she, unconcerned. "Who did this, Mrs. Wright?" said Harry. He said it businesslike—and she stopped pleatin' of her apron. "I don't know," she says. "You don't know?" says Harry. "No," says she. "Weren't you sleepin' in the bed with him?" says Harry. "Yes," says she, "but I was on the inside." "Somebody slipped a rope round his neck and strangled him and you didn't wake up?" says Harry. "I didn't wake up," she said after him. We must 'a' looked as if we didn't see how that could be, for after a minute she said, "I sleep sound." Harry was going to ask her more questions but I said maybe we ought to let her tell her story first to the coroner, or the sheriff, so Harry went fast as he could to Rivers' place, where there's a telephone.

COUNTY ATTORNEY: And what did Mrs. Wright do when she knew that you had gone for the coroner?

HALE: She moved from the rocker to that chair over there *(Pointing to a small chair in the downstage right corner.)* and just sat there with her hands held together and looking down. I got a feeling that I ought to make some conversation, so I said I had come in to see if John wanted to put in a telephone, and at that she started to laugh, and then she stopped and looked at me—scared. *(The* COUNTY ATTORNEY, *who has had his notebook out, makes a note.)* I dunno, maybe it wasn't scared. I wouldn't like to say it was. Soon Harry got back, and then Dr. Lloyd came, and you, Mr. Peters, and so I guess that's all I know that you don't.

COUNTY ATTORNEY: *(rising and looking around)* I guess we'll go upstairs first—and then out to the barn and around there. *(To the* SHERIFF.)* You're convinced that there was nothing important here—nothing that would point to any motive?

SHERIFF: Nothing here but kitchen things.

(The COUNTY ATTORNEY, *after again looking around the kitchen, opens the door of a cupboard closet in right wall. He brings a small chair from right—gets up on it and looks on a shelf. Pulls his hand away, sticky.)*

COUNTY ATTORNEY: Here's a nice mess. *(The women draw nearer upstage centre.)*

MRS. PETERS: *(to the other woman)* Oh, her fruit; it did freeze. *(To the* LAWYER.)* She worried about that when it turned so cold. She said the fire'd go out and her jars would break.

SHERIFF: *(rises)* Well, can you beat the woman! Held for murder and worryin' about her preserves.

COUNTY ATTORNEY: *(getting down from chair)* I guess before we're through she may have something more serious than preserves to worry about. *(Crosses down right centre.)*

HALE: Well, women are used to worrying over trifles. *(The two women move a little closer together.)*

COUNTY ATTORNEY: *(with the gallantry of a young politician)* And yet, for all their worries, what would we do without the ladies?

(The women do not unbend. He goes below the centre table to the sink, takes a dipperful of water from the pail and, pouring it into a basin, washes his hands. While he is doing this the SHERIFF and HALE cross to cupboard, which they inspect. The COUNTY ATTORNEY starts to wipe his hands on the roller towel, turns it for a cleaner place.)

Dirty towels! *(Kicks his foot against the pans under the sink.)* Not much of a housekeeper, would you say, ladies?

MRS. HALE: *(stiffly)* There's a great deal of work to be done on a farm.

COUNTY ATTORNEY: To be sure. And yet *(With a little bow to her.)* I know there are some Dickson County farmhouses which do not have such roller towels. *(He gives it a pull to expose its full length again.)*

MRS. HALE: Those towels get dirty awful quick. Men's hands aren't always as clean as they might be.

COUNTY ATTORNEY: Ah, loyal to your sex, I see. But you and Mrs. Wright were neighbours. I suppose you were friends, too.

MRS. HALE: *(shaking her head)* I've not seen much of her of late years. I've not been in this house—it's more than a year.

COUNTY ATTORNEY: *(crossing to women upstage centre)* And why was that? You didn't like her?

MRS. HALE: I liked her all well enough. Farmers' wives have their hands full, Mr. Henderson. And then—

COUNTY ATTORNEY: Yes—?

MRS. HALE: *(looking about)* It never seemed a very cheerful place.

COUNTY ATTORNEY: No—it's not cheerful. I shouldn't say she had the homemaking instinct.

MRS. HALE: Well, I don't know as Wright had, either.

COUNTY ATTORNEY: You mean that they didn't get on very well?

MRS. HALE: No, I don't mean anything. But I don't think a place'd be any cheerfuller for John Wright's being in it.

COUNTY ATTORNEY: I'd like to talk more of that a little later. I want to get the lay of things upstairs now. *(He goes past the women to upstage right where steps lead to a stair door.)*

SHERIFF: I suppose anything Mrs. Peters does'll be all right. She was to take in some clothes for her, you know, and a few little things. We left in such a hurry yesterday.

COUNTY ATTORNEY: Yes, but I would like to see what you take, Mrs. Peters, and keep an eye out for anything that might be of use to us.

MRS. PETERS: Yes, Mr. Henderson.

(The men leave by upstage right door to stairs. The women listen to the men's steps on the stairs, then look about the kitchen.)

MRS. HALE: *(crossing left to sink)* I'd hate to have men coming into my kitchen, snooping around and criticizing.

(She arranges the pans under sink which the LAWYER *had shoved out of place.)*

MRS. PETERS: Of course, it's no more than their duty. *(Crosses to cupboard upstage right.)*

MRS. HALE: Duty's all right, but I guess that deputy sheriff that came out to make the fire might have got a little of this on. *(Gives the roller towel a pull.)* Wish I'd thought of that sooner. Seems mean to talk about her for not having things slicked up when she had to come away in such a hurry. *(Crosses right to* MRS. PETERS *at cupboard.)*

MRS. PETERS: *(who has been looking through cupboard, lifts one end of a towel that covers a pan)* She had bread set. *(Stands still.)*

MRS. HALE: *(eyes fixed on a loaf of bread beside the breadbox, which is on a low shelf of the cupboard)* She was going to put this in there. *(Picks up loaf, then abruptly drops it. In a manner of returning to familiar things.)* It's a shame about her fruit. I wonder if it's all gone. *(Gets up on the chair and looks.)* I think there's some here that's all right, Mrs. Peters. Yes—here; *(Holding it toward the window.)* this is cherries, too. *(Looking again.)* I declare I believe that's the only one. *(Gets down, jar in her hand. Goes to the sink and wipes it off on the outside.)* She'll feel awful bad after all her hard work in the hot weather. I remember the afternoon I put up my cherries last summer.

(She puts the jar on the big kitchen table, centre of the room. With a sigh, is about to sit down in the rocking chair. Before she is seated realizes what chair it is; with a slow look at it, steps back. The chair which she has

touched rocks back and forth. MRS. PETERS *moves to centre table and they both watch the chair rock for a moment or two.)*

MRS. PETERS: *(shaking off the mood which the empty rocking chair has evoked. Now in a businesslike manner she speaks)* Well, I must get those things from the front room closet. *(She goes to the door at the right, but, after looking into the other room, steps back.)* You coming with me, Mrs. Hale? You could help me carry them. *(They go in the other room; reappear,* MRS. PETERS *carrying a dress, petticoat, and skirt.* MRS. HALE *following with a pair of shoes.)* My, it's cold in there. *(She puts the clothes on the big table, and hurries to the stove.)*

MRS. HALE: *(right of centre table examining the skirt)* Wright was close. I think maybe that's why she kept so much to herself. She didn't even belong to the Ladies' Aid. I suppose she felt she couldn't do her part, and then you don't enjoy things when you feel shabby. I heard she used to wear pretty clothes and be lively, when she was Minnie Foster, one of the town girls singing in the choir. But that—oh, that was thirty years ago. This all you was to take in?

MRS. PETERS: She said she wanted an apron. Funny thing to want, for there isn't much to get you dirty in jail, goodness knows. But I suppose just to make her feel more natural. *(Crosses to cupboard.)* She said they was in the top drawer in this cupboard. Yes, here. And then her little shawl that always hung behind the door. *(Opens stair door and looks.)* Yes, here it is. *(Quickly shuts door leading upstairs.)*

MRS. HALE: *(abruptly moving toward her)* Mrs. Peters?

MRS. PETERS: Yes, Mrs. Hale? *(At upstage right door.)*

MRS. HALE: Do you think she did it?

MRS. PETERS: *(in a frightened voice)* Oh, I don't know.

MRS. HALE: Well, I don't think she did. Asking for an apron and her little shawl. Worrying about her fruit.

MRS. PETERS: *(starts to speak, glances up, where footsteps are heard in the room above. In a low voice)* Mr. Peters says it looks bad for her. Mr. Henderson is awful sarcastic in a speech and he'll make fun of her sayin' she didn't wake up.

MRS. HALE: Well, I guess John Wright didn't wake when they was slipping that rope under his neck.

MRS. PETERS: *(crossing slowly to table and placing shawl and apron on table with other clothing)* No, it's strange. It must have been done awful crafty and still. They say it was such a—funny way to kill a man, rigging it all up like that.

MRS. HALE: *(crossing to left of MRS. PETERS at table)* That's just what Mr. Hale said. There was a gun in the house. He says that's what he can't understand.

MRS. PETERS: Mr. Henderson said coming out that what was needed for the case was a motive; something to show anger, or—sudden feeling.

MRS. HALE: *(who is standing by the table)* Well, I don't see any signs of anger around here. *(She puts her hand on the dish towel which lies on the table, stands looking down at table, one-half of which is clean, the other half messy.)* It's wiped to here. *(Makes a move as if to finish work, then turns and looks at loaf of bread outside the breadbox. Drops towel. In that voice of coming back to familiar things.)* Wonder how they are finding things upstairs. *(Crossing below table to downstage right.)* I hope she had it a little more red–up up there. You know, it seems kind of *sneaking.* Locking her up in town and then coming out here and trying to get her own house to turn against her!

MRS. PETERS: But, Mrs. Hale, the law is the law.

MRS. HALE: I s'pose 'tis. *(Unbuttoning her coat.)* Better loosen up your things, Mrs. Peters. You won't feel them when you go out.

(MRS. PETERS takes off her fur tippet, goes to hang it on chair back left of table, stands looking at the work basket on floor near downstage left window.)

MRS. PETERS: She was piecing a quilt.

(She brings the large sewing basket to the centre table and they look at the bright pieces, MRS. HALE above the table and MRS. PETERS left of it.)

MRS. HALE: It's a log cabin pattern. Pretty, isn't it? I wonder if she was goin' to quilt it or just knot it?

(Footsteps have been heard coming down the stairs. The SHERIFF enters followed by HALE and the COUNTY ATTORNEY.)

SHERIFF: They wonder if she was going to quilt it or just knot it! *(The men laugh, the women look abashed.)*

COUNTY ATTORNEY: *(rubbing his hands over the stove)* Frank's fire didn't do much up there, did it? Well, let's go out to the barn and get that cleared up. *(The men go outside by upstage left door.)*

MRS. HALE: *(resentfully)* I don't know as there's anything so strange, our takin' up our time with little things while we're waiting for them to get the evidence. *(She sits in chair right of table smoothing out a block with decision.)* I don't see as it's anything to laugh about.

MRS. PETERS: *(apologetically)* Of course they've got awful important things on their minds. *(Pulls up a chair and joins MRS. HALE at the left of the table.)*

MRS. HALE: *(examining another block)* Mrs. Peters, look at this one. Here, this is the one she was working on, and look at the sewing! All the rest of it has been so nice and even. And look at this! It's all over the place! Why, it looks as if she didn't know what she was about!

(After she has said this they look at each other then start to glance back at the door. After an instant MRS. HALE has pulled at a knot and ripped the sewing.)

MRS. PETERS: Oh, what are you doing, Mrs. Hale?

MRS. HALE: *(mildly)* Just putting out a stitch or two that's not sewed very good. *(Threading a needle.)* Bad sewing always made me fidgety.

MRS. PETERS: *(with a glance at door, nervously)* I don't think we ought to touch things.

MRS. HALE: I'll just finish up this end. *(Suddenly stopping and leaning forward.)* Mrs. Peters?

MRS. PETERS: Yes, Mrs. Hale?

MRS. HALE: What do you suppose she was so nervous about?

MRS. PETERS: Oh—I don't know. I don't know as she was nervous. I sometimes sew awful queer when I'm just tired. *(MRS. HALE starts to say something, looks at MRS. PETERS, then goes on sewing.)* Well, I must get these things wrapped up. They may be through sooner than we think. *(Putting apron and other things together.)* I wonder where I can find a piece of paper, and string. *(Rises.)*

MRS. HALE: In that cupboard, maybe.

MRS. PETERS: *(crosses right looking in cupboard)* Why, here's a birdcage. *(Holds it up.)* Did she have a bird, Mrs. Hale?

MRS. HALE: Why, I don't know whether she did or not—I've not been here for so long. There was a man around last year selling canaries cheap, but I don't know as she took one; maybe she did. She used to sing real pretty herself.

MRS. PETERS: *(glancing around)* Seems funny to think of a bird here. But she must have had one, or why would she have a cage? I wonder what happened to it?

MRS. HALE: I s'pose maybe the cat got it.

MRS. PETERS: No, she didn't have a cat. She's got that feeling some people have about cats—being afraid of them. My cat got in her room and she was real upset and asked me to take it out.

MRS. HALE: My sister Bessie was like that. Queer, ain't it?

MRS. PETERS: *(examining the cage)* Why, look at this door. It's broke. One hinge is pulled apart. *(Takes a step down to* MRS. HALE*'s right.)*

MRS. HALE: *(looking too)* Looks as if someone must have been rough with it.

MRS. PETERS: Why, yes. *(She brings the cage forward and puts it on the table.)*

MRS. HALE: *(glancing toward upstage left door)* I wish if they're going to find any evidence they'd be about it. I don't like this place.

MRS. PETERS: But I'm awful glad you came with me, Mrs. Hale. It would be lonesome for me sitting here alone.

MRS. HALE: It would, wouldn't it? *(Dropping her sewing.)* But I tell you what I do wish, Mrs. Peters. I wish I had come over sometimes when *she* was here. I—*(Looking around the room.)*—wish I had.

MRS. PETERS: But of course you were awful busy, Mrs. Hale—your house and your children.

MRS. HALE: *(rises and crosses left)* I could've come. I stayed away because it weren't cheerful—and that's why I ought to have come. I—*(Looking out left window.)*—I've never liked this place. Maybe because it's down in a hollow and you don't see the road. I dunno what it is, but it's a lonesome place and always was. I wish I had come over to see Minnie Foster sometimes. I can see now—*(Shakes her head.)*

MRS. PETERS: *(left of table and above it)* Well, you mustn't reproach yourself, Mrs. Hale. Somehow we just don't see how it is with other folks until—something turns up.

MRS. HALE: Not having children makes less work—but it makes a quiet house, and Wright out to work all day, and no company when he did come in. *(Turning from window.)* Did you know John Wright, Mrs. Peters?

MRS. PETERS: Not to know him; I've seen him in town. They say he was a good man.

MRS. HALE: Yes—good; he didn't drink, and kept his word as well as most, I guess, and paid his debts. But he was a hard man, Mrs. Peters. Just to pass the time of day with him—*(Shivers.)* Like a raw wind that gets to the bone. *(Pauses, her eye falling on the cage.)* I should think she would 'a' wanted a bird. But what do you suppose went with it?

MRS. PETERS: I don't know, unless it got sick and died.

(She reaches over and swings the broken door, swings it again, both women watch it.)

MRS. HALE: You weren't raised round here, were you? *(*MRS. PETERS *shakes her head.)* You didn't know—her?

MRS. PETERS: Not till they brought her yesterday.

MRS. HALE: She—come to think of it, she was kind of like a bird herself—real sweet and pretty, but kind of timid and—fluttery. How—she—did—change. *(Silence; then as if struck by a happy thought and relieved to get back to everyday things. Crosses right above* MRS. PETERS *to cupboard, replaces small chair used to stand on to its original place downstage right.)* Tell you what, Mrs. Peters, why don't you take the quilt in with you? It might take up her mind.

MRS. PETERS: Why, I think that's a real nice idea, Mrs. Hale. There couldn't possibly be any objection to it, could there? Now, just what would I take? I wonder if her patches are in here—and her things. *(They look in the sewing basket.)*

MRS. HALE: *(crosses to right of table)* Here's some red. I expect this has got sewing things in it. *(Brings out a fancy box.)* What a pretty box. Looks like something somebody would give you. Maybe her scissors are in here. *(Opens box. Suddenly puts her hand to her nose.)* Why—(MRS. PETERS *bends nearer, then turns her face away.)* There's something wrapped up in this piece of silk.

MRS. PETERS: Why, this isn't her scissors.

MRS. HALE: *(lifting the silk)* Oh, Mrs. Peters—it's—(MRS. PETERS *bends closer.)*

MRS. PETERS: It's the bird.

MRS. HALE: But, Mrs. Peters—look at it! Its neck! Look at its neck! It's all—other side too.

MRS. PETERS: Somebody—wrung—its—neck.

(Their eyes meet. A look of growing comprehension, of horror. Steps are heard outside. MRS. HALE slips box under quilt pieces, and sinks into her chair. Enter SHERIFF and COUNTY ATTORNEY. MRS. PETERS steps downstage left and stands looking out of window.)

COUNTY ATTORNEY: *(as one turning from serious things to little pleasantries)* Well, ladies, have you decided whether she was going to quilt it or knot it? *(Crosses to centre above table.)*

MRS. PETERS: We think she was going to—knot it.

(SHERIFF crosses to right of stove, lifts stove lid and glances at fire, then stands warming hands at stove.)

COUNTY ATTORNEY: Well, that's interesting, I'm sure. *(Seeing the birdcage.)* Has the bird flown?

MRS. HALE: *(putting more quilt pieces over the box)* We think the—cat got it.

COUNTY ATTORNEY: *(preoccupied)* Is there a cat? *(MRS. HALE glances in a quick covert way at MRS. PETERS.)*

MRS. PETERS: *(turning from window takes a step in)* Well, not *now.* They're superstitious, you know. They leave.

COUNTY ATTORNEY: *(to SHERIFF PETERS, continuing an interrupted conversation)* No sign at all of anyone having come from the outside. Their own rope. Now let's go up again and go over it piece by piece. *(They start upstairs.)* It would have to have been someone who knew just the—

(Mrs. Peters sits down left of the table. The two women sit there not looking at one another, but as if peering into something and at the same time holding back. When they talk now it is in the manner of feeling their way over strange ground, as if afraid of what they are saying, but as if they cannot help saying it.)

Mrs. Hale: *(hesitatingly and in a hushed voice)* She liked the bird. She was going to bury it in that pretty box.

Mrs. Peters: *(in a whisper)* When I was a girl—my kitten—there was a boy took a hatchet, and before my eyes—and before I could get there—*(Covers her face an instant.)* If they hadn't held me back I would have—*(Catches herself, looks upstairs where steps are heard, falters weakly.)*—hurt him.

Mrs. Hale: *(with a slow look around her)* I wonder how it would seem never to have had any children around. *(Pause.)* No, Wright wouldn't like the bird—a thing that sang. She used to sing. He killed that, too.

Mrs. Peters: *(moving uneasily)* We don't know who killed the bird.

Mrs. Hale: I knew John Wright.

Mrs. Peters: It was an awful thing was done in this house that night, Mrs. Hale. Killing a man while he slept, slipping a rope around his neck that choked the life out of him.

Mrs. Hale: His neck. Choked the life out of him. *(Her hand goes out and rests on the birdcage.)*

Mrs. Peters: *(with rising voice)* We don't know who killed him. We don't know.

Mrs. Hale: *(her own feeling not interrupted)* If there'd been years and years of nothing, then a bird to sing to you, it would be awful—still, after the bird was still.

Mrs. Peters: *(something within her speaking)* I know what stillness is. When we homesteaded in Dakota, and my first baby died—after he was two years old, and me with no other then—

Mrs. Hale: *(moving)* How soon do you suppose they'll be through looking for the evidence?

MRS. PETERS: I know what stillness is. *(Pulling herself back.)* The law has got to punish crime, Mrs. Hale.

MRS. HALE: *(not as if answering that)* I wish you'd seen Minnie Foster when she wore a white dress with blue ribbons and stood up there in the choir and sang. *(A look around the room.)* Oh, I *wish* I'd come over here once in a while! That was a crime! That was a crime! Who's going to punish that?

MRS. PETERS: *(looking upstairs)* We mustn't—take on.

MRS. HALE: I might have known she needed help! I know how things can be—for women. I tell you, it's queer, Mrs. Peters. We live close together and we live far apart. We all go through the same things—it's all just a different kind of the same thing. *(Brushes her eyes, noticing the jar of fruit, reaches out for it.)* If I was you I wouldn't tell her her fruit was gone. Tell her it *ain't.* Tell her it's all right. Take this in to prove it to her. She—she may never know whether it was broke or not.

MRS. PETERS: *(takes the jar, looks about for something to wrap it in; takes petticoat from the clothes brought from the other room, very nervously begins winding this around the jar. In a false voice)* My, it's a good thing the men couldn't hear us. Wouldn't they just laugh! Getting all stirred up over a little thing like a—dead canary. As if that could have anything to do with—with—wouldn't they *laugh!* (*The men are heard coming downstairs.)*

MRS. HALE: *(under her breath)* Maybe they would—maybe they wouldn't.

COUNTY ATTORNEY: No, Peters, it's all perfectly clear except a reason for doing it. But you know juries when it comes to women. If there was some definite thing. *(Crosses slowly to above table.* SHERIFF *crosses downstage right.* MRS. HALE *and* MRS. PETERS *remain seated at either side of table.)* Something to show—something to make a story about—a thing that would connect up with this strange way of doing it—(*The women's eyes meet for an instant. Enter* HALE *from outer door.)*

HALE: *(remaining upstage left by door)* Well, I've got the team around. Pretty cold out there.

COUNTY ATTORNEY: I'm going to stay awhile by myself. *(To the*

SHERIFF.) You can send Frank out for me, can't you? I want to go over everything. I'm not satisfied we can't do better.

SHERIFF: Do you want to see what Mrs. Peters is going to take in? *(The LAWYER picks up the apron, laughs.)*

COUNTY ATTORNEY: Oh, I guess they're not very dangerous things the ladies have picked out. *(Moves a few things about, disturbing the quilt pieces which cover the box. Steps back.)* No, Mrs. Peters doesn't need supervising. For that matter a sheriff's wife is married to the law. Ever think of it that way, Mrs. Peters?

MRS. PETERS: Not—just that way.

SHERIFF: *(chuckling)* Married to the law. *(Moves to downstage right door to the other room.)* I just want you to come in here a minute, George. We ought to take a look at these windows.

COUNTY ATTORNEY: *(scoffingly)* Oh, windows!

SHERIFF: We'll be right out, Mr. Hale.

(HALE goes outside. The SHERIFF follows the COUNTY ATTORNEY into the other room. Then MRS. HALE rises, hands tight together, looking intensely at MRS. PETERS, whose eyes make a slow turn, finally meeting MRS. HALE's. A moment MRS. HALE holds her, then her own eyes point the way to where the box is concealed. Suddenly MRS. PETERS throws back quilt pieces and tries to put the box in the bag she is carrying. It is too big. She opens box, starts to take bird out, cannot touch it, goes to pieces, stands there helpless. Sound of a knob turning in the other room. MRS. HALE snatches the box and puts it in the pocket of her big coat. Enter COUNTY ATTORNEY and SHERIFF, who remains downstage right.)

COUNTY ATTORNEY: *(crosses to upstage left door facetiously)* Well, Henry, at least we found out that she was not going to quilt it. She was going to—what is it you call it, ladies?

MRS. HALE: *(standing centre below table facing front, her hand against her pocket)* We call it—knot it, Mr. Henderson.

Curtain.

NOTES

party telephone also known as a party line; refers to the old-fashioned practice of having two or more households share one telephone line. If one household was using the line, the other household could listen in on the call.

dunno slang for "don't know"

tippet in this instance, a scarf or covering for the shoulders with long ends that hang in front

ANALYZE AND INTERPRET

1. In your journal, write about the significance of the play's title. What specific references to the word or its meanings can you find within the play itself? Which characters in the play are associated with the title? How is the title related to the play's theme? In what sense might the title be ironic? With a partner, take turns reading your journal entries, and then discuss and compare your ideas.

2. **a)** Sometimes an author gives an object in a literary work a meaning that extends beyond the literal one to take on symbolic significance. In a group, discuss the symbolic significance of the following objects in the story: the bird, the jars of preserves, the apron, the cage, and the quilt. Who or what does each of these items represent? **b)** After your discussion, write an essay about the use of symbolism in this play. Include at least three quotations from the play in your essay. **c)** Ask a classmate to read your essay and give you feedback on how effectively you used quotations to support your ideas and how well you incorporated the quotations into your essay.

3. Write a monologue that Mrs. Peters or Mrs. Hale might deliver at the end of the play, in which the character you choose debates whether to tell the men about the dead bird. In character, consider the following questions: What are your thoughts about Mrs. Wright's life? How does the behaviour of the men at the crime scene affect your decision? How do you justify concealing the evidence? Record your monologue and listen to it carefully to ensure you have captured your character's voice. Make any necessary revisions, and then present your monologue to a group of classmates.

MORE TO EXPLORE

Themes: Self and Culture, Stereotypes, Family, Friends, Rural Life, Intrigue, Moral Questions, Crisis

Elements: characterization, climax, dialogue, pathos, plot, props, set design, tragedy

The Ignoble Knight

Desiderius Erasmus

Knight in armour, c. 15th to 16th century

- Make links between a historic text and the contemporary world.
- Use a text as the basis for research and a visual response.
- Update specific elements of a historic text.

CONTEXT Desiderius Erasmus was born in approximately 1466 in Rotterdam, the Netherlands. Educated in monastic schools, he was ordained as a priest in 1492. He then lived in Paris, France, where he studied philosophy and Greek. Starting in 1499, Erasmus moved among many cities in Europe, working as a tutor and lecturer, and collecting ancient manuscripts. In England, he taught Greek at Cambridge University; he also earned a doctorate at the University of Turin in Italy. The most famous humanist scholar of his time, Erasmus wrote in Latin, displaying in that language his vast knowledge, open-mindedness, and wit. He wrote satire, as well as non-fiction about ethics and corruption. Erasmus died in Basel, Switzerland, in 1536. Although Erasmus lived more than half a millennium ago, many of his views have withstood the test of time. What basic human values do you think are applicable to humanity generally, both now and in the past? Which one of these values is to you the most important? Why? How might a writer use satire to emphasize the importance of these values? ■

HARPALUS: I need your advice. I won't forget it if you help me.

NESTOR: All right, I'll try to help you get ahead.

HARP: If only we could be born nobles.

NEST: That's idle talk. We can always try to live well enough to be given noble rank, which can be passed on to our children.

HARP: But that would take forever!

NEST: Well, you can always *buy* a title, you know. Princes are always looking for money.

HARP: But titles like that are always ridiculed.

NEST: Then why are you so anxious to gain the title of knight?

HARP: I'll tell you why in private if only you'll show me how to act like a knight in public.

NEST: You want to be an imposter?

HARP: When you can't have the real thing, you try to maintain a certain image. But let's go, Nestor, I need your help. When you know my reasons, you'll see why I'm in such a hurry.

NEST: Well, since you feel so strongly, I'll do my best. Now first of all, get away from here; go where you're not known.

HARP: I'm listening.

NEST: Find some young swingers who are real noblemen, who have real titles. Get accepted into their company.

HARP: I'm still listening.

NEST: Once you do that, people will associate you with your noble friends.

HARP: Yes, yes, I see.

NEST: Don't give yourself away; don't look cheap.

HARP: What?

NEST: Watch how you dress. No wool clothes. Wear silk if you can. If that's too expensive, wear good heavy cotton or linen. Never patch your clothes, even if it means wearing rough canvas.

HARP: I've got it.

NEST: Always have a cavalier tear in your garments—a hole in the cap, a rip in the doublet, a slash in the trousers, a nick in the boots—you know. Keep your conversation elegant and elevated. If a Spaniard joins the group, ask him how things are with the Emperor and the Pope, how your cousin Count Nassau is, and what your other royal friends (make them up) are doing.

HARP: Good, good.

NEST: Wear a small, tasteful ring, preferably a signet.

HARP: If I can afford one.

NEST: Oh, fake one. Get a brass ring and pay to have it gilded, then put in some coloured glass that looks like a real gem. And be sure to have a shield, complete with your coat-of-arms.

HARP: What shall I use?

NEST: For you—two milk pails and a beer stein.

HARP: Cut it out. Be serious.

NEST: Have you ever been to war?

HARP: Never even seen a battle.

NEST: At least you've cut the throats of a few geese and chickens?

HARP: Oh yes, and like a professional.

NEST: Then use a silver knife and three gold geese.

HARP: On what colour field?

NEST: Gules, of course, for all the blood you've spilled.

HARP: Well it was just as red as real blood. Keep talking.

NEST: Every time you stop at an inn, be sure the shield is hung outside.

HARP: What about a helmet?

NEST: Glad you remembered. Have it made with a slit across the mouth.

HARP: Why?

NEST: Well for one thing—to breathe. It will also go well with the slits in your clothing. Do you know what should go on top of your helmet, to complete things?

HARP: Tell me, tell me.

NEST: A dog's head—with long ears.

HARP: I've seen *several* like that.

NEST: Then add horns. You haven't seen several like *that*.

HARP: Good. What about animals for the shield though?

NEST: Better not use stags or hunting hounds, or dragons or griffins—they're the property of the real nobility. Why don't you try two *harp*ies on your shield?

HARP: Great! *Harp*ies!

NEST: Now about your name. That must be carefully chosen. "Harpalus Comensis" is too vulgar; it sounds like a begging friar. But "Harpalus von Como"—now *there's* a name fit for nobility.

HARP: I'll remember.

NEST: Do you own anything at all?

HARP: Not even a pig-sty.

NEST: Are you from a good-sized city?

HARP: A little hamlet. I can't lie to you; you're my advisor.

NEST: True. Tell me, is there a mountain near your hamlet?

HARP: Yes.

NEST: Has it a big rock anywhere?

HARP: Yes, a big steep one.

NEST: There it is! You are now "Harpalus, Knight of the Golden Rock."

HARP: One more thing. Knights need a motto don't they? Maximilian used "Follow the Golden Mean," and Philip used "He Who Wills," and Charles used "Further Still." What do you think?

NEST: I think you could appropriately use "Play Every Card."

HARP: Terrific!

NEST: Now to other stratagems. To help convince the townspeople, you must forge letters or pretend you've received news from persons of high estate. Let the letters be addressed "Most Illustrious Sir" or something like that. Let them mention important events, fiefdoms, great castles, wealth, positions, a profitable marriage. Be sure the letters reach you indirectly so people will know of them. Better still, "lose" them or leave them behind as you move around so they will be discovered "by chance." Gossip will do the rest.

HARP: That's easy enough. I can write well, and I can copy anybody else's writing.

NEST: Try leaving the letters in your clothes or purse when you go to a tailor shop for mending. The tailors will quickly spread the news. Of course, then you pretend to be offended, as if a confidence had been broken.

HARP: That's easy too. I'm a great faker.

NEST: Be sure you don't give away the trick. Don't overdo it. If the story spreads naturally through gossip, everyone will believe it.

HARP: Okay, I'll do it that way.

NEST: The next thing you need is someone to act like your servant. In fact, hire a servant if you can. You'll find there are plenty of boys around willing to do this sort of thing. Right here you can find lots of young, would-be authors who will do your writing for you. And there are plenty of starving printers too. One of them will agree to do a news pamphlet announcing you as a great nobleman, probably in capitals. Pamphlets get around, so this source of advertising may be even better than word of mouth or servant's gossip.

HARP: Good idea. But how do I pay a servant?

NEST: Make *him* turn up profitable enterprises for *you*. Get several candidates, in fact, for the honour of serving you. Send them out to prove their worth. If they lose their hands in the process, then they're useless as servants. If they don't, you profit as well.

HARP: I get it.

NEST: And you'll need certain—skills.

HARP: Better tell me about them.

NEST: You'll need to be good with dice, sharp at cards, a known skirt-chaser, a big drinker, a wild spender, a prodigal, and one step out of debtor's prison if you expect to pass for a knight.

HARP: I, I qualify! But I still don't know how I'm going to get along with no bankroll.

NEST: I'm getting to that. Have you any kind of inheritance?

HARP: Not enough to even buy a horse with.

NEST: Well, then concentrate on selling your image. Once people believe you're a knight, they'll begin to trust you. In fact, some of them will be afraid *not* to give you credit. Dodging your creditors later on may prove simpler than you think.

HARP: Oh, I've dodged a few creditors in my day. But what I fear is when they find out I *really* have no money.

NEST: Now think a minute. One of the best ways to rise in society is to owe money to almost everybody.

HARP: What?

NEST: A creditor, first of all, treats you courteously, almost fawningly. He has an investment in you and wants no harm to come to it. Just give him a payment now and then, and he'll be as happy as if you gave him a birthday present.

HARP: Say, I've noticed that too.

NEST: But stay away from poor men or little merchants. They make a big to-do over nothing. The wealthier cause fewer problems. They are ashamed to press you; they always hope to get their money from you; they fear your anger, for after all everyone knows what a terrifying enemy an angry knight makes. Finally, when you are so far in debt there is no way out, then just pick up and move to another city. Keep moving like that whenever you have to. At each new place, you can work the same tricks again. There are no men in the world so deeply in debt as dukes and princes. If anyone presses you too hard, simply pretend you are insulted and shun the fellow. Pay something to *another* debtor and praise him for not being insultful to one of your rank. Just never pay anyone in full, and never pay something to all your debtors at once. Keep up appearances all the while; never let anyone suspect you have no money.

HARP: How do I keep up appearances when I have no money?

NEST: Well, if someone has left something for you to look after, pretend it is yours. Borrow money now and then, and repay it quickly and with ceremony. Pay out of a fat purse stuffed with brass coins. Keep a gold coin or two on top. Surely you can invent other such tricks?

HARP: Probably. But eventually I've got to be ruined.

NEST: Oh, I don't think so—not the way we pamper knights these days.

HARP: That's right. They get away with murder.

NEST: Never keep a lazy or cowardly servant. And never keep one who is a relative. Those kind always need to be supported; they never pay their own way. Alert your servants to watch for merchants who can be held up and traders who can be robbed. Keep them on the watch for goods lying around in inns and homes, on wagons and ships. Let them know why man is equipped with fingers.

HARP: But I don't want them getting caught.

NEST: You are *not* thinking like a knight. If they are well dressed and carrying letters—forged of course—to ranking nobility, no one is seriously going to accuse them of stealing for fear of bringing down your wrath. Now if they take anything by force, you can laugh it off by saying they are just training for battle.

HARP: You're great! What advice!

NEST: There is one fundamental principle of knighthood which you must now understand and master. For a knight to unburden a traveller of his funds is an almost sacred duty. It rebalances the chain of being. It is clearly wrong, you see, for a knight to be insufficiently funded while a mere trader or merchant is unduly fortified in that area. A knight must have his funds to gamble and gambol, if you follow me. And again, remember to insinuate yourself among the noble and wealthy wherever you go. Good places in each town are the finest inns and the reputable baths.

HARP: I've thought of going to those places.

NEST: But remember your business—you may often find a favourable business condition in such places.

HARP: How is that?

NEST: Now and then someone forgets his purse there or leaves his keys behind him—do I have to say more?

HARP: Now wait—

NEST: Will you ever get over your peasant cowardices? Who is going to question a man of your stature, of your speech, conduct, and bearing, you, the Knight of the Golden Rock? Even if there is anyone with the bad taste to question you, who will ever make the concrete accusation? The first suspicion will always fall upon someone innocent, like a guest at the inn who left the day before or that morning. You can always have your servants create a disturbance in the baths or start to fight with the innkeeper. You, of course, remain the soul of dignity, even magnanimously stepping in to calm your righteously indignant, loyal minions. If a shy, decent man has been your victim, he will not raise much fuss. He probably does not want to appear foolish for having left his valuables unguarded, so he will accept his loss.

HARP: You're a genius! Have you heard of the Count of the White Vulture?

NEST: Naturally.

HARP: Well, I heard a good story about him, about how he had a Spanish "nobleman" as guest, and how this Spaniard stole 600 florins, and how the Count never said a word because the Spaniard was supposed to be so noble.

NEST: Exactly! Now another useful scheme is to send one of your servants off to war areas now and then, with instructions to loot whatever churches and monasteries he finds along the way.

HARP: That seems safe enough.

NEST: There is another way to obtain money that I could tell you.

HARP: Tell me! Tell me!

NEST: Find some excuse to quarrel with those who have money. Monks and friars are especially good targets right now; everyone is jealous of them. Say that one of them ridiculed your coat-of-arms or even spat on it. Say that one of them insulted your person. Say that one of them wrote ill of you in a letter. Don't confront them directly, but through an emissary broadcast your grievance. Let threats fly all about the countryside. Rant about war, destruction, even executions. Sooner or later, they will beg for a settlement. Then you ask, again indirectly and with high dudgeon, for an astronomical figure as the price of your dignity. If you hint that you will settle for 3000 guilders, they will be ashamed and afraid to offer less than 200.

HARP: Good, good. After that I will threaten to sue others in the courts, eh? What do you think about that?

NEST: Well, really, that is beneath your station—to use the established legal system. But wait, Harpalus, with all this other talk, I have almost forgotten to advise you of perhaps the most basic step an aspirant to the knighthood must take. You must seek out and woo a girl with a substantial dowry. On the surface, you have certain attractions. You are young, free, not bad looking, and you have a, shall we say, relatively uncomplicated mind and character. Let the word go around that you have actually been received at the Emperor's Court. With those qualities, you will be irresistible to the right kind of women.

HARP: Yes, I know one or two who have married like you say. But what if something goes wrong? What if the creditors gang up on me? Worse yet, what if some knights find out I'm not really a knight? That's a worse crime than looting a church—at least the knights think it is.

NEST: Will you never have any boldness? Without arrogance you will never rise in the world. Just look around. If you are not totally blind, you can see that sheer haughtiness and rank gall are every-where taken for noble character and true wisdom. If ever a ques-tion comes up, you simply must have a story ready. Half the people will believe you right away, especially the socially conscious ones, because they exist by perpetual self-delusion. Many of the real nobility will be too "proper" to admit your story is a hoax. And if things really look dark, you simply invent a war to which you have suddenly been called away. Wars forgive everything. But that is only a last resort. Stay alert. Don't go to small towns where your every fart echoes throughout all the best circles. In the great cities you have room to operate. Always keep your ears open to what people are gossiping about you. When they begin to wonder why you have been around so long, why you seem to be staying away from your own country, why you are neglecting your great estates, and when they begin to look into your noble lineage and the source of your wealth—*then* you had better think about moving on. But of course you must move on with great clamour and ado like the lion you are. Announce that the Emperor himself has sent for you, that you must be off soon with the army on a vital campaign. No one will dare bother you under such circumstances especially not merely to collect a little money you may owe them. I suppose your real ene-mies could be the local poets; they often let their pens speak for them, as many a ruined man has learned. So keep them happy.

HARP: You know, you give the best damned advice there is! Now I'll show you've had a good student and a grateful one. You know what I'm going to do? The first good horse I find grazing I'll send back to you for you to keep.

NEST: How noble. But you made me a promise at the start which I have not forgotten, and I would like to collect while you are still here. Tell me, what is it that so attracts you to the knighthood?

HARP: Well, mainly that they do what they damn well feel like and get away with it! Now doesn't that seem worth it to you?

NEST: Ah, I see. Well, in the end I suppose the worst is simply that you owe the world one death. Even the monks in the great Carthusian Monastery must pay *that* debt. And those men executed upon the wheel really have an easier death than more honest men who die in agony—"naturally" as they say—from any of a thousand different accidents and diseases. For the true knight today, nothing survives a man except his corpse, and that only for a little while.

HARP: There you are—exactly. That's it! That's life. Right?

NOTES

ignoble not noble; base, common

cavalier in this instance, jaunty, nonchalant, carefree, dismissive; from the Old Italian word *cavaliere*, originally from the Latin *caballus*, meaning "horse"

doublet a close-fitting jacket worn by European men between the fifteenth and seventeenth centuries; from the Old French diminutive *double*, originally from the Latin *duplus*, meaning "double"

signet a seal, especially one used to mark documents as official

gules the colour red painted vertically on a coat-of-arms; from the Old French word *goules*, meaning "red fur neckpiece," originally from the Latin *gula*, meaning "throat"

griffins also spelled "gryphons"; a fantastical beast with the head and wings of an eagle and the body of a lion

harpies monsters with the head and trunk of a woman and the tail, wings, and talons of a bird

fiefdom the estate or domain of a feudal lord

minion a subordinate official; an obsequious follower

dudgeon in this instance, a sullen or indignant mood

florin, guilder a British coin worth two shillings

dowry money or property provided by the bride's family for the wedded couple in some cultures

Carthusian Monastery a type of monastery built in some European countries, including England and France, beginning in the twelfth century; the Carthusians were a very strict group of monks and nuns deriving their name from Chartreuse, in southeastern France, where the group was founded

ANALYZE AND INTERPRET

1. In a group, discuss who you consider to be the "nobles" of our modern society. By which route did they attain their nobility: Were they born into it? Have they lived their lives in such a way that they have earned a noble rank? Have they bought their way to nobility? Do you share Harpalus' cynical attitude toward these nobles? Keep notes on your discussion, and share your ideas with the class.

2. Have a class discussion about the meanings of the mottoes Harpalus and Nestor list. What does each of them suggest about the character of the person using it? Next, make up a motto for yourself, and design a shield with a coat-of-arms to display it. In preparation, do research on the Internet about heraldry symbols and their meanings. When you have completed your drawing, share it with your classmates, explaining its significance.

3. With a partner, list the techniques Nestor suggested for fooling people into believing Harpalus was a knight. Use your list to write an original dialogue between a modern would-be celebrity and an image consultant. Practise reading your dialogue with your partner. Then present it to a group of classmates, and ask them to comment on how effectively you have updated the tone and language from the original.

MORE TO EXPLORE

Themes: Self and Culture, Peers, Rebels, Europe, Intrigue, Humour, Eye on the Past

Elements: allegory, anecdote, archetype, caricature, dialogue, foil, satire

Survival in the South

Minnie Aodla Freeman

LEARNING FOCUS

- Select and discuss one element of a play, and present your findings.
- Adapt one genre into another to explore meaning and demonstrate insight.
- Research context as the basis for creating an original script.

CONTEXT Inuit writer Minnie Aodla Freeman was born in 1936 on Cape Hope Island in James Bay, off the coast of Québec. At the age of twenty, she moved to Ottawa, Ontario, to work as a translator for the Canadian government. She later moved to Newfoundland, where she wrote *Survival in the South*. This stage play was later adapted as a radio play for the CBC. Freeman is also a poet and writer of non-fiction. Her book *Life Among the Qallunaat* (1978) explores her experiences living in southern Canada. Freeman co-authored the book *Inuit Women Artists: Voices from Cape Dorset* (1994), reflecting her continued work in sharing aspects of her culture with a wider audience. Have you or has someone you know ever been suddenly placed in a cultural environment that is unfamiliar? What are some of the difficulties and frustrations of such a situation? What strategies might the people in this situation use to improve communication with one another? ■

Dramatis Personae

NARRATOR, *an Inuk woman*

MINNIE AODLA, *a young translator on her first visit to the South*

MR. GORDON ⎫

CHIEF ⎬ *employees of the Department of Indian Affairs*

A WOMAN ⎭

MATRON, *superintendent of the women's residence*

JANE, *Minnie's roommate at the residence*

POLICE OFFICER

RECEPTIONIST *at a hairdressing salon*

Prologue

NARRATOR: There is no doubt that much has been written about Inuit people. There is also no doubt that there is little known about their basic culture.

Traditionally Inuit were nomadic; survival at every season depended on their hunting success. Such was the manner of my early life. My parents belonged to a group that moved around Hudson Bay and James Bay region. According to Qallunaat history books, Henry Hudson had discovered Hudson and James Bay. To me, he visited and saw the region, but my ancestors found it long before him.

My grandfather was the leader of seven families. He had led these people in the late 1800s up to 1940s from the Belcher Islands along the coast of Hudson Bay and James Bay, until he found Cape Hope Island which he named after himself, "Weetaltuk Island." There he settled the seven families. To lead people in our culture one has to have wisdom concerning human nature, knowledge of the weather, and the ability to predict where and when the hunting will be most successful. No moves are made till the leader says so. Though he led the group it does not mean he made every choice for every individual. Family heads still had to lead their own families in matters such as bringing up children. In my culture I was brought up to listen and obey my elders, not to ask but to follow, and not to give advice until I have reached that stage where I am considered to have gained wisdom. Not until I am on my own, such as after marriage, was I allowed to choose my clothing and what I wanted to do. As long as I was with my guardians I had no choice but to take what was given to me.

I came south before I was ever considered in my culture "to be on my own." On arrival in the South, I suddenly found myself in a totally new world, and had to start learning from the beginning once again how to survive each day.

But how does one live in a totally different world and yet survive? My parents always told me, when not knowing what to do, and consequently afraid, I should always put on my best front—that is, smile, use my sense of humour and above all remain curious and alert so as to take every advantage of opportunities to learn new things. Moreover, as I grew older…

…I was taught never to react outwardly to exasperation.

(Sound: train—loud then fade)

I alight from the train on my arrival in the South for the first time.

(Train enters, brakes, changes into people)

So many gates. Which one should I use?...How are people going to know I have arrived? What shall I do?...I wish I was home and see a familiar face...so many people, moving like maggots on rotten meat.

(All stop—continue)

How long am I going to stand here? Oh! the ground is hard on my feet. I suppose I am not allowed to take my shoes off? It is so hot!

MR. GORDON: Miss Aodala? *(All stop)* My name is Gordon. Did you have a good trip? I'll look after your luggage, you will live in a very nice place. You will work with some very nice people, you will have a very nice time. Oh, you have the baggage tickets? Simply follow me.

(All start)

NARRATOR: So many people! doing so many different things...walking...talking...eating...drinking...reading and someone talking in a cupboard!...Oh. I am so hot!, my feet ache...everything is going so fast...

MR. GORDON: Now I'll drive you where you live...you'll like it there, there are over 300 girls. You'll eat there...you'll meet the matron there...you'll get everything you want there...bla bla bla bla...

NARRATOR: I still have to travel?...300 girls? All I want right now is a tent to myself to have a good cry and see my parents.

(Cue for green traffic lights, traffic goes mad)

(Shouting) How does he know which car to take? My first car ride...oh he's going to hit another one...look in front of me...so many cars...where are they going?...

(Cue for red light, traffic stops)

Why have we stopped?

(Cue for green light, traffic starts)

Oh, so many things to see, so many stores…so many walking fast and looking so sad…look at the height of that house.

(Traffic exits)

MR. GORDON: Here we are, only a short trip, I'll take your luggage…

NARRATOR: He is so concerned about my luggage.

MR. GORDON: Ah, matron. *(MINNIE sits)* Inuk! Never been south before, she'll need extra help, you'll have to show her round, explain the rules, etc. *(They both look at her)* Must be tired, been on the train two days—o.k.?—I'll see her in the office tomorrow, make sure she gets there, 8:30 sharp. See ya tomorrow Miss Aodala—Gee, look at the time, I gotta fly—phew—*(Exits)*

MATRON: Miss Aodolah. I am the matron here. Come this way and I'll show you to your room. You will have a roommate but you won't meet her yet as she is still working…Oh, here is the book of house rules—follow me…

NARRATOR: Oh my feet ache—it is so hot.

MATRON: This is your room…here is your locker…the combination is 141256—141256—got that? Your bed will be changed once a week, meals are from 6:30 to 7:30 a.m., 11:30 to 12:30 noon and 5:30 to 6:30 p.m. Make sure you're not late for meals, you pay for your room at the end of each month. Here is your key…just come any time you are having problems, and don't forget to study the house rules.

(Exit)

NARRATOR: So many things I mustn't forget, so many things I must remember: lock combination, change the bed, meal hours, paying my room, I wonder if the girl I room with has to do the same? I will just follow her…she will soon come…Oh I am afraid, I wish to go home and see someone I know and talk to someone oh—someone is coming.

JANE: Hi! *(Loud)*

MINNIE: *(No answer)*

JANE: My name Jane…you…Inuk?!

MINNIE: Yes.

JANE: Really! Uh…where do Inuit come from?

MINNIE: From the Arctic.

JANE: Arctic, eh—uh—I learned in Geography that Inuit rub noses—live in snow houses, and—eat raw meat—Did you do all that?

NARRATOR: This girl has no self control.

MINNIE: Yes!

JANE: Really?

> (Pause)

> Are you shy? You don't say much. I guess you're shy.

NARRATOR: True, no sense of control.

JANE: Say, what's your name? What'll we call you?

MINNIE: Minnie—Minnie Aodla.

JANE: Gee, that's cute, my name's Jane.

> (Pause)

MINNIE: Can I unpack my things?

JANE: Sure! I'll help. Oh, that's real cute—oh—yeah—heh—that's nice—aha—oh yeah. *(She hangs them up)* But, is that all? But…where are your clothes?

MINNIE: There.

JANE: I mean your own…*personal*…clothes.

MINNIE: They are mine.

JANE: No, your clothes where you come from, you know, *SKINS!*

> (Pause)

NARRATOR: This girl is out of control.

JANE: Sorry. I didn't mean to pry into your affairs, I really expected skins.

NARRATOR: I do wish not to be so shy. I would take time to inform her about skin clothing.

JANE: Well, I guess it's bedtime. Are you working tomorrow?

MINNIE: Yes.

JANE: Where? With who?

MINNIE: Department of Indian Affairs.

JANE: Doing what?

MINNIE: Translating.

JANE: From your language to ours?

MINNIE: I guess. I will know better tomorrow.

JANE: Well, time to turn in—

(She begins to undress, turns away from MINNIE, *lights fade)*

Good night Minnie.

MINNIE: Good night Jane.

(Sound of breakfast, etc., all cast enters for breakfast, eat on their feet and go, leaving MINNIE *stranded)*

WOMAN: Oh. I can't remember your name. Matron did tell me yesterday…er—are you the Inuk?

NARRATOR: She is out of control too.

WOMAN: Fine! I'll take you to the office, simply follow me.

(They walk to the street crossing, then stop at the cue for the red traffic lights, enter traffic, rush by and then exit. Exit is cue for green traffic lights, MINNIE *follows woman)*

NARRATOR: Nothing seems to bother her. There is so much to see and yet she doesn't seem to notice anything. She seems to have only one thing in her mind, to get to her destination…my feet ache…how far yet to go? Now, what are we waiting for? A bell?

(All rush into the elevator which ascends)

I'm squashed—I can't breathe—we go upwards—want air—oh.

(Elevator arrives—crowd disperses)

CHIEF: Ah, here we are, glad to meet you again Miss Aodala…Are you ready to work for me?

NARRATOR: He says my name so ugly. Oh I feel shy. What will happen to me now? He looks gentle, but I'm still afraid.

CHIEF: I will have to ask you a few questions just so we have something on our files.

(Pause)

If you prefer I can wait till some other time.

(Freeze)

NARRATOR: He is gentle…How I wish to tell him that I am afraid…that I am not used to what I have gone through for the last twenty-four hours…that I have seen so much that never entered my mind that they exist…that my feet ache…that I have left my family and friends…have endured my first long train ride to a train station…to a car ride…to strange living quarters with strange rules for living…and walked for the first time on a stone path…and for the first time gone up in a strange machine so that my breathing can't seem to take the air outside…Wish this lump in my throat would go away…don't think I can hold those tears anymore…I need to cry…

CHIEF: What's wrong? Did I offend you?…I guess you're tired?…You have to answer me so I can help you. Are you not happy where you're living? Did anything happen yesterday? I know—you have a good cry and I'll get you some coffee. *(He goes for some)*

(Returning with coffee) Here we are—I'll show you where your desk is and leave you some letters to translate. I'd like to see them when you're finished because I have to know how well you do, maybe you'll feel better tomorrow. You can go home at lunch hour, take the afternoon off.

(He motions to secretary, she follows CHIEF, *office stops to look at* MINNIE, *then all continue—slow fade and then back on lunch bell—all rush for elevator to descend) (Bell)*

NARRATOR: *(in elevator)* How will I get back home? If I get lost I must ask a police officer. He wears a blue uniform.

(People rush out)

I'll just follow those people into the street, I won't pay attention to the names of the streets, I will only look at the signs and colours and shapes. That's how I will remember the way.

(Exits then returns to street noises)

MINNIE: Oh!

(Lights change to red and traffic bursts in and then out, lights turn green, MINNIE *moves on)*

NARRATOR: I am very alone…so many tall buildings, I can't see how far the sun has dropped…Ah, there is a police officer. I will ask him where I live.

(She approaches POLICE OFFICER*)*

MINNIE: Can you please tell me where Sussen Street is?

POLICE OFFICER: Speak up ma'am. Where was it?

MINNIE: Please, where is Sussen Street?

POLICE OFFICER: Sussen? That way, ten blocks.

NARRATOR: Ten blocks. *Aukatalangani!* My feet are aching, I am so hot, I have to find my way home. I vow to myself tomorrow I will look at my route better. Tomorrow? What is tomorrow? Today is four, the next is five, so tomorrow is number five.

Ah! Today, I don't care if I'm lost all day…I'm going to see many things…I'll just walk and walk. Look at the shops, tall buildings, I will look at anything I can see.

(Enter revolving door)

Oh! What is that?

(She attempts to enter store but doesn't make it; then the hairdresser's shop materializes)

I will go in here and see what they do. *(Bell)*

(Enters shop)

RECEPTIONIST: Yes. You have an appointment? What is your name? Did you want a wash and set—the works?

(Pause)

Do you speak English?

MINNIE: Yes.

RECEPTIONIST: Did you make an appointment to have your hair done?

MINNIE: No.

RECEPTIONIST: Well, I guess we can fit you in. What is it you want done?

(No answer)

How would you like it done?

MINNIE: What do you do here?

RECEPTIONIST: Curled, cut or just dried?

MINNIE: Everything!

RECEPTIONIST: You don't want it cut, it's such beautiful hair, is it natural, do you dye it? It's so black.

MINNIE: Everything!

RECEPTIONIST: O.K. Marvin! One for the works!

(Lights red for haircutting ritual)

(They exit leaving MINNIE with new hairdo)

MINNIE: My head feels nice and cool, now I'm ready to work.

(Change to boardroom scene)

CHIEF: Now, this meeting is called to discuss our future programs, and top of the list is—er—Miss Aodala—we are planning to begin training some of our people from here in the South to enable them to survive in the North. The title of this program I called—er—"How to survive in the North" *(general reaction)*. Now, Miss—er—Aodala—if you have any suggestions for us—we in this group will be very pleased to consider them.

(Fade to half and focus on Minnie)

NARRATOR: They ask me how to survive, they don't tell me how to survive in the South…I am not worthy for these people…I am nothing to them; it does not matter whether I survive or not in their country; I am nothing to them, therefore, I have to help them in how to survive in my land—ugh, it's hot in this place…

(Fade to END)

NOTES

dramatis personae Latin for "the characters in the play"

Inuk, Inuuk, Inuit used when referring to members of the Inuit First Nation: in the first case, to one person; in the second case, to two people; in the third case, to more than two people

Department of Indian Affairs the branch of the federal government of Canada that deals with Aboriginal issues

Hudson Bay a large gulf or inland sea in the Keewatin and Baffin regions of Nunavut, linked to both the Atlantic and Arctic oceans

James Bay a relatively shallow, saltwater body of water that is the southern extension of Hudson Bay, located between Québec and Ontario

Belcher Islands an archipelago covering 13,000 square kilometres in southeastern Hudson Bay

Aukatalangani an exclamation used either positively or negatively, meaning "amazing" or "beyond belief" in the Inuktitut language

ANALYZE AND INTERPRET

1. With a small group, choose **one** of the following three topics for discussion. After your discussion, select one group member as a spokesperson to present your views to the class. **a)** How was this play similar to or different from other plays you have read? Did anything about this play surprise you? **b)** Consider the structure of this play. How has the playwright set up the sequence of events? Is this structure similar to a play you've seen or read in the past? **c)** What do you notice about the role of the narrator? How does this role add to or detract from your understanding of the plot?

2. Drawing on specific events and images from the play, write a poem that Minnie might have written about her experiences in the South. Demonstrate your understanding of her character and her emotional responses.

3. With a small group, prepare the script for a training video to help workers from the South survive in the North. Begin by rereading the play to identify some of the skills Minnie possesses that would be essential in the North. Add to these by researching to find out more about the daily life of Inuit in the Arctic. In preparing your script, consider how the workers' lack of knowledge of the North may affect their ability to cope when they are transferred. Use your creativity in presenting both the difficulties that future northern workers might face and solutions to these challenges.

MORE TO EXPLORE

Themes: Personal Challenges, Self and Culture, Stereotypes, Peers, Rural Life, Aboriginal Cultures, Canada, Journeys

Elements: characterization, dialogue, narrator, protagonist, setting, sound effects, tone

Wrap-Up

1. Whenever a writer creates a work, she or he is living in a particular time and place, regardless of the time period or location in which the work is set. The environment surrounding a writer provides a context that may influence components of this work. Choose one selection from this unit and research the location and time period in which it was written. Then create a timeline in which you record specific events of that place and era that might have influenced features of the work. Next, analyze what the relationship might be between context and the theme the writer has chosen to explore. Meet with another classmate who selected the same work, and compare your findings.

2. In any dramatic work, dialogue is essential to establishing characterization and developing the plot. To be believable, dialogue must sound realistic. Choose one selection from this unit to analyze in terms of how the writer has created a sense of reality through the effective use of dialogue. Present your findings to a small group.

3. As you read a dramatic work, how essential are the stage or set directions to your understanding? How might these same directions affect you as a viewer of a performance of the work? Use a graphic organizer to compare the use of directions in two selections from this unit. Then write a formal essay in which you analyze how the information in the directions adds to your understanding of each text.

4. Imagine that you are a casting director for one selection in this unit. With a partner, use a graphic organizer to describe the main character. Choose five excerpts from the work that contribute most to your understanding of this character. Explain the significance of each. What qualities would you look for in the actor for this role? Next, describe how you would costume the actor. Discuss which contemporary actor you would choose for the role.

5. In a group, choose one selection from this unit to adapt as a radio drama. Together, reread the play, discussing what modifications you will make so that the script could be understood and enjoyed by a radio audience. Determine and document how you will use narration, sound effects, and music to help your listeners visualize the characters and the action. Then prepare a taped reading of your performance. Play the tape for your classmates and ask for their evaluation.

6. "Elizabethan English," used by Shakespeare, is only one linguistic generation removed from modern English: most of the language we recognize or almost recognize. Reread the excerpt from *Henry V* and find examples of how Shakespeare's English differs from today's in the following areas: vocabulary, verb conjugations, and word order. Rewrite each example as it would be spoken in today's English. Present your findings in chart form.

Glossary

Many of the following elements or features of texts have been cross-referenced to selections in *Viewpoints 11*. In this way, you can use an element as a basis for making connections between selections, exploring how an element is used and expressed in various forms and genres. You will also find below additional terms to use in your study and to enhance your enjoyment of texts.

act   A major division in a dramatic work, larger than a scene or episode.

adaptation   Any work that recreates or redevelops another work in a different medium (e.g., a film based on a novel, a television show based on a stage play).
Related Selection: Sense and Sensibility *474*

allegory   A story with a literal, surface meaning and a second, deeper, usually moral, meaning; traditionally involves **personification.**
Related Selections: The Charmer *100*   ▪   The Gentlemen of the Jungle *185*   ▪   The Ignoble Knight *501*

alliteration   The repetition of the same sound *at the beginning* of nearby words (e.g., "When to the **s**essions of **s**weet **s**ilent thought I **s**ummon…" —Shakespeare).
Related Selections: SOS *212*   ▪   In Progress *220*   ▪   Ode to Autumn *230*   ▪   The Lake Isle of Innisfree *232*   ▪   My Song *238*   ▪   Beautiful Summer *263*   ▪   'Out, Out—' *268*   ▪   A Narrow Fellow in the Grass *272*   ▪   Schooner *276*   ▪   The Titanic *279*   ▪   Macavity: The Mystery Cat *289*   ▪   Sonnet *292*

allusion   A direct or indirect reference in one work to another work or to a historical person or event.
Related Selections: The Charmer *100*   ▪   Love Must Not Be Forgotten *132*   ▪   The Storyteller *159*   ▪   Poetry *248*   ▪   History Lesson *255*   ▪   'Out, Out—' *268*   ▪   Where the World Began *326*   ▪   Surf's Up *392*   ▪   Garbage 101 *396*   ▪   Shakespearean Baseball Game *450*

analogy   A comparison based on partial similarity for the purpose of making something clearer or more powerful (e.g., the growth of a human being to the growth of a tree).
Related Selections: The Pedestrian *153*   ▪   Falling Song *236*   ▪   Henry V *446*

anecdote   A brief story about a single humorous or interesting event.
Related Selections: A Walk to the Jetty *86*   ▪   Canadian Pioneers *310*   ▪   Reaction–Interaction *314*   ▪   The Cartography of Myself *319*   ▪   William Golding *385*   ▪   The Ignoble Knight *501*

antagonist   A **character** who is the **protagonist**'s main opponent.

anti-hero   A **character** who is the **protagonist** of a narrative and is also obviously unheroic, or lacking typical qualities of a **hero**, but for whom an author might arouse sympathy or change the way we view his or her circumstances.

antithesis   A rhetorical device that contrasts ideas that are opposite or at least very different; sometimes parallelism is used to heighten the contrast. In general use, something is said to be the antithesis, or direct opposite, of something else.
Related Selections: Up *246* ▪   King Kong *472*

archetype   Something that represents the essential elements of its category or class of things; Greek for "original pattern" from which all copies are made, a prototype. Certain facts of human life (e.g., birth, death, family), character types (e.g., the rebel, the wanderer), animals (e.g., snake), and themes (e.g., the quest, the descent into the underworld) are considered to be archetypal, forming a part of the collective unconscious (the sum of society's inherited mental images). For example, a movie character might be said to be the archetypal villain.
Related Selections: Ramu and Rani *74* ▪   Holy Sonnet 10 *222* ▪ My Song *238* ▪   The Titanic *279* ▪   Mother and Child *286* ▪ William Golding *385* ▪   Henry V *446* ▪   King Kong *472* ▪   The Ignoble Knight *501*

aside   A **monologue** in which a **character** speaks directly to the audience as though unheard by the other characters onstage. Often it is expressed in a "stage whisper," which is a loud whisper meant to be heard by the audience.

assonance   The repetition of the same or similar vowel sounds *within* nearby words for musical effect (e.g., We ch**a**tted and l**au**ghed as we **a**mbled **a**long).
Related Selections: SOS *212* ▪   In Progress *220* ▪   Falling Song *236* ▪   A Narrow Fellow in the Grass *272* ▪   The Bear on the Delhi Road *282*

ballad   A **narrative poem** about common events and people, typically with four-line **stanza**s and a **refrain**; generally, ballads originate as songs passed by word of mouth, so their creators are unknown. The term is also used broadly to mean romantic songs.

bias   A thought or language that contains a prejudice (an inaccurate, irrational, usually negative perception) against something or someone; bias within a text can exist when information essential to an accurate depiction of a subject has been omitted, thereby prejudicing the unwitting reader's understanding of the subject.

blank verse   A type of unrhymed verse that closely resembles everyday conversation, is usually written in **iambic pentameter**, and is used in some drama.
Related Selection: Henry V *446*

byline   The line at the top of a newspaper or magazine article that provides the writer's name.

camera angle   The relative height or position from which the camera films the subject, thus high (from above), low (from below), flat, normal, or straight (from the same height), etc.
Related Selections: Animation 101   *381*   ▪   Shakespearean Baseball Game *450*   ▪   Sense and Sensibility   *474*

caption   A brief explanation or title given with a photograph, cartoon, chart, or other graphic.
Related Selections: How to Turn a Closed-Down Nuclear Reactor   *400*   ▪ The "Talking" Mace   *409*   ▪   Life Needs Nourishing   *424*   ▪   Life of a Sports Writer   *440*

caricature   A flat **character**, who is often a comic, absurd, or grotesque exaggeration of characteristics.
Related Selections: Shakespearean Baseball Game   *450*   ▪   The Ignoble Knight   *501*

cause-and-effect organization   The arrangement of ideas and information (e.g., in an essay) according to causes and effects, actions and their outcomes, or states of being and their impact (e.g., the effect of an atypical weather pattern on agricultural production).

character   One of the people in a story, either in fiction or drama. The person may be a specific type of character, such as a **stock character**, **protagonist**, **antagonist**, **foil**, **hero**, or **anti-hero**.

characterization   The techniques used to portray or describe a **character** (e.g., in a novel, through the character's **dialogue**, actions, inner thoughts, and direct description).
Related Selections: The Shivering Tree   *4*   ▪   Learning the Language   *17* ▪   Brother Dear   *25*   ▪   Boys and Girls   *44*   ▪   The Lamp at Noon   *62* ▪   The Charmer   *100*   ▪   A Handful of Dates   *123*   ▪   Love Must Not Be Forgotten   *132*   ▪   The Storyteller   *159*   ▪   A Cap for Steve   *167* ▪   Initiation   *198*   ▪   History Lesson   *255*   ▪   Mother and Child   *286* ▪   Albert Einstein   *324*   ▪   Sense and Sensibility   *474*   ▪   Trifles   *484* ▪   Survival in the South   *513*

chorus   In song lyrics, the **refrain** or repeated phrases or lines; in drama, one or more **narrator**-like **character**s, particularly in Greek drama, who comment upon the action of the drama or voice a character's thoughts.

chronological organization   The arrangement of ideas and information (e.g., in a news report) based on the ordering of events (e.g., a crime taking place, its discovery, and the investigation that followed).
Related Selections: Marilyn Bell   *358*   ▪   Japanese Air and Submarine Attack   *368*

cinquain   A **stanza** of five lines.

classification   The arrangement of elements into classes, categories, or groups (e.g., e-mails grouped according to those that are urgent, those needing a response this week, and those to be discarded).

Related Selections: "Where Do You Get Your Ideas From?" *348* ■ Animation 101 *381* ■ Reflections of Girls in the Media *413* ■ Life of a Sports Writer *440*

cliché An overused, timeworn phrase or way of being, generally considered to be ineffective and therefore avoided, but sometimes used for effect in **dialogue**. Certain uses of both **diction** and **characterization** can be considered clichéd.

Related Selection: Sonnet *292*

climax In a **plot**, the height of the tension in the **conflict**; the turning point in the plot; sometimes called the crisis.

Related Selections: The Charmer *100* ■ A Cap for Steve *167* ■ Sunday in the Park *179* ■ Initiation *198* ■ 'Out, Out—' *268* ■ Trifles *484*

colloquial language Words, phrases, and expressions used in ordinary, everyday, familiar conversation; **informal language** that is typically relaxed and plain rather than formal and literary.

comedy A drama (e.g., **satire**, **parody**) that may include misfortunes but ends happily, intending to entertain, but sometimes also to educate or persuade.

Related Selection: Shakespearean Baseball Game *450*

comparison A consideration or description of two or more things in which similarities are identified.

Related Selections: Companions Past and Present *130* ■ My Old Newcastle *306* ■ "Where Do You Get Your Ideas From?" *348* ■ Reflections of Girls in the Media *413*

conflict The central struggle or problem of a narrative, which moves the **plot** forward and motivates the **protagonist**.

Related Selections: Learning the Language *17* ■ Brother Dear *25* ■ Boys and Girls *44* ■ The Charmer *100* ■ A Handful of Dates *123* ■ Love Must Not Be Forgotten *132* ■ The Pedestrian *153* ■ A Cap for Steve *167* ■ Sunday in the Park *179* ■ The Gentlemen of the Jungle *185* ■ Initiation *198* ■ Reaction–Interaction *314* ■ Engineered Food *405* ■ King Kong *472*

connotation An implied meaning of a word or phrase that can be derived from association or frequent use. The connotation extends beyond the **denotation** of the word or phrase, providing additional meaning (e.g., the denotation of "cute" is "appealing in a lovable or dainty way"; the connotation of "cute" often includes "frivolous" or "insignificant").

Related Selection: Branta Canadensis *462*

context In general, the surroundings or circumstances of something. In print, it refers to any element related to communication that influences the creation of a text or the understanding and interpretation of it. These elements include the purpose, the intended audience, and circumstances including time, place, and cultural and gender issues. Examples include the words appearing before and after a phrase, the imagined world that a fiction author creates, and the cultural setting in which a writer works.

couplet   A pair of lines in a poem, one after the other, with rhyming ends; also known as a **rhyming couplet**.
Related Selections: In Progress *220*   ■   My Last Duchess *223*   ■   The Titanic *279*

debate   A formal or informal setting in which two or more participants discuss or argue two conflicting sides of an issue, question, or topic, with one side arguing for a subject, and the other arguing against it.

deck   In a periodical publication, a line explaining (and following on) the **headline**, or title, of an article, thereby acting like a subtitle. It is often used to catch the reader's attention, drawing her or him into a text through the use of a dramatic, controversial, or humorous statement.
Related Selection: Some Paws for Concern *430*

definition   A statement of what a word or phrase means, especially in a specific context (e.g., a discussion on genetically modified foods might require first giving definitions of "genetic modification," "biotechnology," "growth hormones," "irradiation," and "antibiotic residues," etc.).
Related Selections: Wrong Ism *343*   ■   Reflections of Girls in the Media *413*

denotation   A literal, dictionary meaning of a word or phrase (e.g., dove as a bird of the Columbidae family).

dénouement   In a **plot**, the story's end or conclusion; also called the resolution.
Related Selections: Learning the Language *17*   ■   A Handful of Dates *123*   ■   A Cap for Steve *167*   ■   Sunday in the Park *179*   ■   The Gentlemen of the Jungle *185*   ■   'Out, Out—' *268*

description   A style of writing that creates images of people, places, and objects using carefully observed, expressed, and arranged details. These details are perceived by the five senses. Description can range from objective, scientific to subjective and impressionistic.
Related Selections: Silver Mine, Cobalt *42*   ■   Boys and Girls *44*   ■   The Lamp at Noon *62*   ■   Ramu and Rani *74*   ■   A Walk to the Jetty *86*   ■   To Da-duh, in Memoriam *110*   ■   The Pedestrian *153*   ■   Do Seek Their Meat from God *190*   ■   Initiation *198*   ■   Falling Song *236*   ■   You Walked Gently Towards Me *240*   ■   A Flower of Waves *249*   ■   In the Morning (27 May) *262*   ■   Beautiful Summer *263*   ■   The Job of an Apple *270*   ■   The Bear on the Delhi Road *282*   ■   In a Remote Korean Village *296*   ■   Neighbour *298*   ■   My Old Newcastle *306*   ■   The Cartography of Myself *319*   ■   Where the

World Began *326* ▪ Marilyn Bell *358* ▪ Japanese Air and Submarine Attack *368* ▪ Surf's Up *392*

dialect A way of speaking or a variation on language unique to a particular people or to one region or social group.
Related Selection: To Da-duh, in Memoriam *110*

dialogue The conversation of two or more **characters** involving an exchange of ideas or information.
Related Selections: The Shivering Tree *4* ▪ Brother Dear *25* ▪ The Address *35* ▪ Sunday in the Park *179* ▪ Horse-Fly Blue *264* ▪ Reaction–Interaction *314* ▪ The Open Car *334* ▪ William Golding *385* ▪ Shakespearean Baseball Game *450* ▪ Sense and Sensibility *474* ▪ Trifles *484* ▪ The Ignoble Knight *501* ▪ Survival in the South *513*

diction The choice of words and phrases by a writer or speaker.

dramatic monologue A poem in which the speaker addresses an unseen, silent listener. This form is related to the **soliloquy**.
Related Selections: My Last Duchess *223* ▪ You Walked Gently Towards Me *240* ▪ Up *246* ▪ 'Out, Out—' *268* ▪ Schooner *276* ▪ Henry V *446*

elegy Traditionally, a formal poem that is a solemn meditation, written as a lament for the death of a particular person.

empathy The act of mentally (and possibly physically) identifying with a person or object, so comprehending it fully (e.g., knowing a character's struggle because it echoes one's own, involuntarily mimicking a dancer's moves); from the German term *Einfühlung* meaning "feeling into." In general use, sympathy is considered to be compassion, while empathy is the response to a shared (or the *sense* of a shared) feeling or condition.
Related Selections: Brother Dear *25* ▪ Ramu and Rani *74* ▪ Love Must Not Be Forgotten *132* ▪ A Television Drama *147* ▪ Falling Song *236* ▪ William Golding *385*

epic A type of **narrative poem**, long and about historic or legendary people, thus like a legend but not prose (e.g., Homer's *Iliad*).
Related Selection: The Titanic *279*

epigram Originally meant an inscription (from Greek), but was extended to mean any concise statement that is polished and pointed, often with a surprise or twist.

epilogue A closing or concluding section of a drama.

exposition A **style** of writing that is systematically explanatory, and communicates information, as in an expository essay.
Related Selections: Animation 101 *381* ▪ Living Languages, Lasting Cultures *422* ▪ On Boy Trouble *426*

euphemism A vague, indirect term with a positive **connotation** used to replace a more precise or blunt term that may offend or frighten (e.g., garbage collectors can be euphemistically referred to as "sanitation engineers").

figurative language   Language that uses figures of speech, such as **simile**, **personification**, and **alliteration** to create **imagery** (e.g., "Like a pinball in an arcade, she ricocheted again and again down the avenue.").

first-person point of view   Storytelling in which one **character** of the story serves as the storyteller/**narrator**, telling the narrative from his or her point of view. One indication of first-person point of view is that at some point in the text, the speaker refers to her- or himself through words such as "I," "me," "my," "mine," "we," "our," or "us."
Related Selections: The Shivering Tree *4* ▪ Learning the Language *17* ▪ Brother Dear *25* ▪ Boys and Girls *44* ▪ Ramu and Rani *74* ▪ A Walk to the Jetty *86* ▪ The Charmer *100* ▪ Love Must Not Be Forgotten *132* ▪ My Song *238* ▪ The Profile of Africa *258* ▪ In the Morning (27 May) *262* ▪ The Hidden Fence *300* ▪ My Old Newcastle *306* ▪ Canadian Pioneers *310* ▪ The Cartography of Myself *319* ▪ Where the World Began *326* ▪ "Where Do You Get Your Ideas From?" *348* ▪ Japanese Air and Submarine Attack *368* ▪ Surf's Up *392* ▪ Garbage 101 *396* ▪ Engineered Food *405*

flashback   A device used to depict events of the past (e.g., a story of a teenage hero character might contain a flashback to his childhood).
Related Selections: The Address *35* ▪ The Charmer *100* ▪ Love Must Not Be Forgotten *132* ▪ The Cartography of Myself *319* ▪ The Open Car *334*

foil   A **character**, usually minor, who contrasts with, and so sheds light on, the **protagonist**.
Related Selection: The Ignoble Knight *501*

foreshadowing   A device of hinting at the future or events occurring later in the work (e.g., a discovery of an injured bird might foreshadow the main character's accident).
Related Selections: The Address *35* ▪ The Lamp at Noon *62* ▪ A Cap for Steve *167* ▪ Sunday in the Park *179*

form   Broadly, the shape of a communication (e.g., one form of poetry is the **haiku**, one form of business communication is the memorandum); with literary texts, **genres** are the larger divisions, and forms are the smaller divisions.

formal language   Language that is polite and respectful in tone; that rigorously follows conventions; and that is appropriate. It might be used, for example, in a letter of application, in a research paper, or between strangers introduced at a school ceremony.
Related Selections: Holy Sonnet 10 *222* ▪ My Last Duchess *223* ▪ Ode to Autumn *230* ▪ Fear of Science and Love of the Land *402*

free verse   Poetry that follows natural speech **rhythm**s and that has no regular pattern of line length, **rhyme**, or rhythm.

genre   A type or class of literary texts (e.g., novel) within which there are categories or **forms** (e.g., historical, science fiction, fantasy, etc.). Broadly, genre means any type or class, and can refer, for example, to media products (e.g., sitcoms, quiz shows) and formal speeches (e.g., sales presentations, eulogies).

graphics   Pictorial representations or other visual images (e.g., illustration, bar graph). On a Web site, for example, all that is seen can be categorized as either text or graphics.
Related Selections: Animation 101 *381* ▪ How to Turn a Closed-Down Nuclear Reactor *400* ▪ Living Languages, Lasting Cultures *422* ▪ Sustainable Development Information System *436* ▪ King Kong *472*

haiku   A traditional Japanese verse form consisting of three lines, of which the first line is five syllables, the second is seven syllables, and the third is five syllables.

head   A short form for **heading** or **headline**.

heading   The "title" for a section of a text. It is used to introduce a section of text, indicating the topic and offsetting it from other sections.
Related Selections: Reflections of Girls in the Media *413* ▪ Sustainable Development Information System *436*

headline   The title of an article in a periodical publication; sometimes called the **head**. Most often used to refer to the title of a news story, intended to both summarize the article and be "catchy" in order to draw in the reader. It is sometimes followed by a **deck**.
Related Selections: On Boy Trouble *426* ▪ Life of a Sports Writer *440* ▪ King Kong *472*

hero   A **character** who is the **protagonist** and also heroic, demonstrated by such characteristics as bravery and loyalty. Not all protagonists are heroes.

hyperbole   Intended exaggeration, a device often used to create **irony**, humour, or dramatic effect.
Related Selections: To Da-duh, in Memoriam *110* ▪ The Storyteller *159* ▪ The Gentlemen of the Jungle *185* ▪ The Job of an Apple *270* ▪ Sonnet *292* ▪ How to Turn a Closed-Down Nuclear Reactor *400* ▪ Some Paws for Concern *430* ▪ Life of a Sports Writer *440* ▪ Henry V *446*

iambic pentameter   In poetry, a pattern of ten syllables (five **metrical feet**) per line, each foot (pair) beginning with an unstressed ($\cdot$), and ending with a stressed ($\prime$) syllable.
Related Selections: In Progress *220* ▪ Ode to Autumn *230* ▪ Sonnet *292*

idiom   A form of expression unique to a language that has different literal and figurative meanings (e.g., back the wrong horse, wear and tear, better late than never). Some idioms are so appealing that they become overused, **cliché**d.

Related Selections: The Profile of Africa *258* ■ e-phobia? *438*

imagery The collected images that exist in a text. These images include "mental pictures" and any other sensory perceptions that have been created in a text through its use of language. Imagery can be created through words or groups of words that evoke images that are visual (sight), auditory (hearing), tactile (touch), olfactory (smell), gustatory (taste), and kinesthetic (movement). Imagery can be descriptive (literal) or suggestive (metaphorical).

informal language Language that is familiar, intimate, casual, and may include slang terms or other **colloquial language**.
Related Selections: The Open Car *334* ■ On Boy Trouble *426* ■ Some Paws for Concern *430* ■ e-phobia? *438*

irony A literary device involving contrast. The most common type is verbal irony, a statement in which the supposed meaning intended by the speaker is different from (often opposite to) her or his actual meaning.
Related Selections: A Television Drama *147* ■ The Gentlemen of the Jungle *185* ■ Do Seek Their Meat from God *190* ■ Initiation *198* ■ In Progress *220* ■ My Last Duchess *223* ■ History Lesson *255* ■ In the Morning (27 May) *262* ■ Horse-Fly Blue *264* ■ Canadian Pioneers *310* ■ On Boy Trouble *426* ■ Life of a Sports Writer *440* ■ Sense and Sensibility *474*

juxtaposition The practice of placing two elements in a text side-by-side for the specific purpose of creating an effect through their association. Although the two items are not explicitly compared and contrasted, their proximity creates a contrast for the reader.

logical fallacy A falsehood or misunderstanding based on flawed reasoning.

lyric poem A subjective, emotional poem with musical roots (e.g., **rhythm** or **rhyme**). Forms include **ode**s and **sonnet**s.

melodrama A sentimental drama using unrealistic **character**s and **plot** primarily to appeal to emotions; like a farce but not humorous.

metaphor An implied comparison that does not use "like" or "as" (e.g., "your dress is a kite in the wind"), thus connecting two or more usually unlike things that have something in common (dress, kite).
Related Selections: Learning the Language *17* ■ To Da-duh, in Memoriam *110* ■ My Last Duchess *223* ■ The Lake Isle of Innisfree *232* ■ Poetry *248* ■ A Flower of Waves *249* ■ Ode to My Socks *252* ■ The Job of an Apple *270* ■ Schooner *276* ■ Mother *288* ■ In a Remote Korean Village *296* ■ Neighbour *298* ■ The Cartography of Myself *319* ■ Where the World Began *326* ■ Surf's Up *392* ■ Life Needs Nourishing *424*

metre The pattern of **rhythm** (stressed and unstressed syllables in poetry) as examined in **metrical feet**.
Related Selections: An Elegy on the Death of a Mad Dog *214* ■ Holy Sonnet 10 *222* ■ My Last Duchess *223* ■ The Tables Turned *228*

■ The Lake Isle of Innisfree *232* ■ Poetry *248* ■ A Narrow Fellow in the Grass *272* ■ The Titanic *279* ■ Macavity: The Mystery Cat *289*

metrical feet   The units of stressed and unstressed syllables; a way of examining **metre** and identifying the feet according to type and number (e.g., **iambic pentameter**).

mode   In writing, a manner (e.g., narrative), kind (e.g., **comedy**), or way of writing that brings with it certain customs, usual ways of writing (e.g., precise use of detail in descriptive writing, the tragic flaw in **tragedy**).

monologue   In drama, a speech spoken by one **character** (e.g., a **soliloquy**, an **aside**).

mood   The prevailing feeling created in or by a work, also known as the atmosphere.
Related Selections: The Address *35* ■ Silver Mine, Cobalt *42* ■ Fire Down on the Labrador *60* ■ Companions Past and Present *130* ■ The Pedestrian *153* ■ You Walked Gently Towards Me *240* ■ Untitled (Vancouver) *244* ■ Poetry *248* ■ A Flower of Waves *249* ■ Mother *288* ■ My Old Newcastle *306* ■ The Cartography of Myself *319* ■ Albert Einstein *324* ■ Victory! *366* ■ Branta Canadensis *462*

motif   An element (type of incident, device, or formula) that occurs frequently in literature and other artistic works (e.g., in folklore, a young prince or princess disguised as a warty toad or old person). Also, a recurring image, character, or pattern of words that forms a dominant idea in one work (so is part of its theme) can be called a motif (or *Leitmotif*, German for "guiding motif"). For example, in a film about lost innocence, an image of an angel, a child character, or the repeated words "When the child was a child" could all be motifs.
Related Selections: The Pedestrian *153* ■ SOS *212* ■ Ode to Autumn *230* ■ Untitled (Vancouver) *244* ■ Branta Canadensis *462*

myth   A story that involves supernatural beings or powers, and explains why things are as they are—i.e., some aspect of nature (e.g., how the world began, why the beaver's tail is as it is), or of the human condition (e.g., romantic love, greed), *and* of a culture's mythology (its system of stories passed down through generations).
Related Selections: The Shivering Tree *4* ■ Ramu and Rani *74*

narration   A **style** of writing that incorporates **plot** to relay events over time by telling a story.
Related Selections: The Lamp at Noon *62* ■ A Handful of Dates *123* ■ A Television Drama *147* ■ In the Morning (27 May) *262* ■ The Titanic *279* ■ The Open Car *334* ■ Marilyn Bell *358* ■ Victory! *366* ■ Japanese Air and Submarine Attack *368*

narrative poem   A poem that tells a story (e.g., **ballad**, **epic**).

narrator   The storyteller in narrative writing; a function of the point of view. Types include first-person, **omniscient**, and limited omniscient.

Related Selections: Do Seek Their Meat from God *190* ▪ Survival in the South *513*

octave A **stanza** of eight lines.

ode A **lyric poem**, typically long and formal, with a complex structure to offer praise of a scene or to a person.

omniscient narrator An all-seeing, all-knowing storyteller/**narrator** who is "outside" the **characters**; one type of third-person narrator.

onomatopoeia A device in which a word imitates the sound it represents (e.g., the *buzz* of a bee).

oral tradition A custom or long-held practice of composing works orally— i.e., using the spoken word and without putting pen to paper.

Related Selections: The Shivering Tree *4* ▪ The Gentlemen of the Jungle *185* ▪ On Veterans *376*

oxymoron A device that combines contradictory words for dramatic effect (e.g., an honest thief).

Related Selection: Life of a Sports Writer *440*

page layout The physical arrangement of the print and graphics content of a newspaper, magazine, Web site, or book (e.g., the size of type, text that runs in one or more columns, the placement of graphics).

Related Selections: In Progress *220* ▪ A Narrow Fellow in the Grass *272* ▪ The Bear on the Delhi Road *282* ▪ Victory! *366* ▪ The "Talking" Mace *409* ▪ Living Languages, Lasting Cultures *422* ▪ Life Needs Nourishing *424* ▪ Sustainable Development Information System *436*

parable A brief folk tale told to teach an *implied* moral, or lesson.

Related Selections: The Charmer *100* ▪ A Handful of Dates *123* ▪ The Gentlemen of the Jungle *185* ▪ The Hidden Fence *300*

paradox An apparent contradiction or absurdity that is somehow true.

Related Selections: To Da-duh, in Memoriam *110* ▪ A Television Drama *147* ▪ An Elegy on the Death of a Mad Dog *214* ▪ Mother *288* ▪ On Boy Trouble *426*

parody A humorous, exaggerated imitation of a work, **style**, or person.

Related Selections: An Elegy on the Death of a Mad Dog *214* · Macavity: The Mystery Cat *289* ▪ Sonnet *292*

pathetic fallacy A technique of giving human feelings and capacities to inanimate objects, especially nature (e.g., suggesting that a stone weeps); it is often used in poetry and is less formal than **personification**.

Related Selection: The Tables Turned *228*

pathos The quality (e.g., in a novel or play) that evokes pity, sorrow, or tenderness; Greek for "suffering" or "feeling."

Related Selections: Ramu and Rani *74* ▪ A Cap for Steve *167* ▪ Do Seek Their Meat from God *190* ▪ 'Out, Out—' *268* ▪ Off to War *374* ▪ On Veterans *376* ▪ Trifles *484*

personification   A technique in which inanimate objects or concepts are given human qualities, form, or actions.
Related Selections: The Lamp at Noon   *62*   ▪   A Handful of Dates   *123*
▪   Sometimes My Body Leaves Me   *216*   ▪   Ode to Autumn   *230*   ▪
My Song   *238*   ▪   You Walked Gently Towards Me   *240*   ▪   Poetry
248   ▪   In the Morning (27 May)   *262*   ▪   Beautiful Summer   *263*   ▪
The Job of an Apple   *270*   ▪   The Titanic   *279*   ▪   In a Remote Korean
Village   *296*   ▪   Neighbour   *298*   ▪   Branta Canadensis   *462*

persuasion   A style of writing that attempts to convince the audience either to act in a certain way or to adopt a certain opinion, perspective, viewpoint, or belief.
Related Selections: Reaction–Interaction   *314*   ▪   Wrong Ism   *343*   ▪
"Where Do You Get Your Ideas From?"   *348*   ▪   Marilyn Bell   *358*   ▪
On Veterans   *376*   ▪   Fear of Science and Love of the Land   *402*

plain language   Clear, straightforward communication that is intended to be read by the broadest audience, uses concrete and familiar words, avoids using (or explains) jargon, and is organized for easy comprehension.

plot   The series of connected actions and events in a story, written or otherwise, often described as having a course of action and including rising action, **conflict**, **climax**, falling action, and a **dénouement** (or resolution).
Related Selections: Boys and Girls   *44*   ▪   To Da-duh, in Memoriam   *110*
▪   Sunday in the Park   *179*   ▪   The Gentlemen of the Jungle   *185*   ▪
Do Seek Their Meat from God   *190*   ▪   Trifles   *484*

prologue   An opening section of a drama, a kind of introduction.

props   Objects appearing in the action of a drama and used to perform or enhance it. Props, or properties, include furniture, costumes, and so on.
Related Selections: Shakespearean Baseball Game   *450*   ▪   Trifles   *484*

protagonist   The narrative's main **character**.
Related Selection: Survival in the South   *513*

proverb   A brief saying in general use that expresses a general truth (e.g., "It is an ill wind that blows no good."). Some proverbs are the morals of fables.

pun   A play on words using a word with two meanings, two words of similar meanings, or words that are similarly spelled or pronounced.
Related Selections: Some Paws for Concern   *430*   ▪   e-phobia?   *438*

quatrain   A **stanza** of four lines.
Related Selections: The Tables Turned   *228*   ▪   The Lake Isle of Innisfree
232   ▪   A Narrow Fellow in the Grass   *272*

refrain   A phrase, a line, or lines repeated in a poem. In song lyrics, these are often called the **chorus**.

rhetorical question   A question asked for effect and to promote thought and reflection, not to elicit an answer.
Related Selections: Sometimes My Body Leaves Me   *216*   ▪   Horse-Fly
Blue   *264*   ▪   Schooner   *276*   ▪   Neighbour   *298*   ▪   Wrong Ism
343   ▪   Some Paws for Concern   *430*

rhyme   The sound effect of words that have, or end with, the same or similar sounds. Poetry that has a strong rhyming quality may be called rhyme.
Related Selections: An Elegy on the Death of a Mad Dog *214* ▪ In Progress *220* ▪ Holy Sonnet 10 *222* ▪ The Tables Turned *228* ▪ Ode to Autumn *230* ▪ The Lake Isle of Innisfree *232* ▪ Up *246* ▪ Ode to My Socks *252* ▪ The Titanic *279* ▪ Macavity: The Mystery Cat *289* ▪ Sonnet *292*

rhyming couplet   A pair of lines in a poem with rhyming ends to accentuate the unit of thought. Also known as a **couplet**.

rhythm   The sound effect of stressed (accented) and unstressed (unaccented) syllables; the pattern of rhythm is called the **metre**. It sets the beat and tempo of a poem.
Related Selections: SOS *212* ▪ Up *246* ▪ Ode to My Socks *252* ▪ 'Out, Out—' *268* ▪ The Bear on the Delhi Road *282*

sarcasm   Language, often ironic, that is bitter or hurtful toward others. The **connotation** of sarcastic comments or phrases are distinct from their **denotation**; often the explicit meaning is more positive, but a sneering tone or expression reveals a negative **subtext**.
Related Selections: The Shivering Tree *4* ▪ History Lesson *255* ▪ Garbage 101 *396* ▪ Engineered Food *405* ▪ Life of a Sports Writer *440*

satire   A **form** that uses **irony**, ridicule, or sarcasm to expose human flaws.
Related Selections: The Storyteller *159* ▪ Reaction–Interaction *314* ▪ An Elegy on the Death of a Mad Dog *214* ▪ History Lesson *255* ▪ Macavity: The Mystery Cat *289* ▪ Sonnet *292* ▪ Reaction–Interaction *314* ▪ Garbage 101 *396* ▪ Shakespearean Baseball Game *450* ▪ The Ignoble Knight *501*

scene   A division within a dramatic work, usually within an **act**. Typically, a scene takes place in only one time and place.

second-person point of view   A text in which the writer refers directly to the reader(s) as "you" (or an implied "you," as in "Read and analyze this text.") but does not ever refer back to her- or himself.
Related Selection: Ode to Autumn *230*

sestet   A **stanza** of six lines.

set design   Planning and constructing the area in which a drama takes place (e.g., a stage play's backdrops and furniture, a Western movie's imitation frontier town).
Related Selections: Shakespearean Baseball Game *450* ▪ Sense and Sensibility *474* ▪ Trifles *484*

setting   The where and when, place and time, of a narrative.
Related Selections: The Address *35* ▪ Silver Mine, Cobalt *42* ▪ Fire Down on the Labrador *60* ▪ The Lamp at Noon *62* ▪ Ramu and Rani *74* ▪ A Walk to the Jetty *86* ▪ A Handful of Dates *123* ▪

sidebar   A short article, often boxed, appearing beside another article, typically to supplement or give background for the larger, main article.

simile   A stated comparison that uses "like" or "as" (e.g., "your dress is like a kite in the wind").

soliloquy   A **monologue**, often long, in which the lone **character** expresses his or her thoughts and feelings.

sonnet   A **lyric poem** with 14 lines, sometimes written in **iambic pentameter**. The major types of sonnet are the Italian (Petrarchan) and the English (Shakespearean).

sound effects   Any sounds other than speech or music made in a movie, stage play, etc. (e.g., footsteps running down a stair, claps of thunder). Sound effects are imitative and made artificially.

sound track   The recorded sounds of a film; any part of this made available for sale (e.g., the recording of a song that accompanies a part of a movie).

special effects   Illusions created for film, television, or the stage using camera work, props, or computers (e.g., a woman flying out of her body, computer-generated dinosaurs, a man sawn in half).

specialized terms   Words or phrases arising from, or using the precise meanings of, a particular field of study, work, etc. (e.g., "gross domestic product" in economics, *mirepoix* in cookery, "navigation bar" and "cookie" in Web site creation).

Animation 101 *381* ■ How to Turn a Closed-Down Nuclear Reactor *400* ■ Sustainable Development Information System *436*

stage directions In scripts, performance requirements or suggestions (e.g., to say a line angrily, to enter from stage right).

stanza A grouping of lines in a poem, separated by a blank space on the printed page.

stereotype A type of flat **character**, one-dimensional, lacking complexity, and often reflecting some **bias**.

stock character A type of flat **character**, one who the audience will immediately recognize and who serves a familiar function.

storyboard One of a sequence of pictures (sometimes with writing) used to outline or plan, for example, a TV commercial or film.

style An individual's manner of expression. In writing, style is the result of the choices the writer makes regarding such elements as **diction**, sentence structure, and **figurative language**. Style also expresses the writer's personality and way of thinking.

subhead A short form for **subheading**.

subheading A secondary or subordinate **heading**, title, etc., within text (e.g., titled sections of a proposal or research paper); also called **subhead**.
Related Selection: Reflections of Girls in the Media *413*

subplot A secondary course of action in a **narrative**; subplots may provide humour in a **tragedy**, round out minor characters, help to tie up loose ends, and so on.

subtext In a text, a hidden meaning that is not explicit.

summary A brief account; a condensation of a work's content; sometimes called a **synopsis**.

suspense Increasing tension in a narrative caused by uncertainty and excitement about the conclusion, created mainly by the **conflict**.

symbol Something that represents or stands for something else (e.g., a dove for peace, a maple leaf for Canada). Symbolism is many symbols collectively. Symbolic language includes **figurative language** (e.g., **metaphor**, **personification**, etc.), that is representative, metaphorical, not literal, thus including symbols and creating a work's **imagery**.
Related Selections: The Address *35* ■ To Da-duh, in Memoriam *110* ■ Companions Past and Present *130* ■ A Cap for Steve *167* ■ Initiation *198* ■ You Walked Gently Towards Me *240* ■ Poetry *248* ■ The Profile of Africa *258* ■ Beautiful Summer *263* ■ The Hidden Fence *300* ■ The Open Car *334* ■ Branta Canadensis *462*

synopsis A brief outline, summary, or general account (e.g., a synopsis of a **plot**).
Related Selections: Surf's Up *392* ■ Reflections of Girls in the Media *413*

syntax The arrangement of words to form phrases and sentences.

tableau   A "frozen" moment in a drama; the performers freeze in position, motionless and soundless. The plural is tableaux.

target audience   The chosen or intended readers, viewers, or listeners (e.g., of an advertisement); usually a distinct demographic group.

theme   The central insight, idea, focus, or subject matter of a work (especially fiction), stated indirectly or directly.

thesis   The main idea of a work of non-fiction writing. A thesis is focused and is developed with the use of examples and evidence.
Related Selections: Holy Sonnet 10 *222* ▪ The Tables Turned *228* ▪ Wrong Ism *343* ▪ "Where Do You Get Your Ideas From?" *348* ▪ Marilyn Bell *358* ▪ Fear of Science and Love of the Land *402*

third-person point of view   Written text in which the writer never refers either to him- or herself, or directly to the reader as "you."
Related Selections: The Lamp at Noon *62* ▪ A Television Drama *147* ▪ The Pedestrian *153* ▪ The Storyteller *159* ▪ A Cap for Steve *167* ▪ Sunday in the Park *179* ▪ The Gentlemen of the Jungle *185* ▪ Do Seek Their Meat from God *190* ▪ Initiation *198* ▪ A Flower of Waves *249* ▪ History Lesson *255* ▪ The Job of an Apple *270* ▪ The Bear on the Delhi Road *282* ▪ Marilyn Bell *358* ▪ Reflections of Girls in the Media *413*

tone   In a text, the creator's attitude to the subject or audience as conveyed through elements of that text. In writing, the author's tone is often conveyed through **diction** and **style**. In spoken communication, the speaker's tone can be conveyed through her or his diction, volume, pitch, and body language. In visual representations, the artist's tone can be conveyed through the choice of subject matter, medium, technique, composition, emphasis, and balance.
Related Selections: Fire Down on the Labrador *60* ▪ Companions Past and Present *130* ▪ Sometimes My Body Leaves Me *216* ▪ Falling Song *236* ▪ Up *246* ▪ Neighbour *298* ▪ The Hidden Fence *300* ▪ Japanese Air and Submarine Attack *368* ▪ On Veterens *376* ▪ On Boy Trouble *426* ▪ Survival in the South *513*

tragedy   Traditionally, a drama that focuses on the downfall of the **protagonist** (due to a character flaw or a mistake) and that ends unhappily. In the traditional tragedy, the protagonist was of high social status (e.g., a god, a queen) but is often now an ordinary person. Modern usage of the term pertains to any text or event that contains catastrophic occurrences that either seem horribly unfair or seem to have been preventable.
Related Selections: Fire Down on the Labrador *60* ▪ The Lamp at Noon *62* ▪ Love Must Not Be Forgotten *132* ▪ 'Out, Out—' *268* ▪ Trifles *484*

tragic hero   The heroic **protagonist** of a **tragedy**.

tragicomedy   A drama that combines aspects of **tragedy** and **comedy**.

usage   The customary, established, or common manner of using words, phrases, and expression in a language not necessarily reflected yet in dictionaries (e.g., as with computer terminology) *or* the particular manner of using a word, phrase, or expression (e.g., a writer's use of a word that indicates which dictionary definition or which surronding syntax might be appropriate).

visual composition   The artistic arrangement of parts in the whole; the way in which parts are combined and related. For example, a photograph of a farm scene might have the following composition: undulating lines of corn in the foreground and middle ground leading to the barn and silo in the distance (upper left), silhouetted against the sky.
Related Selections: Silver Mine, Cobalt *42*   ▪   Fire Down on the Labrador *60*   ▪   Companions Past and Present *130*   ▪   Untitled (Vancouver) *244*   ▪   Mother and Child *286*   ▪   Albert Einstein *324*   ▪   Victory! *366*   ▪   Off to War *374*   ▪   Animation 101 *381*   ▪   How to Turn a Closed-Down Nuclear Reactor *400*   ▪   The "Talking" Mace *409*   ▪   Living Languages, Lasting Cultures *422*   ▪   Life Needs Nourishing *424*   ▪   Sustainable Development Information System *436*   ▪   e-phobia? *438*   ▪   King Kong *472*

visual scale   Proper proportion; proportional representation of actual objects in a visual work; the relative size of objects in a visual work.
Related Selections: Silver Mine, Cobalt *42*   ▪   Fire Down on the Labrador *60*   ▪   Companions Past and Present *130*   ▪   Untitled (Vancouver) *244*   ▪   Mother and Child *286*   ▪   Victory! *366*   ▪   The "Talking" Mace *409*   ▪   Life Needs Nourishing *424*   ▪   Sustainable Development Information System *436*   ▪   e-phobia? *438*   ▪   King Kong *472*

voice   Broadly, the personality of the speaker or persona (or the author) coming through in a work, created through the combination of **diction**, **point of view**, and **tone**. Narrowly defined, voice can be described as active (e.g., I made a mistake) or passive (e.g., Mistakes were made).
Related Selections: Learning the Language *17*   ▪   A Walk to the Jetty *86*   ▪   "Where Do You Get Your Ideas From?" *348*

voice over   Narration (e.g., in film) in which the speaker is not seen.
Related Selections: Shakespearean Baseball Game *450*   ▪   Branta Canadensis *462*   ▪   Sense and Sensibility *474*

Credits

Every reasonable effort has been made to find copyright holders of the material in this anthology. The publisher would be pleased to have any errors brought to its attention.

Literary Credits

p. 4 From *An Anthology of Canadian Native Literature in English*, 2nd ed., 1998, Oxford University Press; **p. 17** Reprinted by permission of Karen Donnelly; **p. 25** "Brother Dear" by Bernice Friesen from *The Seasons Are Horses* (Thistledown Press, 1995); **p. 35** English translation copyright © 1984 by Jeannette Kalker Ringold. Reprinted by permission of Marga Minco and Jeannette Kalker Ringold; **p. 44** From *Dance of the Happy Shades*, Ryerson Press, 1968; **p. 62** *The Lamp at Noon and Other Stories* by Irving Layton. Used by permission, McClelland & Stewart, Ltd. *The Canadian Publishers*; **p. 74** From *The Opium Eater and Other Stories* by Iqbal Ahmad, published by Cormorant Books Inc.; **p. 86** "A Walk to the Jetty" from *Annie John* by Jamaica Kincaid. Copyright © 1985 by Jamaica Kincaid. Reprinted with permission of Farrar, Straus and Giroux, LLC.; **p. 100** "The Charmer" by Budge Wilson in *Cordelia Clark*, 1994, reprinted by permission of Stoddart Publishing Co. Limited; **p. 110** Reprinted by permission of Paule Marshall; **p. 123** From *African Short Stories*, selected and edited by Chinua Achebe and C.L. Innes, Heinemann Educational Books Ltd.; **p. 132** Reprinted by permission of Chinese Literature Press; **p. 147** "A Television Drama" by Jane Rule. Published in *Literature in Canada, Volume II*, 1975 by Gage Publishing Co. Copyright © 1975 by Jane Rule; **p. 153** Reprinted by permission of Don Congdon Associates, Inc. Copyright © 1951 by the Fortnightly Publishing Company, renewed 1979 by Ray Bradbury; **p. 159** From *The Short Stories of Saki*, published by The Bodley Head Ltd.; **p. 167** © The Estate of Morley Callaghan; **p. 179** Reprinted by permission of Bel Kaufman; **p. 185** From *African Short Stories*, selected and edited by Chinua Achebe and C.L. Innes, Heinemann Educational Books Ltd.; **p. 190** From *The Oxford Book of Canadian Short Stories in English*, edited by Margaret Atwood and Robert Weaver, Toronto, Oxford University Press, 1986; **p. 198** From *Johnny Panic and the Bible of Dream*, 1979, Faber and Faber Ltd, London, reprinted by permission of the publisher; **p. 214** Reprinted by permission from *Archive for Our Times: Previously Uncollected and Unpublished Poems* of Dorothy Livesay, edited by Dean J. Irvine (Arsenal Pulp Press, 1998).; **p. 216** From *Angels of Flesh, Angels of Silence* by Lorna Crozier. Used by permission of McClelland & Stewart, Inc. *The Canadian Publishers*; **p. 220** Found in *A Book of Women Poets from Antiquity to Now*, edited by Aliki Barnstone and Willis Barnstone, Schoken Books, New York; **p. 232** From *Collected Poems*, by W.B. Yeats, Macmillan Co., 1903, renewed 1934; **p. 236** Reprinted by permission of Harbour Publishing Co. Ltd.; **p. 238** From *The Collected Poems and Plays* by Rabindranath Tagore, © 1993, reprinted with permission of Macmillan Ltd.; **p. 240** "You Walked Gently Towards Me" by Ben Okri, in *An African Elegy*, Jonathan Cape, London: 1992; **p. 246** From *Up from Morning in the Burned House* by Margaret Atwood. Used by permission, McClelland & Stewart, Inc. *The Canadian Publishers*; **p. 248** "Poetry" by Sally Ito (From *Frogs in the Rain Barrel*, by Sally Ito. Nightwood Editions, 1995.); **p. 249** Translated by Etsuko Terasaki and Irma Brandeis. Found in *A Book of Women Poets from Antiquity to Now*, edited by Aliki Barnstone and Willis Barnstone, Schocken Books; **p. 252** From *Neruda and Vallejo: Selected Poems*, edited and translated by Robert Bly, reprinted in *The Rag and Bone Shop of the Heart*, edited by Robert Bly, James Hillman, and Michael Meade, HarperCollins, 1992, by Robert Bly; **p. 255** From *Seventh Generation Contemporary Native Writing*, edited by Heather Hodgson, 1989 Theytus Books, Ltd.; **p. 258** Maxine Tynes is a poet, writer, and educator who lives and works in Dartmouth, Nova Scotia; **p. 262** "In the Morning (27 May)" by Elizabeth Brewster is reprinted by permission of Oberon Press; **p. 263** "Beautiful Summer" from *Day has no equal but the night*, English translation copyright © 1997 by House of Anansi Press. Reprinted by permission of Stoddart Publishing Co. Limited; **p. 264** From *A Really Good Brown Girl*, Brick Books 1996, reprinted in *An Anthology of Canadian Native Literature in English*, 2nd ed., edited by Daniel David Moses and Terry Goldie, Toronto: Oxford University Press 1998; **p. 268** From *The Poetry of Robert Frost* edited by Edward Connery Lathem, © 1969 by Henry Holt and Company, LLC. Reprinted by permission of Henry Holt & Co., LLC.; **p. 270** McGill-Queen's University Press, Ronna Bloom, "The Job of an Apple" from *Fear of the Ride*; **p. 272** Reprinted by permission of the publishers and the Trustees of Amherst College from *The Poems of Emily Dickinson*, Thomas H. Johnson, ed., Cambridge, Mass.: The Belknap Press of Harvard University Press, Copyright © 1951, 1955, 1979 by the President and Fellows of Harvard College; **p. 276** Reprinted by permission of Kamau Brathwaite; **p. 279** From *E.J. Pratt: Complete Poems*, Edited by Sandra Djawa & R.G. Moyles, 2 volumes, © University of Toronto Press 1989. Reprinted with permission; **p. 282** From *Ghost in the Wheels: Selected Poems* by Earle Birney. Used by permission, McClelland & Stewart Ltd. *The Canadian Publishers*; **p. 288** Translated by Kenneth Rexroth and Ikuko Atsumi from *The Burning Heart: Women Poets of Japan*. Translated and edited by Kenneth Rexroth and Ikuko Atsumi. English language translation copyright 1977 by The Seabury Press, Inc.; **p. 289** "Macavity: The Mystery Cat" from *Old Possum's Book of Practical Cats* by T.S. Eliot, published by Faber and Faber Limited. Copyright © 1939, 1953 by T.S. Eliot. Copyright renewed 1967 by Esme Valerie Eliot. Reprinted by permission; **p. 292** From *Canadian Author and Bookman*, Winter 1972, reprinted in *Theme in Canadian Lit: Canadian Humour and Satire*, edited by Theresa Ford, Toronto: Macmillan, 1976; **p. 296** Reprinted by permission of Chang Soo Ko; **p. 298** "Neighbour" by Christine Churches, from *My Mother and the Trees*, reprinted with permission of HarperCollins Publishers Australia; **p. 300** From *Lnu and Indians We're Called*, Ragweed Press, P.E.I. Copyright © Rita Joe, 1991;